ETHNIC ATLANTA

Denise Black and **Janet Schwartz** are also the authors of *Around Atlanta with Children: A Guide for Family Activities.* They and their families live in Atlanta.

ETHNIC ATLANTA

THE COMPLETE GUIDE TO ATLANTA'S ETHNIC COMMUNITIES

JANET SCHWARTZ / DENISE BLACK

LONGSTREET PRESS
Atlanta, Georgia

Published by LONGSTREET PRESS, INC.
A subsidiary of Cox Newspapers,
A division of Cox Enterprises, Inc.
2140 Newmarket Parkway
Suite 118
Marietta, GA 30067

Printed in the United States of America

1st printing, 1993

Library of Congress Catalog Number: 92-84010

ISBN: 1-56352-063-X

This book was printed by R. R. Donnelley & Sons, Harrisonburg, Virginia.
The text was set in New Baskerville

Cover and book design by Jill Dible

Front cover photo credits (left to right):
Janice Morrill, Mark Byrne, Linda Schaefer, Linda Schaefer

TABLE OF CONTENTS

acknowledgments

We would like to express our appreciation to the many individuals who have helped us with our book. We were overwhelmed that so many people graciously and enthusiastically shared their cultural and personal histories with us, telling heartwarming stories and amusing anecdotes, describing special cultural festivities, and often providing us with a much-needed community contact or reviewing a section of the book pertaining to their ethnic heritage.

Many thanks to: Peter Bardoul, Dennis Carlson, Stephanie C. Davis, Surin and Pou Jung, Pete Kongthaborn, Joanna and Shigehisa Kuriyama, Jay and Livi Lee, Nicholas Moraitakis, Clarence Moritz, Ziad Nassar, Phuc Nguyen-Dinh, Subash Razdan, Else Shewmake, Irina Supruniuk, Leslie Perry Wingate, Claire and James Yang, and Thomas Yatabe.

We gratefully acknowledge our husbands, Ira and Bruce, for their countless contributions to this book; and our children, Allison and Daniel, David and Nathan, for their spirited enthusiasm for our project.

INTRODUCTION

Atlanta is receiving increased national and international attention as a sophisticated city known for the diversity of its population, its accessibility, affordability and other attractive amenities. Yet very little is known about Atlanta's multiculturalism — its reputation appears to be based more on a vague notion of numbers than upon actual information and knowledge about the communities themselves. Gathering meaningful information about the city's rich cultural diversity is not an easy task because Atlanta's ethnic communities are spread throughout the metropolitan area (a notable exception being the DeKalb Peachtree Airport area which has truly become an international village). But people are preserving their heritage in families, social clubs, civic organizations and religious institutions, places where people have always proudly gathered to find support and community. And in recent years, individuals who closely identify with their heritage have successfully opened grocery stores, restaurants, small retail shops, and emporiums all over our city. These commercial establishments have quickly become focal points for information about community events. Posters on store windows announce upcoming film festivals, colorful flyers announce club meetings, association newsletters are stacked on store counters and business cards advertising the opening of new offices are tacked on bulletin boards. Finally, there are local neighborhood centers to disseminate information to community members.

And, even more exciting, our ethnic and international communities, realizing how eager Atlantans are to learn and partake of the cultural traditions of their neighbors, are reaching out. Groceries, bakeries and restaurants are encouraging everyone to sample locally prepared, yet authentic dishes and delicacies. International and ethnic festivals have emerged where all of Atlanta may enjoy traditional arts and crafts, food, music and dance and celebrate colorful national holidays. Through these and other efforts, members of the many international and ethnic groups in our city sincerely hope that other Atlantans will become more aware of the friendliness and warmth of their neighbors and acknowledge the countless contributions each community has made to our collective culture.

During our very enjoyable research we drove (and walked!) all over the city, met wonderful people, attended dozens of festivals and sampled delicious food in countless restaurants. We have compiled a well-rounded sampling of area amenities. We apologize that we could not list every restaurant, shop, club or festival — there are more than you would imagine. And remember, a handful of new ethnic restaurants opens each week, as do new galleries, markets and emporiums. And unfortunately, others close. Write to us and let us know what we should sample for our next edition. Also, telephone numbers change, as do presidents of organizations and days and hours that restaurants are open. So please call ahead if you are charting unfamiliar territory.

With these few thoughts in mind, both of us wish you a *bon voyage, buona fortuna, safiri salama, buena suerte* and *"a jolly good time"* as you set forth to explore *Ethnic Atlanta* with this guidebook in hand!

ETHNIC ATLANTA

The Sheaf Toss is one of the contests at the Scottish Highland Games in Stone Mountain.

UNITED KINGDOM & IRELAND

(England, Scotland, Wales & Ireland)

HISTORY

Spanish, English and French settlements flourished in the Georgia area in the 16th and 17th centuries. Then, in the early 18th century, James Oglethorpe, a respected member of the English Parliament, was pivotal in fashioning a royal charter and convincing King George II to establish the colony of Georgia under the supervision of a board of trustees. The original purpose of the colony was to create a refuge for European Protestants and help alleviate the unemployment situation in England. To this end, prospective settlers were carefully screened, and about 120 small-businessmen, tradesmen and unemployed laborers were approved for the journey. (Contrary to popular belief, the first settlers were, for the most part, not debtors or indentured servants.) Oglethorpe, one of the trustees, agreed to accompany the first mission and, while on board ship, quickly emerged as a strong and compassionate leader of men. The settlers arrived in Savannah on February 12, 1733, officially seizing the area for Britain.

Oglethorpe's leadership was solidified by the sweeping originality of his vision for the colony, which included thoughtfully planning the city of Savannah as a prototype for other cities and establishing Georgia as a bastion for the middle class (not wealthy landowners). His novel ideas included banning slavery, building a diversified economic base, regulating trade with Native Americans, permitting Jewish settlers (against the wishes of the trustees in London) and forbidding all liquor except wine and English ale and beer. (The liquor prohibition was requested by the Indian chiefs.) Though some of Oglethorpe's ideas were later undermined by other colonists and British Parliamentary trustees, as well as his own shortcomings, General Oglethorpe's influence certainly shaped Georgia's early years and permitted Britain to remain in control throughout the colonial period.

Though never legally a "governor" (the original charter forbade any trustee from assuming the role), General Oglethorpe is considered to have been the first chief executive of Georgia (1733-1743). To commemorate his role in shaping the destiny of Georgia, a bust of Oglethorpe is on permanent display in the Georgia State Capitol in Atlanta.

Oglethorpe and his successors in Georgia during the colonial period encouraged **Scottish Highlanders** to settle in the Savannah area and serve as a buffer between the Spanish Floridians and the English in the Carolinas. (The Carolinas had a different form of government from Georgia, one which Oglethorpe considered economically and militarily weak, so the two were constantly at odds.) As more Scottish settlers arrived, they began moving up the coast toward the mountains and then into Atlanta where they felt more at home. By the end of the 19th century, the Scotch-Irish were the largest single European group in the South. (An interesting tidbit: Did you know that the phrases "might could" and "fixin'" have Scottish roots?)

The first **Irish** settlers in Georgia were mainly railroad workers, many of whom settled in Atlanta when they got injured. The Irish community grew, and by the 1850s Atlanta had a large Irish population. The Irish supported the Confederacy, and, in fact, it was the heroic efforts of Father Thomas O'Reilly which convinced the Union troops to spare City Hall and several downtown churches from destruction. A plaque now stands outside Holy Transfiguration Church (across from Underground Atlanta) commemorating the priest's successful efforts, and The Hibernian Society of Atlanta was given a special burial plot in Oakland Cemetery by the City of Atlanta in appreciation of his bravery.

Some evidence exists that an expedition from **Wales** landed at Mobile Bay as early as the 12th century and attempted to establish a colony in the South. Rumor has it that the stone wall at Fort Mountain State Park, near Chatsworth, may have been built by Welshmen. Also, Van Wert in Polk County was settled by Welsh miners who came to work the slate mines. (Did you know that Button Gwinnett and Thomas Jefferson were of Welsh descent?)

Approximately 10,000 British nationals and 3,000 Irish nationals are estimated to reside in the Atlanta area, with about 25 percent of the families living here for business-related purposes. British citizens are easily assimilated into Atlanta's culture, so for the most part, the community has not found it necessary to form many clubs and societies for social companionship. Recent census figures indicate that approximately 971,000 Georgians claim to be of

Irish ancestry, 192,000 of Scotch-Irish ancestry, 890,000 of English ancestry and 142,000 of Scottish ancestry. Not surprisingly, there is a wealth of social, charitable and cultural organizations comprised of Atlantans eager to preserve and promote the customs and traditions of their Celtic ancestors.

HISTORICAL SITES & MUSEUMS

■ **Fort Peachtree**, 2630 Ridgewood Rd., NW, Chattahoochee Water Treatment Plant Facility, Atlanta (609-7100). You can visit a replica of the original Fort "Peach Tree" built by the British on the shores of the Chattahoochee River as a buffer against the Creek Indians. There are no exhibits, artifacts or documents at the replica of the fort, but a visit to the historical site may be of interest to British and American history buffs. Hours: Mon.–Fri. 8:00am–4:00pm. Free.

■ **Georgia State Museum of Science and Industry**, Georgia State Capitol Building, NW, Atlanta (656-2844). Tours of the State Capitol and the Museum of Science and Industry on the fourth floor include information about General James Oglethorpe and the early British settlers in Georgia. Hours: Mon.–Fri. 8:00am–5:30pm. Tours are conducted Mon.–Fri. at 10:00am, 11:00am, 1:00pm and 2:00pm. Free.

■ **High Museum of Art**, Robert Woodruff Arts Center, 1280 Peachtree St., NE, Atlanta (892-HIGH). Besides the numerous pieces of British art and antiquities in the museum's permanent collection, special collections of work by British artists often find their way to Atlanta, such as the spectacular Fitzwilliam Collection which visited Atlanta in past years. Hours: Tues., Wed., Thurs. and Sat. 10:00am–5:00pm; Fri. 10:00am–9:00pm; and Sun. 12noon–5:00pm. Admission fee.

■ **Oakland Cemetery**, 248 Oakland Ave., SE, Atlanta (688-2107). The 88-acre Victorian cemetery is an open-air museum of Atlanta history filled with mausolea, statuary and the graves of thousands of early Atlantans, rich and poor. The Hibernian Society of Atlanta was given a special burial plot in the cemetery by the City of Atlanta in appreciation of the heroic acts of Father Thomas O'Reilly during the Civil War. Hours: Daily from 7:00am–7:00pm. Visitor Center is open Mon.–Fri. from 9:00am–5:00pm. Free.

■ **Robert Burns Cottage**, Alloway Pl. (off Confederate Ave. east of Grant Park), Atlanta. In 1910, the Burns Club of Atlanta built a replica of the birthplace of the Scottish poet Robert Burns — the only replica of its kind in the world. Now on the National Register of Historic Places, the Cottage was constructed from plans taken from the original, so that even the bend in the middle is authentic. Tours of the interior are hosted during special occasions, such as the club's annual *ceilidh,* an evening of Scottish music and dance, held on a Saturday in late September.

And keep in mind . . . the **Atlanta Botanical Garden**, 1345 Piedmont Rd. (Piedmont Park at The Prado), Atlanta (876-5858) often presents lectures and slides highlighting some of the famous gardens in Great Britain and Ireland. Call for a schedule of upcoming programs and events. Hours: Tues.–Sat. 9:00am–6:00pm; Sun. 12noon–6:00pm. (Extended hours during summer months.) Admission fee.

GALLERIES & ANTIQUES

■ **Bennett Street** houses several galleries and antique shops packed with British art and antiquities, including **Beaman Antiques** (352-9388), **Woodward & Warwick Antiques** (355-6607), **Bennett Street Antiques** (351-4633) and **Bittersweet Antiques, Ltd.** (351-6594).

■ **Miami Circle** is also the site of many British galleries and antique shops such as **Barrington Antiques** (231-8595), **British American Antiques** (231-4454), **Burroughs Wellington** (264-1616), **Thames Valley Antiques** (262-1541) and **Bureau International, Ltd.** (266-1600).

A sampling of other galleries: **Irish Country Pine**, 511 E. Paces Ferry Rd., NE, Atlanta (261-7924); **Morgan & Allen Gallery**, 2300 Peachtree Rd., NW, Atlanta (355-5799); **O'Karma Jones, Inc.**, 450 14th St., NW, Atlanta (874-9461); and **Englishman's**, 2050 Hills Ave., NE, Atlanta (351-4464).

COMMUNITY, RELIGIOUS & CULTURAL ASSOCIATIONS

BRITISH ASSOCIATIONS

■ **Daughters of the British Empire** (482-7252). The social and philanthropic society is open to female citizens of the British Commonwealth, including Canada, Australia and New Zealand, as well as their proven ancestors. Chapters of the club meet monthly for luncheon or evening meetings and engage in a multitude of fund-raising activities to support homes for the elderly in the U.S.

■ **English Speaking Union** (636-4009). The Atlanta chapter of this international organization has monthly evening meetings featuring programs about the English-speaking world's cultures and traditions. The Union also engages in fund-raising to support students who wish to study in the U.K. Social activities include a celebration on the Queen's Birthday in June and a seasonal party during the Christmas holidays.

- **Lions & Eagles Social Club** (591-2488). Membership in the social club is open to British nationals (the "lions") and their American spouses (the "eagles"). Friendly get-togethers are held monthly at members' homes and special events are scheduled throughout the year.

SCOTTISH ASSOCIATIONS

- **St. Andrews Society of Atlanta** (979-1010). The society's purpose is the perpetuation of Scottish traditions, culture and heritage and the promotion of fellowship among its 300 or so members. Membership is open to those Atlantans of Scottish descent who live within a 75-mile radius of the city. Activities are planned throughout the year, such as a Saint Andrews Dinner in November and a Burns Dinner in January. The society also plays a prominent role in the Celtic Festival and Stone Mountain Highland Festival and Tattoo.
- **Scottish-American Military Society.** The society's purpose is the preservation and promotion of Scottish and American armed forces customs, traditions and heritage. Membership is open to honorably discharged, retired, active duty reserves, service academy cadets and college-level ROTC members of the U.S. military, and equivalent members of the British Commonwealth armed forces. Contact the St. Andrews Society for more information.
- **The Society of Scottish Clan Associations.** The society aims to preserve and promote the customs, traditions and heritage of the Scottish people through assistance to and support of Scottish-oriented organizations. Contact the St. Andrews Society for more information.

IRISH ASSOCIATIONS

- **The Hibernian Benevolent Society of Atlanta** (299-9399). The charitable, cultural and social society is one of the city's oldest, having been formed in 1858 to assist newly arrived Irish immigrants. A monthly meeting of the society may consist of a lecture, cultural performance or discussion group. The Society also has many charitable causes and sponsors the annual Hibernian Ball and St. Patrick's Day Parade in downtown Atlanta.
- **Children's Friendship Program for Northern Ireland** (427-3968). The program assists peace efforts by pairing two children from Northern Ireland between the ages of 14-17, one Protestant and one Catholic, together in the U.S. in the environment of a compassionate and caring American family with the hope that the 6-week summer exchange program will help bring about mutual understanding and friendship for these children. To find out more about being a host family or supporting this most extraordinary program, call the above number.

WELSH ASSOCIATIONS

■ **St. David's Welsh Society of Georgia** (953-1040). The society, named in honor of the patron saint of Wales, was formed to encourage the preservation of Welsh culture, language and history. Membership is open to anyone whose heritage is Welsh or who is interested in learning more about Wales. The society meets at 2:00pm, the second Sunday of each month, at Skyland United Methodist Church, 1850 Skyland Ter., NE, Atlanta. And don't forget the annual Welsh St. David's Day Dinner held in March of each year.

CELTIC ASSOCIATIONS

■ **Celtic Heritage Centre — *On the Horizon.*** The Celtic community is actively raising funds to build a Celtic Heritage Centre which will house a museum, library, space for cultural activities and classes, and meeting rooms for Atlanta-area Celtic organizations. It is hoped that the realization of a Celtic Centre will provide Atlantans with a means to appreciate the cultural heritage of the Celts including their language, art, history, music and dance.

LITERARY & OTHER CLUBS

■ **Atlanta Sherlock Holmes Society** (231-1258). Sherlockians meet monthly and sponsor annual social functions.

■ **The Jane Austen Society of North America** (924-3922). Meetings are held the second Thursday of every other month at the Oxford Too Bookstore, 2395 Peachtree Rd., NE, Atlanta, where society members discuss the works of this great British writer.

■ **Burns Club of America**, Alloway Pl. (off Confederate Ave. east of Grant Park), Atlanta (381-2136). The Robert Burns Cottage is the location for the literary meetings of 100 Atlantans dedicated to the works and spirit of the great Scottish bard, Rabbie Burns. Meetings feature readings from Burns and other prominent literary figures, lectures, informal discussions and, of course, the singing of "Auld Lang Syne." Each September, on a Saturday evening, the cottage is the location for an authentic *ceilidh,* an evening of piping, singing and dancing.

■ **The Society for Creative Anachronism** (627-6416). The Atlanta chapter of this national organization is devoted to the research and re-creation of the Middle Ages and Renaissance. Members dress in reproductions of costumes and weaponry from these periods and hold public demonstrations, tournaments, mock wars and festivals. All interested Atlantans are encouraged to attend fighter practice Sunday from 11:00am–3:00pm at the Georgia Hill Neighborhood Facility Lawn or attend weekly meetings on Wednesday at 8:00pm at the same location.

SCHOOLS, CLASSES, LANGUAGE

■ **Earthsong Dulcimer Works**, 464 Grant St., SE, Atlanta (688-1377) offers classes in dulcimer, guitar and auto harp.
■ **Irish Arts of Atlanta Dancers** (873-5621) sponsors Irish language classes throughout the year.

NEWSPAPERS, MAGAZINES, BOOKS, VIDEOS

■ **The Celtic Connection of Atlanta**, 5 Whitlock Ave., Marietta (426-5521) has a large selection of Irish, Scottish and Welsh books, gift items, music and videos.
■ **Taste of Britain**, 73 S. Peachtree St., Norcross (242-UKUK) carries Scottish music tapes.
■ **Oxford Book Store**, 2345 Peachtree Rd., NE, Atlanta (364-2700) and 360 Pharr Rd., NE, Atlanta (262-3333); and **Borders Book Shop**, 3655 Roswell Rd., NE, Atlanta (237-0707) have a large selection of British newspapers and magazines, including *The Times of London*, *Punch* and *The Economist*. Other area bookstores such as **BookStar**, 4101 Roswell Rd., NE, Marietta (578-4455); and **Brentano's**, 4400 Ashford-Dunwoody Rd. (Perimeter Mall), Atlanta (394-6658) occasionally carry British newspapers and magazines. Of course, books and popular music by British authors and rock stars may be found in almost every Atlanta area book or music store.

SHOPPING CENTERS, IMPORT STORES, HOTELS

ENGLISH DESIGNERS

A sampling: **Alfred Dunhill of London, Inc.**, 3393 Peachtree Rd. (Lenox Square), Atlanta (231-2142) sells men's clothing and furnishings; **Burberry's of London**, 3393 Peachtree Rd. (Lenox Square), Atlanta (231-5550) carries men's and women's clothing and coats from Britain; **Churchill's English Shoes**, 3393 Peachtree Rd. (Lenox Square), Atlanta (231-3155) stocks a large selection of men's shoes; **Laura Ashley**, 3393 Peachtree Rd. (Lenox Square),

Atlanta (231-0685) and 4400 Ashford-Dunwoody Rd. (Perimeter Mall), Atlanta (395-6027) sells women's and children's designer clothes and fabric; and **Laura Ashley Home**, 1 West Paces Ferry Rd. (Peachtree Rd.), Atlanta (842-0102) showcases designer home furnishings and accessories such as fabrics, wallpaper and furniture.

BRITISH IMPORTS

■ **The English Shop,** 5360 Peachtree Industrial Blvd., Atlanta Flea Market, Chamblee (454-9755) has a selection of British gifts, pub ware, crystal, postcards, clothes and a few grocery items. Open only on Friday, Saturday and Sunday.

■ **Taste of Britain**, 73 S. Peachtree St., Norcross (242-UKUK), a delightful import store on the square in Norcross, has a large selection of British gifts such as teacups, teapots, place mats, pictures, tartan ties and stationery, along with a small selection of British, Scottish and Irish groceries.

■ **The Waterford Wedgwood Store**, 3393 Peachtree Rd. (Lenox Square), Atlanta (365-0110) stocks a full selection of Wedgwood china, Waterford crystal and Reed and Barton silver.

IRISH IMPORTS

■ **Irish Crystal Co.**, 3168 Peachtree Rd. (Peachtree Plaza), Atlanta (266-3783) carries a large selection of fine Irish crystal and linens.

CELTIC SHOPS

■ **The Celtic Connection of Atlanta**, 5 Whitlock Ave., Marietta (426-5521) specializes in Irish, Scottish and Welsh gift items. The store also stocks pipe band supplies, Irish dance pumps, hard shoes, kilts to order, music tapes and videos, sweaters, shirts, jewelry, crystal and lots of St. Patrick's Day supplies.

■ **History of Names**, Glover Enterprises, 4584 Q. Valley Pkwy., Smyrna (961-5127) can provide you with a scroll or coat of arms bearing information about the history of your surname.

■ **PFR Reproductions**, 1345 Spring St., Atlanta (881-1646) sells quality replicas from the ancient world, including Celtic, Roman and Medieval carvings and tiles.

MUSICAL INSTRUMENTS

■ **Classic Bagpipes**, 4046 Brymond Ct., Tucker (934-3016) carries used sets of Scottish bagpipes; **Robert Cunningham**, 446 Clifton Rd., Atlanta (373-0955) handcrafts Celtic harps, early keyboard instruments and, occasionally, dulcimers; **Earthsong Dulcimer Works**, 464 Grant St., SE, Atlanta (688-1377) sells dulcimers, guitars and auto harps; **Guy A. Gaddis**, 13340 Providence Rd., Alpharetta (475-7240) handbuilds fretted and hammered dulcimers and bowed psalteries; and **Handcrafted Dulcimers**, 913 S. Main St., Suite J, Stone Mountain (469-5529) carries handcrafted mountain and hammered dulcimers, harps, autoharps and bowed psalteries, books, lessons, tapes and accessories.

GROCERIES, MARKETS, BAKERIES

■ **The English Shop,** 5360 Peachtree Industrial Blvd., Atlanta Flea Market, Chamblee (454-9755) carries a small selection of British grocery items. Open only on Friday, Saturday and Sunday.

■ **Scottish Specialty Foods**, 2523 Roosevelt Hwy., Suite B6, College Park (762-1002) sells specialty foods from Great Britain, including tinned (canned) goods, condiments, chocolates, frozen pastries, bangers, kidney pies and Scottish kippers. Call ahead, but usual hours are afternoons Monday–Friday and all day Saturday.

■ **Taj Mahal Imports, Indian, Pakistani & British Grocery**, 1594 Woodcliff Dr., NE, Atlanta (321-5940) carries a broad selection of British food products for those who miss such British specialties as salad cream, biscuits (cookies), Marmite, Bovril, Ribena and Cadbury chocolates.

■ **Taste of Britain**, 73 S. Peachtree St., Norcross (242-UKUK), located on the square in Norcross, has a large selection of groceries from the British Isles, such as tinned (canned) goods, chocolates, teas, sausages, bacon and frozen meat pies.

RESTAURANTS

BRITISH-STYLE RESTAURANTS

■ **Atlanta Shakespeare Tavern**, 499 Peachtree St. (4 blocks south of the Fox Theatre), Atlanta (874-5299). The home of the Atlanta Shakespeare Company serves a pub-style meal during its evening performances of Shakespearean plays (and occasional works by other British playwrights). Open: Dinner: Wednesday–Saturday.

■ **Prince of Wales Pub**, 1144 Piedmont Ave. (between 13th & 14th Sts. across from Piedmont Park), Atlanta (876-0227). The English-style pub serves a large selection of British ales and offers typical pub fare during lunch hours, including Cornish pastries and steak and mushroom pie. Hot snacks are available evenings. Open: Daily.

■ **Reggie's British Pub & Restaurant**, 317 CNN Center (Marietta Blvd.), Atlanta (525-1437). The Victorian-style pub is where Anglophiles in Atlanta relax after hours, enjoy a large selection of British ales and spirits, and dine on prime ribs of beef and other pub fare. The pub is also the location for the British community's special celebrations, such as the annual celebration of the Battle of Britain and the annual July 4th "Grand-Losers" party saluting George Washington with lots of jolly good fun. Open: Lunch and Dinner: Daily.

■ **Ugly Mug Pub**, 3585 Peachtree Industrial Blvd. (before Pleasantdale Rd./Howell Ferry Center), Duluth (497-1459). The Scottish pub serves specialties like fish and chips, Scotch eggs, shepherd's pie, prime rib and British ale. Special Sunday Brunch. Open: Lunch and Dinner: Daily.

IRISH-STYLE RESTAURANTS

■ **County Cork Pub**, 56 E. Andrews Dr. (Irby Ave. near Roswell Rd.), Suite 16, Atlanta (262-2227). Authentic Irish fare, such as lamb stew, Irish sausage, corned beef sandwiches and soda bread, may be enjoyed at this very Irish pub. A full line of Irish ale and spirits is also available. Open: Dinner: Daily.

TEAS

■ **Ritz-Carlton Atlanta**, 181 Peachtree St. (Ellis St. across from Macy's), Atlanta (659-0400). A traditional tea is served daily from 3:00pm–5:00pm in the hotel lobby with tea sandwiches, fruit tarts and pastries.

■ **Ritz-Carlton Buckhead**, 3434 Peachtree Rd. (across from Lenox Square), Atlanta (237-2700). A traditional tea complete with tea sandwiches, scones and pastries is served daily from 3:00pm–5:00pm in the hotel lobby.

ENTERTAINMENT: THEATRE, DANCE, MUSIC, CLUBS, FILMS, T.V. & RADIO, SPORTS

THEATRE

■ **The Atlanta Shakespeare Company**, Atlanta Shakespeare Tavern, 499 Peachtree St. (4 blocks south of the Fox Theatre), Atlanta (874-5299) presents Shakespearean works and, on occasion, works by other British playwrights on Wednesday through Saturday evenings. You may also enjoy a pub-style meal during performances.

■ **Georgia Shakespeare Festival**, Oglethorpe University, 4484 Peachtree Rd., NE, Atlanta (264-0020), produced every summer by the Georgia Shakespeare Festival Society (233-1717), presents three outdoor performances of Shakespearean plays in repertory. "Camp Shakespeare," a one-day summer acting workshop for children, is also held at Oglethorpe University during summer months.

■ **Neighborhood Playhouse**, 430 W. Trinity Pl., Decatur (373-5311) presents at least one British mystery each year, such as a recent production of *Cards on the Table* by Agatha Christie.

■ **Southeastern Savoyards**, 6840 Ramundo Dr., Doraville (396-0620) has performed light operas, mainly Gilbert & Sullivan, for the last ten years. These operas are full-scale lavish productions supported by a 14-piece orchestra. Productions are usually presented at the Georgia Tech Theatre for the Arts.

■ **Theatre Gael**, P.O. Box 77156, Atlanta 30357 (876-1138) presents plays, poetry, music and films offering Atlantans an opportunity to experience the rich cultural traditions of Ireland, Scotland and Wales. At least one children's show is offered each year. Performances are at different locations, such as the 14th Street Playhouse, Agnes Scott College and The Theatrical Outfit.

Other local theatre companies often perform works by or about British, Scottish and Irish authors, such as **Callanwolde Fine Arts Center's** recent performance of *The Minstrel and the Shirra,* a one-man drama about the life of Sir Walter Scott, one of Scotland's most celebrated writers.

DANCE & MUSIC — LOCAL

■ **Irish Arts of Atlanta** (873-5621) is the local affiliate of the Irish cultural organization *Comhaltas Ceoltoiri Eireann,* and promotes traditional Irish music, song, dance and culture with special emphasis on the Irish language. Anyone interested in Irish cultural traditions is welcome to attend. The club has also brought to Atlanta a special tour called "The Comhaltas Ceoltoiri Eireann Annual North American Tour," one of the most celebrated exchange programs between Ireland and North America. The tour featured the cream of Irish traditional musicians, singers and dancers.

■ **Royal Scottish Country Dance Society**, P.O. Box 33905, Decatur 30033 (982-9438) seeks to perpetuate Scottish country dances. Classes of various levels are held throughout the metropolitan Atlanta area, and each year the society sponsors social dances, workshops and a Fall Gala. The bimonthly newsletter *The Petronella Paper* has a variety of articles of interest to Scottish country dancers.

- **Glencoe School of Highland Dancing** (934-3016) has as its top priority the enjoyment of Scottish dancing heritage and offers dance classes at all levels. Students also perform at various Celtic and international festivals throughout the city.
- **English Country Dance Group** (876-3456) holds monthly dances at the Beacon Hill Dance Studio in Decatur the second Saturday of every month. Included are country (contra) dances from England and New England, as well as round and square dances. Emphasis is on sociability, not performance.
- **The Drake School of Irish Dance** (876-0048) and **The Mulligan School of Irish Step Dancing** (926-9059) offer Irish dancing lessons for children and adults. Students often perform at local festivals.
- **Fiddler's Green Coffee House**, Garden Hills Recreation Center (at Pinetree Dr. and Rumson Rd.), Atlanta (875-8942) is sponsored by the Atlanta Area Friends of Folk Music and often features Celtic folk songs and harp music. Get-togethers are on the third Saturday of every month. Other coffeehouses featuring contemporary and traditional Celtic music are: **Lena's Place Coffeehouse**, Central Congregational Church, 2676 Clairmont Rd., Atlanta (936-4102) held on the second Saturday of every month; **Northwest Unitarian Congregation Coffeehouse**, 1025 Mt. Vernon Hwy., Sandy Springs (951-5500) held on the first Saturday of every month; **Pat's Place**, St. Patrick's Episcopal Church, 4755 N. Peachtree Rd. (outside I-285), Atlanta (455-6523) held on the third Friday of every month; and **Trinity Coffeehouse**, Trinity United Methodist Church, 265 Washington St. (near the State Capitol), Atlanta (659-6236) held on the fourth Saturday of every month.
- **In-Town Down-Home Dulcimer Club** (634-3578) welcomes mountain dulcimer players of all levels at their monthly meetings held the second Sunday of each month.
- **Scottish Harp Society of Atlanta** (659-3936) promotes Scottish tradition through the perpetuation and enjoyment of traditional Scottish and Celtic harp music.
- **Welsh Choir** (953-1040), which will perform at society events and at festivals in Atlanta, is presently being formed by The St. David's Welsh Society.
- **Sacred Harp Singing Schools** (923-5817), sponsored by The Atlanta Area Friends of Folk Music, offer classes taught by nationally known master singers. (Sacred Harp is a 200-year-old form of a capella singing.) Call for information about this year's schedule.

Atlanta has a large number of entertainers who perform traditional folk music from England, Ireland and Scotland and/or play the bagpipes and other Celtic instruments. A sampling: **Atholl Highlanders Pipe Band** (299-3096); **The Atlanta Pipe Band** (394-0334/378-2757); **Bagpipes by John Recknagel** (934-3016); **Gan Ainm** (378-5808/378-2757); **Greenway Sparks** (659-3936); **John and Patti McIlroy** (623-9792); **John Mohr MacKintosh Pipes and Drums** (469-4212/469-0803); and **Buddy O'Reilly Band** (373-0448).

■ **James W. Flannery**, Emory University professor of theatre and film studies and founder of The Yeats International Festival and Abbey Theatre in Dublin, is a specialist in the dramatic works of W.B. Yeats and a singer and performer of Irish and Celtic folk music. He hopes to start a Celtic and Irish Studies Center at Emory. Look for announcements about concerts by this world-renowned performer who was named one of the 100 most prominent Irish-Americans.

DANCE & MUSIC —
INTERNATIONAL PERFORMERS

World-class performers may be enjoyed year-round in Atlanta. A sampling of recent performances: **The Scholars of London Chamber Singers** performed French chansons, English folk songs, madrigals, classical glees and contemporary songs at Oglethorpe University; **Scottish Chamber Orchestra**, one of the most sought after orchestras in the world, was brought to Atlanta by the Spruill Center for the Arts; **The Tallis Scholars**, a British vocal ensemble, performed sacred music from the Renaissance; **Boys of the Lough**, a Celtic quintet, performed at the Variety Playhouse; and **Avon Schools Symphonic Wind Band of Great Britain** performed at the Woodruff Children's Art Festival and Symphony Hall.

■ **Windstorm Productions** (874-2232) presents high-quality English, Irish, Scottish and Celtic folk, traditional and rock music throughout the year at various locations in Atlanta including Emory University and The Variety Playhouse.

BRITISH-STYLE PUBS

■ **The Churchill Arms**, 3223 Cains Hills Pl., NW, Atlanta (233-5633); **Churchill's Pub**, 1401 Johnson Ferry Rd., NE, Marietta (565-2739); **Prince of Wales Pub**, 1144 Piedmont Ave. (between 13th & 14th Sts. across from Piedmont Park), Atlanta (876-0227); **Ugly Mug Pub**, 3585 Peachtree Industrial Blvd., Duluth (497-1459); and **Reggie's British Pub & Restaurant**, 317 CNN Center, Atlanta (525-1437) are all reasonable facsimiles of British pubs, complete with dart boards and a large selection of imported ale and spirits.

IRISH-STYLE PUBS

■ **County Cork Pub**, 56 E. Andrews Dr., Suite 16, Atlanta (262-2227) offers Irish ale and spirits, pub-style food, dart teams, Irish entertainers and a gift shop, making this pub the undisputed center of Irish night life in Atlanta.

■ **Limerick Junction**, 822 N. Highland Ave., Atlanta (874-7147) in Virginia-Highlands features Irish ale and spirits along with live music and an outside seating area. The Irish-style bar also serves a small selection of "pub grub," such as hamburgers, fish and chips and Irish stew.

■ **Kelly's Tap Room**, 1598 Roswell Rd., Marietta (578-6872) features a few brands of Irish ale and spirits, dart teams and occasional Irish entertainment. This Irish-themed bar will soon be introducing shepherd's pie and Irish stew to its snack menu.

T.V. & RADIO

■ **WRFG–FM (89.3)** airs "The Celtic Hour" on Sunday between 12:00noon–1:00pm, featuring Irish, British and European Celtic music. The show is hosted by John Maschinot of the Buddy O'Reilly Band.

■ **WABE–FM (90.1)** broadcasts "My Word," a delightful BBC quiz show featuring Frank Muir and Dennis Norden, on Thursdays at 6:30pm.

■ **BBC (British Broadcasting Company World Service)** may be heard on short-wave radio, at varying frequencies, throughout the day. You may subscribe to *London Calling* for monthly program guides at a cost of $20.00/year. Write: *London Calling*, P.O. Box 76S, Bush House, Strand, London, England WC2B 4PH. The British Consulate General (524-5856) will also send you a less detailed program guide.

■ **British Mysteries, Comedies** and **Soap Operas** may be viewed on public television throughout the year.

SPORTS

■ **Atlanta Cricket League** (971-6094/381-0727/447-9248) began in 1989 and has already grown from just two teams to nine. British expatriates, Indians, Pakistanis, South Africans and West Indians compete every Sunday, May–October, at four fields in metro Atlanta. Call for more information.

FEBRUARY

■ **Oglethorpe Ball**, British-American Business Group (920-2224). The British-American Business Group celebrates the founding of Georgia by James Oglethorpe by throwing a lavish ball with an actor from the Royal Shakespeare Company flown in specially to portray the General himself.

MARCH

■ **Welsh St. David's Day Dinner** (953-1040). The annual celebration of the birth of St. David, the patron saint of Wales, includes dinner and lots of camaraderie.

■ **The Hibernian Society's Ball** (299-9399). This annual function of the Hibernian Benevolent Society of Atlanta features traditional Irish pipers and singers, along with great all-American dance music.

■ **St. Patrick's Day Festival and Parade**, Friendly Sons of St. Patrick, Atlanta (392-1272). The Buckhead Parade usually begins at Frankie Allen Park and proceeds down Pharr Road to Bolling Way, to East Paces Ferry Road, to Maple Drive and then back to the Park. An old-fashioned carnival is held at the corner of East Paces Ferry Road and Bolling Way with rides, games, amusements, children's activities and food.

■ **St. Patrick's Day Parade**, Hibernian Benevolent Society of Atlanta (378-1255). For over 108 years, the exciting St. Patrick's Day Parade has proceeded down Peachtree Road to Underground Atlanta, ending up in Woodruff Park. In more recent years, the celebration has continued with an all-night party at Underground Atlanta.

■ **St. Patrick's Day Celebration**, Stone Mountain Village (498-2097). The Village celebrates St. Patrick's Day with Irish dances, "specials" in the Village restaurants and Irish cultural events.

■ **St. Patrick's Day Celebration**, Chateau Élan, Georgia (800/233-WINE). Celebrate St. Patrick's Day at Chateau Élan and enjoy Irish entertainment, afternoon tea, craft demonstrations and an evening medieval feast.

■ **St. Patrick's Day County Cork Irish Festival**, Buckhead, Atlanta (262-2227). A celebration of St. Patrick's Day at the Buckhead tavern includes Irish entertainment, jugglers, pipers, food and lots of beer.

■ **St. Patrick's Day at Limerick Junction**, Virginia-Highlands, Atlanta (874-7147). Food, drink, live remote music in the pub's back parking lot and Irish folk singers are the usual events held during the holiday celebration.

SPRING

■ **Atlanta Celtic Festival** (394-4081). The annual celebration of Irish, Scottish, Welsh and Celtic heritage features Celtic food, beer, exhibits, wares, music, dance, theatre, folklore and workshops. The festival has also featured an *Irish Feis*, a competitive music festival with Irish step dancing. A fund-raiser for the festival, Celtic Cabaret, is held close to St. Patrick's Day and features five hours of continuous entertainment including Scottish and Irish dancing, Welsh singing, Scottish pipers and readings from Dylan Thomas.

■ **Scottish Days**, Indian Springs, Georgia (706/775-6734). Indian Springs welcomes visitors to the historic Indian Springs Hotel for a celebration of 18th century Oglethorpe Highlanders camp life. Cooking, musket drills, bagpipe music, and Scottish dance and music are some of the featured events.

■ **Georgia Renaissance Festival**, Fairburn, Georgia (964-8575). For six weekends and Memorial Day Weekend, Atlantans may enjoy an authentic 30-acre Renaissance Village complete with jugglers, magicians, fire-eaters, comedian troupes and minstrels. Knightly games and activities, an authentic crafts village, and food and drink round off this very unusual festival.

SEPTEMBER

■ **Commemoration of the Battle of Britain**, Reggie's British Pub & Restaurant, Atlanta (525-1437). Reggie's Pub commemorates the Battle of Britain with a special evening featuring British sing-alongs and other entertainment including videos with footage of the Battle of Britain. Members of the RAF and other prominent members of Atlanta's British community are often present.

■ **The Burns Club of Atlanta's Annual Ceilidh** (KAY-lee), Alloway Place, Atlanta (381-2136). The Burns Club of Atlanta hosts an authentic *ceilidh* in late September featuring an evening of Scottish piping, singing, dancing, fiddling and food.

OCTOBER

■ **Stone Mountain Highland Games and Scottish Festival & Tattoo**, Stone Mountain Park, Atlanta (396-5728/498-5702). Kilted clans compete in highland athletic events, while pipe-and-drum band competitions, Scottish folk dancing, sheep herding contests, parades and pageantry entertain the crowds. Clan and Tartan information tents, Scottish shops and food abound.

■ **Scottish Presbyterian Heritage Fair**, Norcross Presbyterian Church, Norcross (448-7744). This celebration of the history and heritage of Scotland and the Presbyterian Church in the U.S. includes Scottish music and dance, Scottish-American food, entertainment, a "kirking of the tartans," a tartan tea

16

room, genealogy experts, Scottish merchants and programs in the sanctuary.
■ **Olde English Festival**, St. Bartholomew's Church, Atlanta (634-3336). The festival recaptures the flavor of Merry Old England, complete with Renaissance art, antiques, a flea market, a book sale, children's activities, music, dance, drama, food, decorations and other period activities.

DECEMBER

■ **Christmas at Callanwolde**, Callanwolde Fine Arts Center, Atlanta (873-3256). The annual Christmas celebration may sometimes feature a Scottish night co-hosted by the St. Andrew's Society. Activities include a Christmas *ceilidh* with pipers, dancers, singers, Celtic instrumentalists, harp music, storytellers and a roll call of the clans.

RESOURCES

BRITISH OFFICES

■ **British Consulate General**, 245 Peachtree Center Ave., Suite 2700, Atlanta 30303 (524-5856); **British American Business Group**, 6472 Church St., Suite E, Douglasville 30134 (920-2224); and **British Tourist Authority**, 2580 Cumberland Pkwy., Suite 470, Atlanta 30339 (432-9635).

IRISH OFFICES

■ **Industrial Development Authority of Ireland**, P.O. Box 190129, Atlanta 31119 (351-8474); **Irish Trade Board**, 240 Peachtree St., Suite 2214, NE, Atlanta 30303 (524-1765); and **Irish Tourist Board**, 1201 W. Peachtree St., 49th Floor, Atlanta 30309 (875-1496).

Bastille Day celebration sponsored by Alliance Française d'Atlanta.

tbe frencb community

HISTORY & NEIGHBORHOODS

The French expatriate community in Atlanta, presently numbering about 400, is very loosely connected. Most of the French residents are here for business purposes, and the temporary nature of their stay in Atlanta has not made it necessary for them to seek each other out or form clubs for social companionship and support. Atlantans of French descent and Francophiles frequent the Alliance Francaise, where they are offered an opportunity to speak French and utilize the many resources offered by the cultural and social center. Recently, the French American Chamber of Commerce has assumed an active role in promoting French cultural activities and has become an excellent source for information about the community's activities.

HISTORICAL SITES & MUSEUMS

■ **High Museum of Art**, Robert Woodruff Arts Center, 1280 Peachtree St., NE, Atlanta (892-HIGH). The museum's permanent collection includes French porcelains and ceramics, impressionist paintings and Rodin sculpture. Special traveling exhibits of French impressionist and postimpressionist art often visit the museum, such as the recent exhibit "Impressionist and Post-Impressionist Prints," featuring prints by Gauguin, Cassatt, Renoir and Toulouse-Lautrec. French language films sponsored by the Alliance Française and other organizations are often screened at the museum's auditorium. Hours: Tues., Wed., Thurs. and Sat. 10:00am–5:00pm; Fri. 10:00am–9:00pm; and Sun. 12noon–5:00pm. Admission fee.

■ **Chateau Élan, Ltd. Vineyards**, Route 1 (30 minutes north of Atlanta on I-85/Exit 48) Hoschton (800/233-WINE or 706/867-8200). The European-

French-style winery is often the location for the French community's social and cultural events. The Chateau itself sponsors French-themed events, such as an annual Bastille Day Celebration in July and year-round wine appreciation classes and cooking demonstrations. The Chateau also maintains an art gallery and golf course; hosts automobile shows and races; maintains a European-style health spa; and serves afternoon teas Monday–Saturday, deluxe brunches on Sunday and elegant dinners Thursday–Sunday in Le Clos, its French-oriented formal dining room. Future plans for the Chateau include the addition of a resort hotel, conference center and expanded golf course. Hours: Daily 10:00am–10:00pm. Tours of the winery are from 11:00am–4:00pm. Free.

GALLERIES

■ Antique shops and galleries carry large selections of French paintings, antiques and collectibles. A sampling: **Antique Shop of Paris,** 631 Miami Cir., Suite 18, Atlanta (231-1238); **Galerie Timothy Tew**, 75 Bennett Street (TULA), Atlanta (352-0655); **Gallery de France**, 351 Peachtree Hills Ave., Atlanta (262-9612); **Woodward & Warwick Antiques**, 22 Bennett St., NW, Atlanta (355-6607); and **Bureau International Ltd.**, 690 Miami Cir., NE, Atlanta (266-1660).

COMMUNITY, RELIGIOUS & CULTURAL ASSOCIATIONS

■ **Alliance Française**, 1360 Peachtree St. (One Midtown Plaza), Suite 200, NE, Atlanta (875-1211). The Alliance Française encourages the study of French language and culture and fosters friendly relations between French-speaking and American people. The cultural center sponsors French language films, lectures, concerts, classes, festivals, luncheon get-togethers and other social gatherings, all with a French flavor. Members of the Alliance receive a quarterly newsletter and have use of the library which houses a collection of French language books, magazines, newspapers, records, and audio and video tapes.

■ **French American Chamber of Commerce**, 999 Peachtree St., Suite 2095, NE, Atlanta (874-2602). Although chartered to serve as a business organization for the Atlanta community, the chamber recently began cosponsoring numerous special events throughout the year, including: "Passport to France," an annual elegant dinner party in May, a Bastille Day celebration in July, the Beaujolais Nouveau Wine Festival in November and wine appreciation classes year-round. Feel free to contact the chamber for more information about the community and its special events.

■ **Friends of Vieilles Maisons Françaises – Friends of Old French Homes** (252-6497). The historical preservation association meets regularly to socialize and engage in fundraising activities for the restoration of French architectural treasures. Membership is open to all Francophiles in the city.

■ **Blerancourt Museum of French-American Friendship** (252-6497). The local chapter of this non-profit association raises money for the Blerancourt Museum of French-American Friendship, lying to the north of Paris. This unusual museum contains collections of paintings, sculptures and archives illustrating 200 years of the alliance between France and the U.S.

■ **Atlanta-Toulouse Sisters City Committee** (237-5311/894-4590). The committee promotes cultural and social interactions between the citizens of Atlanta and its sister city in France, including the sponsorship of an annual visit to Toulouse.

schools, classes, language

LANGUAGE CLASSES

■ **Alliance Française School**, 1360 Peachtree St. (One Midtown Plaza), Suite 200, NE, Atlanta (875-1211) offers a wide range of French language conversational courses at 14 different levels with small classes and native-speaking teachers experienced in teaching French as a second language. Private lessons and special classes for business persons also can be arranged.

■ **The French Institute**, 4421 Tree Haven Dr., NE, Atlanta (252-9347) offers group and private classes for adults at different levels year-round.

■ **Artplay, Inc.** (607-9660) offers an after-school French language program for children ages 5 and older. During summers, it cosponsors a camp program at the International School for children ages 4 and older.

WINE TASTINGS

■ **French American Chamber of Commerce**, 999 Peachtree St., NE, Atlanta (874-2602) sponsors wine appreciation classes and tastings throughout the year.

■ **Wine Seminars** and **Private Tastings** are offered by Atlanta's wine connoisseurs, the most popular being presided over by **Yves Durand** (993-4337), former owner of Rue de Paris French restaurant, author of *A Connoisseur's Guide to Bordeaux Wines,* first-prize winner of the Sommelier's Blind Wine-Tasting championships in Paris and winner of the French Medal *Mérite Agricole.* Year-round he conducts wine seminars and courses for groups. During winter months, he conducts wine "savourings," which offer Atlantans an opportunity to enjoy his private wine collection and learn more about French wines. Monsieur Durand also leads wine-tasting tours to the regions of Bordeaux and Burgundy, twice annually.

NEWSPAPERS, MAGAZINES, BOOKS, VIDEOS

■ **Alliance Française**, 1360 Peachtree St. (One Midtown Plaza), Suite 200, NE, Atlanta (875-1211). Members are entitled to free use of the library's collection which includes about 1,200 books and magazines, newspapers, records, audio tapes and videos.

■ **Oxford Book Store**, 2345 Peachtree Rd., NE, Atlanta (364-2700) and 360 Pharr Rd., NE, Atlanta (262-3333); and **Borders Book Shop**, 3655 Roswell Rd., NE, Atlanta (237-0707) have a few French-language newspapers, a large selection of French fashion magazines, and some French-language books for children and adults. Other area bookstores such as **BookStar**, 4101 Roswell Rd., NE, Marietta (578-4455); and **Brentano's**, 4400 Ashford-Dunwoody Rd. (Perimeter Mall), Atlanta (394-6658) occasionally carry French fashion magazines.

SHOPPING CENTERS, IMPORT STORES, HOTELS

FRENCH IMPORTS

■ **The Country French Connection**, 3211 Cains Hill Pl., NW, Atlanta (237-4907), a French-style boutique and antique gallery, sells antiques, linens, crystal, china and decorative arts. Most gifts are imported from France.

■ **Giftissimo**, 3500 Peachtree Rd. (Phipps Plaza), Atlanta (233-4563) offers a selection of unusual gifts from France and specializes in GAULT ceramics.

■ **Pierre Deux**, 111 W. Paces Ferry Rd., NW, Atlanta (262-7790) carries exquisite Country-French fabrics and linens as well as boxes, picture frames, luggage, tote bags and other items that can be decoratively covered in fabric. The store also stocks a selection of French china, crystal and other decorative arts.

FRENCH DESIGNERS

■ **Cartier**, 3393 Peachtree Rd. (Lenox Square), Atlanta (841-0840) offers for sale designer jewelry, scarves, belts, crystal, china and handbags; **Louis Vuitton**, 3393 Peachtree Rd. (Lenox Square), Atlanta (266-3674) sells expensive designer luggage and accessories including handbags, attaches and suitcases; **Petit Mom**, 3500 Peachtree Rd. (Phipps Plaza), Atlanta (266-1203) sells pricey French and Italian clothes for children; and **Rodier of Paris**, 3393 Peachtree Rd. (Lenox Square), Atlanta (261-5033) carries designer clothing for the career woman including knit, silk, wool and tweed separates.

GROCERIES, MARKETS, BAKERIES

■ **Alon's**, 1394 N. Highland Ave., Atlanta (872-6000). Continental and French-style breads, croissants and pastries are baked daily at this bakery in the Virginia-Highlands neighborhood. Scrumptious sandwiches on homemade bread, such as roasted chicken with pesto sauce and roast beef with rosemary mayonnaise, are also available.

■ **Joli Kobe French Bakery**, 5600 Roswell Rd., Atlanta (843-3257). The French-Japanese bakery in the Prado Shopping Center creates croissants, tartes and gourmet pastries blending French and Japanese culinary tastes. The small luncheon area serves a light luncheon fare of salads, meats and sandwiches.

■ **Le Gourmet**, 2341 Peachtree Rd., Atlanta (266-8477). The French-style bakery in Peachtree Battle Shopping Center sells breads, croissants and other French pastries in the bakery section and Italian and Continental fare in the restaurant section.

■ **Maison Gourmet**. 2581 Piedmont Rd., Atlanta (231-8552). The bakery portion of this restaurant sells French and European-style cakes and tarts, but orders must be placed one day in advance.

■ **Maison Robert**, 3867 Peachtree Rd., Atlanta (237-3675). French and European pastries may be enjoyed at this deluxe bakery, including fruit tarts, marzipan creations, macaroons, rum balls, luscious cakes and homemade chocolates. A lovely tea room to the rear of the bakery offers a light lunch of Country-French cuisine.

■ **Pain de Lyon**, 2625 Piedmont Rd., Atlanta (814-0827). A large selection of French-style baked goods are prepared daily. A lilmited sandwich menu is also offered.

FRENCH RESTAURANTS

■ **Anne Marie's**, 3340 Peachtree Rd. (Tower Place/Piedmont Rd.), Atlanta (237-8686). Classic French fare is served in this small, intimate French restaurant designed as a replica of a 300-year-old French country home. Specialties include Mediterranean Seafood and Duck Grandmother's Style. Open: Lunch: Mon.–Fri.; Dinner: Mon.–Sat.

■ **Bernard's Restaurant**, 1193 Collier Rd. (near DeFoors Ave.), Atlanta (352-2778). The small restaurant in Collier Hills specializes in French-Continental fare. Open: Lunch: Mon.–Fri.; Dinner: Mon.–Sat.

■ **Café de la Place**, 2140 Peachtree Rd. (Brookwood Square), Atlanta (351-3792). The French-style bistro, featuring an open exhibition kitchen, serves Country-French cuisine in a "casual elegant" atmosphere. A selection of rabbit, veal, seafood, duck and pasta entrees are prepared daily. Special weekend brunch. Open: Lunch and Dinner: Daily.

■ **Cassis**, Hotel Nikko Atlanta, 3300 Peachtree Rd. (Piedmont Rd.), Atlanta (365-8100). Hotel Nikko's elegant restaurant serves Continental cuisine "influenced by the South of France" in a dining area overlooking a traditional Japanese garden. Mussel soup and rack of lamb are two specialties. Special Sunday brunch. Open: Breakfast, Lunch and Dinner: Daily.

■ **Ciboulette**, 1529 Piedmont Rd. (Monroe Dr.), Atlanta (874-7600). Ciboulette features the combined culinary talents of Jean Barchet, award-winning former City Grill chef, and Tom Cochill, former owner and chef of the 5-star La Française in Chicago. The upscale bistro serves high quality but reasonably priced French-American dishes. Food critics highly recommend the bouillabaisse and Capon Coq au Vin. Open: Dinner: Tues.–Sun.

■ **Claudette's French Restaurant**, 315 W. Ponce de Leon Ave. (Wachovia Bank Tower), Decatur (378-9861). Loyal customers continue to enjoy Country-French cuisine served in an Old European-style dining room. Specialties include Veal á la Creme, Lobster Bisque and Coq au Vin. Open: Lunch: Mon.–Fri.; Dinner: Tues.–Sat.

■ **La Café Crêpe**, Marietta Station Walk (Marietta Depot), Marietta (426-8003). Crêpes, onion soup, salads and other French specialties are served at this charming restaurant on Marietta Square. Open: Lunch: Mon.–Fri.; Dinner: Thurs.–Sat. (Open for dinner Monday–Wednesday for large groups.)

■ **Le Clos**, Chateau Élan Vineyards, Route 1, Hoschton (800/233-WINE or

706/867-8200). Chateau Élan's formal dining room has a French chef and French orientation. Five-course fixed meals pair entrees with the vineyard's premium wines. Open: Dinner: Thurs.–Sun.

■ **The Restaurant, Ritz-Carlton**, Ritz-Carlton Atlanta, 181 Peachtree St. (Ellis St. across from Macy's), Atlanta (659-0400). The deluxe, elegant and expensive restaurant serves "French-inspired" fare, earning this restaurant the title "Best French Restaurant in Atlanta" year after year by almost every restaurant guide. Special weekend brunch. Open: Lunch: Mon.–Fri.; Dinner: Daily.

■ **Resto des Amis**, 3060 Peachtree Rd. (Buckhead Plaza/W. Paces Ferry Rd.), Atlanta (364-2170). Internationally known chefs Guenter Seeger of the Ritz Carlton in Buckhead and Jean Palladin of the Jean Lois at Washington, D.C.'s Watergate Hotel are part-owners of this new bistro opening in early 1993. Under the supervision of the two chefs' combined culinary talents, the restaurant will feature moderately-priced casual French cuisine. A huge rotisserie grill suspended from the ceiling over an open hearth will dominate the dining room area. Outdoor patio seating will also be available.

■ **South of France Restaurant**, 2345 Cheshire Bridge Rd. (La Vista Rd.), Atlanta (325-6963). Country-French fare and European specialties are served in a cozy country-inn atmosphere, complete with wood-burning fireplaces. The chef's creations include Saumon Aux Artichauts En Crabe Bernaise and Crevettes en Croute. Open: Lunch: Mon.–Fri.; Dinner: Mon.–Sat.

■ **Violette**, 3098 Briarcliff Rd. (Clairmont Rd.), Atlanta (633-3323). Violette, one of Atlanta's best-kept secrets, serves inexpensive but delicious patés, crêpes, salads, pastas and Country-French fare in a comfortable and charming atmosphere. Open: Lunch: Mon.–Fri.; Dinner: Daily.

CONTINENTAL RESTAURANTS

Atlanta boasts numerous top-quality restaurants specializing in innovative Continental cuisine with a French accent. A complete listing of restaurants is not possible, so here is a small sampling:

■ **The Abbey**, 163 Ponce de Leon Ave. (North Ave.), Atlanta (876-8532). The converted church in Midtown features waiters dressed in authentic monk robes, 60-foot stained glass windows, a harpist in the choir loft and award-winning contemporary Continental cuisine. The restaurant boasts that it has one of the finest wine cellars in the country. Open: Dinner: Daily.

■ **The Bistro at Andrews Square**, 56 E. Andrews Dr. (W. Paces Ferry Rd.), Atlanta (231-5733). Regional cuisine from Europe is featured at this bistro-style restaurant in Andrews Square. Delicious French-style desserts are the restaurant's specialty. Open: Dinner: Tues.–Sat.

■ **City Grill**, 55 Hurt Plaza (Edgewood Ave.), Atlanta (524-2489). The elegant dining room in downtown Atlanta has been praised for its nouvelle Continental cuisine and spectacular dessert pastries. A variety of veal, lamb, beef and game entrees served with light sauces are always offered. Open: Lunch: Mon.–Fri.; Dinner: Daily.

■ **Country Place**, 1197 Peachtree St. (Colony Square), Atlanta (881-0144). This popular restaurant, like others in the Peasant Restaurant chain, serves creative American and Continental cuisine in a Country-French atmosphere. Special Sunday brunch. Open: Lunch: Mon.–Fri.; Dinner: Daily.

■ **La Tour**, 3209 Paces Ferry Pl. (W. Paces Ferry Rd.), Atlanta (233-8833). European-style dishes with a French flair are prepared at this restaurant where the interior "reflects the grandeur and opulence of the French empire." Soufflés and paté foie gras are two specialties. Live piano music is featured. Open: Lunch: Mon.–Fri.; Dinner: Mon.–Sat.

■ **Le Rendez-Vous**, 3120 Roswell Rd. (Peachtree and Roswell Rds.), Atlanta (231-2073). The bistro-style restaurant has received solid reviews for its Continental cuisine which includes a few Country-French specialties. Open: Lunch: Sun.–Fri.; Dinner: Daily.

■ **103 West**, 103 W. Paces Ferry Rd. (Peachtree Rd.), Atlanta (233-5993). Often called the most glamorous of Atlanta's restaurants, 103 West features Continental cuisine "with a French influence." The baroque setting, extensive wine list and excellent service have earned this restaurant Mobil's Four Star rating and numerous titles as "Atlanta's Best Restaurant." Open: Dinner: Mon.–Sat.

■ **Pano's & Paul's**, 1232 W. Paces Ferry Rd. (Northside Pkwy.), Atlanta (261-3662). Luxurious and continental, this restaurant receives superior reviews for its attentive service and excellent food. Specialties include Escalopes de Veau Epicure, Supremes de Poularde en Daube and paté foie gras. Open: Dinner: Mon.– Sat.

■ **The Patio by the River**, 4199 Paces Ferry Rd. (across the Chattahoochee River), Atlanta (432-2808). This beautiful restaurant, overlooking the Chattahoochee River, uses the flavors of classic Italian and French cooking to create innovative Continental fare. Enjoy a stroll through the riverbank gardens before or after your meal. Special Sunday brunch. Open: Lunch: Mon.–Fri.; Dinner: Mon.–Sat.

■ **Les Saisons**, 590 W. Peachtree St. (The Penta Hotel), Atlanta (881-6000). Continental cuisine is served in an elegant "European art deco ambience." Specialties include cioppino, rack of lamb and paté fois gras. Open: Lunch: Mon.–Fri.; Dinner: Mon.–Sat.

THEATRE & MUSIC

- Theatre productions of work by French playwrights are occasionally presented by companies in Atlanta. For example, in the last year, Theater Emory presented a **Molière Festival** consisting of the two plays, *School for Wives* and *Flying Doctors*, performed in repertoire; and Classic TheaterWorks at Kennesaw State College presented a contemporary translation of Molière's comedy, *Le Misanthrope*.
- French music recitals and concerts may be enjoyed at various Atlanta locations. A sampling: Agnes Scott College hosted a baritone recital of "French Art Songs" sung by **Gerard Souzay;** and Windstorm Productions presented an **Old World Music Series** of French and Celtic folk music at Emory University and The Variety Playhouse.

FILMS

- **The Francophone Film Series** at the High Museum of Art (892-HIGH) and Emory University (727-6562) is often cosponsored by The Alliance Française and French American Chamber of Commerce. Films are screened throughout the year.
- French film fans should keep an eye on **Garden Hills Cinema**, 2835 Peachtree Rd., NE, Atlanta (266-2202); **Plaza Theatre**, 1049 Ponce de Leon Ave., Atlanta (873-1939); and **The Screening Room**, 2581 Piedmont Rd. (Lindbergh Plaza), Atlanta (231-1924) — the three movie theatres in Atlanta that frequently screen foreign language films. Also, the **Metropolitan Film Society** (729-8487) screens independent and foreign language films at the Cinevision Screening Room, 3300 NE Expressway Office Park, Building 2, Atlanta.

MAY

- **Passport to France**, French American Chamber of Commerce, Atlanta (874-2602). France is brought to Atlanta each year during an elegant dinner party featuring French vintage wines, cuisine, entertainment, fashion shows, silent and live auctions, and lots of French atmosphere and camaraderie.

JULY

■ **La Fête du 14 Juillet (Bastille Day)** (874-2602). The various French organizations in Atlanta often host an outdoor soirée commemorating the start of the French revolution. French dancing, singing, caricaturists, mimes, jugglers, and delicious food are featured.

■ **Spirit of France Festival (Bastille Day)**, Chateau Élan, Braselton (800/233-WINE). Chateau Élan Winery's celebration of Bastille Day includes French flags, artists, music, gourmet luncheons, wines, breads, pastries, chocolates and hot-air balloon rides.

NOVEMBER

■ **Beaujolais Nouveau Festival** (874-2602). The wine-tasting festival offers Atlantans an opportunity to sample the year's new batch of Beaujolais wine flown in from France especially for the event.

RESOURCES

■ **French Consulate General**, 285 Peachtree Center Ave., Suite 2800, NW, Atlanta 30303 (522-4226); **French American Chamber of Commerce**, 999 Peachtree St., NE, Suite 2095, NE, Atlanta 30309 (874-2602); **French Trade Commission**, 285 Peachtree Center Ave., NE, Building 2, Suite 2801, Atlanta 30303 (522-4843); **Lorraine Development Office**, USA Division, 57 Forsyth St., NW, Healy Building, Suite 1110, Atlanta 30303 (659-2353); and **MIRCEB** (Brittany), Representative for the Southeast Region, 825-F Franklin Ct., Marietta 30067 (424-5111).

German specialties prepared by restaurateur Mary Ann Wilson.

GERMANY, AUSTRIA, SWITZERLAND & LIECHTENSTEIN

HISTORY & NEIGHBORHOODS

One of the original purposes for the formation of the colony of Georgia was to create a haven for European Protestants suffering religious persecution in their native countries. This vision always included room for refugees from countries other than England. Thus, when the Lutheran Salzburgers were suffering a fierce persecution by the Catholic clergy in March of 1734, James Oglethorpe helped direct about 300 Salzburgers to Savannah, where they founded Ebenezer (Rock of Help), one of the first settlements in the colony of Georgia. Because the original Ebenezer was inaccessible and the marshy land was less than desirable, the settlement relocated about 25 miles north of Savannah, on the Savannah River, in 1736. It was renamed New Ebenezer. Further immigration brought the population of New Ebenezer up to 1,200 by 1741, and the colony quickly began to grow. Because the Salzburgers were industrious, directed and disciplined, the colony prospered better than most of the early Georgian settlements.

Later in the 1700s, Palatines, Swabians, other Germans and Austrians, and a handful of Swiss settled in Georgia. As the number of Germans and Salzburgers arriving in Georgia began to grow, the Germans soon became Georgia's second largest national group after the British. It was not surprising that the first governor of Georgia, John Adam Treutlen, hailed from the Rhine Palatine. To commemorate his role in the early days of Georgia as Governor and Revolutionary War leader, a portrait of Governor Treutlen is on permanent display in the Georgia State Capitol in Atlanta.

Today, Atlantans of German, Austrian and Swiss descent, together with the estimated 2,500 German and Swiss expatriates temporarily residing in the metro Atlanta area, keep alive the traditions, culture and celebrations of their native countries. More and more Fasching Karnivals, Mayfest Celebrations and Oktoberfests spring up each year. All Atlantans are encouraged to attend these lively gatherings and partake of the abundant food, beer and Bavarian entertainment.

HISTORICAL SITES & MUSEUMS

■ **High Museum of Art**, Robert Woodruff Arts Center, 1280 Peachtree St., NE, Atlanta (892-HIGH). The museum's permanent collection includes German porcelains and ceramics from the Cocke & Scott-Allen Collections, as well as an extensive collection of German expressionist lithographs and works on paper. Hours: Tues., Wed., Thurs. and Sat. 10:00am–5:00pm; Fri. 10:00am–9:00pm; and Sun. 12noon–5:00pm. Admission fee.

■ **Helen, Georgia**, North Georgia Mountains (706/878-2181). This north Georgia mountain city has re-created an Alpine village, and although the community is by no means a genuine Bavarian settlement, the townsfolk have done their best to put together about 150 Bavarian and Scandinavian gift shops and restaurants specializing in Bavarian food, clothes and gift items. Bavarian festivals abound, and it is rare when Bavarian entertainment cannot be found on any given weekend.

GALLERIES

■ **Goethe-Institut of Atlanta**, 1197 Peachtree Street, Colony Square – Plaza Level, Atlanta (892-2388). The Goethe-Institut, which is the cultural and resource center for the German community in Atlanta, houses a gallery whose changing exhibits portray various aspects of German culture. For example, the gallery has exhibited: "Cartoons: Die Deutchen im Ausland," drawings by German cartoonists portraying "typical" German behavior during their vacations; and "The Wall," a photographic display chronicling the "coming down" of the Berlin Wall. Hours: Mon.–Thurs. 9:00am–5:00pm; Fri. 9:00am–2:00pm. Free.

■ And don't forget . . . occasionally Atlanta-area galleries will feature work of German, Swiss or Austrian content. For example, in 1991, which was the 700th birthday of Switzerland, the **Ann Jacob Gallery**, 3500 Peachtree Rd. (Phipps Plaza – First Floor), Atlanta (262-3399) featured Swiss paintings and sculptures in celebration of the birthday; and **Emory University's Schatten Gallery**, Woodruff Library, 540 Ashby Cir., Atlanta (727-6868/727-6861) displayed photos and documents depicting 700 years of democracy and chronicling the political climate of Switzerland from its inception. **Schatten Gallery** was also the location for an exhibit entitled "Mozart," sponsored by the Austrian Cultural Institute.

GERMAN

■ **Goethe-Institut of Atlanta**, 1197 Peachtree Street, Colony Square – Plaza Level, Atlanta (892-2388).   The Goethe-Institut is the primary cultural and research center for the German community in Atlanta. Its goal is to promote German language and culture, strengthen ties, and improve understanding between the people of Georgia and Germany. Gallery exhibits, musical events, films, lectures and social activities proliferate. Call to receive a copy of their quarterly calendar of events, which is full of information about events in Atlanta and the Southeast.

■ **Friends of German Language and Culture** (422-9956). The society is primarily a social group whose activities include a dance on the first Saturday of each month at the Knights of Columbus on Buford Highway. Members also sponsor a Fasching Karnival in January, a Mayfest Celebration in the spring, an Oktoberfest Festival in the fall and a Christmas Gala in December.

■ **Salzburger Society – Atlanta Chapter** (427-2287). The Atlanta Chapter of the Georgia Society has recently formed so local Salzburgers may have an opportunity to interact socially and culturally with other descendants of the Savannah Salzburger colonial settlements. There are three classes of membership: (1) documented descendants of the original Salzburger colonial settlers in the Ebenezer settlement near Savannah; (2) associate members who are spouses of such descendants; and (3) friends of the Society who may be Atlantans interested in the history and culture of the Salzburgers. The Georgia Salzburger Society sponsors a large Labor Day Celebration in Ricon, Georgia.

■ **Southside German Culture Club** (961-9322). The social and cultural club meets the fourth Thursday of each month at the Officer's Club at Fort Gillem and gathers annually for an Oktoberfest celebration and traditional Christmas dinner featuring entertainment by the German Lieder Kreis.

■ **Deutsche Kirchengemeinde (German Church)** (373-1682). Plans are underway to build a church in Atlanta which will be part of the Evangelical Lutheran in America – Southeastern Synod and offer regular German language worship services. Until such time, a congregation led by a German pastor meets monthly for German language services at the **Lutheran Church of the Messiah** at 465 Clairmont Ave., Decatur (373-1682) which also conducts a special German language service on Easter Sunday. Also, **Grace Lutheran Church**, 115 N. Highland Ave., NE, Atlanta (875-5411) holds a German language Christmas Eve service; and **Prince of Peace Lutheran Church of Fayetteville**, 257 Hwy. 314, Fayetteville (461-3403) conducts a German and English Christmas service featuring the German Lieder Kreis.

SWISS

■ **The Swiss-American Society of Atlanta**, 3343 Peachtree Rd., NE, Atlanta (264-2689). The society hosts social events for Atlanta's Swiss community, including a Swiss Independence Day (August 1st) picnic at Lake Allatoona featuring Swiss folkdance, music, traditional food and wine. During Christmas, the group hosts a large party where members of the society may enjoy Swiss pastries and chocolates and a visit from Santa Claus.

schools, classes, language

LANGUAGE

■ **Goethe-Institut of Atlanta**, 1197 Peachtree Street, Colony Square – Plaza Level, Atlanta (892-2316) offers language classes for beginning, intermediate and advanced students, as well as a "learn German in Germany program" for children ages 10–13 years and teenagers ages 14–18 years.

■ **German/English Language Association**, 1436 Womack Rd., Dunwoody (394-7420) offers private German language classes at different levels for adults during daytime hours.

■ **German School of Atlanta**, Dickerson Middle School, 317 Woodlawn Dr., Marietta (642-0822) is an intensive Saturday morning language program for children K–12th grade. The school also sponsors organized play groups for parents who wish to speak German with their preschool children. Adult language classes at three different levels are available.

■ **Artplay, Inc.** (607-9660) offers an after-school German language program for children ages 5 and older and cosponsors a summer camp program at the International School for children ages 4 and older.

WINE TASTINGS

■ **The German Wine Society** (393-4584) sponsors wine tastings, classes and formal dinners featuring German wines. Call to be placed on the society's mailing list.

- **Goethe-Institut of Atlanta**, 1197 Peachtree Street, Colony Square – Plaza Level, Atlanta (892-2226) has a library housing over 10,000 books in German and English on literature, language, history, art, film and German affairs. The Institut library also houses language learning material, children's books, periodicals, cassettes, slides and documentary videos. Use of the library is free and open to the public.
- **Oxford Book Store**, 2345 Peachtree Rd., NE, Atlanta (364-2700) and 360 Pharr Rd., NE, Atlanta (262-3333); and **Borders Book Shop**, 3655 Roswell Rd., NE, Atlanta (237-0707) carry a large selection of German newspapers, fashion magazines and some German language books. Other area bookstores such as **BookStar**, 4101 Roswell Rd., NE, Marietta (578-4455); and **Brentano's**, 4400 Ashford-Dunwoody Rd. (Perimeter Mall), Atlanta (394-6658) occasionally carry German fashion magazines.
- **Helen, Georgia** has a large number of Bavarian gift shops stocking books, music and videos from Germany and Europe.

HOTELS

- **Penta Hotel**, 590 W. Peachtree St., NW, Atlanta (881-6000). With the recent opening of the contemporary 25-story hotel, Atlanta now has another hotel featuring "European elegance and superior service." Included among the Penta's five restaurants are the Rathskeller, an authentic *Bierstube* serving German specialties and authentic draft beer; and Les Saisons, an elegant Continental-style restaurant.
- **Swissôtel Atlanta**, 3391 Peachtree Rd., NE, Atlanta (365-0065). The Swissôtel's European atmosphere has made it a favorite location for special events and festivities sponsored by the Swiss and European community. Café Gamay and Opus, the hotel's two restaurants, are consistently praised by Atlanta's food critics for their creative Continental cuisine and Swiss-style pastries. During special

occasions, such as Switzerland's 700th birthday celebration, Opus offers deluxe dinners of contemporary Swiss cuisine paired with Swiss wines.

IMPORT STORES

■ **Bally of Switzerland**, 3393 Peachtree Rd. (Lenox Square), NE, Atlanta (231-0327) sells expensive and conservative fashioned luggage, belts, travel accessories and shoes; and **Mondi International**, 3393 Peachtree Rd. (Lenox Square), NE, Atlanta (262-1694) features designer women's clothes imported from Germany.

■ **Helen, Georgia** has about 150 Bavarian and Scandinavian gift shops specializing in imported Alpine gift items. A sampling: **House of Tyrol**, Main Street, Helen (706/878-2264) & Hwy. 75N (between Helen and Cleveland) (706/865-2951) carries fine import gifts, clothing, porcelain, jewelry, food delicacies, books, videos and music from around the world; **Opa's Chalet Imports**, Main Street, Helen (706/878-2090) sells Alpine clothing, personalized beer steins, cuckoo clocks, Austrian wood carvings, candles, gnomes, music boxes and other fine imports; and **Wesson's Alpine Sportsman**, Gesellschaft Mall, Main Street, Helen (706/878-3544) offers pewter, hummel figurines, cuckoo clocks, steins, gnomes, porcelain and other Alpine import items.

SWISS CHOCOLATES

■ **Classic Confections**, 75-H Mendel Dr., SW, Atlanta (696-8536). Rolf Schittli and Hans Wenger manufacture Swiss chocolate dessert cups. Although the gourmet dessert cups are primarily sold to Swissair and gourmet restaurants, the public is also welcome to shop.

■ **Monchelle Lamoure, Inc.**, 75-G Mendel Dr., SW, Atlanta (691-1211). Hans Wenger is the creator of award-winning Swiss-style chocolate truffles which are supplied to Swissair and gourmet restaurants. The public is also welcome to shop.

■ **Swiss Gourmet Chocolates** may be found throughout Atlanta at various gourmet grocery stores, boutiques, farmers markets and even department stores.

GROCERIES, MARKETS, BAKERIES

GERMAN BAKERIES & DELICATESSENS

■ **Best of Europe Deli**, 3393 Peachtree Rd. (Lenox Square Food Court),

Atlanta (261-3806). The European-style delicatessen has a selection of European sausages and hard-to-find delicatessen meats.

- **The German Bakery, Inc.**, 2914 White Blvd., Decatur (296-4336). A large selection of German baked goods and breads (try the sourdough bread or Black Forest loaf) may be enjoyed at this 30-year-old bakery, along with a variety of German delicatessen meats and sausages.
- **Taste of Europe**, 6631 Roswell Rd. (Abernathy Square), Atlanta (255-7363). The attractive European-style deli specializes in European meats and sausages of all kinds. There is a small seating area.
- **Willie's German Bakery**, 4808 Flat Shoals Rd., Decatur (987-3298). On weekends, the bakery offers a large selection of breads, coffee cakes and other German-style baked goods.
- **Hofer's Bakery**, 334 Sandy Springs Cir., NW, Atlanta (255-8200). Members of the German and Swiss community continue to flock to Sandy Springs to purchase the large selection of German pastries, breads, cold cuts and sausages sold by this long-standing institution. Try one of the coffee cakes or strudels — they are delicious.

SWISS BAKERIES

- **Confis Products and Services, Inc.**, 75-H Mendel Dr., SW, Atlanta (696-8536). Rolf Schittli's award-winning Swiss tortes and confections are sold to Swissair and gourmet restaurants. The public is also welcome, but orders should be placed in advance.
- **Swiss Café**, 3000 Windy Hill Rd., Marietta (984-9110). French and Swiss-style gourmet baked goods are served at this dessert cafe. A luncheon menu is also offered.
- **Swissôtel Atlanta**, 3391 Peachtree Rd., NE, Atlanta (365-0065, ext. 2482). The gift shop at the continental Swissôtel sells Swiss/European-style breads prepared by Swissôtel's executive pastry chef.

RESTAURANTS

GERMAN RESTAURANTS

- **Edelweiss**, 85 Mill St. (Roswell Mill), Roswell (993-2306). Reasonably priced German specialty foods, such as sauerbraten, venison and apple strudel, may be enjoyed at this restaurant located in the historic Roswell Mill complex. Live entertainment by The German Alpine Band is offered every Friday and

Saturday evening. Special Oktoberfest dinners are offered during the fall. Open: Dinner: Tues.–Sun.

- **Kurt's at River Manor**, 4225 River Green Pkwy. (between Pleasant Hill Rd. and Hwy. 120 off Peachtree Industrial Blvd.), Duluth (623-4128). Restaurant critics give high marks to this restaurant featuring Continental cuisine with a "German accent." A selection of excellent German wines may also be enjoyed. Open: Lunch: Mon.–Fri; Dinner: Mon.–Sat.
- **Petite Auberge**, 2935 N. Druid Hills Rd. (Toco Hills Shopping Center), Atlanta (634-6268). On Friday and Saturday evenings, the restaurant also serves "Essvergnugen," a menu of German specialties, in addition to the regular French and Continental menu. Special Oktoberfest dinners are featured during the months of September and October. Open: Lunch: Mon–Fri.; Dinner: Mon.–Sat.
- **Rathskeller**, 590 W. Peachtree St. (North Ave.), Atlanta (815-5008). Authentic German fare is offered at this *Bierstube* located in the Penta Hotel. Specialties include frankfurters, bratwurst and wienerschnitzel. During Oktoberfest, the restaurant serves special dinners featuring authentic Bavarian dishes accompanied by live entertainment. Open: Lunch and Dinner: Daily.
- **Zur Bratwurst Bavarian Restaurant**, 529 N. Central Ave. (across the tracks from the Ford plant), Hapeville (763-4068). Restaurant critics unanimously recommend that Atlantans travel south to sample the authentic wursts, soups, salads, potatoes and breads served by this German restaurant. Open: Lunch: Tues.–Fri.; Dinner: Tues.–Sat.
- Helen, Georgia has many German-style restaurants. A sampling: **Alt Heidelberg Restaurant & Lounge** (706/878-2986), **Hofer's Bakery & Konditorei Café** (706/878-8200), **Gessellschaft Haus Restaurant & Lodge** (706/878-2136), **Hofbrauhaus Inn Restaurant and Lounge** (706/878-2248) and **Restaurant Edelweiss & Lounge** (706/878-3466).

SWISS & SWISS-STYLE RESTAURANTS

- **The Hedgerose Heights Inn**, 490 E. Paces Ferry Rd. (between Piedmont and Peachtree Rds.), Atlanta (233-7673). For the last ten years, Swiss-born chef Heinz Schwab has prepared spectacular continental cuisine at this award-winning restaurant, including seafood, steaks and specialty game entrees followed by dessert soufflés. Open: Dinner: Tues.–Sat.
- **Dante's Down the Hatch**, Underground Atlanta (between Lower Alabama and Lower Pryor Sts.), Atlanta (577-1800) and 3380 Peachtree Rd. (across from Swissôtel between Piedmont and Lenox Rd.), Atlanta (266-1600). Fondue entrees, live jazz and live crocodiles (at the Buckhead location) may

be found at this Atlanta institution. Open: Dinner: Daily.

- **The Dining Room**, Ritz-Carlton Buckhead, 3434 Peachtree Rd. (across from Lenox Square/Lenox Rd.), Atlanta (237-2700). Atlanta's premier restaurant features exceptional continental cuisine "with a Swiss and German flavor" prepared by star chef Guenter Seeger. Impeccable service, real silver and china and an extensive wine list have helped earn this restaurant the accolade of "Georgia's Best Restaurant," year after year. Open: Lunch: Mon.–Fri.; Dinner: Mon.–Sat.
- **Melting Pot Restaurant**, 857 Collier Rd. (Howell Mill Rd.), Atlanta (351-1811) and 3610 Satellite Blvd. (Gwinnett Mall Corners), Duluth (623-1290). The Swiss-style fondue restaurant has been enjoyed by Atlantans for many years. Lunch is available for large groups only. Open: Dinner: Daily.
- **Swissôtel**, 3391 Peachtree Rd. (next to Lenox Square), Atlanta (365-0065). The two restaurants in the Swissôtel have consistently received praise by food critics for their continental-style cuisine with a heavy concentration on Swiss-style baked goods and pastries. **Café Gamay**: Breakfast, Lunch and Dinner: Daily. **Opus**: Breakfast and Lunch: Mon.–Sat.; Dinner: Daily.

AUSTRIAN-STYLE RESTAURANTS

- **Café Intermezzo**, 4505 Ashford-Dunwoody Rd. (Park Place across from Perimeter Mall), Atlanta (396-1344). The café features light continental fare and a dazzling selection of coffees, espresso, cappuccino, liquors and Viennese and German pastries. The restaurant suggests you "close your eyes and you could be in Vienna." Open: Breakfast: Mon.–Sat.; Lunch and Dinner: Daily. Also, try **Café Intermezzo**, 1845 Peachtree Rd. (Collier Rd.), Atlanta (355-0411) which features a large variety of coffees, espresso, cappuccino, liquors and unique desserts. Special weekend brunch. Open: Lunch and Dinner: Daily.

ENTERTAINMENT: THEATRE, DANCE, MUSIC, CLUBS, FILMS, T.V. & RADIO, SPORTS

THEATRE & PUPPETRY

- Atlanta theatre groups occasionally perform plays by German playwrights. For example, Seven Stages Performing Arts Center recently performed *Carmen Kittel* by **Georg Seidel**; The Actor's Express performed *The Caucasian Chalk Circle* by **Bertolt Brecht**; and Theater Emory hosted a **Brecht Fest**.
- **The Center for Puppetry Arts**, 1404 Spring Street, Atlanta (874-0398) is often the location for special puppet shows of German content such as a

recent show for adults entitled *Anne & Enno Podehl: Theater in Wind Hermann — A German Story,* a moving puppet show recounting memories of life during the Third Reich.

DANCE & MUSIC

■ **Metro Atlanta Lieder Kreis** (963-6330), a unique performing group led by Else Shewmaker, preserves German and Austrian culture through the presentation of traditional folk songs, lieder (art songs), classical and choir pieces. Look for the group at Atlanta-area festivals, benefits and religious services.

■ **Atlanta Bach Choir**, 1026 Ponce de Leon Ave., NE, Atlanta (872-2224) may be enjoyed at various events throughout the year and during "Bach Around the Clock," the choir's annual festival featuring day-long performances of compositions by Bach.

■ **Pro-Mozart Society** (934-6330) sponsors a selection of concerts of music by Mozart (of course) throughout the year at various locations. The Mozart lovers' society also participates in special celebrations such as a **Mozart Festival** at the Ritz Carlton in Buckhead, celebrating the composer's 200th birthday with authentic Austrian luncheons, teas and dinners accompanied by Mozart-era music.

■ Classical music concerts featuring German and Austrian compositions may be enjoyed almost every night of the year somewhere in Atlanta. A sampling: **Atlanta Musica Antiqua** (476-1725) performs programs featuring high Baroque ambiance with period instruments and costumes; **Atlanta Chamber Players** (651-1228) often performs works by Schubert, Beethoven and Brahams; and **Choral Guild of Atlanta** (435-6563) frequently performs works by Bach and other period composers.

■ World-renowned German performers often find their way to Atlanta, such as the dance group **Tanzgruppe Maja Lex,** which performed at Seven Stages Performing Arts Center. (The performers, who are proponents of *Ausdruckstanz*, a rhythmic modern dance movement, were primarily from Cologne, Germany and Basel, Switzerland.) Also, tenor **Peter Schieier** accompanied by pianist **Armen Guzelimian** performed at Emory University.

■ **Helen, Georgia** (706/878-2181) features Bavarian entertainment year round at all of its special events.

FILMS

■ **Goethe-Institut of Atlanta**, 400 Colony Square, Atlanta (892-2388) screens award-winning German language films every Wednesday evening. Call for a schedule.

- **The German Film Series at Emory University** (727-6562) presents German language films with English subtitles.
- The Consulate General of Switzerland sponsored a Swiss evening at Emory University celebrating the 700th birthday of the founding of Switzerland. The event featured an art exhibit and a screening of the Swiss film *Messidor*. Look for announcements about other screenings of Swiss films.

MISCELLANEOUS

- **Liechtenstein Circus**, "The World's Smallest Complete Circus," visited Emory University and entertained for free. Keep your eye out for return visits!

festivals & special events

JANUARY & FEBRUARY

- **Fasching Karnival**, Knights of Columbus Hall, Buford Hwy., Atlanta (422-9956). The Friends of the German Language and Culture sponsors a Fasching Karnival celebration, complete with German entertainment, food and beer.
- **German Mardi Gras Celebration**, The German-American Business Stammitisch and the Atlanta Penta Hotel (454-0442). The Penta Hotel is often the location for a Fasching costume party featuring a German buffet dinner and music by The German Alpine Band.
- **The German School of Atlanta** (993-4766). The German School's annual benefit concert is usually held at Callanwolde Fine Arts Center. Look for announcements in the Goethe-Institut's newsletter.
- **Fasching Karnival**, Helen, Georgia (706/878-2181). Every weekend in January and February, the Helen retail community sponsors a celebration of the German "Mardi Gras" to welcome the coming spring.

MARCH

- **Bach Around the Clock**, Atlanta (872-2224). Bach lovers delight in this festival featuring day-long choral groups, orchestral performances, organ music, chamber and vocal recitals, movies, a coffeehouse, souvenirs, German food, a performance of the Brandenburg Concert and a candlelight evening performance.

MAY

- **MayFest Celebration**, Knights of Columbus Hall, Buford Hwy., Atlanta (422-9956). The Friends of the German Language and Culture sponsors a MayFest dance and celebration.
- **MayFest Celebration**, Helen, Georgia (706/878-2181). During two weekends in May, Helen celebrates MayFest in the mountains with Bavarian food, music and dance.

SEPTEMBER & OCTOBER

- **Atlanta's Oktoberfest**, Knights of Columbus Hall, Buford Hwy., Atlanta (422-9956). Members of the Friends of German Language and Culture celebrate Prince Ludwig of Bavaria's 1810 marriage to Princess Theresa with an Oktoberfest Festival featuring beer drinking, food, pastries, polka music and a Bavarian band. A Bavarian market is also occasionally featured.
- **Oktoberfest at the Penta Hotel**, Atlanta (815-5008). During Oktoberfest, the Rathskeller in the Penta Hotel features special evening menus featuring German delicacies and Bavarian breads, accompanied by live Bavarian entertainment.
- **Oktoberfest of Atlanta**, Sun Valley Beach, Powder Springs (944-6265). During the fall, Sun Valley Beach hosts a family Oktoberfest celebration with rides, games, entertainment and a German buffet.
- **Oktoberfest in Roswell**, Canton Street, Roswell (642-2055). Arts and crafts, samplings of German cuisine, carriage rides, live entertainment and children's activities highlight this Oktoberfest celebration.
- **Oktoberfest**, Helen, Georgia (706/878-2181). The mountain village of Helen celebrates the fall harvest with Bavarian food, music, sing-alongs and lots of dancing. Held Thursday, Friday and Saturday in September; and Monday–Saturday in October.

NOVEMBER & DECEMBER

- **Magical Alpine Christmas in Helen** (706/878-2181). Helen celebrates a Bavarian Christmas in the mountains from late November through December and presents an Altstadt Christmas Market on Friday, Saturday and Sunday throughout December.

GERMANY

■ **Consulate General of the Federal Republic of Germany**, 285 Peachtree Center Ave., NE, Suite 901, Atlanta 30303 (659-4760); **German American Chamber of Commerce**, 3475 Lenox Rd., Suite 620, NE, Atlanta 30326 (239-9494); **German American Trade Center**, 5139 S. Royal Atlanta Dr., Tucker 30084 (493-9305); and **German-American Business Stammitisch, Inc.** (454-0442).

SWITZERLAND

■ **Consulate General of Switzerland**, 1275 Peachtree St., NE, Suite 425, Atlanta 30309 (872-7874); and **Swiss-American Chamber of Commerce**, 3343 Peachtree Rd., NE, Suite 1800, NE, Atlanta 30326 (264-2689).

AUSTRIA

■ **Honorary Consulate of Austria**, 4200 Northside Pkwy., Building 10, Atlanta 30327 (264-9858); and **Austrian Trade Commission**, 240 Peachtree St., Suite 2214, Atlanta 30303 (524-4022).

Queen Beatrix of the Netherlands visits the King Center in Atlanta.

NETHERLANDS, BELGIUM & LUXEMBOURG

HISTORY & NEIGHBORHOODS

Approximately 1,000 Belgian and 1,500 Dutch citizens reside in the north Atlanta area (Buckhead, Sandy Springs and Roswell) on a temporary basis. The Atlanta-Holland Club and the Pelletier Club offer companionship and support for these Dutch and Belgian expatriates, as well as those Atlantans of Dutch and Belgian descent eager to have an opportunity to speak their native language and socialize with members of their communities. All Atlantans who wish to learn more about the Dutch or Belgian communities are welcome to participate in the many social get-togethers, cultural events and holiday celebrations sponsored by the clubs.

HISTORICAL SITES & MUSEUMS

■ **High Museum of Art**, Robert Woodruff Arts Center, 1280 Peachtree St., NE, Atlanta (892-HIGH). The permanent collection of the museum includes works by Rembrandt and other Dutch masters. Occasionally there are lectures and special exhibits featuring Dutch artists. Hours: Tues., Wed., Thurs. and Sat. 10:00am–5:00pm; Fri. 10:00am–9:00pm; and Sun. 12noon–5:00pm. Admission fee.

■ **Atlanta Botanical Garden**, 1345 Piedmont Rd. (Piedmont Park at The Prado), Atlanta (876-5858). The garden occasionally presents lectures and slide shows showcasing the summer gardens of Holland, including those in Amsterdam, The Hague and Hetloo Palace. Recently, the garden cosponsored a tour of the gardens of Europe, which included the Floridae Horticultural Exhibition in Amsterdam, an event that is held only once every ten years. Call for a schedule of upcoming programs and events. Hours:

Tues.–Sat. 9:00am–6:00pm; Sun. 12noon–6:00pm. (Extended hours during summer months.) Admission fee.

GALLERIES

■ Galleries in the Atlanta area often have special exhibits featuring aspects of Dutch history, culture or art, such as a recent exhibit at **Emory University's Schatten Gallery**, Woodruff Library, 540 Ashby Cir., Atlanta (727-6868/727-6861) entitled, "Anne Frank in the World: 1929-1945," which presented 800 photographs and pages from the diary of Anne Frank, building a picture of life in Nazi Germany and occupied Holland. Another exhibit at **Georgia State's University Art Gallery**, Peachtree Center Ave. at Gilmer St., Atlanta (651-3424) was called "Point of View: Contemporary Dutch Jewelry and Design."

COMMUNITY, RELIGIOUS & CULTURAL ASSOCIATIONS

■ **Atlanta-Holland Club** (634-3302/394-3981). The social group has about 560 members who are either direct descendants of Dutch ancestors, ex-residents of Holland, or were themselves born and raised in Holland. The club meets the first Thursday of each month from 6:00-8:00pm for a *Borrel-Tafel* (beer table or get-together) at the Terrace Garden Inn and often sponsors special events throughout the year, including auto rallies, picnics, and film and video screenings. Membership is open to Dutch citizens and friends of the Dutch community.

■ **The Pelletier Club**. The social club of the Belgian community has monthly get-togethers where natives and friends of the community have an opportunity to relax and feel at home speaking their native languages — Flemish and French. The club also sponsors parties, auto rallies and special events throughout the year. Call the Consulate General of Belgium (659-2150) or the Belgian-American Chamber of Commerce (231-5985) for information about the location of the next meeting.

SCHOOLS, CLASSES, LANGUAGE

■ **Oglethorpe University's Continuing Education Department** (364-8383) usually offers evening Dutch language instruction at different levels.

■ Members of the **social clubs** may be able to provide names of individuals who are willing to tutor children and adults.

NEWSPAPERS, MAGAZINES, BOOKS, VIDEOS

■ **The Belgian-American Chamber of Commerce**, 3333 Peachtree Rd., Suite 222, NE, Atlanta (231-5985) has Belgian newspapers and magazines in its office which may be perused.

■ **Oxford Book Store**, 2345 Peachtree Rd., NE, Atlanta (364-2700) and 360 Pharr Rd., NE, Atlanta (262-3333); and **Borders Book Shop**, 3655 Roswell Rd., NE, Atlanta (237-0707) carry *The European,* an international newspaper featuring events in European countries including Belgium, the Netherlands and Luxembourg.

SHOPPING CENTERS, IMPORT STORES, HOTELS

HOTELS

■ **Swissôtel Atlanta**, 3391 Peachtree Rd., NE, Atlanta (365-0065). The Swissôtel's European atmosphere has quickly made it a favorite location for special events and festivities sponsored by the Dutch, Belgian and other European communities.

IMPORT STORES

■ **Godiva Chocolatier, Inc.**, 3393 Peachtree Rd. (Lenox Square), Atlanta (262-2108) and 4400 Ashford-Dunwoody Rd. (Perimeter Mall), Atlanta (671-9650) specializes in scrumptious Godiva-brand chocolates. Godiva and a selection of other divine Belgian chocolates may be found at various gourmet grocery stores, boutiques, large farmers markets and department stores.

■ **Flowers from Holland, Ltd.**, 3393 Peachtree Rd. (Lenox Square), Atlanta (237-4001) features top-quality flowers from all over the world, specializing, of course, in Dutch tulips and bulbs; and **Holland Blossom Flower Market**, 1230 Peachtree St. (Promenade Two at 15th St.), Atlanta (876-5220) creates exotic flower designs featuring Dutch tulips and bulbs.

■ **Tropical Foods**, 5165 Buford Hwy. (Pinetree Plaza), Doraville (451-4355). The pleasant, spacious market carries several teas, spices and grocery products from West Africa (especially Nigeria) and the Caribbean, as well as a selection of beautiful fabric made in Holland.

■ **Windmill Shop**, White Horse Square, Helen (706/878-3444) has a large selection of imports from Holland, such as Delft china, Dutch tiles, clocks, jewelry, miniatures, windmills and wooden shoes. Sometimes the store carries a small selection of Dutch chocolates and cookies and Indonesian spices.

GROCERIES, MARKETS, BAKERIES

■ **The Royal Bagel**, 1544 Piedmont Rd., Atlanta (876-3512). Recently, a Belgian baker has been added to the bakery's staff, so in addition to bagels and New York-style baked goods, Belgian pastries, such as éclairs and peach-upside-down cake, may be enjoyed at this popular Ansley Mall establishment.

■ **The Wooden Shoe**, Towers Hotel on Main Street, Helen (706/878-3530). The small Helen restaurant has a selection of Dutch and German groceries, pastries and other imported food items.

■ Individual members of the Dutch community often sell **Dutch cheeses** and other imported specialty items. This information is usually announced during Atlanta-Holland Club meetings.

RESTAURANTS

DUTCH CUISINE

■ **Maison Gourmet**, 2581 Piedmont Rd. (Lindbergh Plaza), Atlanta (231-8552). Although the restaurant primarily serves French and continental-style cuisine, occasionally it presents a unique *Rijst-Tafel* (Rice Table), a feast of Dutch and Indonesian specialties requiring days of preparation. In the past, the *Rijst-Tafel* was offered on the last Sunday of each month. Call to find out if it will be offered this year.

■ **The Wooden Shoe**, Towers Hotel on Main Street, Helen (706/878-3530). The small Helen restaurant serves American sandwiches and a few authentic Dutch dishes. Try *Saucyzenbroodjes* (bread puffs filled with homemade sausage and topped with a mustard sauce) — they come highly recommended by food critics. Open: Breakfast, Lunch and Dinner: Daily (except in the winter months when it's only open Saturday and Sunday).

■ **Cafe Brussels**, 5975 Roswell Rd. (Hammond Springs Shopping Center), Atlanta (256-0100). The European cafe, owned by a Belgian family, features freshly baked kosher food, Belgian waffles, pastries, crêpes, soups, salads and imported coffees. Live classical and jazz music may be enjoyed on the patio. Open: Lunch: Sun.–Fri.; Dinner: Sat.–Mon. (Closes late Friday afternoon before sundown for the Sabbath and reopens after sundown on Saturday.)

■ **Il Centro**, 3500 Peachtree Rd. (Phipps Plaza – Lower Level), Atlanta (364-9313). The European-style coffee bar specializes in premium imported coffee and espresso and handmade Druart pralines from Belgium. Open: Mall Hours (9:00 am-9:30 pm Mon.-Sat.; 12 noon-6:00 pm Sun.).

■ And keep in mind . . . some of the chefs in Atlanta's finest restaurants hail from Belgium and often include Belgian dishes on their menus, such as *waterzoo* (aromatic fish or chicken soup), poached turbot topped with a mousseline sauce or traditional pastries.

ENTERTAINMENT: THEATRE, DANCE, MUSIC, CLUBS, FILMS, T.V. & RADIO, SPORTS

■ Presently, there are no traditional **Klog Folkdance** groups in Atlanta, but the community does hope to assemble a troupe in the near future.

■ World-renowned Dutch musicians occasionally find their way to Atlanta, such as **Amsterdam Loeki Stardust Quartet's** performance at Clayton State College's Spivey Hall; **Pia Beck's** concert during the KLM Birthday celebration; and **Kitchens of Distinction**'s appearance at the Cotton Club during the rock group's international tour. Dutch dancers have also performed in Atlanta, such as **Onafhankelijk Toneel** from Rotterdam, who was brought to Seven Stages Performing Arts Center by Several Dancers Core.

■ Belgian entertainers, including world-famous musicians and mimes, have performed in Atlanta for Taste of Belgium and other special events, such as **Children's Choir Rondinella of Knokke**.

■ The Consulate General of Belgium is one of the cosponsors of **Emory University's Francophone Film Series** (727-6562) which sometimes screens French language films produced by Belgian filmmakers.

APRIL

■ **Queen's Birthday** (634-3302). The Atlanta-Holland Club celebrates the Queen's birthday on April 30th with a special get-together and party.

JUNE

■ **Touch of Dutch Festival**, North Atlanta Community Church, Roswell (587-2460). This Dutch Reform Church sometimes celebrates its heritage by hosting an open-air market featuring authentic Dutch crafts, entertainment and foods. A drawing for a free trip to the Netherlands has also been featured.

MISCELLANEOUS

■ **Taste of Belgium**, Atlanta (231-5985). In the past, this festival has included a buffet of Belgian foods and imported beers, exhibits of antique lace, diamonds and imported luxury items, and fine art by Flemish artists. Fashion shows, Belgian entertainment, visits by foreign dignitaries and demonstrations by some of Belgium's famous chefs are also featured. Call for information about the date and location of this year's event.

■ **World War II Liberation Celebration**, The Atlanta-Holland Club, Atlanta (394-3981). Every five years, the Dutch, Belgium, French and Luxembourg communities jointly sponsor a formal dinner honoring the World War II veterans who fought in Europe. Entertainment and reenactments are part of the celebration honoring the veterans and their spouses. The next (and perhaps last) celebration in September of 1995 will be the 50th anniversary of the liberation.

■ **KLM Events** (523-5900). Occasionally, KLM will sponsor social and cultural bashes such as its celebration of the 10th Anniversary of KLM in Atlanta. The week-long event included parties, jazz concerts, ethnic costumes and cosponsorship of "Art in Bloom" at the High Museum of Art.

RESOURCES

NETHERLANDS

■ **Consulate of the Netherlands**, 133 Peachtree St., NE, Suite 2500, Atlanta

30303 (525-4513); and **Netherlands Chamber of Commerce in the United States**, 233 Peachtree St., Suite 404, NE, Atlanta 30303 (523-4400).

BELGIUM

■ **Consulate General of Belgium**, 225 Peachtree St., Suite 800, Atlanta 30303 (659-2150); and **The Belgian-American Chamber of Commerce**, 3333 Peachtree Rd., Suite 222, NE, Atlanta 30326 (231-5985).

Inger Stover, president of the Norwegian Women's Club of Atlanta, greets a visiting Norwegian poet.

The ScanÐinavian Communities

(Sweden, Norway, Denmark, Finland & Iceland)

HISTORY & NEIGHBORHOODS

Approximately 3,000 Scandinavians reside in the Atlanta area and actively participate in the many community events sponsored by the Scandinavian clubs and societies. The communities are eager for Atlantans of Scandinavian descent, as well as those interested in learning more about the countries, to participate in the many social get-togethers, folk dancing activities, cultural events and holiday celebrations sponsored by the organizations. As the 1996 Atlanta Olympics approach, the Scandinavian-American Foundation of Georgia is eagerly seeking ways that the community can participate in the many cultural events that will take place in Georgia, especially those activities involving Atlanta's tribute to Lillehammer, Norway, host of the 1994 Winter Olympics.

Although there are no Scandinavian neighborhoods per se, recently, Swedish developers have undertaken ambitious projects in the midtown area. One of these projects is the GLG Grand, 75 14th Street, Atlanta, developed by Gullstedt Gruppen, which is a 600-foot multi-use tower that reflects an international focus. It houses the Occidental Grand, a 250-room hotel featuring Café Opera, an elegant continental-style resturant, plus office space and luxury residential apartments. The same developer has announced plans to renovate the five-block area surrounding Atlanta's historical Biltmore Hotel on West Peachtree into a mixed-use community called GLG Park Plaza. Another Swedish group has renovated two large buildings near Crawford Long Hospital and named the complex Scandinavian House; long-term plans for the residential, office and retail complex may include the development of a Scandinavian retail mall.

■ **High Museum of Art**, Robert Woodruff Arts Center, 1280 Peachtree St., NE, Atlanta (892-HIGH). The museum is the location for special exhibits of work by Scandinavian artists, such as a recent exhibit, "Edvard Munch: Master Prints From the Epstein Family Collection," featuring more than 90 paintings, lithographs, etchings, mezzotints and woodcuts by the renowned Norwegian artist. Hours: Tues., Wed., Thurs. and Sat. 10:00am–5:00pm; Fri. 10:00am–9:00pm; and Sun. 12noon–5:00pm. Admission fee.

■ **Fernbank Museum of Natural History**, 767 Clifton Rd., NE, Atlanta (378-0127). In 1993, the Museum was honored by a visit from Queen Sonja of Norway, who introduced a special exhibit called "Olympic Winterland: Encounters With Norwegian Cultures." The exhibit featured 102 pieces of art by Norwegian artists, including work by Norway's best-known artist Edvard Munch. Two months of theatre performances, film screenings, concerts, lectures, demonstrations and fiction readings in different venues throughout Atlanta accompanied this event, which was the official opening of Atlanta's Cultural Olympiad. Hours: Mon.–Sat. 9:00am–6:00pm; Sun. 12noon–6:00pm. Admission fee.

GALLERIES

■ **Atlanta International Museum of Art and Design**, Marquis Two Tower – Garden Level, 285 Peachtree Center Ave., Atlanta (688-2467). The small gallery showcases dimensional art, design and craftsmanship for everyday use by the world's societies, both past and present. An exhibit of Scandinavian furnishings and crafts is planned for the near future. Hours: Tues.–Sat. 11:00am–5:00pm; Sun. 1:00pm–5:00pm. Free, but a donation is suggested.

■ **Jon Eric Riis Designs, Ltd.** (881-9847). Jon Riis, one of the founders of the Atlanta International Museum of Art and Design, is himself an artist specializing in textiles and fiber work. The artist's tapestries are sought by numerous private and corporate collectors. Please call for an appointment.

■ Other Atlanta galleries often feature work by Scandinavian artists, such as **The Arts Connection** at Oxford Books, 360 Pharr Rd., Atlanta (237-0005) which recently exhibited work by Finnish artists; and **Emory University's Schatten Gallery**, 540 Ashby Cir., Atlanta (727-6868/727-6861) which exhibited "Pehr Kalm and His Voyage to America: 1747-1751."

■ **Scandinavian-American Foundation of Georgia**, P.O. Box 1166, Decatur 30031-1166 (377-4825). The Scandinavian-American Foundation promotes the interchange of ideas and culture among the five Scandinavian countries and serves as a liaison to the general Atlanta community. The foundation's quarterly newsletter, *Insights,* is an excellent resource for information about the Scandinavian community, club meetings, special activities, language classes, literature discussion groups and holiday celebrations. The well-organized foundation continues to develop more programs and encourages anyone interested in Nordic people and culture to become involved.

■ **Nordic Lodge 708** (355-8807). The Nordic Lodge is the local chapter of the international organization Vasa Order of America, a Swedish-American cultural and fraternal organization for persons of Scandinavian birth or descent, as well as non-Scandinavians married to a member. The Lodge sponsors numerous social and cultural events throughout the year. **Young Vikings** is the children's culture club associated with the Nordic Lodge.

■ **Embla** (449-1325). The Swedish women's club meets monthly for luncheons and special programs.

■ **Svenska Damklubben** (237-1517). The Swedish women's social club meets monthly on Monday evenings for coffee and conversation.

■ **Atlanta Suomi-Finland Society** (343-9753). The society is primarily a social and cultural organization which strives to disseminate information about Finland and Finnish culture and create opportunities for contacts between Atlantans and people of Finnish descent. Membership is open to anyone interested in Finland and Finnish culture.

■ **Ladies of Norway Club** (483-0378). The club is an informal group of women of Norwegian origin who meet monthly on the last Tuesday of each month to speak their native language, indulge in Norwegian customs, and celebrate Norwegian holidays.

SCHOOLS, CLASSES, LANGUAGE

■ **Scandinavian-American Foundation of Georgia** (522-1458/377-4825) offers Danish, Finnish, Norwegian and Swedish language classes throughout the year at several different levels. Recently, a class on Nordic cultures was added to the program.

■ **Oglethorpe University's Continuing Education Program** (364-8383) offers beginners and intermediate Swedish language courses during evening hours.

■ **Swedish Conversation Group** (422-9120) meets at members' homes on the last Thursday of each month. These friendly meetings end with refreshments.

NEWSPAPERS, MAGAZINES, BOOKS, VIDEOS

■ **Norway House of Vinings**, 2950 Paces Ferry Rd. (Vinings Jubilee Shopping Center), Atlanta (435-1502) stocks a selection of English language books written by Scandinavian authors, Scandinavian coffee-table books, children's books and cookbooks.

■ **Scandinavian Gift Shop**, Old Sautee Store, Sautee-Nacoochee (706/878-2281) sells a large number of English language books written by Scandinavian authors, Scandinavian coffee-table books, children's books, travel books and cookbooks.

SHOPPING CENTERS, IMPORT STORES, HOTELS

MODERN FURNITURE

■ **Bova Scandinavian Furniture**, 6500 Dawson Blvd., NW, Norcross (242-6666) carries a large selection of imported, modern Scandinavian furniture; **House of Denmark**, 6248 Dawson Blvd., Norcross (449-5740) has a large selection of imported Scandinavian furniture, rugs, business furniture and household furnishings; and **Scan Haus**, 6358 Dawson Blvd., NW, Norcross (840-0844) also has a large selection of imported, modern Scandinavian furniture.

GIFTS & IMPORTS

■ **Bang & Olufsen**, 3500 Peachtree Rd. (Phipps Plaza), Atlanta (233-5445). Ultra-modern electronics, gifts and specialty items are sold at this very upscale Danish shop.

■ **Norway House of Vinings**, 2950 Paces Ferry Rd. (Vinings Jubilee Shopping Center), Atlanta (435-1502) sells a well-rounded selection of Scandinavian gifts, including sweaters and other hand-knit items, trolls, jewelry, crystal and china, books, linens, candles and imported food delicacies.

■ **Helen, Georgia**, in the North Georgia Mountains, has a few Scandinavian gift shops specializing in the arts and crafts of Sweden, Norway, Denmark, Finland and Iceland. A sampling: **Old Norway House**, Troll St., Helen (706/878-2475) sells a small selection of handmade sweaters and lots of inexpensive gift items such as trolls of all sizes and Viking hats; and **Scandinavian Gift Shop**, Old Sautee Store, Sautee-Nacoochee (706/878-2281) is filled with Scandinavian ski sweaters, knit-goods, hand-carved trolls, crystal, dinnerware, pewter, jewelry, embroideries, books, cheeses and gourmet foods.

GROCERIES, MARKETS, BAKERIES

■ **Offshore Seafood, Inc.**, 5522 N. Peachtree Rd., Chamblee (451-6443). Fresh and smoked salmon, gravlax (salted salmon), mackerel, herring, Scandinavian-style shrimp and crayfish, and other specialty fish are sold at this market year-round. During the holiday season, you may also purchase dried Scandinavian mushrooms, *Västerbotten* cheese and other imported specialty food products. Although the market is primarily for wholesale customers (a lot of Atlanta's best restaurants shop here), the general public is always welcome.

■ **Norway House of Vinings**, 2950 Paces Ferry Rd. (Vinings Jubilee Shopping Center), Atlanta (435-1502). The Scandinavian gift shop has a small selection of Scandinavian cheeses and imported specialty foods, such as cookies, preserves, chocolates and beverages.

■ **Scandinavian Gift Shop**, Old Sautee Store, Sautee-Nacoochee (706/878-2281). The gift shop stocks a large selection of Scandinavian cheeses, chocolates, crackers, cookies, *glogi* (a beverage) and other gourmet specialties.

■ **Potatiskorv** (Potato Sausage), a traditional Christmas food, is sometimes made available to the community during the holiday season. Check the Scandinavian-American Foundation of Georgia's newsletter for announcements or try **Sausage World & Deli**, 5353 Lawrenceville Hwy., Lilburn (925-4493).

RESTAURANTS

■ Since the closing of the Midnight Sun Restaurant several years ago,

Atlantans have eagerly been awaiting the opening of another quality restaurant specializing in Scandinavian cuisine. In the meantime, we may still enjoy such Scandinavian delicacies as fresh or smoked salmon, gravlax, Swedish meatballs and delectable pastries, often appearing on the menus of Atlanta's finest restaurants. And, don't forget . . . the very popular *smörgåsbord*, which we have adopted as our own, actually originates from Sweden.

ENTERTAINMENT: THEATRE, DANCE, MUSIC, CLUBS, FILMS, T.V. & RADIO, SPORTS

■ The **Georgia Scandinavian Folkdancers** (442-9120) has established itself as an important performing group in Atlanta's international folkdance community, and its repertoire includes dances from Denmark, Finland, Norway and Sweden. Although the group is presently inactive, it does hope to perform again in the near future.

■ Performances featuring the work of **Hans Christian Andersen** may often be enjoyed in the Atlanta area, including The Atlanta Ballet's *The Red Shoes* and A Comic Cafe's adaptation for children of *The Ugly Ducking*.

■ The Scandinavian-American Foundation of Georgia has formed a film committee for those interested in bringing **Scandinavian Films** to Atlanta. Look for announcements about future film screenings.

■ World-Class Scandinavian Performers often perform in Atlanta, such as the **Danish National Radio Symphony Orchestra,** which appeared at the Fox Theatre as part of the Coca-Cola International Series.

FESTIVALS & SPECIAL EVENTS

SPRING

■ **Valkpurgis Eve Celebration** (355-8807). The Swedish community's annual spring celebration is often held at Chastain Park. Call for more information.

■ **17th Day of May** (483-0378). Norwegian Independence Day is celebrated by the community. Call for information about the location of this year's celebration.

SUMMER

■ **MidSummer Party** (377-4825). Many of the Scandinavian associations join together to celebrate the summer season with sporting activities, a picnic and a traditional dance around the Maypole.

WINTER

- **Scandinavian Christmas Arts & Crafts Festival** (432-2587/377-4825). The Scandinavian community presents a large arts and crafts festival each year featuring holiday crafts and gifts.
- **Finnish Independence Day Celebration** (343-9753). Finnish Independence Day is celebrated by the community. Call for information about the location for this year's event.
- **Lucia Festival** (279-6440). The Swedish-American Chamber of Commerce celebrates Lucia, the "Queen of Lights," with an elegant dinner and ball.
- **Lucia Celebration** (355-8807). The Nordic Lodge celebrates Lucia, featuring a performance by the Young Vikings at St. John's Lutheran Church. Light refreshments are served afterwards.
- **Family Christmas Celebration** (923-8950). The Atlanta Suomi-Finland Society's annual Christmas celebration includes a drink of glogi followed by a Finnish smorgasbord of traditional baked goods, live entertainment, children's activities, caroling and an appearance by *Joulupukki*, the Finnish Santa Claus.
- **Scandinavian Christmas Morning Service** (377-4825). The Scandinavian-American Foundation of Georgia sponsors a Christmas Morning Service conducted in five Scandinavian languages and English. Coffee, juice and traditional baked goods are served following the service.

RESOURCES

DENMARK

- **Honorary Consulate of Denmark**, 225 Peachtree St., Suite 201, Atlanta 30303 (614-5207); and **Danish Trade Office**, 229 Peachtree St., NE, Suite 1008, Atlanta 30303 (588-1588).

FINLAND

- **Honorary Consulate of Finland**, 9240 Huntcliff Trace, Dunwoody 30305 (993-6696); and **Finnish-American Chamber of Commerce of the Southeast**, P.O. Box 100160, Roswell 30077-7160 (640-2601).

ICELAND

- **Honorary Consulate General of Iceland**, 1677 Tullie Cir., NE, Suite 118, Atlanta 30329 (321-0777).

NORWAY

- **Honorary Consulate of Norway**, 300 Northcreek, Suite 650, 3715 Northside Pkwy., Atlanta 30327 (239-0885).

SWEDEN

- **Honorary Consulate of Sweden**, 3343 Peachtree Rd., Suite 1420, Atlanta 30326 (261-1187); and **Swedish-American Chamber of Commerce**, P.O. Box 56169, Atlanta 30343 (279-6440).

Polish Christmas celebration

EASTERN EUROPE, RUSSIA & THE FORMER SOVIET UNION

HISTORY & NEIGHBORHOODS

The Eastern European and Central Asian population has been growing in Atlanta, and we can expect continued growth given the incredible, revolutionary changes taking place in the former USSR that, hopefully, will grant more freedoms to the people. Currently there are approximately 5,000 Soviet émigrés in Atlanta, most of whom are Jewish, the others largely Pentecostal. Since the spring of 1987, over 1,000 Soviet Jews have resettled in Atlanta with the aid and support of Atlanta's Jewish community. (See our "Jewish Community" chapter.) Many Soviets live in "Little Russia," a series of apartment complexes along Buford Highway, and along LaVista and Briarcliff Roads. Chamblee, Doraville, Tucker, and Norcross all have concentrations of Soviet families. Many notable Russians live here, including the painter Constantin Chatov, the coloratura Medea Ruhadze-Namoradze, and gymnast Olga Korbett. As of this writing, the granddaughter of Eduard Shevardnadze attends Emory University.

The broader Ukranian and Eastern European community in Atlanta includes about 100 families of Ukranian heritage, people from the now independent (August 20, 1991) Baltic States, Hungarians, Poles, Czechs, Armenians and Romanians. The members of these communities primarily meet and socialize around churches and through community associations. There is not an official count of the numbers of Atlantans who are from Eastern Europe, but their numbers certainly reach into the tens of thousands. The artistry of a recent émigré from Kiev, Igor Raikhline, can be seen on the walls of the new Fernbank Museum of Natural History in the great dinosaur hall.

MUSEUMS

- **Atlanta History Center**, 3101 Andrews Dr., NW, Atlanta (814-4000). The Atlanta History Center boasts 32 beautiful acres of gardens with plants and nature trails labeled for botanical and historical interest. The Swan Woods Trail features the Garden For Peace with its "Peace Tree" sculpture created by an artist from Soviet Georgia. Hours: Mon.–Sat. 9:00am–5:30pm; Sun. 12noon–5:30pm. Admission fee.

- **Center for Puppetry Arts**, 1404 Spring St., Atlanta (873-3391). The center is the most comprehensive puppetry center in the entire nation, attracting masters of puppetry from all over the world, producing shows and workshops for adults and children, and housing a puppet museum that features one of the largest exhibits of puppets in North America. The permanent collection of the museum exhibits puppets from the former Soviet Union. A recent show was "Pinokio Uncensored" by Theatre DRAK of Czechoslovakia. Hours: Mon.–Sat. 9:00am–4:00pm and evenings on performance nights. Admission fee.

- The major museums in Atlanta periodically host art exhibitions by East European and especially Russian artists. For example, **High Museum at Georgia-Pacific Center**, 133 Peachtree St., NW, Atlanta (577-6940) recently displayed the contemporary "Poster Art of the Soviet Union," portraying the important role posters play in a society of pedestrians and the modern techniques many artists are using to communicate with their audience. In conjunction with the exhibit, the Museum held lectures and video presentations and hosted the Atlanta Ballet (demonstrating early Russian dance technique still in wide use all over the world) and Troika Balalaikas (a musical performance group). Ukranian art, traditional costumes, eggs (*pysanka*) and artifacts have also been exhibited on loan from the Ukranian Museum in New York. Hours: Mon.–Fri. 11:00am–5:00pm. Free.

GALLERIES

Galleries throughout Atlanta feature outstanding traveling exhibits from around the world, including Eastern Europe and The Commonwealth of Independent States, and also exhibit the art of recent émigrés. Some galleries to keep your eyes on follow:

- **The Arts Connection**, Oxford Book Store, 360 Pharr Rd., Atlanta (262-3333) hosted "Russian Émigré Artists," which featured a collection of wooden nesting dolls, lacquered boxes, photography and paintings. Hours: Sun.–Thurs. 9:00am–12midnight; Fri.–Sat. 9:00am–2:00am.

- **Emory University Schatten Gallery**, Woodruff Library, 540 Ashby Cir., Atlanta (727-6868/727-6861) hosted "Poster Art of the Soviet Union" and "A

Kind of Journal," which featured works by Polish illustrator and painter Wojciech Wolynski. These and many exhibits and related activites throughout the year are sponsored by Emory's Department of Soviet, Post-Soviet and East European Studies (727-6582). Call for hours as they vary throughout the year.

- **Kennesaw State College Gallery**, 3455 Frey Lake Rd., NW, Kennesaw (423-6139) inaugurated its "Year of Eastern Europe International Studies" with Hungarian food, music and the art exhibit, "Metaphors: Contemporary Hungarian Art." Art department gallery hours: Mon.–Fri. 10:00am–4:00pm; and library gallery hours: Sat. 1:00pm–5:00pm.
- **The Russian Art House**, 3078 Roswell Rd., NE, Suite 103, Atlanta (266-9328). Newly imported contemporary socialist realist paintings by the Russian artist Lansky, landscapes by Lazarov, and paintings and wooden sculpture pieces by other Russian artists are on exhibit. Hours: Mon.–Sat. 10:00am–6:00pm.

COMMUNITY, RELIGIOUS & CULTURAL ASSOCIATIONS

ARMENIAN COMMUNITY ASSOCIATIONS

- **Armenian Independent Cultural Association** (518-4982). This group preserves and promotes Armenian culture and heritage through various cultural programs and festivals, lectures and language lessons. Visiting Armenian priests conduct religious services in Armenian several times a year.

HUNGARIAN COMMUNITY ASSOCIATIONS

- **Hungarian Cultural Foundation** (377-2601/491-3960). Founded by a native Hungarian who has lived in Atlanta for more than 25 years, the foundation assists incoming Hungarians relocating to Atlanta. The group provides information on Hungary to schools and participates in the Festival of Trees held annually at the World Congress Center.
- **Hungarian-American Heritage Society** (978-2652). The group meets monthly to socialize and preserve their Hungarian culture. Call to receive information on the date of the next get-together.

LATVIAN COMMUNITY ASSOCIATIONS

- **Atlanta Latvian Community** (292-6779). The Latvian community is a loose-knit group of people who are in the process of trying to develop a more formal organization. They have the capability of exhibiting traditional arts and crafts and displaying many of the several dozen varieties of authentic Latvian folk dresses. Since Latvia has been readmitted to the International Olympic Committee, this association is acting as a support group for Latvian pre-Olympic shows and exhibits, as well as other efforts in support of Latvian athletes.

LITHUANIAN COMMUNITY ASSOCIATIONS

■ **Lithuanian-American Community of the U.S., Georgia Chapter** (454-7629). This social and cultural group holds bimonthly meetings to preserve and promote Lithuanian heritage.

POLISH COMMUNITY ASSOCIATIONS

■ **Komitet Parafialny**, Catholic Shrine of the Immaculate Conception, 48 Martin Luther King, Jr. Dr., SW, Atlanta (642-6542). This social and religious Committee has regular meetings, publishes a Polish language newsletter and celebrates traditional Polish holidays.

■ **Polish-American Heritage Society** (972-0503). Open to everyone, this organization meets quarterly to preserve Polish heritage and culture and provide travel and educational information on Poland. Members are bringing Polish National team competition to Gwinnett County and are forging pre-Olympic relationships which will, among other things, hopefully bring Polish swimmers to Atlanta each summer until the Olympics.

UKRANIAN COMMUNITY ASSOCIATIONS

■ **Ukranian Association of Georgia** (475-1084). This is primarily a family-oriented association for Ukranian families, especially children, to get together to preserve and share their rich cultural heritage. The association is associated with the Ukranian National Women's League of America.

■ **Ukranian National Women's League of America, Atlanta Branch** (475-1084). The league meets once a month with the goal of preserving the language, culture and heritage of the Ukraine and promoting an understanding of the 5,000-year history of the Ukraine. Members participate in international festivals around Atlanta, performing on the Bandura (a 56-string musical instrument), explaining the art of *pysanka* (coating eggs in beeswax in an elaborate, colorful batik-style manner) and displaying traditional costumes. They also host lectures, provide educational programs to schools (elementary and high school) and assist refugees. Of special concern to the Women's League is the tragic situation facing Ukranian children who are suffering from acute leukemia in the aftermath of the nuclear disaster at Chernobyl.

CULTURAL EXCHANGE

■ **The Friendship Force** (24-hour hotline: 222-2001). The organization sponsors a "Friend-To-Friend" citizen exchange program to develop improved relationships between the people of Moscow and Atlanta. Participants may choose to live with a host family in Moscow and deliver food and medical supplies or serve as a host for Russians coming to Atlanta. Trips to Moscow are scheduled between December and April for a set, all-inclusive fee. For more information, write to: Friend-To-Friend, The Friendship Force, 575 South Tower, One CNN Center, Atlanta 30303.

RELIGIOUS ORGANIZATIONS

A sampling of the many, diverse ministries that serve the former Soviet and Eastern European communities are listed below. For a comprehensive listing of Jewish synagogues, see our chapter "Jewish Atlanta."

■ **ARMENIAN & LATVIAN: Lutheran Church of the Messiah**, 465 Clairmont Ave., Decatur (292-6779).

■ **MORAVIAN: First Moravian Church of Georgia**, 4950 Hugh Howell Rd., Stone Mountain (491-7250). Moravians comprise the oldest Protestant denomination in the world, originating in the area of Czechoslovakia, although worshipers are now multi-ethnic. About 225 Moravians attend services regularly at this church.

■ **POLISH: Shrine of the Immaculate Conception**, 48 Martin Luther King, Jr. Dr., SW, Atlanta (521-1866). This church has a Polish priest and parish.

■ **ROMANIAN: First Baptist Church of Atlanta**, 754 Peachtree St., Atlanta (347-8300); **First Baptist Church of Norcross**, 706 N. Peachtree St., Norcross (923-2950); **Atlanta North Seventh Day Adventist**, 5123 Chamblee-Dunwoody Rd., Dunwoody (399-6884); **Duluth Seventh Day Adventist**, 2959 Hwy. 120, Duluth (426-2709); **First Romanian Baptist Church**, 220 Worthington Hills Trace, Roswell (992-4274); **Romanian Pentecostal Church** c/o First Baptist Church of Lilburn, 3445 Lawrenceville Hwy., Lawrenceville (923-4222); and **Stone Mountain Seventh Day Adventist**, 1350 Silver Hill Rd., Stone Mountain (469-0111).

■ **RUSSIAN: Mountain West Church of God**, 4818 Hugh Howell Rd., Stone Mountain (491-0228); **St. Elias Antiochian Orthodox Church**, 2045 Ponce de Leon Ave., NE, Atlanta (378-8191); and **St. Mary of Egypt Orthodox Church**, 925 Beaver Ruin Rd., Norcross (923-7790).

■ **UKRANIAN: Epiphany Byzantine Catholic Church**, 2030 Old Alabama Rd., Roswell (993-0973); and **St. Andrew's Orthodox Mission**, 2755 Kenwood Ct., Duluth (476-0351).

■ **Emory University's Department of Soviet, Post-Soviet and East European Studies (SEES)**, Box 21774, Emory University, Atlanta 30322 (727-6582) offers students an undergraduate minor and a graduate certificate from this program. SEES also sponsors films, exhibits, lectures and performances on topics related to the Soviet Union and Eastern Europe. Faculty members are also available for presentations to interested organizations in the Atlanta metropolitan area. Call to receive their bulletin announcing upcoming events.

■ The following universities and colleges offer Russian language evening classes: **DeKalb College** (551-3064); **Evening at Emory** (727-6000); **Kennesaw State College** (423-6765); and **Oglethorpe University** (364-8383).

■ **U.S. Soviet Global Thinking Project** was developed by the Association for Humanistic Psychology and was field-tested at Dunwoody High School and Kittredge School for High Achievers during the 1991-92 school year. The exciting and innovative curriculum was developed by a team of U.S. and Soviet teachers who traveled throughout both countries. Through computer linkage, American and Soviet students investigate such global issues as the greenhouse effect, drug abuse and waste disposal, and explore possible solutions.

newspapers, magazines, books, videos

■ *Russia House*, a semi-monthly Russian language newspaper published in Atlanta is available at **Oxford Book Store**, 360 Pharr Rd., NE, Atlanta (262-3333).

■ *Svorboda (Freedom)*, the Ukranian daily newspaper, and *Our Life*, a magazine for Ukranian women, are sometimes available at **Oxford Book Store**.

shopping centers, import stores, hotels

■ Many oriental rug stores in Atlanta carry Romanian and/or Russian handmade rugs. Look in the *Yellow Pages* for listings of stores near you.

■ **Mountain Memories**, Town Square, Dahlonega (800/535-2641). This store offers Russian Lacquers (miniature paintings on lacquered eggs and boxes), especially at Christmas time.

■ Since it is difficult to find imported Russian and East European clothing, jewelry, records, and *matryoshka* in Atlanta, you might take a look at two catalogue import companies: **The Original Rooskie Trading Company, Inc.**, P.O. Box 32, Lexington, Kentucky 40501 (800/237-8400, ext. 1); and **The Daily Planet/Russian Dressing**, P.O. Box 1313, New York, New York 10013 (212/334-0006).

GROCERIES, MARKETS, BAKERIES

■ **International Food Market**, 6045 S. Norcross-Tucker Rd., Suite 103, Atlanta (493-7088). Owned and operated by a Russian émigré, this market features imported borscht, caviar, herring and more.

■ To sample Zakuski (Russian snacks), attend one of the **Atlanta Balalaika Society Orchestra's** performances, where you can enjoy an evening of music followed by delicious tidbits.

■ **Jewish Delicatessens** in Atlanta carry food that is native to Russia and Eastern Europe. For a listing, see our chapter "Jewish Atlanta."

RESTAURANTS

■ **European Buffet**, 5885 Glenridge Dr. (Hammond Dr.), Sandy Springs (252-4198). Owned by a Czech, this southern-style deli carries sausages and a few Czechoslovakian specialties. Open: Breakfast and Lunch: Daily.

■ **Hovan**, Lenox Square Mall Food Court, 3393 Peachtree Rd., Atlanta (231-9018); Perimeter Mall Food Court, 4400 Ashford-Dunwoody Rd., Atlanta (396-1770); and Underground Atlanta Food Court, Old Alabama St. (Peachtree St./Central Ave.), Atlanta (577-4770) offers Armenian sausage and unusual, tasty fast-food sandwiches. Open: Lunch and Dinner: Daily.

■ **Janousek's Restaurant**, 1475 Holcomb Bridge Rd. (Holcomb 400 Shopping Center/Old Alabama Rd.), Roswell (587-2075) and 5454 Peachtree Pkwy. (Winn Dixie Shopping Center/Spaulding Rd.), Norcross (449-8585). These two family-owned Eastern European restaurants will, with one day's advance notice, cook just about any Czech or Hungarian dish a patron requests, such as Hungarian goulash, sauerbrauten or schnitzel. Give them a call! Dumplings are available on the daily menu, as is American continental food. Open: Lunch: Mon.–Fri.; Dinner: Mon.–Sat.

■ **Nikolai's Roof**, 255 Courtland St. (The Atlanta Hilton & Towers), Atlanta (659-2000). This coat-and-tie restaurant has been the recipient of the Mobil Four Star Award every year since 1983 and is noted for its elegance, romantic Russian ambience and skyline view of Atlanta. The restaurant, reflecting the time when Czar Nikolas II was in power and imported French wines and top French chefs were in vogue, features French continental cuisine and Russian specialties, such as piroshkis and Ukranian borscht. Reserve well in advance for weekends and holidays. Open: Dinner: Daily. (Seatings are at 6:30pm and 9:30pm.)

■ **Papa Pirozki's**, 4953 Roswell Rd. (Belle Isle St.), Atlanta (252-1118). A recipient of local awards and a Mobile Three Star Award, the Russian cafe serves traditional Russian fare, such as homemade piroshkis and their famous flavored iced vodkas, in a dressy, romantic setting of Russian art and music. Open: Lunch: Mon.–Fri.; Dinner: Mon.–Sat.

■ **Romanian Restaurant**, 3081 E. Shadowlawn Ave. (E. Paces Ferry Rd./Peachtree St.), Atlanta (365-8220). Formerly Little Bucharest, this cozy restaurant features outstanding stuffed cabbage, homemade sausages, Mititei and Romanian coffee. Fresh breads and pastries are prepared daily. Open: Lunch and Dinner: Mon.–Sat.

■ Keep an eye out for: **Babushka's Peasant Cooking**, formerly of 469 N. Highland Ave., Atlanta, which is expected to reopen in a new location in the same neighborhood. The restaurant offers "the flavors of Eastern Europe," featuring a hearty Hunter's Stew (a rice, bean, chicken, sausage, ham and lamb dish), Baba Yoga Roasted Chicken and Salmon Metzia & Golamkis.

> ## ENTERTAINMENT:
> ## THEATRE, DANCE, MUSIC, CLUBS,
> ## FILMS, T.V. & RADIO, SPORTS

LOCAL DANCE & MUSIC

■ **International Ballet Rotaru**, 3162 Maple Dr., Atlanta (365-0488) was founded by Pavel Rotaru, a Romanian native, who is also artistic director of this highly regarded classical ballet troupe of 45 dancers. Recently, the Atlanta based group has had the good fortune to tour Romania and perform at the Georgia Enescu International Arts Festival in Bucharest. (BRAVO, the ballet's support group, made the tour possible.)

- **Atlanta Balalaika Society Orchestra** (292-7176) is a colorful group of 25 musicians dressed in traditional folk costumes who play instruments, including the domra, bayan and balalaika (some hand-carried from the Soviet Union), to preserve the folk music of Russia and Eastern Europe. Call for the location of their next performance, to be placed on their mailing list and to receive their newsletter, *Balalaikas, Borscht & Blackeyed Peas.*
- **The Atlanta Polka Band** (979-1038), led by Big John Cwiek, plays all over Atlanta, including the "Great Southeast Regional Pierogi Eating Contest" at the Hellenic Community Center. Polka parties are also held around Atlanta frequently.
- **Great American Gypsy Band** (982-9035), comprised of a prima balalaika, contrabass balalaika, guitarist and singer, and cymbalon, plays a range of music from Europe and even some American bluegrass. The group is available for concerts, parties and festivals.
- **Izvornia Folk Ensemble** (284-0106) is a group of singers, dancers and musicians who perform traditional Eastern European productions from such countries as Hungary and Romania.
- **Troika Balalaikas** performs Russian and Eastern European folk music at various events around Atlanta, including the Dogwood Festival and special events such as the "Poster Art of the Soviet Union" exhibition at the High Museum at Georgia-Pacific. Dressed in traditional costumes, the artists perform on a collection of instruments. They have toured throughout the United States for over 15 years and have released two albums, *Standing Room Only* and *Troika Balalaikas.*
- **Ukranian Bandura Ensemble** (261-3722) is sponsored by the Ukranian Association of Georgia and performs at various events in Atlanta. (The Bandura is a 56-stringed musical instrument.)

INTERNATIONAL PEFORMERS

- The Fox Theatre, 660 Peachtree St., Atlanta (249-6400) is often the location for peformances by world renowned international performers. For example, in recent years: **Andreyev Balalaika Orchestra**, a company of 70 Soviet artists originally from the Imperial Russian Court; **Red Army Chorus and Dance Ensemble**; **Donetsk Ballet**, a dance group from the Ukraine; and **Mazowsze Folk Dance Troupe**, Poland's national dance troupe, all performed at the Fox.
- Also, **Alliance Studio Theatre** (892-2414); **Callanwolde Fine Arts Center** (872-5338); and **Emory University** (727-6562) have all hosted several programs featuring Russian and East European artists in recent years. Keep your eye on announcements about future events.

- **Clowns of Russia: Ambassadors of Peace** recently visited Atlanta and delighted school children. Hopefully, the troupe will return in the near future.

FILMS

- **Emory University** is the location for several international film series, including: **Russian Film Series** and **East European Film Series** sponsored by the Soviet, Post-Soviet & East European Studies program (727-6582); and **Soviet Film Series** sponsored by the Emory Center for International Studies (727-6562) screening Russian, Armenian, Georgian and Lithuanian films. Also, **Emory's Soviet & East European Studies Resource Center** has a series of videos available on the Soviet Union, produced by PBS (Public Broadcasting Service).

SOVIET TELEVISION

- Hear live broadcasts of the Russian evening news program *Novosti* at Emory University in Candler Library. The broadcast lasts about 45 minutes. Call 727-6582 for hours.

FESTIVALS & SPECIAL EVENTS

MAY

- **DeKalb International Arts Festival**, Old Courthouse Square, Decatur (371-8386). This Memorial Day festival for adults and children has an international flavor, including Ukranian artifacts, handcrafted art, *pysanka* and ethnic food.
- **Tour of World Figure Skating**, OMNI Coliseum, Atlanta (249-6400). Champion skaters from around the world, including the former Soviet Union, perform in this spectacular ice show.

SUMMER

- **Atlanta Balalaika Society** (292-7176). The society holds an annual concert in Presser Hall at Agnes Scott College at which the Atlanta Balalaika Society Orchestra and special guests perform.
- **DeKalb International Choral Festival**, DeKalb Convention & Visitors Bureau (378-2525). Billed as the largest choral festival in the U.S., this event has featured the Tallin Chamber Choir from Estonia, the Plovdiv Female Students Chamber Choir from Bulgaria, and an ensemble from Soviet Georgia. Concerts occur in various sites around Atlanta culminating in a grand finale at

Stone Mountain Park. Although a selection process is involved to determine which groups from around the world will perform here, look each year for representatives from Eastern Europe and the former Soviet Union.

FALL

■ **Fall Bazaar**, First Moravian Church of Georgia, Stone Mountain (491-7250). Traditional Moravian baked goods such as sugar cake, cookies and yeast bread, as well as Moravian crafts, are featured during this annual event Decorated shirts, advent stars, beeswax candles, jewelry, baskets and exquisite quilts are for sale.

■ **Georgia-To-Georgia Friendship Fest** (423-6153). The Georgian National Dance Company, The Pirosmani Quartet, The Dariali Boys Choir, puppeteers, a chef, silversmith, photographer and film director all traveled to Atlanta from our sister city Tbilisi under the auspices of various Atlanta organizations. These groups and individuals shared their talents in various locales throughout Atlanta. It is hoped that this will become an annual event.

■ **World Fest**, Cobb County (475-1084). In past years, the Atlanta chapter of the Ukranian Women's League of America participated in World Fest by selling ethnic food, artifacts, handcrafted art, traditional costumes and more. Although the festival was not held in 1992, the league hopes to participate in World Fest 1993, or other international festivals.

DECEMBER

■ **Moravian Christmas**, Vann House Historic Site, Spring Place (706/695-2598). The historical house is decorated as it would have appeared in 1805, and candlelight tours are held on two evenings.

RESOURCES

■ **Atlanta Chamber of Commerce, International Department**, 234 International-al Blvd, Atlanta 30301 (586-8460); **Representative Office of the Chamber of Commerce and Industry of the Georgian SSR** (586-8460); **Eastern European Small Business Development Association**, 2670 Arbor Glen Pl., Marietta (509-0308); and **Eastern European Social Adjustment Services** (622-2235).

Festa Italiana, Atlanta's annual Italian-heritage festival.

The Italian
Community

history, neighborhoods,
historical sites,
museums & galleries

HISTORY

The most visible evidence of the influence of Italian culture in America may be the food we eat in our everyday lives and the vocabulary that accompanies it. In fact, most of us probably eat spaghetti or pizza once a week, either in an Italian restaurant, cooked at home or for take-out. *Pasta* is now a household word, and is there anyone in our health-conscious society who doesn't know that olive oil is a monosaturated fat? Though Italian cooking, not to mention wine, should never be taken lightly, there are many more ways we can learn about and partake of the rich heritage of Italy right here in Atlanta.

Atlantans of Italian descent number in the tens of thousands (with approximately 1,500 being recent immigrants) and their influence is all around us. We can eat in over 100 Italian restaurants, visit museums and galleries to view art created by some of the world's greatest masters, become involved in several community associations, attend the Atlanta Opera, purchase Italian products or enjoy ourselves at a festival sponsored by community members.

MUSEUMS & GALLERIES

■ **High Museum of Art**, Robert Woodruff Arts Center, 1280 Peachtree St., NE, Atlanta (892-HIGH). The museum exhibits Italian art in its permanent European collection. Hours: Tues., Wed., Thurs. and Sat. 10:00am–5:00pm; Fri. 10:00am–9:00pm; and Sun. 12noon–5:00pm. Admission fee.

■ Other museums and galleries around Atlanta exhibit Italian art throughout the year. A sampling: **Michael C. Carlos Museum** (formerly Emory University Museum of Art and Archaeology), Emory University, Main Quadrangle, 571 S. Kilgo Cir., Atlanta (727-4282) has obtained art on loan from Italy, such as works from the Museo Egizio in Turin and from May–October in 1993 will display "A Roman Muse from the Capitoline Museums, Rome"; and the **High Museum at Georgia-Pacific Center**, 133 Peachtree St., NE, Atlanta (577-6940) hosted an exhibition of contemporary Italian art entitled "Eternal Metaphors: New Art From Italy."

COMMUNITY, RELIGIOUS & CULTURAL ASSOCIATIONS

■ **Italian Cultural Society** (634-8690). This service organization preserves and promotes the study of Italian culture and language, and works toward enhancing relationships between Italy and the United States.

■ **Italian Friendship Club** (434-1459). The club meets at 7:30pm the second Thursday of each month at All Saints Church, Mt. Vernon Rd., Dunwoody, for the purpose of preserving and encouraging the growth of Italian culture. The club hosts the Italian Festival held annually at the Helenic Center in October.

■ **La Societa Italiana** (392-1499). The thrust of La Societa is the preservation and promotion of Italian heritage and culture through involvement in civic and social activities and events. Membership is open to everyone interested in pursuing this goal. This Italian-American club hosts an annual masquerade ball in February.

■ **Sons of Italy** (333-3113). Despite its name, this fraternal organization accepts both men and women of Italian descent, and their families, into its membership. Italian language classes are offered and up-to-date information may be obtained through their newsletter. Meetings are held monthly.

SCHOOLS, CLASSES, LANGUAGE

■ **Sons of Italy** (333-3113) and **Kennesaw State College Division of Continuing Education** (423-6765) offer Italian language classes.

■ **Evening at Emory** (727-6000) often offers a variety of courses, such as "Italian Peasant Cooking" and "Italian for Travelers."

■ **The Atlanta Opera**, 999 Peachtree St., Atlanta (261-4722) presents an annual operatic educational series, which includes operas by Italian composers, on five consecutive Wednesday evenings for $5.00 per class. Call for the dates of the next series.

- Pick up Italian language fashion and sport magazines at **Oxford Book Store**, 2345 Peachtree Rd., NE, Atlanta (364-2700) and 360 Pharr Rd., NE, Atlanta (262-3333). **BookStar**, 4101 Upper Roswell Rd. (Providence Square Shopping Center), Atlanta (578-4455); and **Borders Book Shop**, 3655 Roswell Rd., NE, Atlanta (237-0707) sometimes carry Italian periodicals as well.

CLOTHING & ACCESSORIES

- Imported Italian clothing and accessories can occasionally be purchased in Atlanta's larger department stores, or in smaller specialty shops that have a reputation for carrying high-quality items. A sampling: **Giorgio Brutini Shoes**, 48 Marietta St., Atlanta (577-2898) sells shoes for men; **Gucci**, 3500 Peachtree Rd. (Phipps Plaza), Atlanta (261-7910) carries very high quality Italian clothing and accessories; **La Bottega Handbags**, 3500 Peachtree Rd. (Phipps Plaza), Atlanta (261-2944) sells Italian leather handbags; **Milan Couture**, 3078 Roswell Rd., NW, Atlanta (264-9105) showcases Italian designer clothes and French jewelry; **Nazareno Gabrielli**, 3500 Peachtree Rd. (Phipps Plaza), Atlanta (842-0081) carries fine Italian men's and women's fashions; **Pappagallo**, 4200 Paces Ferry Rd., NW, Atlanta (333-0705) and 4400 Ashford-Dunwoody Rd. (Perimeter Mall), Atlanta (394-4844) carries Italian leather shoes and purses; **Petit Mom**, 3500 Peachtree Rd. (Phipps Plaza), Atlanta (266-1203) carries pricey Italian and French clothes for children; and **Sasha Frisson**, 3094 E. Shadowlawn Ave., NE, Atlanta (231-0393) has Italian women's clothing.

FURNISHINGS

- Many furniture stores sell Italian furniture and home accessories. A sampling: **Henry-Benger Galleries**, 670 Miami Cir., NE, Atlanta (237-8052) has contemporary Italian furnishings for the home; **International Terracotta**, 351 Peachtree Hills Ave., NE, Atlanta (261-4061) carries Italian pottery; and **Legatto**, 6348 Roswell Rd. NW, Atlanta (847-9750) and 2140 Peachtree Rd., NW, Atlanta (355-4305) carries a good selection of finer quality imported leather furniture.

- **Brio** (518-7956). This company imports the Italian caffeine-free soft drink of the same name and will deliver in quantity to your home.
- **Buckhead Bread Company**, 3070 Piedmont Rd., NE, Atlanta (237-2941). Formerly located behind the Italian restaurant Pricci, the bakery offers highly rated chocolate boule, pane bello, farmer bread (plain and whole wheat), focaccia and other baked goods. *Atlanta Magazine* deems the bakery to have the "Best Bread" in Atlanta.
- **Caffè Donatello**, 3500 Peachtree Rd. (Phipps Plaza). Atlanta (233-2333). Fresh bread, pasta, cheeses and sauces, as well as packaged gourmet items may be purchased inside the Caffe Donatello restaurant.
- **Costa's Pasta**, 2145 Roswell Rd. (East Lake Shopping Center), Marietta (971-2771). This store sells numerous unique items to the public, such as pimiento angel hair pasta, saffron and black linguini, and oils, cheeses and sauces. Bring your children along to watch the pasta being made.
- **East 48th Street Market Italian Food Specialties**, 2462 Jett Ferry Rd., Suite 340, Dunwoody (392-1499). A very broad selection of food includes bread, pasta, fresh mozzarella, imported cheeses, sausages and Brio (an Italian soft drink). The top-rated deli offers large sandwiches, pizza slices, lasagna, salad, wine and beer. Cooking classes are also offered.
- **Harry's Farmers Market**, 1180 Upper Hembree Rd, Alpharetta (664-6300) and 2025 Satellite Blvd., Duluth (416-6900); **International Farmers Market**, 5193 Peachtree Industrial Blvd., Chamblee (455-1777); and **Your DeKalb Farmers Market**, 3000 Ponce de Leon Ave., Decatur (377-6400), all sell coffee beans, fresh pasta, Italian cheeses (including fresh mozzarella), fresh Italian parsley, sausages, pesto, marinara and other sauces, imported items such as tomato paste, dried tomatoes, dried spaghetti and macaroni, extra virgin olive oil and Perugina chocolates. The markets have deli sections with fresh Italian meats and cheeses, and Harry's has a pre-packaged take-out section that usually has lasagna and other Italian entrees.

PIZZA

Before you peruse our extensive sampling of top Italian restaurants, let's take note of some of the special places Atlantans frequent for pizza.

■ **Aglio e Olio/The Bread Garden** 1035 N. Highland Ave., NE (Virginia Ave.), Atlanta (607-1492/875-5599). Enjoy pizza made with fresh herbs and spices at Aglio e Olio, a business under the auspices of Fellini's. The Bread Garden sells unique fresh breads such as rosemary pane integrale and walnut baguette. Lunch and Dinner: Tues.–Sun.

■ **Athens Pizza Express**, 1788 Clairmont Rd. (Mason Mill Rd.), Decatur (634-8646). The take-out restaurant is known for swift deliveries and a unique Greek pizza. Open: Lunch and Dinner: Daily.

■ **Broadway Danny's Pizza**, 2391 Peachtree Rd. (Peachtree Battle Shopping Center), Atlanta (231-4946). This establishment compares its pizzas to those of New York's Little Italy and serves calzones that many consider to be the best in Atlanta. Open: Lunch and Dinner: Daily.

■ **Everybody's Pizza**, 1593 N. Decatur Rd. (Emory Village), Atlanta (377-7766) and 1040 N. Highland Ave. (Virginia Ave.), Atlanta (873-4545). Everybody's is popular among the Emory University crowd for its atmosphere and unique toppings. Open: Lunch and Dinner: Daily.

■ **Jagger's**, 1577 N. Decatur Rd. (Emory Village), Atlanta (377-8888). The Emory Village restaurant serves square-shaped award-winning pizza in a comfortable setting. Open: Lunch: Mon.–Sat.; Dinner: Daily. (Open Sun. at 4:00pm.)

■ **New York Pizza Exchange**, 2810 Paces Ferry Rd. (Exit #12 off I-285), Atlanta (434-9355). The pizzeria bakes an award-winning "white pizza." Open: Lunch and Dinner: Daily.

■ **Pizza by Tomaselli**, 365 Pat Mell Rd. (Olive Springs Rd.), Marietta (438-1819). This restaurant is considered by *Atlanta Magazine* to serve the "Best Traditional Pizza" in the metropolitan area. Open: Lunch and Dinner: Thurs.–Sat.

■ **Rocky's Brick Oven Pizza**, 1170 Peachtree St. (26th St.), Atlanta (876-1111); 3210 Roswell Rd. (Buckhead), Atlanta (262-7625); 1395 N. Highland Ave. (University Ave.), Atlanta (262-7625); and 7887 Roswell Rd. (Morgan Falls), Atlanta (262-7625). Rocky's is a top-rated newcomer to the Italian restaurant scene, serving pizzas with unique toppings. Open: Lunch and Dinner: Daily.

■ **Sal's Pizza & Pasta**, 2581 Piedmont Rd. (Lindbergh Plaza), Atlanta (237-5560). The pizzeria offers a highly recommended "white pizza." Open: Lunch: Mon.–Fri.; Dinner: Mon.–Sat.

RESTAURANTS

Fine Italian restaurants may be found in every corner of Atlanta. Here is an extensive list of well-regarded restaurants:

■ **Abruzzi Ristorante**, 2355 Peachtree Rd. (Peachtree Battle Shopping Center), Atlanta (261-8186). This popular, sophisticated restaurant (owned by the spouse of Broadway Danny's) features Northern Italian specialties with a New York influence. The menu offers pastas, seafood and veal, with fresh desserts to finish the meal. Open: Lunch: Mon.–Fri.; Dinner: Mon.–Sat.

■ **Aldo's Italian Restaurant**, 4450 Hugh Howell Rd. (Heritage Place Shopping Center), Tucker (270-5286) and 2550 Sandy Plains Rd. (Roswell Rd./I-75), Marietta (977-1343). Aldo's serves Italian and continental cuisine in a sophisticated family environment. Open: Dinner: Mon.–Sat.

■ **Alfonzo's Italian Cuisine**, 4859 Hwy. 78 (River Cliff Plaza), Lilburn (972-6500). A variety of foods, including pasta, pizza, seafood, veal and chicken, are offered. Open: Lunch and Dinner: Daily.

■ **Alfredo's Italian Restaurant**, 1989 Cheshire Bridge Rd. (Piedmont Rd.), Atlanta (876-1380). Regional Italian cuisine includes pastas, spicy mussels marinara, garlic spinach and veal specialties, with an extensive wine list. Reservations are suggested. Open: Dinner: Daily.

■ **Altobeli's**, 3000 Old Alabama Rd. (Haynes Market Shopping Center), Alpharetta (664-8055) and 5370 Hwy. 78 (Stone Mountain Square), Stone Mountain (413-1111). Voted "best Northside Italian restaurant," Altobeli's serves all entrees made to order, including homemade desserts. Half portions of pastas are available for children. Take-out is also available. Open: Lunch: Mon.–Fri.; Dinner: Daily.

■ **Antoinetta's**, 4285 Roswell Rd. (Hwy. 120), Atlanta (973-3368). This is a traditional family-style restaurant, offering such delights as muffaletta sandwiches, gourmet pizzas, frittas and desserts made in their own bakery. Open: Lunch: Mon.–Sat.; Dinner: Daily.

■ **Asti Trattoria**, 3199 Paces Ferry Pl. (Peachtree Rd.), Atlanta (364-9160). This new homey restaurant, a local favorite, occupies the space of former Trattoria 515. Open: Lunch: Fri.; Dinner: Daily.

■ **Avanti's Pescivino**, 3401 Northside Pkwy. (W. Paces Ferry Rd./I-75), Atlanta (266-1094). Established in 1975, this spacious restaurant offers a large selection of fish and veal dishes. Pastas are made-to-order and desserts are baked fresh on the premises. The piano lounge is accessible from the dining room and patio for listening and dancing. Open: Lunch: Mon.–Fri.; Dinner: Mon.–Sat.

■ **Avanzare**, 265 Peachtree St. (Hyatt Regency), Atlanta (588-4135). This restaurant features an extensive selection of unique pasta, seafood, veal and beef dishes in a contemporary Italian setting defined by an 1,800-gallon salt water aquarium. Open: Lunch and Dinner: Mon.–Fri.

■ **Azio**, 220 Pharr Rd. (Bolling Way), Atlanta (233-7626). Located in a popular Buckhead area frequented by singles, Azio's offers country Italian pizza and pasta served in a pleasant atmosphere. Special Sunday brunch. Open: Lunch and Dinner: Daily.

■ **Bambinelli's**, 3236 Northlake Pkwy. (Northlake Village Shopping Center), Tucker (493-1311). This New York-style family-owned restaurant serves pasta, seafood, veal, eggplant and more. Open: Lunch and Dinner: Mon.–Sat.

■ **Bardi's Restaurant**, 182 Courtland St. (across from The Radisson), Atlanta (659-4848). This elegant, quaint restaurant located in the heart of the financial district downtown serves Northern Italian cuisine, with grilled fish as a specialty. Reservations suggested. Open: Lunch: Mon.–Fri.; Dinner: Daily.

■ **Bellini's**, 5525 Chamblee-Dunwoody Rd. (Dunwoody Village Shopping Center), Dunwoody (668-0558). Enjoy an evening meal by candlelight in this cozy restaurant or take the family for a pizza or hero at lunchtime. Open: Lunch: Mon.–Fri.; Dinner: Mon.–Sat.

■ **Benedetti's Italian Restaurant**, 2064 N. Decatur Rd. (Clairmont Rd.), Decatur (633-0480). Daily dinner specials are offered to supplement their traditional Italian menu. Open: Lunch and Dinner: Daily.

■ **Bice Ristorante**, 1100 Peachtree St. (between 10th and 14th Sts.), Atlanta (874-4445). The first Bice was founded in 1926 in Milano by Ruperto Ruggeri. The new Atlanta location offers impressive mahogany and brass surroundings and complements the several Bice's around the United States. The menu varies, offering many tantalizing specials to choose from, including a special business lunch weekdays. House accounts are available for regular individual and corporate customers, and a fax service provides the inquirer with the daily menu. Open: Lunch: Mon.–Fri.; Dinner: Sat.–Sun.

■ **Bugatti Restaurant**, 100 CNN Center (OMNI Hotel/Marietta St.), Atlanta (659-0000). The Northern Italian cuisine features homemade pasta, daily specials and a new "healthy fare." Reservations suggested. Open: Lunch: Mon.–Fri.; Dinner: Daily.

■ **Café Prego**, 4279 Roswell Rd. (Chastain Square), Atlanta (252-0032). The small, chic restaurant offers homemade pasta, veal and seafood dishes. Open: Dinner: Mon.–Sat.

■ **Cafe San Remo**, 3375 Buford Hwy. (Northeast Plaza), Atlanta (320-3226). Neopolitan-style pasta, spaghetti, lasagna and more can be enjoyed in this new cafe. Open: Lunch and Dinner: Daily.

■ **Caffè Donatello**, 3500 Peachtree Rd. (Phipps Plaza), Atlanta (233-2333). Fine Tuscan meals, an antipasto bar, and a small Italian mercato and delicatessen with fresh bread, cheeses, pasta, sauces and gourmet items are the hallmark of the second additon of the Four-Star San Francisco-based restaurant. Open: Lunch and Dinner: Daily.

■ **Camille's**, 1186 N. Highland Ave. (Virginia Ave.), Atlanta (872-7203). This popular restaurant (owned by Camille Sotis of New York, who also owns San Gennaro) serves traditional ethnic Italian food in cozy, family-style surroundings. *Atlanta Magazine* deems the fried calamari the "best" in Atlanta. Open: Dinner: Daily.

■ **Cappuccino Time**, 3039 Bolling Way, Suite 301 (Pharr Rd./Buckhead Ave.), Atlanta (816-3318). Bask in the ambience of a European coffee house cafe while enjoying espresso, cappuccino, salad, pizza and desserts. Order from Azio's and they will serve you here, if you wish. Open: Lunch and Dinner: Daily.

■ **Capri Ristorante Italiano**, 5785 Roswell Rd. (Carpenter Dr.), Atlanta (255-7222). The cozy northern Italian restaurant specializes in homemade pasta, shrimp "ala caprese" and unique veal entrees. A wide selection of Italian and California wines is offered. No casual attire. Open: Lunch: Mon.–Fri.; Dinner: Mon.–Sat.

■ **Carlucci's**, 605 Indian Trail Rd. (Lilburn Rd.), Lilburn (925-4943/carry-out 925-3883). This intimate restaurant serves both northern and southern Italian entrees. Open: Lunch: Mon.–Fri.; Dinner: Daily.

■ **DePalma's Italian Cafe**, 2072 Defoors Ferry Rd. (Collier Rd.), Atlanta (352-0082) and 1205 Johnson Ferry Rd. (Woodlawn Square Shopping Center), Marietta (509-7777). Italian-American food, including pizza with unique toppings, fresh pasta, calzones with homemade sauce and Italian sandwiches, are served in a neighborhood ambience. Take-out is available. Open: Lunch and Dinner: Daily.

■ **Fellini's Pasta**, 1174 Euclid Ave. (Little Five Points), Atlanta (525-5525). Live jazz is featured at this trendy restaurant on Friday–Monday evenings. Fellini's also has several pizza restaurants in Atlanta. Open: Lunch and Dinner: Daily.

■ **Filamia's Upstairs**, 4975 Jimmy Carter Blvd. (Green's Corner Shopping Center), Norcross (925-8430). Known for its homemade garlic rolls and family salad, Filamia's also serves veal, pasta, seafood and individual pizzas. Open: Lunch: Mon.–Fri.; Dinner: Mon.–Sat.

■ **Frankie's Italian Restaurant & Pizza**, 3085 Canton Hwy. (E. Piedmont Rd.), Marietta (419-8931). Owned and operated by Italians, Frankie's serves pasta, chicken, veal and seafood entrees. Open: Dinner: Daily.

■ **Gene & Gabe's The Lodge Italian Restaurant**, 936 Canton St. (Hwy. 9), Roswell (993-7588). Gene & Gabe's has been known to Atlantans for a long time, and the restaurant continues to serve well-regarded Italian and American cuisine in a cozy atmosphere. Open: Lunch and Dinner: Mon.–Sat.

■ **Gianni's Ristorante Italiano**, 630 LaVista Rd. (Northlake Square Shopping Center), Tucker (934-6501). This small restaurant, decorated in the colors of the Italian flag, serves luncheon pasta specials at a low price. Open: Lunch and Dinner: Daily.

■ **Gina's Italian Restaurant and Pizzeria**, 710 Peachtree St. (Third Ave.), Atlanta (875-4019). Catering to the lunch and Fox Theatre crowd, the restaurant serves traditional Italian food and pizza. Open: Lunch and Dinner: Daily. (If there is no show at the Fox Theatre on Sat. or Sun., the restaurant opens at 5:00pm.)

■ **Grissini**, 1800 Sullivan Rd. (Hyatt Atlanta Airport), College Park (991-5906). Northern Italian food is served at dinner only: American grill for breakfast and lunch. Open: Breakfast, Lunch and Dinner: Daily.

■ **Ippolito's Family Style Italian Restaurant**, 1425 Holcomb Bridge Rd. (King's Market), Roswell (992-0781). Order pizza and calzones made from scratch at this neighborhood restaurant or enjoy other authentic Italian specialties (chicken florentine, alfredo and mussels marinara). Try the "best calzone" in town (*Atlanta Magazine*). Open: Lunch: Mon.–Fri.; Dinner: Mon.–Sat.

■ **Ital-B-Greek**, 895 Indian Trail-Lilburn Rd. (Market Center Plaza), Lilburn (921-7665). As the name implies, the menu has been influenced by traditional Italian and Greek foods. Buffet is served Monday–Friday. Open: Lunch: Mon.–Sat.; Dinner: Daily.

■ **JoHanna's Ristorante Italiano & JoHanna's Upstairs**, 1578 Piedmont Rd. (Monroe Dr.), Atlanta (885-1816). Traditional Italian food, such as pasta, veal and seafood dishes, are prepared with a "Brooklyn flair." Upstairs is a variety club open every night. Special Sunday brunch. Open: Dinner: Daily.

■ **Joni's Italian Restaurant**, 2140 N. Decatur Rd. (Clairmont Rd.), Decatur (728-0041). Generous salads and fresh bread are served with entrees at this southern Italian restaurant. Open: Lunch and Dinner: Daily.

■ **LaGrotta Ristorante Italiano**, 2637 Peachtree Rd. (W. Wesley Dr.), Atlanta (231-1368) and 647 N. Atlanta St. (north of Upper Roswell St.), Roswell (998-0645). At the Buckhead location, you can choose your drink from an impressive list of Italian wines, and dine by candlelight in a beautiful, romantic setting.

The Roswell diner may have an intimate meal by firelight in a historic cottage. Both locations have a northern Italian menu of veal, seafood, homemade pastas and more. Reservations suggested. Dressy – jackets for men. Open: Dinner: Mon.–Sat (except at the Roswell location, which is closed Monday). (Note: The Roswell location is now **Villa D' Este**.)

■ **La Strada Restaurant**, 2930 Johnson Ferry Rd. (Lassiter Rd.), Marietta (640-7008) and 8550 Roswell Rd. (Northridge Rd.), Dunwoody (552-1300). This popular, family-oriented restaurant consistently receives good reviews. It has junior dinners for children, and for adults, a varied menu that includes several kinds of focaccia, squid steak and a rigatoni special, all at reasonable prices. The chocolate desserts are a specialty. Take-out is available. Open: Dinner: Daily.

■ **Lindy's**, 10 Kings Circle (Peachtree Hills Ave.) Atlanta (231-4112). Popular with the locals, this neighborhood cafe has both indoor and roof garden dining. The specialty is veal that is butchered on the premises. Open: Lunch: Mon.–Fri.; Dinner: Daily.

■ **Lombardi's**, 94 Upper Pryor St. (Underground Atlanta), (522-6568). Loud, lively and friendly, the restaurant is known for its pastas and meats. To feed your imagination, crayons are offered with the white paper tablecloth. Open: Lunch: Mon.–Fri.; Dinner: Daily.

■ **Mad Italian Restaurant**, 5 locations: 2245 Peachtree Rd. (Collier Rd.), Atlanta (352-1368); 2071 N. Druid Hills Rd. (I-85), Atlanta (315-6231); 2145 Roswell Rd. (East Lake Center), Atlanta (977-5209); 2520 Windy Hill Rd. (Windy Hill Plaza), Marietta (952-1806); and 2197 Savoy Dr. (I-285), Chamblee (451-8048). Traditional Italian food is served that pleases many palates, including children's. Open: Lunch and Dinner: Daily.

■ **Mama Mia's**, 5805 Buford Hwy. (McLeroy Rd.), Doraville (457-1113). This is a family-run restaurant with veal and pasta specialties on the menu. Open: Lunch: Mon.–Fri.; Dinner: Mon.–Sat.

■ **Mama Mia's Pasta & Pizza**, 961 Main St. (Stone Mountain Village), Stone Mountain (469-1199). This down-home restaurant offers pasta and pizza made with old-world recipes. Open: Lunch and Dinner: Mon.–Sat.

■ **Mama's Italian Cuisine**, 451 Cherokee Ave. (Grant Park), Atlanta (523-2420). This intimate neighborhood restaurant serves southern Italian food and pizza. Local delivery. Open: Dinner: Tues.–Sat.

■ **Marchello's Cafe Italiano**, 4805 Lawrenceville Hwy. (Indian Trail-Lilburn Rd. at Market Place), Lilburn (381-9722) and 4015 Holcomb Bridge Rd. (Spaulding Woods Village Shopping Center), Norcross (242-9919). Traditional Italian entrees are offered in pleasant surroundings. Look for a new

Marchello's in Alpharetta in 1993. Lunch and Dinner: Sun.–Fri.

- **Marchello's Italian Restaurant**, 3634 Satellite Blvd. (Mall Corners Shopping Center), Duluth (476-8787). Homemade Italian food, including pasta, chicken, veal, seafood and pizza, can be enjoyed. Open: Lunch: Mon.–Fri.; Dinner: Mon.–Sat.

- **Mario's of Atlanta**, 736 Johnson Ferry Rd. (Olde Towne Shopping Center), Marietta (578-8009). The "spirit of nouvelle cuisine" is offered at this new restaurant that promises to serve top quality Italian dishes . . . oh, and pizza, too. Open: Dinner: Daily.

- **Mario's Restaurant**, 3644 Shallowford Rd. (Buford Hwy), Doraville (451-0979). Listen to Balalaika music Wednesday through Saturday evenings while dining at this casual Italian restaurant. Open: Lunch: Mon.–Fri.; Dinner: Daily.

- **Meatballs Italian Restaurant**, 510 Piedmont Rd. (Rio Shopping Center), Atlanta (874-2691). They have "everything Italian" from sandwiches to pizzas to entrees. Open: Lunch: Mon.–Fri. (opens at 1:00pm on Sat. and 2:00pm on Sun.); Dinner: Daily.

- **Mi Spia**, 4505 Ashford-Dunwoody Rd. (Park Place Shopping Center), Atlanta (393-1333). The popular, contemporary Italian bistro specializes in Tuscan cuisine, with desserts made on the premises. Reservations are suggested. Enjoy a special Sunday Brunch on the outdoor patio. Open: Lunch and Dinner: Daily.

- **Nino's Italian Restaurant**, 1931 Cheshire Bridge Rd. (Piedmont Rd.), Atlanta (874-6505). This long-standing favorite serves authentic Italian cuisine of veal, seafood and pasta in a romantic environment. Open: Dinner: Mon.–Sat.

- **Old Spaghetti Factory**, 249 Ponce de Leon Ave. (east of Peachtree St.), Atlanta (872-2841). The Factory is a unique restaurant where kids will thrill to eat aboard a replica of a trolley car or a booth made from an antique bed. The opulent decor includes a 674-piece Viennese crystal chandelier, elaborately carved mahogany, and other turn-of-the-century pieces from light fixtures to chairs and couches. Children can stay happily occupied during the sometimes long wait for a table. Special features are spaghetti with five sauces, pasta dishes made from scratch and a child's dinner plate. Open: Lunch: Mon.–Fri.; Dinner: Daily.

- **Olive Garden Restaurant**, nine metro Atlanta locations including 6317 Roswell Rd. (Mount Vernon Hwy.), Atlanta (851-9070); 2077 Northlake Pkwy (LaVista Rd./outside I-285), Tucker (938-6904); 2467 Cobb Pkwy. (outside I-285), Smyrna (933-8971); 3565 Mall Blvd. (I-85), Duluth (497-0594); 905 Holcomb Bridge Rd. (GA 400), Roswell (642-0395); and 429 Earnest W. Barrett

Pkwy. (Cobb Pkwy.), Kennesaw (424-3668). Manicotti, lasagna, veal and chicken dishes are the features at this very popular chain restaurant. The menu offers daily lunch specials and children's meals. Open: Lunch and Dinner: Daily.

■ **Oscario's**, 4225 Roswell Rd. (Wieuca Rd.), Atlanta (392-7940). Yes, there is a real Oscar who also owns Oscar's Villa Capri. Housed in a cozy cottage with three separate dining rooms, a wine room, lobster tank and espresso machine, Oscario's serves Neapolitan cuisine, including seafood, chicken and veal, with an artichoke appetizer, highly rated sausage dishes (Capellini Alla Oscario), and generous portions offered with an extensive wine list. Open: Lunch: Mon.–Sat.; Dinner: Daily.

■ **Oscar's Villa Capri Restaurant**, 2090 Dunwoody Club Dr. (Jet Ferry Rd.), Dunwoody (392-7940). Oscar's prides itself on its Neapolitan-style seafood, chicken and veal dishes. Specials are offered every night, along with an extensive wine list. Open: Dinner: Daily.

■ **Paisano's**, 5975 Roswell Rd. (Hammond Springs Center, outside I-285), Sandy Springs (843-2181); 2967 Cobb Pkwy. (Akers Mill Square), Atlanta (956-0523); and 1570 Holcomb Bridge Rd. (Ga. 400/ Holcomb Woods Village), Roswell (640-0260). Enjoy authentic Italian background music while dining on traditional Northern and Southern Italian fare prepared from scratch in Paisano's kitchens; or, eat a quick lunch at the pizza bar. Join them for a Feast of San Gennaro in September. Open: Lunch: Mon.–Fri.; Dinner: Daily.

■ **Pero's Pizza & Pasta Restaurant**, 3521 Northside Pkwy. (W. Paces Ferry Rd.), Atlanta (261-5077). Eat in or have pizza, pasta and other traditional Italian fare delivered. Open: Lunch: Mon.–Fri.; Dinner: Daily.

■ **Pricci**, 500 Pharr Rd. (Maple Dr.), Atlanta (237-2941). Formerly Capriccio, this contemporary Italian restaurant has a casual cafe motif and offers a top-rated pizza rustica and authentic entrees, such as osso buco and tortelloni. The former Buckhead Bread Company space located behind Pricci will be used as a pasta factory for in-house and retail sale. Open: Lunch and Dinner: Daily.

■ **Provino's Italian Restaurant**, 4387 Roswell Rd. (Wieuca Rd.), Atlanta (256-4300); 5231 Memorial Dr. (Stonemont Center), Stone Mountain (292-3617); 3606 Satellite Blvd. (Mall Corner Shopping Center), Duluth (497-8841); and 1255 Grimes Bridge Rd. (Grimes Square), Roswell (993-5839). Home-cooked traditional Italian meals keep patrons returning for more. Open: Dinner: Daily.

■ **Raffaello's**, 3102 Piedmont Rd. (Peachtree St.), Atlanta (233-8123). A sophisticated, romantic, northern Italian restaurant that specializes in home-made pasta and sauces, veal and seafood dishes, a gnocci with four cheeses and a ricotta cheesecake. Desserts are made on the premises. Reservations preferred; jacket required. Open: Lunch: Mon.–Fri.; Dinner: Daily.

■ **Romano's Macaroni Grill**, 770 Holcomb Bridge Rd. (1 mi. west of GA400), Roswell (993-7115). There are several Macaroni Grills in the South, and the owners plan to open additional restaurants in metropolitan Atlanta. Open: Lunch: Sun.; Dinner: Daily.

■ **Romeo's Pasta**, 2980 Cobb Pkwy. (Cumberland Festival Mall), Atlanta (956-8755). Using all-natural, low-salt, low-fat ingredients, the owner fashions homemade pasta and homemade sauces at reasonable prices. Take-out available. Open: Lunch and Dinner: Mon.–Sat.

■ **Sal's Restaurant**, 6889 Peachtree Industrial Blvd. (Winters Chapel Rd.), Norcross (448-0200). Traditional Italian food, including pastas and pizza, are served. Open: Lunch: Mon.–Fri.; Dinner: Mon.–Sat.

■ **Sal's Pasta & Pizza**, 2581 Piedmont Rd. (Lindbergh Plaza), Atlanta (237-5560). Take-out is offered at this small restaurant with a big, varied Italian menu. Open: Lunch: Mon.–Fri.; Dinner: Mon.–Sat.

■ **San Gennaro**, 2196 Cheshire Bridge Rd. (LaVista Rd.), Atlanta (636-9447). The upscale restaurant serves traditional Italian entrees at reasonable prices. The owner is Camille Sotis (of Camille's Restaurant), who brings a New York Italian atmosphere to the restaurant. Open: Dinner: Daily.

■ **Scalini's**, 2390 Cobb Pkwy. (Loehmann's Plaza/north of Cumberland Mall), Smyrna (952-7222). Northern and Southern Italian entrees are served in the casual-dress restaurant. Desserts are made on the premises — a specialty is *Tiramisu.* Open: Dinner: Daily. The second and newest location at 3365 Piedmont Rd. (Tower Place/Peachtree Rd.) is well-rated and features live music. Open: Lunch: Mon.–Fri.; Dinner: Daily.

■ **Spaghetti Warehouse**, 2475 Delk Rd. (Exit #111 east of I-75), Atlanta (953-1175). Lots of spaghetti with 11 different sauces, a 15-layer lasagne, garlic bread with *Tigerini* cheese and peanut butter moussecake for the kids are available at good prices. Open: Lunch and Dinner: Daily.

■ **Spike's Brick Oven Pizzeria, Bar and Bocce Ball Galleria**, 1115 Powder Springs St. (Natchez Place), Marietta (422-6821). This new restaurant serves pizza that has been cooked in wood-fired brick ovens. Adjoining the restaurant is a bocce ball court. Open: Lunch and Dinner: Daily.

■ **Three-Fifty Pizza and Pasta**, 3155 E. Ponce de Leon Ave. (just east of Your DeKalb Farmers Market), Scottdale (378-2828) and 3246 Hwy. 23 (Hwy. 120), Duluth (476-7887). Spaghetti and noodles are made from scratch, sauces are made fresh daily, and bread and rolls are made fresh on the premises. Open: Lunch and Dinner: Daily.

■ **Toni's Casa Napoli**, 2486 Mount Vernon Rd. (Jet Ferry Rd.), Dunwoody

(394-9359). A cozy restaurant, Toni's serves an authentic Italian cuisine in a family atmosphere. Open: Dinner: Daily.

■ **Torino Italian Restaurant**, 3342 Clairmont Rd. (Buford Hwy.), Atlanta (634-5805). The pleasant, family restaurant serves traditional Italian fare with a personal touch. Open: Lunch: Mon.–Fri.; Dinner: Mon.–Sat.

■ **Tuscano Italian Eatery**, 4060 Peachtree Rd. (Windsor Station Shopping Center), Atlanta (237-9838). An extensive selection of antipasti, daily specials, pizza and humongous desserts characterize this restaurant. Entrees from the central Tuscany region of Italy predominate. Open: Dinner: Daily.

■ **Veni Vidi Vici**, 41 14th St. (One Atlanta Center/W. Peachtree St.), Atlanta (875-8424). Dine in an elegant atmosphere on authentic, yet creative, Italian cuisine. The appetizer, verdure alla grillia, has been highly rated. Bocce ball is played every day on the green. Open: Lunch: Mon.–Fri.; Dinner: Daily.

■ **Village Inn Pizza 'N' Pasta**, 3920 Fulton Industrial Blvd. (Shalimar Airport), Atlanta (691-3484) and 306 S. Cobb Pkwy. (next to Wal-Mart Shopping Center), Marietta (422-8681). Village Inn offers lunch and dinner buffets. Dine-in or carry-out. Open: Lunch and Dinner: Daily.

DESSERTS AND GELATO

■ **Café Intermezzo**, 1845 Peachtree Rd. (Collier Rd.), Atlanta (355-0411) and 4505 Ashford-Dunwoody Rd. (Park Place Shopping Center), Atlanta (396-1344). The European-style cafe with a pasta-based entree menu features a capuccino and dessert bar. The Buckhead location has a new garden terrace and **Café Gelateria** (owned separately) serves gelato and capuccino. Open: Lunch and Dinner: Daily.

■ **Cafe Zabaglione**, 85 Mill St., Suite 206, Roswell (640-6464). Located at Roswell Mill overlooking Vickery Creek, this dessert cafe serves sandwiches, espresso, cappuccino, mokkaccino, Italian ice cream and other desserts. Open: Lunch and Dinner: Tues.–Sun.

■ **Cappuccino Time**, 3039 Bolling Way, Suite 301 (Pharr Rd./Buckhead Ave.), Atlanta (816-3318). This cafe is noted for its desserts. Open: Lunch and Dinner: Daily.

■ **Il Cappuccino Café**, 57 Forsyth St. (Healy Bldg.), Atlanta (523-6068). Highly regarded cappuccino can be enjoyed with breakfast, with luncheon sandwiches or with daily specials. Open: Breakfast and Lunch: Mon.–Fri.

■ **Le Gourmet**, 2341 Peachtree Rd. (Peachtree Battle Shopping Center), Atlanta (266-8477). The French and Italian pastry restaurant serves Italian pastries (including kahlua with chocolate pieces and baci chocolate with hazelnuts), espresso and capuccino. Open: Lunch and Dinner: Mon.–Sat.

■ **Leonardo's Gelato**, 3039 Bolling Way (Pharr Rd.), Atlanta (237-8090). Leonardo's serves gelato, sorbettos, sandwiches, espresso, capuccino, cookies and pastries. Open: Mon.–Fri. 12noon–11:00pm; Sat. 12noon–1:00am; and Sun. 1:00pm–10:00pm.

ENTERTAINMENT: THEATRE, DANCE, MUSIC, CLUBS, FILMS, T.V. & RADIO, SPORTS

MUSIC

■ **The Atlanta Opera**, 1800 Peachtree St. NW, Suite 620, Atlanta (355-3311). The Atlanta Opera performs in Symphony Hall at the Woodruff Arts Center, under the supervision of Artistic Director William Fred Scott. This opera company is attracting larger audiences every year as it presents high quality performances and develops innovations, such as supertitles, to make opera more accessible to a wider audience. A recent season included Puccini's *Tosca* (with English supertitles), Verdi's *Un Ballo In Maschera* (with English supertitles), and Donizetti's *The Elixir Of Love* (sung in English). Season ticket prices range from $15-$160.

■ **The Atlanta Opera** also has a special **Studio Program** to bring a taste of opera to children in K–12th grade. The Opera performs 200 one-act operas a year in the public schools and at community centers. The productions are carefully tailored to the age group, yet professional quality is maintained as the performers sing in English. To enhance the scene, the singers are dressed in ornate period costumes and perform on specially designed stage sets. To arrange a visit, call 355-3311.

FILM

■ Italian film aficionados should keep an eye on **Garden Hills Cinema**, 2835 Peachtree Rd., NE, Atlanta (266-2202); **Plaza Theatre**, 1049 Ponce de Leon Ave., Atlanta (873-1939); and **The Screening Room**, 2581 Piedmont Rd. (Lindbergh Plaza), Atlanta (231-1924) — the three movie theatres in Atlanta which frequently screen foreign language films. Also, **the Metropolitan Film Society** (729-8487) screens independent and foreign language films at the Cinevision Screening Room, 3300 NE Expressway Office Park, Building 2, Atlanta.

BOCCE BALL

■ Bocce ball (a bowling-type game) is played at two Atlanta restaurants: **Spike's Brick Oven Pizzeria, Bar & Bocce Ball Galleria**, 1115 Powder Springs

St. (Natchez Place), Marietta (422-6821); and **Veni Vidi Vici**, 41 14th St. (One Atlanta Center/W. Peachtree St.), Atlanta (875-8424). Bocce ball is featured at some special events, such as the **Bocce Ball Benefit** held in May and the **Italian Festivals** in October.

FESTIVALS & EVENTS

FEBRUARY

■ **Carnevale** (392-1499). La Societa Italiana hosts its annual charity masquerade ball with contests, music and door prizes.

OCTOBER

■ **Festa Italiana** (988-8085). Held at Galleria Gardens behind Galleria Mall, the huge festival includes entertainment, a bocce ball tournament, cultural exhibits, Italian jewelry and marble, children's activities, games and rides, fireworks, delicious Italian food and more. Also, local Italian clubs set up booths to provide everyone with information about their organizations.

■ **Italian Festival**, Hellenic Community Center, 2124 Cheshire Bridge Rd., NE, Atlanta (434-1459). This annual festival features Italian crafts and cultural items, folk dancing, a bocce ball tournament, children's entertainment and Italian food from some of Atlanta's best restaurants. The event is sponsored by the Italian Friendship Club.

RESOURCES

■ **Italian Consul** (305/374-6322); and **Italian Trade Commission**, 233 Peachtree St., NE, Suite 2301, Atlanta 30303 (525-0660).

Troupe Hellas performs at the Atlanta Greek Festival.

GREECE &
CYPRUS

HISTORY & NEIGHBORHOODS

Although it is not clear when the first Greek immigrant arrived in Georgia (scholars believe circa 1870), Greek archives indicate that the first document-ed Greek immigrant to arrive in Atlanta was Alexander Carolee from Argos, who arrived in 1890. Thus, the Greek community has adopted the year of 1890 as the official start of their community in Atlanta.

The first wave of Greek immigration was comprised of settlers from Argolis and Peloponnesus and, later, from other parts of Greece. In little time, these settlers formed the Annunciation Society, whose primary purpose was to establish a place of worship for the Greek Orthodox community. This goal was accomplished in 1905, when the society rented space in a building south of Five Points, and Greek Orthodox services were conducted on a regular basis. After the church moved two more times to accommodate the growing number of members in the parish, funds were raised by members of the Greek community for the purchase of $7^1/2$ acres on Clairmont Road near Emory University and, in 1965, groundbreaking ceremonies were held at the new church site. Now, almost thirty years later, the stunning Greek Orthodox Cathedral of the Annunciation erected at that site continues to play a signifi-cant role in the religious, social and cultural activities of the community. Recently, the Holy Transfiguration Greek Orthodox Church in Marietta has assumed a similar central role for members of the Greek community residing in northern Atlanta.

Atlanta's Greek community is close-knit and well-organized. Atlanta's Greeks share a strong sense of cultural and community identity and have established many support organizations focusing on the elderly, the youth

and the indigent. In the fall of 1974, the membership of the Greek Orthodox Cathedral of the Annunciation initiated the first Atlanta Greek Festival,
which has continued to grow in size throughout the years. This exciting
four-day event offers the rest of Atlanta an opportunity to learn more about
the community and its heritage. And thanks to its tremendous success, other
ethnic groups have become inspired to host their own festivals and share
their heritage with all of Atlanta.

HISTORICAL SITES, MUSEUMS & GALLERIES

■ **Michael C. Carlos Museum** (formerly Emory University Museum of Art &
Archeology), Emory University, Main Quadrangle, 571 S. Kilgo Cir., Atlanta
(727-4282). The museum's permanent collection includes art, artifacts,
coins, jewelry and everyday objects from ancient Greece. From the spring of
1993 through August 1996, the newly renovated museum will house "Sacred
Spaces, Famous Faces," an exhibit showcasing the history of athletic competition and ceremonies in ancient Greece. Special lectures, films, classes and
workshops offered throughout the year, also highlight Greek art and archeology. Hours: Tues.–Sat. 10:00am–4:30pm; Sun. 12noon–5:00pm. Free, but a
donation of $3.00 is suggested.

■ Occasionally, Atlanta's galleries exhibit work by Greek artists or of Greek
content, such as **The Arts Connection** at Oxford Book Store, 360 Pharr Rd.,
Atlanta (237-0005) which recently displayed a photodocumentary of Greek
villages, along with abstract paintings by Greek artist Sotos Zahariadis.

COMMUNITY, RELIGIOUS & CULTURAL ASSOCIATIONS

GREEK COMMUNITY

■ **Greek Orthodox Cathedral of the Annunciation**, 2500 Clairmont Rd., NE,
Atlanta (633-5870/633-7358). The cathedral is the religious and cultural center of the Greek community in Atlanta. The magnificent sanctuary houses
some of the world's most beautiful Byzantine mosaic iconography. (The
dome, created by artist Sirio Tonelli, is covered with a mosaic of Christ and is
made up of over three million pieces of glass.) The general population is
welcome to tour the cathedral and learn more about the Greek Orthodox
religion during the cathedral's annual Greek Festival. Sunday worship services are conducted in both Greek and English.

■ **Hellenic Community Center of Atlanta**, 2124 Cheshire Bridge Rd., NE,

Atlanta (636-1871/321-9783). The Hellenic Center is a division of the Greek Orthodox Cathedral and serves as a center for social, cultural and sporting events for the Greek community. The large complex is the location for dances, athletic leagues, special holiday celebrations and meetings for church groups and service organizations, including:

—**The American-Hellenic Educational Progressive Association** (A.H.E.P.A.) provides many social services to the Greek community and participates in activities on a local and national level. **Sons of Pericles** is the auxiliary of the A.H.E.P.A. for young men ages 13-21 years.

—**Daughters of Penelope–Menelaos Chapter** is the Women's Auxiliary of A.H.E.P.A. and is involved in a wide range of local and national charities. **Maids of Athena** is the Daughters of Penelope auxiliary for young women ages 13-21 years.

—**Hellenic Women's Cultural Association** is open to Greek-American and Greek-born women eager to promote Greek language and culture in Atlanta. Monthly meetings are conducted in Greek.

—**Junior Orthodox Youth** (J.O.Y.) meetings are for 5th, 6th and 7th graders, and activities include Christmas caroling, pizza parties and programs for spiritual and intellectual development.

—**Golden Group** is an organization for senior citizens which holds regular meetings and is involved in a variety of organizations.

—**Greek Orthodox Youth of America** (G.O.Y.A.) is an organization for 8th through 12th graders where activities may include a religious retreat, assisting at the annual Greek Festival or participating in a regional basketball tournament.

—**Philoptochos Society** participates in many charitable activities for the needy and offers scholarships for college and theological students. Membership is open to any woman in the parish.

—**Young Adult League** (Y.A.L.) includes members 18-35 years and sponsors various church activities, such as the Hellenic Tower Christmas party, religious retreats and the annual Labor Day softball tournament.

■ Regional groups gather for regular meetings and special functions throughout the year. Contact the Annunciation Greek Orthodox Cathedral for the names and numbers of current organization leaders for the: **Santa Ekaterini Society** (Greeks from the Kalamata region); **Danaos Society** (descendants from the province of Argolis in the Peloponnesian peninsula); and **Pan Laconian Society** (Greeks descended from the province of Laconia).

■ **Holy Transfiguration Greek Orthodox Church**, 2692 Sandy Plains Rd. (Sprayberry Crossing Shopping Center), Marietta (977-1350). Mailing Address: P.O. Box 669834, Marietta 30066. This Greek Orthodox religious center was founded in 1989 to serve the northern metropolitan Greek community and has quickly become another important center for religious, social and cultural activities. The annual Greek Glendi held in May continues to grow in size and popularity as Atlantans take advantage of this lively festival to discover more about Greek life. Sunday services are conducted in Greek and English.

■ **Greek Orthodox Diocese of Atlanta**, 2801 Buford Hwy., NE, Atlanta (634-9345). This is the headquarters for the Greek Orthodox Diocese serving the Atlanta area.

CYPRIAN COMMUNITY

■ **The Georgia Cyprus Friendship Association**, 895 Somerset Dr., Atlanta (941-3764/231-3699). The association's goal is the promotion of closer ties between Georgia and the Republic of Cyprus.

SCHOOLS, CLASSES, LANGUAGE

■ **Greek Orthodox Cathedral of the Annunciation**, 2500 Clairmont Rd., NE, Atlanta (633-5870/633-7358) offers Sunday religious instruction for both children and adults. It also conducts a Greek language school for children in the 2nd grade and up, where students learn to read, speak and write the Greek language.

■ **Holy Transfiguration Greek Orthodox Church**, 2692 Sandy Plains Rd. (Sprayberry Crossing Shopping Center), Marietta (977-1350) offers religious instruction as well as a Greek school for children and adults focusing on the heritage, traditions, language and culture of Greece.

■ **Troupe Hellas – Eleni Hopes** (493-9096). The Greek folkdancer offers instruction for children and adults in Greek dance, song, history, legends, tradition and geography.

NEWSPAPERS, MAGAZINES, BOOKS, VIDEOS

■ The bimonthly newsletter of the Greek Orthodox Cathedral of the Annunciation, the *Annunciator,* lists announcements about the many activities of the church and Greek community.

■ **The Greek Orthodox Cathedral of the Annunciation** houses a library containing a large number of books in Greek and English focusing on the community's religious and cultural heritage. The library is open during church hours or by special appointment.

■ *The Key to Greek Cooking* is an excellent cookbook compiled by members of the Greek Orthodox Cathedral of the Annunciation which may be purchased at the annual Atlanta Greek Festival or at the cathedral's office throughout the year.

SHOPPING CENTERS, IMPORT STORES, HOTELS

■ A highlight of both **Greek Festivals** is a marketplace area featuring art work, imported gift items, jewelry, clothing, authentic Greek sailor hats, ceramics, copper, icons, needlepoint tapestry, stationery, musical tapes, videos, CDs, T-shirts, ancient coins, ingredients for Greek cooking and anything else "Greek." Also, both **Greek Orthodox Churches** sell religious items in their gift shops.

GROCERIES, MARKETS, BAKERIES

■ **Happy Herman's**, 2299 Cheshire Bridge Rd., NE, Atlanta (321-3012) and 204 Johnson Ferry Rd., Atlanta (256-3354). Atlanta's longest-standing gourmet grocery store sells a large selection of Greek grocery items. The delicatessen has a constant supply of Greek specialties, such as spanakopita, salads, feta cheese, grape leaves, fresh baklava and sweets.

■ **International Bakery**, 2165 Cheshire Bridge Rd., Atlanta (636-7580). The superb bakery specializes in pastries from around the world, including a large selection of Greek and Mediterranean sweets. Also available are Greek and Mediterranean groceries, olives, cheeses and other specialty items.

■ **International Groceries & Deli**, 585 Franklin Rd., Marietta (499-7608). This unusual delicatessen and grocery store stocks a variety of groceries, delicatessen items and gifts from Greece, the Middle East, India and Persia.

■ **Acropolis Greek Cuisine & Pizza**, 4853 Memorial Dr. (Rockmor Plaza), Stone Mountain (292-2092). Greek pizza, gyros, Greek salads, spanakopita, saganaki (flaming cheese), stuffed grape leaves and other Greek specialties are served at this comfortable restaurant. Open: Lunch and Dinner: Mon.–Sat.

■ **Athens Pizza House**, 1369 Clairmont Rd. (N. Decatur Rd.), Decatur (636-1100); 5550 Peachtree Industrial Blvd. (Chamblee Plaza), Chamblee (452-8282); 1565 Hwy. 138, Conyers (483-6228); 1255 Johnson Ferry Rd. (Market Plaza), Marietta (509-0099); and 245 Johnson Ferry Rd. (Roswell Rd.), Atlanta (257-0252). Specialty pizza, gyros and Greek salads are served together with other Greek and Italian-style dishes. The informal atmosphere makes this restaurant a favorite for families with small kids. Open: Lunch and Dinner: Daily.

■ **Basil's Mediterranean Cafe**, 2985 Grandview Ave. (Pharr Rd.), Atlanta (233-9755). Unusual specialities blending traditional and original Greek and Lebanese cooking styles are featured at this popular Buckhead restaurant. Specialties include Greek salads and a variety of lamb, seafood, beef and chicken dishes prepared Mediterranean-style. Open: Lunch: Tues.–Sat.; Dinner: Tues.–Sun.

■ **Cafe Dimitri**, 3714 Roswell Rd. (Powers Ferry Square), Atlanta (842-0101). A combination of Greek and Italian specialties are served in casual elegant surroundings. Traditional Greek pastry dishes such as Lamb and Artichoke in Pastry and Chicken and Eggplant in Pastry are featured. Open: Lunch and Dinner: Daily.

■ **Chris's Pizza House**, 2911 N. Druid Hills Rd. (Toco Hills Shopping Center), Atlanta (636-7544). This restaurant serves Greek-style pizza, gyros and salads along with other Greek-American specialties, such as moussaka and roasted chicken. Special weekend brunch. Open: Lunch: Mon.–Sat.; Dinner: Daily.

■ **Colossus Pizza**, 5383 Five Forks Trickum Rd. (Rockbridge Rd.), Stone Mountain (923-9852). Enjoy Greek-style pizza, salads, gyros, kabobs, moussaka and souvlaki in this friendly and casual restaurant. Open: Lunch: Mon.–Sat.; Dinner: Daily.

■ **Dimitri's Restaurant**, 4651 Woodstock Rd. (Sandy Plains Rd./Hwy. 92), Roswell (587-2700). The restaurant features a unique blend of Greek and Italian cuisines. Most entrees are moderately priced. Open: Lunch and Dinner: Daily.

■ **The Downwind**, 1951 Clairmont Rd. (DeKalb Peachtree Airport), Chamblee (452-0973). The restaurant, located near the observation deck at DeKalb Peachtree Airport, primarily serves American fare; however, on weekends, the Greek owners prepare ethnic specialties for the dinner menu, such as spanakopita, kalamari and octopus. Open: Breakfast: Mon.–Fri.; Lunch and Dinner: Mon.–Sat.

■ **Evelyn's Cafe**, 3853-F Lawrenceville Hwy. (Brockett Rd.), Tucker (496-0561). The charming restaurant has been highly praised by food critics for its full menu of traditional Greek fare, including Greek salads, spanakopita, gyros and moussaka. Open: Lunch and Dinner: Daily.

■ **Grecian Gyro**, 855 Virginia Ave. (1/2 mile off I-85), Hapeville (762-1627). The small, informal Greek restaurant is rumored to have the best gyro sandwich in town and also serves souvlaki, cheese sandwiches, meat platters, Greek salads, baklava and Greek pastry. Open: Lunch and Dinner: Mon.–Fri.

■ **Gyro Wrap Cafe**, 3027 N. Druid Hills Rd. (Toco Hills Shopping Center), Atlanta (320-7580). Gyro wrap sandwiches, souvlaki and platters are the restaurant's most popular fare, but the Greek/Middle Eastern restaurant also serves spanakopita, Greek salads and Mediterranean-style pizza. There is live entertainment on weekends. Open: Lunch and Dinner: Daily.

■ **Ital-B-Greek**, 895 Indian Trail-Lilburn Rd. (Market Center), Lilburn (921-7665). Greek specialties, such as gyros, kabobs, moussaka and spanakopita, are served along with Italian cuisine at this informal restaurant. Open: Lunch: Mon.–Sat.; Dinner: Daily.

■ **Jaffa Gate**, 245 Peachtree Center Ave. (Marquis One – Gallery Level), Atlanta (577-0352) and 1197 Peachtree St. (Colony Square), Atlanta (876-0094). The Mediterranean-style cafe serves tasty Middle Eastern and Greek specialties, such as felafel, hummus, gyros, shish kabob, moussaka, spanakopita, salads and sweets. Open: Breakfast, Lunch and Dinner: Daily.

■ **Niko's Greek Restaurant**, 1789 Cheshire Bridge Rd. (Piedmont Rd.), Atlanta (872-1254). Authentic Greek cuisine, including house specialties, saganaki (flaming cheese) and kalamarakia (stuffed squid), make this restaurant a long-standing favorite for Greek food enthusiasts. Live Greek entertainment is offered on Friday and Saturday evenings. Open: Lunch: Mon.–Fri.; Dinner: Mon.–Sat.

■ **Papa Nick's Greek Pizza & Restaurant**, 1799 Briarcliff Rd. (Sage Hill Shopping Center), Atlanta (875-9677). This friendly restaurant in the Emory area features reasonably priced Greek-style pizza, salads, gyros, kabobs, moussaka and souvlaki, plus some authentic village-style casseroles. Open: Lunch and Dinner: Daily.

■ **Parthenon Greek Restaurant**, 6125 Roswell Rd. (Sandy Springs Shopping Center), Atlanta (256-1686). The Sandy Springs Greek restaurant is owned by the Tasos family and serves the same fine Greek cuisine that may be enjoyed at the award-winning Tasos restaurant. Live music on weekends is featured. Open: Lunch: Mon.–Fri.; Dinner: Daily.

■ **Pizza by Nitsa**, 1255 Grimes Bridge Rd. (Grimes Square Shopping Center), Roswell (587-1100). Greek-style pizza may be enjoyed at this casual restaurant in Roswell. Open: Lunch and Dinner: Mon.–Sat.

■ **Sahara Cafe**, 710 Peachtree St. (3rd St./Scandinavian House), Atlanta (876-4750). Sahara Cafe has the same menu as the other Jaffa Gate restaurants, plus an extended dinner menu. Specialties include tabouli, Moroccan couscous and Greek salad. Belly dancing and live Arabic music may be enjoyed on weekends. Special Sunday brunch. Open: Lunch and Dinner: Daily.

■ **Shipfeifer's Gyro Wrap**, 1814 Peachtree Rd. (Palisades St.), Atlanta (875-1106). Gyro wrap sandwiches, souvlaki and platters are the mainstay of this restaurant, but other Greek and Middle Eastern dishes, such as hummus, felafel, Greek salads and spanakopita, are also quite popular. Enjoy a large selection of vegetarian meals. Open: Lunch and Dinner: Daily.

■ **Sparta Pizza & Gyros**, 3021 Peachtree St. (Buckhead Ave.), Atlanta (364-0960). This Buckhead restaurant serves Greek-style gyros, pizza, baklava and a few Middle Eastern dishes. Open: Lunch and Dinner:

■ **Tasos**, 5277 Buford Hwy. (Pinetree Plaza), Atlanta (451-3188). All of Atlanta's restaurant critics praise the authenticity and quality of the taverna dishes served in the casual, family-owned restaurant. The kalamari, moussaka, Greek sausage and souvlaki specialties have been called "true delights" by restaurant critics. Open: Lunch and Dinner: Mon.–Sat.

■ **Gyro Fast Food Booths** may be found in the food courts of almost every shopping mall and large office building in Atlanta, offering the uninitiated an easy way to sample these delicious sandwiches.

**ENTERTAINMENT:
THEATRE, DANCE, MUSIC, CLUBS,
FILMS, T.V. & RADIO, SPORTS**

THEATRE, DANCE & MUSIC

■ Greek classics, whether they be afforded traditional or contemporary treatment, are often performed by area theatre companies, such as The Actor's Express' contemporary treatment of the Euripides' classic, *The Bacchae*, performed recently as *The God of Ecstasy: A Retelling of the Bacchae.*

■ Greek bands perform weekend evenings at **Niko's Greek Restaurant**, 1789 Cheshire Bridge Rd. (Piedmont Rd.), Atlanta (872-1254); and **Parthenon Greek Restaurant**, 6125 Roswell Rd. (Sandy Springs Shopping Center), Atlanta (256-1686).

■ The **Hellenic Community Center** (636-1871/321-9783) is the location for year-round concerts, dances and performances featuring Greek music and dance.

■ Byzantine choral selections, bouzouki music and folkdances may be enjoyed at various international and Greek festivals throughout the city. Keep your eye out for **Troupe Hellas** and **Odyssey Dance Troupe**.

T.V. & RADIO

■ **WGKA-AM (1190)** (261-3684) broadcasts "Echoes of Athens," a bilingual program featuring Greek music and announcements of interest to the Greek community on Sunday from 1:30pm–2:30pm.

FESTIVALS & SPECIAL EVENTS

SPRING

■ **B.C. Fest!**, Michael C. Carlos Museum (formerly Emory Museum of Art & Archeology), Atlanta (727-4282). The one-of-a-kind festival and educational experience introduces children to the life and culture of ancient worlds. Past festival events have included Greek drama and comedy performances, pottery making, hands-on arts and crafts activities, ancient sporting events, gift stalls and authentic Greek food.

MAY

■ **Greek Glendi Festival**, Cobb County Civic Center, Marietta (977-1350/971-6015). Authentic Greek bands, folk dancing, food, wine, pastries, artwork, costumes, religious gifts, jewelry, imported gifts, records, tapes, CDs, great T-shirts (Raise Hellus!) and entertainment for children highlight this annual Greek *Glendi* (festival) hosted by the Holy Transfiguration Greek Orthodox Church in Marietta.

SEPTEMBER

■ **Atlanta Greek Festival**, Greek Orthodox Cathedral of the Annunciation,

2500 Clairmont Rd., NE, Atlanta (633-5870). The four-day festival has, over the years, become a favorite for Atlantans who eagerly take advantage of this unique opportunity to experience Greek culture. Festivities usually include continuous Greek entertainment, travel movies, lectures about Greece and Atlanta's Greek community, tours of the cathedral and a *Bakaliko* (large marketplace) selling all sorts of Greek art, clothing, jewelry, handbags and imported items. Large quantities of Greek food, wine and pastries are served continuously throughout the festival.

RESOURCES

GREECE

■ **Consulate of Greece**, 3340 Peachtree Rd., Suite 1670, NE, Atlanta 30326 (261-3313).

CYPRUS

■ **Honorary Consulate of the Republic of Cyprus**, 1790 Mulkey Rd., Suite 6A, Austell 30001 (941-3764/231-3699).

MARTHA NELSON

A musician plays the oud at Atlanta's Middle Eastern Festival.

The Middle Eastern Communities, Turkey, Iran & North Africa

HISTORY & NEIGHBORHOODS

Atlanta's Middle Eastern community is estimated to number over 10,000, including individuals from Morocco and other North African countries. Those of Lebanese descent are the largest group, followed by Palestinians and Syrians. Members of the Middle Eastern organizations are eager to include the general population in their many social gatherings, cultural events, festivals and holiday celebrations. Each year, the Mideastern Festival at St. Elias Antiochian Orthodox Church continues to grow in size thanks to the community's openness and willingness to allow visitors to share in a part of their culture and lives. We cannot think of a more friendly place for Atlantans to start their exploration of the exotic food, art, dance and music originating from this region of the world.

Another 5,000–10,000 Persians are estimated to reside in the Atlanta area (unfortunately, estimates vary widely). The Persian Community Center has actively pursued activities to further inter-ethnic relationships, including its recent sponsorship of an international music festival at the Center where musicians from many other community groups joined together to present a very special multicultural performance.

The Turkish-American Cultural Association of Georgia estimates that approximately 2,000 Turkish-Americans reside in the Atlanta area, many of whom participate in the association's social and cultural activities. Turkish Hospitality Night, usually held in the spring, offers the general population an opportunity to experience Turkish hospitality, food and culture.

■ **Michael C. Carlos Museum** (formerly Emory University Museum of Art & Archeology), Emory University, Main Quadrangle, 571 S. Kilgo Cir., Atlanta (727-4282). Egyptian art, artifacts and mummies constitute the core of the museum's permanent collection, along with other pieces of art, artifacts, sculpture, pottery, coins and everyday objects from the many ancient cultures of the Mediterranean. The museum has also been fortunate to be able to exhibit spectacular special collections, such as "Islamic Art and Patronage: Treasures from Kuwait," a recent exhibit of about 100 pieces of art, jewelry, books, rugs and artifacts from the 8th–18th centuries, representing works from the major cultural centers of the Islamic world. These pieces were on exhibit in St. Petersburg during the Iraqi occupation of Kuwait in 1990, and may be the only treasures remaining from the National Museum of Kuwait. Contact the museum for information about the Greater Atlanta Archaeology Society, which sometimes meets at the museum or elsewhere on the Emory campus. Hours: Tues.–Sat. 10:00am–4:30pm; Sun. 12noon–5:00pm. Free, but a donation of $3.00 is suggested.

■ **Center for Puppetry Arts,** 1404 Spring St., Atlanta (874-0398). The center's puppetry museum has an extensive collection of puppets from around the world, including many of the Middle Eastern cultures. Recently, the center's special exhibit of shadow puppets from the Karagoz theatre of Turkey featured traditional characters from the plays and offered a glimpse of Turkish social life during the Ottoman Era. (*Karagoz* or "Black-Eye" refers both to the Turkish shadow theatre and to the protagonist of this puppet tradition, dating from the 14th century.) Hours: Mon.–Sat. 9:00am–4:00pm and evenings on performance nights. Admission fee.

■ **Museum of the Jimmy Carter Library**, One Copenhill Ave., Atlanta (331-3942). An exhibit at the museum includes photographs and memorabilia memorializing the Camp David peace conferences brought about by Jimmy Carter during his Presidency and addresses issues relevant to politics in the Middle Eastern region. Hours: Mon.–Sat. 9:00am–4:45pm; Sun. 12 noon–4:45pm. Admission fee.

■ **High Museum at Georgia-Pacific Center**, 133 Peachtree St., NW, Atlanta (577-6940). The attractive extension to the High Museum occasionally houses special exhibits of Middle Eastern content, such as the recent exhibit "Traditional Crafts of Saudi Arabia," which featured more than 150 unusual pieces of Bedouin jewelry, weavings, weapons, riding accoutrements for camels and utensils from the vanishing nomadic culture. In conjunction with the exhibit, the museum offered workshops for children in Islamic design, a program on the ancient art of belly dancing and a storytelling session featuring Akbar Imhotep, who wove magical tales from *One Thousand and One Arabian Nights.* Hours: Mon.–Fri. 11:00am–5:00pm. Free.

■ **Atlanta Museum**, 537 Peachtree St., NE, Atlanta (872-8233). The museum's collection includes some artifacts from the ancient civilizations of the Middle East, such as a genuine stone from King Tut's tomb. Hours: Mon.–Fri. 10:00am–5:00pm and weekends by appointment only. Admission fee.

COMMUNITY, RELIGIOUS & CULTURAL ASSOCIATIONS

ARAB ASSOCIATIONS

■ **Arab American Fund of Georgia, Inc.**, P.O. Box 52052, Atlanta 30355. The fund is both an educational and cultural organization which promotes better understanding of the people and culture of the Middle East and disseminates educational material for the improvement of relationships between Arabs and Americans.

■ **Arab American Women's Society of Georgia**, P.O. Box 451276, Atlanta 30345 (448-9190). The organization fosters an appreciation of Arab history and culture and the accurate projection of the image of the Arab woman. The society supports an Arabic school which teaches Arabic language, culture and heritage; has informational programs available to community groups; and sponsors numerous festivals and special events throughout the year. Membership is open to any woman of Arab heritage or married to an Arab.

■ **Georgia Committee on U.S.–Arab Relations**, P.O. Box 404, Carrollton 30117 (706/834-2751). The Atlanta chapter of the National Council on U.S.–Arab Relations is comprised of educators who have participated in the Joseph J. Malone Faculty Fellows Program in Arab and Islamic Studies, a unique program providing American educators with an opportunity to visit one of eight participating Arab countries for an intensive program in Arab and Islamic studies. Fellows from the program gain firsthand insight into the region and its people and share their experiences through community outreach activities. The bimonthly newsletter is an excellent source of information about films, lectures, conferences, special events and teaching material available in Georgia, focusing on topics and events pertaining to the Middle East.

■ **National Association of Arab Americans – Georgia Chapter**, 2774 Jasmine Ct., Atlanta 30345 (493-4725). Membership in the social, cultural and educational organization is open to Arab-Americans, as well as those interested in

Arab countries who wish to work toward Arab and American friendship, goodwill and peace.

■ **Arab American Anti-Discrimination Committee**, P.O. Box 29132, Atlanta 30329. The ADC's goal is the protection of the human and civil rights of Arab-Americans.

DRUZE ASSOCIATIONS

■ **American Druze Society – Georgia Chapter** (633-1161). The society perpetuates the teachings of the Tawhid faith and serves as an educational and cultural organization for the Druze community in Atlanta.

LEBANESE ASSOCIATIONS

■ **Cedar Club of Atlanta** (498-2597). Membership in the social group is open to Americans of Lebanese and Syrian descent. The club meets year-round for social gatherings featuring music, dance and food, and for a major convention on Labor Day weekend. There is also a Women's Auxiliary section.

■ **The National Alliance of Lebanese Americans – Atlanta Chapter (NALA)**, 3087 Henderson Rd., Tucker 30084 (493-1670). NALA's goals are the preservation of the culture, heritage and identity of Lebanese-Americans, the support of fellow Lebanese in their quest for freedom and peace, humanitarian support to war victims in Lebanon, and the conveyance of information to the American people about the contributions of the Lebanese population to civilization. The Atlanta chapter is quite active and willing to provide Atlantans with information about Lebanese culture and the society's social events. Members are often available to speak, write and provide information about Lebanon. NALA's dabkeh dance group, The Lebanese Dance Troupe, may frequently be enjoyed at international festivals throughout Atlanta.

■ **American University of Beirut Alumni Association** (936-0113). Alumni from the American University of Beirut meet regularly for social and fund-raising activities.

PALESTINIAN ASSOCIATIONS

■ **Palestinian Human Rights Campaign**, P.O. Box 831072, Stone Mountain 30083 (496-9844). The political organization provides or sponsors lectures, slides, cultural displays and discussion groups for the purpose of educating Atlantans about the plight of the Palestinians in the West Bank and Gaza Strip.

PERSIAN ASSOCIATIONS

■ **Persian Community Center**, 6890 Peachtree Industrial Blvd., Doraville (409-8966). The center's goal is the preservation of Iranian heritage, language, culture and traditions, by sponsoring social activities, language classes, concerts and other cultural events for the Persian community. The community organization is also involved in many charitable concerns, including the organization of a food bank for Atlanta's needy, and providing free medical, dental and eye-screening for community members. The center also pursues activities to further inter-ethnic relationships. Contact the center for a copy of the bimonthly newsletter.

TURKISH ASSOCIATIONS

■ **Turkish American Cultural Association** (971-5095). The association serves Atlanta's Turkish community, estimated to be about 2,000 strong. Members are eager to educate and expose the general population to Turkish culture, art, history, politics and travel information. Association meetings are conducted in Turkish and English. The association also hosts a Turkish Hospitality Night, usually held in the spring.

ARABIC, ARAMAIC & EASTERN ORTHODOX CHURCHES

■ A sampling: **St. Elias Antiochian Orthodox Church**, 2045 Ponce de Leon Ave., NE, Atlanta (378-8191) (Sunday services in Arabic and Lebanese); **St. Joseph's Maronite Eastern Rite Church**, 502 Seminole Ave., NE, Atlanta (525-2504) (portions of the 11:00am service during Sunday mass are in Arabic and Aramaic); **St. John's Crysostom Melkite Catholic Church**, 1428 Ponce de Leon Ave., NE, Atlanta (373-9522) (portions of Sunday services are in Arabic and Greek); **Briarlake Arabic Baptist Church**, 3715 LaVista Rd., Decatur (325-4214) (Sunday services at 5:00pm); and **St. Mary's Coptic Orthodox Church**, 11450 Houze Rd., Roswell (642-9727) (Arabic, Coptic and Greek services held on Saturdays).

MOSQUES

■ **Al-Farooq Masjid of Atlanta**, 442 14th St., NW, Atlanta (874-7521). Atlanta's largest mosque (in membership) is a place of worship for all Moslems and a cultural and educational center for the Islamic community in Atlanta. Friday congregational prayers are at 1:45 pm. With its recent expansion, the mosque now offers two Islamic schools, as well as weekend Islamic classes for adults and children. A newsletter, *Al Él Aan,* provides a calendar of upcoming religious, cultural and special events. One of the schools houses a library and Islamic bookstore.

■ A sampling of other mosques: **Atlanta Masjid of Al Islam**, 560 Fayetteville Rd., SE, Atlanta (378-1600) (besides congregation prayers each Friday at 1:00pm, and educational meetings each Sunday at 2:00pm, the mosque has both an elementary school and high school forming the second largest Islamic educational facility in the U.S.); **Community Masjid of the West End**, 1128 Oak St., SW, Atlanta (758-7016); **Masjid Al-Muminuum**, 735 Capitol Ave., Atlanta (586-9562); **Masjid Momeneen**, 3777 Church St., Stone Mountain (294-4058); **Masjid Al-Hidayah**, 9 Perimeter Way, NW, Suite 152, Atlanta (953-6806); and **Ismali Center**, 6944 Hwy. 85, Riverdale (996-0755), and 685 DeKalb Industrial Way, Decatur (299-9226).

OTHER RELIGIOUS GROUPS

■ **Zoroastrianism** (876-2818). The informal society provides information about the Zoroastrian religion founded by the Persian prophet Zarathustra.

schools, classes, language

■ **Al-Farooq Masjid of Atlanta – Masjid Dar Un Noor School**, 442 14th St., NW, Atlanta (874-7521) presently offers religious instruction for adults, a children's weekend Islamic school, a full-time Islamic day school for children Pre-K through 6th grade, and an early-morning school where children memorize the Koran.

■ **Atlanta Masjid of Al Islam**, 735 Fayetteville Rd., SE, Atlanta (378-4219) runs Sister Clara Mohammed Elementary School and W.D. Mohammed High School, that, together, form the second largest Islamic educational facility in the U.S.

■ **Persian Community Center**, 6890 Peachtree Industrial Blvd., Doraville (409-8966) offers Farsi language classes for children and adults on Saturdays, as well as a children's music program.

■ **Oglethorpe University's Continuing Education Program** (364-8383) usually offers beginning Arabic during evening hours.

■ **Mercer University Atlanta**, 3001 Mercer University Dr., Atlanta (986-3375/986-3109) often offers Saturday morning classes for adults in Arabic I and II.

■ *American Arab Business Directory for the Southeast of the U.S.A.* Published by Middle East Advertising Agency (416-6620). The bilingual business directory provides information about Middle Eastern associations, restaurants, businesses, schools, groceries, bakeries and professionals in Georgia, Virginia, Maryland and Washington, D.C. Cost is $1.50.

■ *PAKE Monthly*, 10440 Colony Glen Dr., Alpharetta (842-0549). The monthly magazine contains news, articles and announcements of interest to the Persian community. Although most of the articles are in Farsi, most of the advertisements are also in English, so the magazine can be a source for discovering new Persian restaurants and business establishments.

■ **Al-Farooq Masjid of Atlanta**, 442 14th St., NW, Atlanta (874-7521). One of the schools at the Mosque houses an Islamic library and bookstore.

■ **Islamic Book Center Service of Al-Furqan Academy**, 5675 Jimmy Carter Blvd. Flea Market, NW, Norcross (840-7900). The booth in the flea market has a selection of Islamic books for children and adults. It also carries an English language Islamic magazine.

■ The **Middle Eastern Groceries** and **Import Stores** listed below, for the most part, carry a selection of Arabic or Farsi reading material, cookbooks, newspapers and sheet music, as well as audio cassettes, CDs and rental videos.

■ **International Groceries and Delicatessen**, 585 Franklin Rd., SE, Marietta (499-7608) sells a small selection of imported gifts, such as Egyptian papyrus scrolls, from Middle Eastern and North African countries.

■ **Leon International Foods (Middle East Baking Company)**, 4000-B Pleasantdale Rd., NE, Atlanta (416-6620) stocks a few household goods, kitchen supplies and gifts from the Middle East.

■ **Shahrzad International, Co.**, 215 Copeland Rd., Atlanta (843-0549). The grocery has a small selection of religious and small gift items from Iran.

■ **Super Bahar**, 5920 Roswell Rd., Sandy Springs (252-2210). The Persian grocery store, adjacent to Salar Restaurant, has a small selection of gift items.

ORIENTAL RUGS & KILIMS

■ Luxurious oriental rugs from Persia, Turkey and other Middle Eastern countries may be found in the many oriental rug stores throughout the city. For example, **Kilim Collection, Ltd.**, 22-A Bennett St., Atlanta (351-1110) specializes in high-quality Kilim rugs and pillows, vests, pocketbooks and other decorative arts from the Middle East; and **Kilim Kreations**, 800 Miami Cir., Atlanta (231-0580) sells pillows, wall-hangings and a large selection of rugs from the Middle East, Turkey, Persia and Russia. Look in the *Yellow Pages* for additional listings.

GROCERIES, MARKETS, BAKERIES

(H) Designates that the establishment carries Halal (kosher) meat.

BUTCHERS

■ *(H)* **Almadina Certified Halal Market**, 536 Fayetteville Rd., Atlanta (370-0270); **Georgia Halal Meat**, 1594 Woodcliff Dr., NE, Atlanta (315-7224); and **S.K. Grocery Store**, 3996 Pleasantdale Rd., Suite 101, Doraville (447-5326) sell halal chicken, beef, goat, lamb and processed meats.

BAKERIES, GROCERIES & DELICATESSENS

■ *(H)* **Asian Trade Co.**, 6034 S. Norcross-Tucker Rd., Norcross (840-1009). This grocery stocks a selection of Indian, Pakistani, Bangladeshi, Middle Eastern and African groceries, as well as halal meat, fresh produce, breads and spices.
■ **The Cedar Tree**, 1565 N. Decatur Rd., NE, Atlanta (373-2118). The Lebanese deli serves delicious Middle Eastern dishes, such as stuffed grape leaves, spinach pie, hummus, babaghanoush, labneh dip, felafel, shish kabob, grilled kabobs, tabbouleh, fattoush and even bagels. There is also a small selection of groceries, baked goods and sweets for sale.
■ **Gyro & Felafel Stop**, 2250 Cobb Pkwy., Smyrna (984-0888). The Middle Eastern fast-food restaurant serves gyro wraps, felafel, ful medammes, spinach pies and sweets.
■ **International Groceries and Delicatessen**, 585 Franklin Rd., Marietta (499-7608). The deli/restaurant sells a selection of groceries and deli items from the Middle East, Greece, India and Persia.
■ **Leon International Foods**, 4000-B Pleasantdale Rd., Doraville (416-6620). Owned by the Middle Eastern bakery, a wholesale bakery in Atlanta, the

attractive grocery store sells breads of all kinds, Middle Eastern pastries, nuts, cheeses, spices, dried fruits, canned groceries and delicatessen items. There is a small seating area.

■ **Middle Eastern Groceries**, 2250 Cobb Pkwy., Suite 11, Smyrna (984-0888). The grocery store is jam-packed with groceries, spices, dried fruits, nuts, cheeses, canned groceries, pastries and sweets.

■ **Pyramid Pita Market & Deli**, 3965 Rockbridge Rd., Stone Mountain (297-0768). The restaurant/market sells top quality Lebanese and Middle Eastern grocery items, including fresh deli items (gyro, felafel, hummus, grape leaves, etc.), coffees, spices, cheeses, nuts, olive oil, breads and pastries.

■ *(H)* **Shahrzad International, Co.**, 215 Copeland Rd., Atlanta (843-0549). The Persian grocery is packed with Persian and Middle Eastern delicacies, such as fresh feta cheese, nuts, spices, teas, pastries, canned goods and anything else you may need for a genuine Persian feast.

■ *(H)* **Shalimar**, 5265 Jimmy Carter Blvd., Norcross (409-1720). The Pakistani, Indian, Arabic and Bangladeshi grocery store is well- stocked with halal meat and a large selection of Indian and Middle Eastern groceries.

■ *(H)* **S. K. Grocery Store**, 3996 Pleasantdale Rd., Suite 101, Doraville (447-5326). The Indian, Pakistani and Arabic grocery store sells halal meat, Middle Eastern groceries, spices, nuts and more.

■ **Super Bahar**, 5920 Roswell Rd., Sandy Springs (252-2210). The small Persian grocery store, adjacent to Salar, has a selection of Persian groceries, cheese, nuts, spices, breads and sweets.

RESTAURANTS

■ **Basil's Mediterranean Cafe**, 2985 Grandview Ave. (Pharr Rd.), Atlanta (233-9755). Mediterranean and Middle Eastern specialties are featured at this Buckhead restaurant, including Greek and Lebanese-style entrees of lamb, beef, seafood and chicken. Tabbouleh, hummus, felafel and grape leaves are also favorites. Open: Lunch: Tues.–Sat.; Dinner: Tues.–Sun.

■ **Emah's**, 5920 Roswell Rd. (Parkside Shopping Center–Lower Level), Atlanta (255-2686). The Israeli-owned restaurant features authentic Middle Eastern–Moroccan fare, such as couscous, shish kabob, hummus and felafel. Critics have given this restaurant high ratings. Specials change daily. Open: Lunch and Dinner: Daily.

■ **Gyro Wrap Cafe**, 3027 N. Druid Hills Rd. (Toco Hills Shopping Center),

Atlanta (320-7580). Gyro wrap sandwiches and platters are the most popular fare at this Greek/Middle Eastern-style restaurant, but other specialties include spanakopita, hummus, felafel, Greek salads and Mediterranean pizza. Live entertainment on weekends. Open: Lunch and Dinner: Daily.

■ **Jaffa Gate**, 245 Peachtree Center Ave. (Marquis One – Gallery Level), Atlanta (577-0352) and 1197 Peachtree St. (Colony Square), Atlanta (876-0094). The Mediterranean-style cafe serves Middle Eastern and Greek specialties, such as felafel, hummus, gyros, shish kabob, spanakopita, espresso and sweet desserts. Open: Breakfast, Lunch and Dinner: Daily.

■ **Lawrence's Cafe and Restaurant**, 2888 Buford Hwy. (N. Druid Hills Rd.), Atlanta (320-7756). The romantic Lebanese restaurant has an excellent selection of Middle Eastern appetizers, including hummus, tabouli salad, babaghanoush and Turkish salad. Entree specialties include mezza, grilled seafood specialties, lamb, kabobs and couscous. Authentic (and tasteful) belly dancing may be enjoyed on weekends. Open: Lunch: Mon.–Fri.; Dinner: Daily.

■ **Nicola's**, 1602 LaVista Rd. (Briarcliff Rd.), Atlanta (325-2524). The friendly neighborhood restaurant serves Lebanese specialties, such as stuffed grape leaves, fatoush salad, tabbouleh, babaghanoush, kabobs, stuffed eggplant, kibbe and honeyed pastries. Restaurant critics agree that this restaurant is one of Atlanta's best Middle Eastern restaurants. Open: Lunch: Mon.-Fri., Dinner: Daily.

■ **Oasis Cafe – Mediterranean Cuisine**, 752 Ponce de Leon Ave. (across from Kroger Plaza), Atlanta (881-0815) and 1799 Briarcliff Rd. (Sage Hill Shopping Center), Atlanta (876-1280). House specialties include kibbi, felafel, schwarma, kabobs, hummus, babaghanoush and Turkish coffee. Low prices and friendly atmosphere have made this restaurant a popular spot. Open: Lunch and Dinner: Daily.

■ **Pyramid Pita Market & Deli**, 3965 Rockbridge Rd. (Rockbridge Market Place), Stone Mountain (297-0768). The restaurant/deli serves a full menu of Middle Eastern specialties, including gyro wraps, felafel, hummus, grape leaves and kabobs. Open: Lunch & Dinner: Daily.

■ **Sahara Cafe of Jaffa Gate**, 710 Peachtree St. (3rd St./Scandinavian House), Atlanta (876-4750). Sahara Cafe has the same menu as the other Jaffa Gate restaurants, featuring Middle Eastern and Greek specialties, plus an extended dinner menu. Tasteful belly dancing and live entertainment may be enjoyed on weekends. Special Sunday brunch. Open: Lunch and Dinner: Daily.

■ **Shipfeifer's Gyro Wrap**, 1814 Peachtree Rd. (Palisades Rd.), Atlanta (875-1106). Gyro wrap sandwiches and platters are the mainstay of the restaurant's fare, but other Greek and Middle Eastern dishes, such as hummus, felafel, Greek salads and spanakopita, are also very popular. A large selection of vegetarian entrees is always offered. Open: Lunch and Dinner: Daily.

■ **Gyro Fast Food Booths** may be found in the food courts of almost every shopping mall and large office building in Atlanta, offering the uninitiated an easy way to sample these delicious sandwiches.

PERSIAN RESTAURANTS

■ **Pars Persian Cuisine**, 215 Copeland Rd. (Roswell Rd. at I-285/Copeland Village Shopping Center), Atlanta (851-9566). Generous portions of grilled shish kabobs, *tahdeeg* (Persian-style rice pilaf), Persian stews, stuffed grape leaves, chicken with pomegranate sauce and marinated vegetables are served Persian-style at this very distinctive restaurant. Open: Lunch and Dinner: Daily.

■ **Salar**, 5920 Roswell Rd. (Parkside Shopping Center), Atlanta (252-8181). This Sandy Springs Persian restaurant features an extensive menu of Persian food and Mediterranean cuisine, including a large selection of Persian stews, grilled Cornish hen and kabobs (tenderloin, chicken, lamb and turkey) cooked over an open pit. Children are very welcome. Open: Lunch and Dinner: Daily.

NORTH AFRICAN RESTAURANTS

■ **African Brown Bag**, 699 Ponce de Leon Ave. (Ford Factory Square), Atlanta (642-3434). Geneva Francais constantly receives praise for her cooking at this most unusual restaurant. Entrees are prepared using a blend of Tunisian and Moroccan spices with a touch of "French technique." Chicken stews, lamb dishes, couscous, Tunisian eggplant and vegetarian specialties are some of the entrees which may be offered at any given time. Lunch: Sun. (1:00pm–6:00pm); Dinner: Tues.–Sat.

■ **The Imperial Fez**, 2285 Peachtree Rd. (south of Peachtree Battle Ave.), Atlanta (351-0870). Customers who enter the tent setting of this unusual restaurant are seated on deep pillows and presented with elaborate five-course Moroccan dinners. Critics rave about the Cornish hen with honey and lemon, lamb brochette and vegetarian couscous entrees, all accompanied by aromatic mint tea. Authentic belly dancing and other live entertainment is available upon request. Open: Dinner: Daily.

DANCE, MUSIC & STORYTELLING

■ **Belly Dancing** may be enjoyed at **Lawrence's Cafe and Restaurant**, 2888 Buford Hwy. (N. Druid Hills Rd.), Atlanta (320-7756); and **Sahara Cafe of Jaffa Gate**, 710 Peachtree St. (3rd St./Scandinavian House), Atlanta (876-4750) on Friday and Saturday evenings. **The Imperial Fez**, 2285 Peachtree Rd. (south of Peachtree Battle Ave.), Atlanta (351-0870) presents belly dancing on request. From time to time, various dancers in the Atlanta area will offer classes in belly dancing. Check *Creative Loafing* or your neighborhood newspapers for announcements.

■ **The Lebanese Dance Troupe** (252-3463) may be enjoyed at various ethnic festivals throughout the year. A performance may contain a traditional *dabke* (group dance), a modern dance or a belly dance. Some of the Middle Eastern churches also have their own *dabke* dance groups.

■ **Turkish American Cultural Association Folkdance Ensemble** (634-0043) and the **Turkish American Music Choir** (294-8768) appear at international and cultural festivals throughout Atlanta. The Folkdance Ensemble presents an afternoon workshop on Turkish folk dance during Turkish Hospitality Night.

■ **B.J. Abraham** (633-3277), a professional storyteller and member of the Southern Order of Storytellers, appears at international festivals throughout the year, enchanting children and adults alike with her tales from the Middle East. Recently, she and another storyteller, Fiona Page, performing as The Tellers Two, have developed a repertoire of multicultural and international folk tales for all ages.

■ **Persian Music Classes, Concerts and Dances** are offered at the Persian Community Center year-round. There is also a music program for children. Persian concerts may be enjoyed at various locations in Atlanta, such as Emory University, where the **Persian Classical Music Society** (252-2210) sponsors concerts by masters of Persian traditional music. Recently, the society hosted a performance by a traditional Persian Ensemble with **Hossein Alizadech**, composer.

■ *Pastoos* (Persian Dance Disco's) may be enjoyed throughout the year at various locations in Atlanta. Look for flyers in the Persian grocery stores announcing upcoming dances.

Ponce de Leon Ave., Atlanta (373-9522). The church occasionally h
international festival featuring exotic food from Lebanon and Syria, i.
ing baklava and other honeyed pastries. Display booths, food and dance
formances by many of Atlanta's other communities are also featured.

FALL

■ **Mideastern Festival**, St. Elias Antiochian Orthodox Church, 2045 Ponce de
Leon Ave., NE, Atlanta (633-5749). Delicious food and pastries, imported gift
items, performances of traditional music, song and folkdance, cultural displays,
tours of the sanctuary and children's activities highlight this annual festival.
■ **Egyptian Food and Craft Fair**, St. Mary's Coptic Orthodox Church, Roswell
(642-9727). The Orthodox Church often hosts a festival in celebration of
Egyptian heritage featuring hot foods, sweets and crafts.

OTHER

■ **Al-Farooq Masjid of Atlanta** and other Atlanta mosques have religious services and feasts during Ramadan. Call the mosques for more information if
you are seriously interested in attending these religious celebrations.

RESOURCES

■ **Honorary Consulate General of Turkey**, 569 Emory Oaks Way, Decatur
30033 (325-3174).

FILMS

■ Middle Eastern films may be found throughout the year at various locations. For example: **The Iranian Movie Series** (296-2598) screens Iranian films, such as *The Runner, Broken Columns* and *Roonama Dance* at Cinevision, 3300 NE Expressway, Building 2, Atlanta; and **The Near Eastern Film Series** (727-6562) screens at Emory University. Look for advertisements about upcoming films in *PAKE* and *Creative Loafing*.

T.V. & RADIO

■ **WGUN-AM** **(1010)** (491-1010) airs a radio show called "Arabic Voice o Gospel" on Sunday from 2:15pm–2:30pm.

fEStIVALS & spEcIAL EVENTS

SPRING

■ **B.C. Fest!**, Michael C. Carlos Museum (formerly Emory Museum of A Archeology), Emory Quadrangle, Atlanta (727-4282). The one-of-a-kind val and educational experience introduces children to the life and cultu the ancient worlds. Annual festival events have included Middle Ea music and belly dancing, pottery making, mummy wrapping demonstra hieroglyphic coloring walls, pyramid building, hands-on arts and crafts ties, ancient sporting events, gift stalls and wonderful Middle Easter prepared by The Cedar Tree.

■ **Persian New Year Celebration**, Persian Community Center, Doravil 8966). The Persian New Year falls on the first day of spring, and the nity celebrates with a large festival featuring traditional food, m dance. A community picnic is also part of the New Year celebrati general public is invited to join in the celebration.

SUMMER

■ **Turkish Hospitality Night**, Unitarian Universalist Church (Cliff and I-85), Atlanta (971-5095). During the annual Turkish Hospi usually held in the spring, The Turkish American Cultural Associ the public to experience Turkish food, culture, dance and theatr more about the people and history of their country. There a dance workshops and cooking demonstrations.

■ **International Festival**, St. John's Crysostom Melkite Catholic

Pakistani child at the gathering of the Pakistan Society of Atlanta.

INDIA, PAKISTAN, BANGLADESH, AFGHANISTAN & NEPAL

HISTORY & NEIGHBORHOODS

Approximately 30,000 individuals of Indian, Pakistani or Bangladeshi descent are estimated to reside in Atlanta, the majority of which are either professionals or are involved in trade or business activities in the city. The India Cultural and Religious Center in Smyrna plays an important role in the Indian community, serving as a center for religious, social and cultural activities. And, now that the construction of the Hindu Temple of Atlanta in Riverdale has been completed, approximately 1,000 of Atlanta's Hindu families and another 30,000 Hindus from all over the Southeast, journey to the southside of Atlanta to join in prayer at the new facility. Similarly, the Al-Farooq Masjid of Atlanta, in midtown, serves as an important religious center for those members of the community who are of the Moslem faith.

Northeast DeKalb County has quite a few strip shopping centers which house clusters of business establishments dealing in Indian/Pakistani foods, fabrics, clothing, reading material, appliances, music, videos and imported gifts. And lately it seems as if a new Indian restaurant or grocery is opening in some corner of the county every month! One of the largest of the shopping centers is Woodcliff Shopping Center, located at the intersection of Briarcliff and North Druid Hills Roads. Those who are unfamiliar with Indian spices should visit Taj Mahal Grocery for a wonderful exploration of the smells and flavors emanating from this part of the world. If you become inspired by the store's aromas, go next door to Chat Patti and sample a samosa or another flavorful dish from this excellent and inexpensive fast-food restaurant. Perhaps this adventure will spark an interest in Indian food that will lead you to explore more of Atlanta's fine Indian restaurants or encourage you to buy a cookbook and begin experimenting with curries and other Indian dishes at home.

Most of Atlanta's Afghani community members, estimated to number about 1,200, were political refugees, who after fleeing to India, Pakistan or Germany in the early 1980s, have resettled in Atlanta. Lutheran Ministries of Georgia, Inc. and the Afghan Community of Georgia play a significant role in providing job placement and other support services to the newly arrived families. Since most community members are of the Moslem faith, both the Al-Farooq Masjid of Atlanta and the Masjid Momeneen in Clarkston assist newly arrived Afghanis by offering English language classes, religious instruction and opportunities for Afghanis to socialize with one another.

HISTORICAL SITES, MUSEUMS, & GALLERIES

■ **Fernbank Science Center**, 156 Heaton Park Dr., NE, Atlanta (378-4311). One of the shows at Fernbank Planetarium is called "Stars of India." Occasionally, the Science Center will simultaneously display an exhibit of Indian art, artifacts and jewelry in conjunction with the show. Call to find out when the program will be presented next. Planetarium admission fee.

■ Atlanta area galleries periodically house exhibits featuring the art, history, culture or religion of India. A sampling of recent exhibits: **Emory University's Schatten Gallery**, Woodruff Library, 540 Ashby Cir., Atlanta (727-6868/727-6861) housed a cultural and religious exhibit called "Living Gods, Hindu Faces;" and **Kennesaw State College's Library Art Gallery**, 3455 Frey Lake Rd., NW, Kennesaw (423-6139) displayed a special exhibit, "The Art of India."

COMMUNITY, RELIGIOUS & CULTURAL ASSOCIATIONS

COMMUNITY ASSOCIATIONS

■ **India American Cultural Association (IACA)** (436-3719) promotes Indo-American friendship and serves the cultural, educational and religious needs of Atlanta's Indian community. The **India Cultural & Religious Center (ICRC)** at 1281 Cooper Lake Rd., Smyrna (436-4272) is owned and operated by IACA for the benefit of its members. This 7-acre center houses a 280-seat auditorium, a Hindu temple and religious school, a 2,000-volume library on India, and a dance and music academy. The center is also the venue for year-round concerts, films, lectures, religious celebrations and social events. You may also contact the IACA for information about the **National Federation of Indian Associations**, **The Indian Women's Association** and **Indian Youth of Atlanta** (age 13–23 years).

■ Here is a sampling of some of the regional groups that are active in Atlanta: **Aligarh Association** espouses the cultural and social philosophy of Sir Sayed Ahmad Khan and holds social gatherings, Urdu poetry symposia and other cultural events year-round; **Bangladesh International Association** sponsors year-round activities, including a celebration on December 16th (Liberation Day), an Independence Day celebration on March 25th and religious holiday observances throughout the year; **Bengali Association of Greater Atlanta** is a Bengali-speaking organization which meets regularly throughout the year; **Gujarati Samaj** is a religious and cultural association for people from Gujarat State; **Kannada Koota** is a regional group from Karnataka State; **Kashmiri Overseas Group, Atlanta Chapter** consists of individuals from Kashmir; **Maharashtra Manbal** is a Marathi-speaking group from Maharashtra State (Bombay); **Pakistan Club** and the **Pakistan Society of Atlanta** sponsor activities for members; and **Pujari Group** is a cultural group which celebrates the Bengali New Year and Hindu religious holidays. Contact the IACA for the names and telephone numbers of current contact people for each association or check the latest edition of the *Atlanta Multicultural Directory* (378-3719).

■ **Afghan Community of Georgia** (875-0201). The association's members meet regularly to celebrate religious holidays, such as Éid, the Afghani New Year (March 21st) and the Christian New Year.

HINDU CENTERS

■ **Hindu Temple of Atlanta**, 5851 Ga. Hwy. 85, Riverdale (907-7102). The congregation of the newly constructed Hindu Temple is primarily of South Indian origin and consists of about 1,000 of Atlanta's Hindu families and close to 30,000 other Hindus from Alabama, Tennessee, Florida and other southern states. The temple conducts daily Hindu services and has recently begun Sunday religious instruction for children and adults.

■ **India Cultural & Religious Center**, 1281 Cooper Lake Rd., SE, Smyrna (436-4272/436-3719). The ICRC houses a Hindu temple where Indians, primarily of North Indian origin, worship on Sundays. Religious instruction for children and adults is also offered.

■ A sampling of other Hindu Temples: **Bochasanwasi Swaminarayan Sanstha Hindu Temple**, 3518 Clarkston Industrial Blvd., Clarkston (297-0501) is open every day and conducts a religious service on Sundays at 5:00pm; **Greater Atlanta Vedic Temple Society**, 492 Harmony Grove Rd., Lilburn (564-3003) offers Hindu worship, a Sanskrit School and training for Hindu priesthood; **Vishwa Hindu Parishad of America–Atlanta Chapter** (458-2661) teaches Hindu cultural heritage and language and supports the Regional Hindu Family Camp in the Southeast each summer; **International Swaminarayan Sapsang Organization** (433-9878) is a very small religious group whose members are from Gujarat State; and **Hare Krishna Temple (ISKCON-Atlanta)**, 1287 S. Ponce de Leon Ave., NE, Atlanta (377-8680) is a group whose religious and spiritual philosophy is derived from the ancient Vedic literatures, although members of ISKCON are not necessarily members of the Indian community.

ISLAMIC CENTERS

■ **Al-Farooq Masjid of Atlanta**, 442 14th St., NW, Atlanta (874-7521). Atlanta's largest mosque (in membership) is a place of worship for all Moslems and a cultural and educational center for the Islamic community in Atlanta. Friday congregational prayers are at 1:45 pm. With its recent expansion, the mosque now offers two Islamic schools, as well as weekend Islamic classes for adults and children. A newsletter, *Al Él Aan,* provides a calendar of upcoming religious, cultural and special events. One of the schools houses a library and Islamic bookstore.

■ A sampling of other mosques: **Atlanta Masjid of Al Islam**, 560 Fayetteville Rd., SE, Atlanta (378-1600) (besides congregation prayers each Friday at 1:00pm, and educational meetings each Sunday at 2:00pm, the mosque has both an elementary and high school, forming the second largest Islamic educational facility in the U.S.); **Community Masjid of the West End**, 1128 Oak St., SW, Atlanta (758-7016); **Masjid Al-Muminuum**, 735 Capitol Ave., Atlanta (586-9562); **Masjid Momeneen**, 3777 Church St., Clarkston (294-4058); **Masjid Al-Hidayah**, 9 Perimeter Way, NW, Suite 152, Atlanta (953-6806); and **Ismali Center**, 6944 Hwy. 85, Riverdale (996-0755) and 685 DeKalb Industrial Way, Decatur (299-9226).

OTHER RELIGIOUS CENTERS

■ **Sikh Study Circle**, 1821 S. Hairston Rd., Stone Mountain (808-6320). Approximately 500 Sikhs have recently opened the first *gurd wara* (temple) in Atlanta. Besides being a center of worship, the temple offers Sunday classes and summer camp activities for Sikh children, providing an opportunity to study their native culture.

■ **Vedanta Society of Atlanta** (636-7942). Vedanta is a world-wide movement under the spiritual guidance of the Ramakrishna Order of India. This society is based upon the Vedic literature but is not necessarily comprised of members of the Indian community.

■ **First India Baptist Church**, Clairmont Hills Baptist Church, 1995 Clairmont Rd., Decatur (636-6595). The quickly growing church encourages Indian traditions and language by conducting services in Hindi, rather than English, and using traditional Indian musical instruments. Sunday school classes also incorporate Indian culture. Baptist congregations are forming elsewhere in the city.

schools, classes, language

■ **Hindu Temple of Atlanta**, 5851 Ga. Hwy. 85, Riverdale (907-7102) has begun offering religious instruction for both children and adults.
■ **India Cultural & Religious Center**, 1281 Cooper Lake Rd., SE, Smyrna (436-4272/436-3719) presently offers weekly classes where children are taught Indian history, culture and customs. Gujarati and Hindi language classes are also available. Swadhyay is an adult study group at the ICRC which meets regularly to study religion and philosophy. Hindi Jagat, a Hindi literary society, offers language classes, maintains a small Hindi language library at the ICRC and publishes *Parichay*, a quarterly literary magazine.
■ **Masjid Dar Un Noor School** (Al-Farooq Masjid of Atlanta), 442 14th St., NW, Atlanta (874-7521) presently offers religious instruction for adults, with classes in both Arabic and English, a children's weekend Islamic school, a full-time Islamic day school for children Pre-K through 4th grade, and an early-morning school where children memorize the Koran.
■ **Atlanta Masjid of Al Islam**, 735 Fayetteville Rd., SE, Atlanta (378-4219) runs Sister Clara Mohammed Elementary School and W.D. Mohammed High School, that, together, form the second largest Islamic educational facility in the U.S.
■ **Vishwa Hindu Parishad of Atlanta** (458-2661) provides Hindu religious and cultural instruction for children age six and older every other Sunday. The society also sponsors a summer Regional Hindu Family Camp.

newspapers, magazines, books, videos

■ *Voice of India* is a publication of the India American Cultural Association containing news articles, announcements and advertisements of interest to the community. Each of the regional associations and clubs publish small newsletters and/or distribute flyers announcing upcoming events.

■ **Khabar Classifieds**, 2376 Shallowford Terr., Chamblee (451-7666), an Indian-Pakistani direct mail advertising company, publishes an events calendar which is included in its mailings, containing chronological listings of events and happenings around Atlanta and its environs. Call to be placed on the mailing list.

■ Hindi Jagat, a Hindi literary society, maintains a small Hindi language library at the ICRC and publishes *Parichay*, a quarterly literary magazine.

■ National Indian Newspapers, such as *News India, India Abroad* and *India Tribune,* may sometimes be found in local Indian/Pakistani grocery stores and are available by subscription.

■ **Hindu Temple of Atlanta**, 5851 Ga. Hwy. 85, Riverdale (907-7102) is opening a library which will house books on religion, Hinduism and Indian culture.

■ **Hare Krishna Books & Boutique (ISKCON)**, 1287 S. Ponce de Leon Ave., NE, Atlanta (378-9234) has a store which carries a large selection of Vedic literature.

■ **Priya Imports**, 3090 Briarcliff Rd., NE, Atlanta (633-5603) rents a large number of Indian videos, and sells snacks and small gift items.

■ The **Indian Groceries** and **Import Stores** listed below, for the most part, sell Hindi and/or Urdu reading material. Most also have Hindi, Gujarati and Urdu video tapes and some CDs. Some groceries, such as Taj Mahal Imports at Woodcliff Shopping Center, also rent Bengali and some African-language videos.

ShoppING CENTERS, IMPORT STORES, hOTELS

SHOPPING CENTERS

■ **Woodcliff Shopping Center** (Briarcliff and N. Druid Hills Rds.) houses a large selection of Indo-Pakistani retail establishments, such as: **Taj Mahal Imports**, carrying a large supply of English and Indian/Pakistani spices, groceries, sweets, reading material, audio tapes, CDs and rental videos; **Texas Sari Sapne**, an emporium stocking sari and Indian fabrics; **Vitha Jewelers**, selling Indian-style fine jewelry; **Chat Patti**, serving inexpensive but delicious fast-food; and **Georgia Halal Meats**, a meat market selling halal (kosher) meat.

■ Other pockets of Indian/Pakistani businesses and retail stores are quickly forming in Decatur at Scott Plaza (at the intersection of Lawrenceville Hwy. and Church St.); in Tucker at LaVista Road (just south of Northlake

Shopping Mall); and in Norcross at the intersection of Jimmy Carter Boulevard and S. Norcross-Tucker Road.

IMPORT STORES

- **Asia Jewelers**, 1707 Church St., Suite C-7, Decatur (294-1646) specializes in 22K gold jewelry in Indian designs.
- **Cherians**, 1707 Church St., C-10, Decatur (299-0842), an Indian grocery store, also stocks saris, Indian fabrics and a selection of handicrafts, brass items, gifts, toys and appliances.
- **Highglow Jewelers**, 2968 N. Decatur Rd., Decatur (296-2714) specializes in 22K gold jewelry in Indian designs.
- **India Apparels**, 4445 Commerce Dr., SW, Atlanta (691-4516) sells imported Indian clothing for women, perfume and jewelry.
- **J.K. International – Import Emporium**, Buford Highway Flea Market, 5000 Buford Hwy., Chamblee (454-6434) carries a very large selection of trendy Indian-American clothing for women. Open only on Friday, Saturday and Sunday.
- **Kala Niketan**, 1707 Church St., Decatur (296-1001) sells Indian silk saris, fabric and ready-made clothing.
- **Laxmi Sari**, 2968 N. Decatur Rd., Decatur (292-7100) sells Indian saris, salwar khameez sets and imported fabrics.
- **Lotus International**, 3450 Jones Mill Rd., Norcross (368-9141) sells ladies salwar khameez sets, gold plated silver jewelry, paintings on silk, handcrafted cushion covers and more.
- **Sanrig Styles**, 3900 LaVista Rd., Tucker (723-1022) specializes in Indian outfits and accessories.
- **Sona Imports**, 1248, Suite 2D, Clairmont Rd., Decatur (636-7979), an Indian grocery store, also carries saris, Indian fabrics and imported gifts.
- **Taj Mahal Imports**, 1594 Woodcliff Dr., NE, Atlanta (321-5940), an Indian grocery store, also has a selection of jewelry, appliances and electronic equipment.
- **Texas Sari Sapne**, 1594 Woodcliff Dr., NE, Atlanta (633-7274) sells Indian fabrics, saris and men's clothing, as well as electronics, appliances, luggage and housewares.
- **Vitha Jewelers, Inc.**, 1594 Woodcliff Dr., Suite B, Atlanta (320-0112/633-5496) has a large selection of 22K gold jewelry in Indian artistic designs.

ORIENTAL RUGS & DHURRIES

- Authentic rugs and dhurries from India, Pakistan and Afghanistan may be found in most oriental rug stores throughout the city. Look in the *Yellow Pages* for listings of stores near you.

(H) Designates that the establishment carries Halal (kosher) meat.

BUTCHERS

■ *(H)* **Almadina Certified Halal Market**, 536 Fayetteville Rd., Atlanta (370-0270); **Georgia Halal Meat**, 1594 Woodcliff Dr., NE, Atlanta (315-7224); and **S.K. Grocery Store**, 3996 Pleasantdale Rd., Suite 101, Doraville (447-5326) sell halal chicken, beef, goat, lamb and processed meats.

BAKERIES & GROCERIES

■ *(H)* **Asian Trade Co.**, 6034 S. Norcross-Tucker Rd., Norcross (840-1009). This grocery stocks a selection of Indian, Pakistani, Bangladeshi, Middle Eastern and African groceries, as well as halal meat, fresh produce, breads and spices.

■ **Cherians**, 1707 Church St., C-10, Decatur (299-0842). The Indian grocery store stocks a large selection of Indian spices, canned goods, groceries, breads and sweets.

■ **Dana Bazar**, 1875 Cobb Pkwy., SE, Marietta (980-0527). The moderately sized Indian/Pakistani grocery sells spices, groceries, sweets, snacks, frozen foods, fresh vegetables and some household goods.

■ **Globe Foods & Video**, 2179 Lawrenceville Hwy. , Decatur (633-6540). Indian and Pakistani grocery products are available at this market, along with fresh sweets, snacks, household goods, CDs, audio tapes and rental videos.

■ **India Bazar**, 1525 E. Park Place Blvd., Suite 2000, Stone Mountain. This Indian grocery store stocks Indo-Pak groceries, snacks, sweets, audio tapes, CDs, rental videos and a few small gift items.

■ **India Imports**, 6030 Hwy. 85, Riverdale (996-6956). A selection of spices, groceries and other specialty items may be purchased at this grocery store.

■ **International Groceries and Delicatessen**, 585 Franklin Rd., Marietta (499-7608). The deli/restaurant sells a selection of groceries and deli items from India, the Middle East, Greece and Persia.

■ **Naya Bazaar**, 3900 LaVista Rd., Tucker (491-6700). The Indian market, adjacent to Maharaja Lounge and Restaurant, sells a large selection of Indian and international groceries, including many homemade sweets. There is a large selection of Hindi and Gujarati video tapes for rental.

- **New Delhi Import Store**, 4025 Satellite Blvd., Duluth (623-9560). Indian groceries, spices, daals, snacks, household items and small gifts may be purchased at this Indian grocery. Audio cassettes, CDs and rental videos are also available.
- **Patel Brothers**, 2968 N. Decatur Rd., Decatur (292-8235). The small Indian grocery store is packed with Indian spices, groceries and specialty items.
- *(H)* **Shalimar**, 5265 Jimmy Carter Blvd., Norcross (409-1720). The Pakistani, Indian, Arabic and Bangladeshi grocery store is well- stocked with halal meat and a large selection of Indian and Middle Eastern groceries.
- *(H)* **S. K. Grocery Store**, 3996 Pleasantdale Rd., Suite 101, Doraville (447-5326). The Indian, Pakistani and Arabic market sells halal meat and a selection of Indian/Pakistani groceries.
- **Sona Imports**, 1248, Suite 2D, Clairmont Rd., Decatur (636-7979). The Indian grocery store stocks Indian groceries, spices, sweets, breads and specialty items.
- **Taj Mahal Imports**, 1594 Woodcliff Dr., Suite G, NE, Atlanta (321-5940). Atlanta's largest Indian, Pakistani and British grocery store is filled with every kind of spice and grocery item imaginable from India and Pakistan. There is also a selection of breads, bakery products and sweets.

RESTAURANTS

(H) Designates that the establishment serves only Halal (kosher) meat.

- **Bombay Palace**, 68 W. Paces Ferry Rd. (Peachtree Rd.), Atlanta (233-0335). This elegant restaurant features specialties from the Punjab and northwest regions of India. Luncheon buffet on weekdays. Open: Lunch and Dinner: Daily.
- **Calcutta Restaurant**, 1138 Euclid Ave. (near Moreland Ave.), Atlanta (681-1838). Recently remodeled and expanded, the restaurant serves a variety of tasty curries and tandoori dishes. Open: Lunch and Dinner: Daily.
- *(H)* **Chat Patti**, 1594 Woodcliff Dr. (N. Druid Hills and Briarcliff Rds.), Atlanta (633-5595). Inexpensive and delicious fast-food Indian specialties are served at this small cafeteria-style restaurant in Woodcliff Shopping Center. There is always a large selection of vegetarian dishes. Take-out service is available. Open: Lunch and Dinner: Daily.

- *(H)* **The Clay Oven**, 1829 Peachtree Rd. (Palisades Rd.), Atlanta (355-9411). The Clay Oven specializes in kabobs and tandoori-style Indian food using marination recipes from East India, Afghanistan and Soviet Georgia. You may also enjoy a large selection of curries and other Indian specialties. Weekday Lunch Buffet. Open: Lunch and Dinner: Daily.
- **Curry House**, 451 Moreland Ave. (Euclid Ave.), Atlanta (688-0005). The restaurant serves authentic Indian food and specializes in tandoori dishes, vegetarian specialties and, of course, curries. Open: Lunch: Mon.–Sat.; Dinner: Daily.
- **Dawat Indian Cafe**, 4025 Satellite Blvd., Duluth (623-6133). The cafeteria-style vegetarian restaurant serves samosa, bhel puri, curry, dosa, biryani and many more Indian specialties. Take-out service is available. Open: Lunch: Daily; Dinner: Tues.-Sun.
- **International Society for Krishna Consciousness (Hare Krishna)**, 1287 S. Ponce de Leon Ave. (Briarcliff Rd.), Atlanta (373-4817). The Hare Krishna Dinner Club is an "international dining experience" featuring natural vegetarian and "karmafree" international cuisine. There is a special feast on Sunday. The suggested donation is $4.50/meal or $3.00 without an entree. Open: Dinner: Daily.
- *(H)* **Haveli**, 2706 Cobb Pkwy. (north of Cumberland Mall), Smyrna (955-4525). This restaurant is considered the most elegant of Atlanta's Indian restaurants and is often praised for its luncheon buffet and vegetarian specialties. Special dinner menus are offered during Hindu holidays. Open: Lunch: Mon.–Sat.; Dinner: Daily.
- *(H)* **Heera of India**, 595 Piedmont Ave. (Rio Shopping Center), Atlanta (876-4408). Specializing in Northern Indian cuisine, the award-winning restaurant's specialties include tandoori dishes and stuffed breads. Luncheon buffet on weekdays. Open: Lunch: Mon.–Fri.; Dinner: Daily.
- **Himalayas Indian Tandoori Restaurant**, 5520 Peachtree Industrial Blvd. (Chamblee Plaza), Chamblee (458-6557/455-9616). The restaurant's stuffed breads, tandoori dishes and Indian sweets have won it many "Best Indian Restaurant" awards through the years. Open: Lunch and Dinner: Daily.
- **Indian Delights**, 1707 Church St. (Lawrenceville Hwy.), Decatur (296-2965). The small, inexpensive, vegetarian restaurant receives rave reviews from all of Atlanta's restaurant critics, as well as those who are familiar with North Indian cuisine. Take-out service is available. Open: Lunch and Dinner: Tues.–Sun.
- **Jewel of India**, 1529 Piedmont Rd. (Clear Creek Center/Monroe Dr.), Atlanta (875-0633). This restaurant boasts that it has the city's most comprehensive menu of traditional Indian food and vegetarian dishes. A weekend

buffet brunch offers an excellent opportunity to sample some of the well-prepared dishes served by this restaurant. Open: Lunch and Dinner: Daily.

■ **Kabobish**, 6034 S. Norcross-Tucker Rd. (Jimmy Carter Blvd.), Norcross (729-1745). Specializing in Pakistani and Indian cuisine, this cafeteria-style restaurant features unique dishes plus a large selection of dosas and other vegetarian dishes. Open: Breakfast: Sat.–Sun: Lunch & Dinner: Daily.

■ **Khan's Indian Restaurant**, 3115 Piedmont Rd. (E. Paces Ferry Rd.), Atlanta (264-0980). This small restaurant serves Northern Indian dishes and features mughlai specialties. Open: Lunch: Mon.–Sat.; Dinner: Daily.

■ **Maharaja Lounge & Restaurant**, 3900 LaVista Rd. (one block south of LaVista Rd./Northlake Plaza), Tucker (414-1010). This beautifully decorated, upscale restaurant serves a wide-range of regional Indian dishes. An observation window allows diners to look into the clay oven where many specialties are cooked. The attentive service, generous portions and well-prepared food make this restaurant a real find for Indian food enthusiasts. Weekday lunch buffet and weekend brunch buffet. Banquet facilities are available. Open: Lunch and Dinner: Daily.

■ *(H)* **Mehfil**, 3965 Rockbridge Rd. (Rockbridge Market Place/Memorial Dr.), Stone Mountain (294-0274). Indian and Pakistani food is served with a "traditional touch." Chicken tikka, seekh kabob and South Indian vegetarian dishes are specialties. Open: Lunch and Dinner: Daily.

■ **Moghul Salute**, 114 East Trinity Pl. (east of DeKalb County Courthouse), Decatur (371-9554). This Indian restaurant in downtown Decatur specializes in South Indian cuisine. Indian classical music may be enjoyed on weekends. Open: Lunch and Dinner: Daily.

■ *(H)* **Passage to India**, 5050 Jimmy Carter Blvd. (Carter's Rockbridge Plaza), Norcross (729-0303). One of Atlanta's newer Indian restaurants has been well received for its authentic Northern Indian cuisine. Open: Lunch and Dinner: Daily.

■ **Poona**, 1630 Pleasant Hill Rd. (Club Dr. at the Wal-mart Center), Atlanta (717-1053). Authentic Indian cuisine is served at this relatively new restaurant, including many vegetarian dishes and traditional desserts. Children ten and under may eat at half price. Live sitar music is featured most Friday and Saturday evenings. Special weekend brunch. Open: Lunch and Dinner: Daily.

■ **Raja Indian Restaurant**, 2919 Peachtree Rd. (south of Pharr Rd.), Atlanta (237-2661). The small restaurant has been a Buckhead favorite for years, and loyal customers rave about the unusual Indian fare with a heavy concentration on tandoori food preparation. Open: Lunch: Mon.–Sat.; Dinner: Daily.

■ **Razia Dining Indian Cuisine**, 3741 Roswell Rd. (north of Piedmont Rd.),

Atlanta (262-1395). North Indian cuisine along with a sampling of dishes from all over the Indian subcontinent are featured at this Buckhead restaurant. Open: Lunch: Mon.-Fri.; Dinner: Daily.

■ **Roopa's Vegetarian Indian Food**, 3420 E. Ponce de Leon Ave. (N. Decatur Rd.), Scottdale (501-0019). Authentic Indian vegetarian food is served in a cafeteria-style restaurant that also features a small sit-down area. Open: Lunch: Daily; Dinner: Wed.-Mon.

■ **Samrat**, 5920 Roswell Rd. (Parkside Shopping Center), Atlanta (252-1644). The intimate restaurant specializes in Indian curries, stuffed breads and tandoori dishes. Open: Lunch and Dinner: Daily.

■ **Sitar Indian Restaurant**, 884 Peachtree St. (7th St./across from the Fox Theatre), Atlanta (885-9949). The restaurant serves a variety of moderately priced dishes from different regions of India and specializes in tandoori, curries, breads and vegetarian dishes. Open: Lunch: Mon.–Sat.; Dinner: Daily.

■ **Tajmahal Indian Restaurant**, 1152 Spring St. (Red Carpet Inn), Atlanta (875-6355). Authentic Mughlai entrees, curries, and vegetarian specialties are served in the authentically decorated North Indian restaurant. Weekday lunch buffet. Take-out service is available. Open: Lunch: Daily; Dinner: Mon.–Sat.

■ **Touch of India Tandoori and Curry Restaurant**, 962 Peachtree St. (Peachtree Pl.), Atlanta (876-7777) and 2065 Piedmont Rd. (I-85), Atlanta (876-7775). The moderately priced restaurant consistently serves well-prepared Indian food with tandoori and vegetarian specialties. Open: Lunch and Dinner: Daily.

ENTERTAINMENT: THEATRE, DANCE, MUSIC, CLUBS, FILMS, T.V. & RADIO, SPORTS

THEATRE, DANCE & MUSIC

■ Indian Theatrical Performances may occasionally be enjoyed in the Atlanta area at the India Cultural and Religious Center (436-4272), where Indian ballets, musicals and drama productions are presented throughout the year. Also, the classic epic, *Mahabharata*, was performed at the Hare Krishna Temple during the Festival of India.

■ **Academy of Indian Dance and Music** (433-1885) offers instruction at the ICRC in Indian classical and folk dance, as well as classical vocal and instrumental music from India. Students of the academy perform at area international festivals, such as the Festival of Cultures at Underground Atlanta.

■ **Bhangrha Dance Group** (396-5033) performs the Bhangrha, a lively and exciting folk dance from the Punjab; and **Radha Dance Group** (396-5033) performs classical and folk dances from India. Both groups may be enjoyed at international festivals in the Atlanta area.

■ There are many local musicians who perform classical Indian music, such as **Studio East,** an orchestral musical group which performs violin, sitar, tabla, zheng, zither and guitar pieces; and **Sangeetkar,** also specializing in classical Indian music.

■ **The Indian Classical Musical Society of Greater Atlanta** (320-1567) holds several classical music concerts each year. Call for further information.

■ Some of the Indian restaurants listed above feature live Indian music on weekends, such as **Moghul Salute**, 114 East Trinity Pl., Decatur (371-9554); and **Poona**, 1630 Pleasant Hill Rd., Atlanta (717-1053).

■ Indian, Pakistani and Bangladeshi performers may be found throughout the year at the ICRC and other locations. A sampling of recent performances includes: **An Evening of Music from Pakistan** at Center Stage Theatre; an **East Indian Concert** at the Civic Center; a concert by **Vijay Raghav Rao**, flutist, poet, choreographer, composer and musicologist who performed at Spivey Hall; **Abhinet Pagla Ghoda**, who performed in Hindi at Agnes Scott College in Clayton County; and **Vishnamohan Bhatt**, a classical guitarist, whose concert was presented by the Indian Association of Georgia State College.

FILMS

■ **Indian Film Series**, Twin Theater, 5805 Buford Hwy. (Treasure Village Shopping Center), Doraville (498-8888) screens newly released Indian motion pictures every weekend. Films are accompanied by Indian snacks and tea. Call the above number for a schedule of upcoming films.

T.V. & RADIO

■ **WGUN–AM (1010)** (491-1010) broadcasts "Music From Asia," a mix of music, gossip, news and features about the Indian subcontinent on Sundays between 1:15pm–2:15pm. "Jiwan Jyoti" (Light of Life), a Hindustani language program, is broadcast Sundays from 5:15pm–5:30pm.

■ **WRFG–FM (89.3)** (523-3471) airs "Music From India" Friday evenings from 8:00pm–10:30pm.

SPORTS

■ **The Atlanta Cricket League** (971-6094/381-0727/447-9248) began in 1989, and it has already grown from just two teams to nine. British expatriates, Indians, Pakistanis, South Africans and West Indians compete each Sunday, May–October, at four fields in metro-Atlanta. Call for more information.

FESTIVALS & SPECIAL EVENTS

JANUARY

■ **Republic Day**, India Cultural and Religious Center, Smyrna (477-4272/436-3719). The India American Cultural Association holds a large Republic Day celebration at the center each year.

MARCH

■ **Holi – The Festival of Colors**, Stone Mountain Park (477-4272/436-3719). The India-American Cultural Association sponsors this festival of colors featuring Indian games (kabaddi, tug of war, seven tiles, volleyball, kho-kho and races), lunch, gulal and lots of color. Look for announcements in the ICAC newsletter or at Indo-Pak grocery stores.

■ **Afghani New Year's Day**, Afghan Community of Georgia (875-0201). The Afghani community celebrates the New Year (March 21st) with a large party featuring traditional foods and lots of fellowship.

JUNE

■ **Festival of India**, Hare Krishna Temple (ISKCON), S. Ponce de Leon Ave., Atlanta (378-9234). The temple's New Panihati Festival of India focuses on East Indian culture, cuisine, music, arts and crafts, astrology, religion and theatre. In the past, a replica of an Indian village with bamboo huts and water holes was created, where ancient crafts of weaving, pottery, rice flour decoration and face-painting were demonstrated. A well-stocked shopping bazaar featuring Indian crafts, clothing, jewelry, art, crystals, posters and books is a lot of fun for international shoppers. Some Indian restaurants and businesses participate in this festival.

AUGUST

■ **Indian Independence Day – Anand Mela**, India Cultural and Religious Center, Smyrna (477-4272/436-3719). The Indian-American Cultural Association sponsors an evening of Indian music, song, dance, food, carnival games and children's activities in celebration of India's Independence Day. A special exhibit of art is also part of the festivities.

OTHER

■ Hindu and Moslem holidays are celebrated by the community and religious groups throughout the year at the Hindu Temple of Atlanta, India Cultural & Religious Center, Gujarat Samaj, Al-Farooq Masjid of Atlanta Mosque, Indian restaurants and other locations in Atlanta. For example, the India-American Cultural Association and the Gujarat Samaj host celebrations during **Diwali** (The Festival of Lights) each year; and Al-Farooq Masjid of Atlanta Mosque holds special services and feasts during **Ramadan**. If you are seriously interested in celebrating any of these religious holidays, contact the religious institutions for more information.

RESOURCES

■ **Honorary Consulate General of Nepal**, 212 15th St., NE, Atlanta 30309 (892-8152); and **Indian Business Association (IBA)** (457-8634).

Vietnamese New Year's celebration.

ThE ASIAN
COMMUNITIES

(China, Taiwan, Korea, Thailand, Philippines, Vietnam, Laos, Cambodia, Indonesia & other Southeast Asian Communities)

HISTORY & NEIGHBORHOODS

The **Asian** communities are the fastest growing populations in Atlanta. Recent figures estimate that there are more than 120,000 Asians (including those from Japan and the Indian subcontinent), hailing from over fourteen different countries, in the area. Because of the diversity of national origins, there is not, as of yet, a strong sense of Asian community. Yet each of the different ethnic groups has tried hard to provide support — culturally, socially, politically and economically — to others from their own countries. Asian communities are spread throughout the metro-Atlanta area and, luckily for us, Asian grocery stores and restaurants are accessible to almost every area of town. The DeKalb Peachtree Airport area (Buford Highway around Chamblee and Doraville) is Atlanta's largest Asian enclave, and it promises to grow even larger as Asian developers continue to construct attractive malls housing more and more Asian businesses, groceries and restaurants.

Approximately 30,000 **Chinese-Americans** presently reside in the metro-Atlanta area, and estimates indicate that another 3,000 have permanent resident status, are students, or are residents in Atlanta for temporary business purposes. Community members range from first generation immigrants to fourth and fifth generation native-born citizens, some of whom can claim that their ancestors fought in the Civil War, worked on the transcontinental railroad or were members of canal construction crews along the Savannah River. From the 1940s (after the repeal of the Chinese Exclusion Act of 1882), a large influx of Chinese immigrants began arriving in Atlanta, quickly assimilating into the mainstream Atlanta community. Today Chinese-Americans are professionals, business proprietors and restaurant owners. Did you know that there are over 400 Chinese restaurants in the metro-Atlanta area?

The **Korean-American** community presently numbers about 30,000, and it is estimated that five to ten new families arrive in the city every day. The fast-growing population is hard-working and presently owns about 500 businesses in the Atlanta area. (Latest reports suggest there are over 300 Korean-owned groceries in metro-Atlanta.) Buford Highway has become the focal point for the business community, and strip shopping centers such as Pinetree Plaza, Northwoods Shopping Center and the recently opened Koreatown Plaza have an interesting mix of Korean retail and office establishments.

The **Thai-American** community in Atlanta presently numbers about 2,000 and is quickly growing. Members of the community are spread throughout the metro-Atlanta area, and Thai-owned businesses and restaurants are opening all over town. At last count, there were nearly 20 restaurants in Atlanta specializing in Thai cuisine. The Wat Buddha Temple and the Thai Association of Georgia have brought the community a little closer and created opportunities for Thai families to meet and socialize with one another. This community has made it quite clear that they are eager for Atlantans to join in and be a part of the community's various celebrations and functions.

The **Filipino-American** community is 6,000 strong, and thanks to the community's willingness to participate in Atlanta's international and cultural events, Atlantans have an opportunity to savor a small taste of traditional Filipino culture. The Filipino-American Association of Greater Atlanta plays a significant role in Atlanta's cultural activities and has been visible at numerous area festivals and special events. Their dance troupe, the Filipino-American Dance Group, should not be missed; and if you are lucky, you may have a chance to join in the tricky bamboo dances. One well-known member of the community is Maniya Barredo, the prima ballerina for the Atlanta Ballet, who year after year has delighted Atlantans with her artful dance performances.

Atlanta is quickly becoming a major resettlement site for **Southeast Asian** refugees. Recent figures indicate that approximately 4,000 Vietnamese, 4,500 Laotians and Hmongs, and 3,500 Cambodians reside in the Atlanta area, the majority of which have come to this city as refugees. Although there is no particular area where the community's presence is dominant, south Fulton County, Chamblee and Decatur are popular destinations for new arrivals. Numerous community associations and refugee resettlement agencies have been established to assist refugees in orienting themselves to life in Atlanta. Services offered include assistance in locating jobs and homes, immigration and legal services, educational facilities for the children and language assistance for adults, and health care. Most importantly, these agencies, along with churches and community groups, provide a source of emotional support to families who may be ill-prepared for the many changes that face them in their new country.

HISTORICAL SITES & MUSEUMS

■ **Atlanta History Center**, 3101 Andrews Dr., Atlanta (261-1837). The Atlanta History Center's Cherry-Sims Asian-American Garden compares native plants from the southeast with their Asian counterparts in China, Korea and Japan. Magnolias, dogwoods, azaleas and other species native to the southeast are planted in close proximity to their Asian twins so similarities and differences may be compared. Hours: Mon.–Sat. 9:00am–5:30pm; Sun. 12 noon–5:30pm. Admission fee.

■ **Center for Puppetry Arts**, 1404 Spring St., Atlanta (874-0398). The center's puppet museum houses an extensive collection of puppets from Asia past and present, including a large number of exquisite Japanese and Chinese puppets and delicate Indonesian shadow puppets. Hours: Mon.–Sat. 9:00am–4:00pm and evenings on performance nights. Admission fee.

■ **High Museum of Art**, Robert Woodruff Arts Center, 1280 Peachtree St., NE, Atlanta (892-HIGH). The High Museum's permanent collection includes some pieces of Japanese and Chinese porcelains, as well as Japanese furniture. Hours: Tues., Wed., Thurs. and Sat. 10:00am–5:00pm; Fri. 10:00am–9:00pm; and Sun. 12noon–5:00pm. Admission fee.

GALLERIES

■ Chinese export porcelain, antiques and other fine arts may be viewed by special appointment at upscale galleries. A sampling: **The Asia Center** (876-7260) has a permanent exhibit of museum quality artwork from China and Japan, including figurines, screens, scrolls and photographs; **Chinese Export Porcelain – Charles Perry** (364-9731) specializes in 17th & 18th century export porcelain; **International Art Properties, Ltd.**, 351 Peachtree Hills Ave. (ADAC), Atlanta (237-6990) sells Oriental screens, porcelains and fine arts; and **H. Moog Antique Porcelains**, 2271 Peachtree Rd., NE., Atlanta (351-2200) collects Chinese export porcelains from the 17th, 18th and early 19th century.

■ **Kiang Gallery**, 75 Bennett Street, Atlanta (351-5477). This gallery in the TULA complex exhibits work by Asian artists. Recent exhibits have included paintings and ink washes by Xie Zhigao, work by Song Yali and a special exhibit, "Ethnic Minorities of China," featuring work by six Chinese artists. Open: Wed.–Sat. 11:00am–5:00pm.

■ More and more galleries are displaying exhibits of Asian content. A sampling: **The Durham Reading Room** of Pitts Theology Library on Emory University's Quadrangle, Atlanta (727-4166) exhibited work by Hong Min Zou; **Merrill Chase Galleries** in Lenox Square, 3393 Peachtree Rd., Atlanta (266-1199) displayed work by Jiang Tie-Feng; and **Ariel Gallery** at TULA, 75 Bennett Street, Atlanta (352-5753) exhibited handmade paperwork by He-Seung Chong.

COMMUNITY, RELIGIOUS & CULTURAL ASSOCIATIONS

ASIAN COMMUNITY

■ **Asian/Pacific American Council of Georgia, Inc.** A/PAC is a non-profit corporation whose stated purposes are to promote the full participation of Asian-Pacific Americans in American society while simultaneously maintaining Asian-Pacific cultural heritage, to facilitate cultural and religious practices, to provide facilities and resources for cultural education, and to encourage and promote the participation of Asian-Pacific Americans in American cultural and civic activities. The Atlanta chapter of A/PAC presently has seven member associations and hopes that more Asian communities will soon become involved. Group activities, family picnics and an annual dinner in May during "Asian/Pacific – American Heritage Month" are some of the social activities sponsored by the council. Call either the Organization of Chinese Americans, the Korean Association of the Greater Atlanta Area, or the Filipino-American Association of Greater Atlanta for more information.

CHINESE COMMUNITY

■ **Chinese Community Center**, 5377 New Peachtree Rd., Chamblee (451-4456). Financially funded by the Taiwanese government, the community center's large facility behind Chinatown Square is the location for many social functions and events for the Asian communities, including a large Chinese New Year celebration held every January or February. The center offers the public an array of classes for adults and children in Chinese dance, cooking, painting, wrestling, singing, exercise and language. A weekend school for Chinese children is also offered to enhance the child's education in math and Chinese language and culture. Chinese language newspapers, magazines and books are available for perusal at the center, and a wide-screen television frequently shows current Taiwanese videos. The bimonthly newsletter, *The Chinese Community News,* offers the community an opportunity to keep abreast of the center's many activities.

■ **Organization of Chinese Americans, Inc**., Georgia Chapter, P.O. Box 95792, Atlanta, Georgia 30347 (Hotline: 498-2430). This national organization, which has an active Atlanta chapter of about 300 members, strives to promote the active participation of Chinese-Americans in civic affairs at all levels, and campaigns to secure equal treatment and opportunity for Chinese-Americans. Members are also concerned with the preservation of the cultural heritage of Chinese-Americans and sponsor numerous social and cultural events in metro-Atlanta. The telephone hotline and the bilingual bimonthly newsletter are excellent resources for information about upcoming events. A campaign is underway to raise money for a permanent home for the Atlanta headquarters, so even more fund-raising events should be forthcoming in the next few years. Membership is open to anyone of Chinese ancestry. A Young OCA affiliate has recently formed, and an OCA Professional Network is in the works.

■ **National Association of Chinese Americans** (252-7750). The local chapter of this national association is presently comprised of 100 or so members of Chinese ancestry, whose primary goal is the normalization of relations with the People's Republic of China and the promotion of the welfare of Chinese-Americans in the U.S. Besides sponsoring occasional get-togethers, the association has participated in the national association's biannual convention, as well as conferences and programs concerning Chinese politics, philosophy and culture. Occasionally, the association provides assistance to Chinese artisans and performers appearing in Atlanta and tries to attract Chinese trade delegations to Atlanta.

■ **Atlanta Taiwanese Association** (449-8649). The Atlanta chapter of the national organization sponsors at least four social get-togethers during the year, including a large Chinese New Year celebration. Members also have regular meetings featuring Taiwanese guest lecturers and cultural performances. The association's newsletter highlights upcoming events and news of interest to the Taiwanese community.

■ **Atlanta Association for Democracy in China**, 525 Tellwood Dr., Stone Mountain 30083 (894-2773). The association seeks to promote democracy in the People's Republic of China. Past activities have included holding a candlelight vigil in Woodruff Park on the first anniversary of the Tiananmen Square massacre, inviting prominent figures in China's democracy movement to speak in Atlanta, and briefing politicians on the democracy movement in China.

- **The Chinese American Lions Club** (249-5361/688-3533). The small chapter of this service organization is concerned with leadership training and assisting Chinese senior citizens, children and the needy.
- There are many regional and smaller groups that are active in Atlanta. A sampling: **The Hakka Association of Atlanta** (325-9226) is a social club comprised of Hakka-speaking Asians from Tiawan, Canton, Malaysia and elsewhere; **Kwong Tung Association of Atlanta** (993-1017) is a social organization comprised of individuals from Hong Kong and Kwong Tung Province; and **The Cantonese Association of Atlanta** (993-1017) is a social club comprised of Cantonese-speaking individuals. Members meet regularly for social gatherings and sponsor cultural activities at the Chinese Community Center. Some, like the Kwong Tung Association, also provide assistance to newly arrived members of their community.
- Chinese congregations are scattered throughout Atlanta. A sampling: **Atlanta Buddhism Association**, 5383 New Peachtree Rd., Chamblee (414-0485) (Sunday services at 10:00am at Chinatown Square); **Chinese Congregation of Briarlake Baptist Church**, 3715 LaVista Rd., Decatur (325-4214/564-1575) (Sunday services at 11:00am in Mandarin); **First Chinese Baptist Mission of Atlanta**, North Peachtree Baptist Church, 4805 Tilly Mill Rd., Doraville (451-8793) (Sunday services at 11:00am in Cantonese); **Oak Grove Chinese United Methodist Church**, Oak Grove United Methodist Church, 1722 Oak Grove Rd., Decatur (636-7558/634-7212) (Sunday services in Mandarin); and **Atlanta Taiwanese Presbyterian Church**, 1039 Rays Rd., Stone Mountain (294-0498) (Sunday services in Taiwanese).

KOREAN COMMUNITY

- **The Korean Association of the Greater Atlanta Area**, 5302 Buford Hwy. (Koreatown Plaza), Doraville (458-7798). The association is the umbrella organization of over 80 different organizations and clubs, all offering Korean-Americans in Atlanta a variety of services. For example, the association helps promote Korean businesses in Atlanta, runs a Saturday school program for Korean children, organizes a large number of sports leagues for children and adults, and sponsors numerous social and cultural events throughout the year. Another of the organizations, **Korean Community Service Center**, 5302 Buford Hwy. (Koreatown Plaza), Doraville (936-0969), serves as a resettlement agency for newly arrived immigrants and assists the families by providing them with social services and arranging for classes in English.
- **Korean American Wives Association** (296-1736). Membership is open to Korean women married to Americans or American wives of Korean men.

American acculturation skills are taught at the association's monthly meetings.

- **Society of 87** (763-4473). The society serves as an advisory council to the Korean community.
- Korean religious institutions number over 40. Almost all religious services are in Korean. A sampling: **Chil Bo Sa Buddhist Temple**, 5516 Green Wing Pl., Lithonia (593-2355); **Kum Kang Sa Buddhist Temple**, 5464 Old Dixie Rd., Forest Park (392-0918); **Bethany Korean Presbyterian Church**, 771 Elberta Dr., Marietta (427-6792); **Hung San First Methodist Church**, 1523 Church St., Decatur (378-4273); **The Korean Church of Atlanta**, 2197 Peeler Rd., Dunwoody (395-1751); **Korean Community Presbyterian Church**, 4877 Lawrenceville Hwy., Tucker (939-4673); and **Korean Catholic Apostolate of the Archdiocese of Atlanta**, 6003 Buford Hwy., Doraville (455-1380).

THAI COMMUNITY

- **Thai Association of Georgia**, P.O. Box 47115, Atlanta 30362 (493-1175/717-7909, ext. 1992). The association is comprised of about 100 families who gather for special occasions throughout the year, including a Thai New Year celebration and a formal dinner party during the December holiday season. The association's newsletter is a good source for information about the community and upcoming events.
- **Wat Buddha Bucha (Wat Buddha Temple)**, 3094 Rainbow Dr., Decatur (284-2416). The Hinayana Buddhist Temple and Monastery is open on Sunday afternoons for special ceremonies and on a regular basis for chanting and meditation. During the summer, the temple is the location for a special children's program offering instruction in Thai language and culture. During the Thai New Year celebration in April, a Buddhist priest conducts special services, and the community participates in *Songkran* (water blessing). The public is welcome.

FILIPINO COMMUNITY

- **Filipino-American Association of Greater Atlanta** (478-2057). The association, which presently consists of about 300 families, provides a very active social life for Atlanta's Filipino-American community. In addition to a spring Easter Egg Hunt, fall picnic, New Year's Eve party and Independence Day celebration, members have monthly meetings and social get-togethers.
- **The Filipino Charity Foundation of Georgia** (478-2057). This very productive foundation raises money for indigent Filipinos living in Atlanta, for victims of the Mt. Pinatubo eruption in the Philippines and for the American Red Cross. Numerous fund-raising events are held by the charity, including

the sponsorship of performances by Filipino entertainers at the Clayton County Performing Arts Center.

- **Philippine International Baptist Church**, Clarkston Baptist Church, 3895 Church St., Clarkston (292-7256). The congregation holds Sunday services at 6:00pm. Portions of the service are in Tagalog.

VIETNAMESE COMMUNITY

- **Georgia Association for Vietnamese-American Education**, 1862 Candler Rd., Decatur (289-4556). The association's purpose is to promote an understanding of Vietnamese and American cultures and languages, support quality education programs for Vietnamese-Americans, encourage Vietnamese-Americans to maintain their cultural heritage, and provide resettlement services for newly arrived Vietnamese.

- **World Relief's Operation Homecoming** (294-4352). Operation Homecoming provides long-term social and cultural support services to Amerasians resettling in the Atlanta area, so they may achieve self-sufficiency in their new home.

- A sampling of Vietnamese religious institutions: **Vietnamese Buddhist Association of Georgia**, Chua Quang Minh Temple, 1168 Benteen Ave., SE, Atlanta (624-9782) (Sunday services at 11:00am in Vietnamese); **Vietnamese Baptist Church in Atlanta**, Second Ponce de Leon Baptist Church, 2715 Peachtree Rd., NE, Atlanta (266-8111); and **Our Lady of Vietnam Catholic Church**, 4265 Thurman Rd., Forest Park (361-3741) (Sunday masses at 9:00am and 11:00am in Vietnamese).

CAMBODIAN COMMUNITY

- **United Cambodian Society** (991-9146). The society assists with the cultural orientation of refugees and offers a variety of social services to community members.

- A sampling of Cambodian congregations: **Cambodian Buddhist Society**, 6533 Rock Springs Rd, Lithonia (482-5563); **Brookvalley Church of Christ**, 1146 Sheridan Rd., NE, Atlanta (633-9373); **First Baptist Church of Decatur**, 308 Clairmont Ave., Decatur (373-1653); **Holy Cross Lutheran Church**, 377 Valley Hill Rd., SW, Riverdale (478-LAOS/478-9324); and **Liberty Cambodian Baptist Mission**, 1070 Flat Shoals Rd., College Park (991-0493).

HMONG & LAOTIAN COMMUNITIES

- **Asian Community Service, Inc.**, 145 New St., Decatur (370-0113/370-1560). Although this organization primarily provides short-term resettlement services to newly arrived Hmong refugees, it is also concerned with helping Hmongs adjust socially and culturally to their new lives in Atlanta. Therefore, a variety of long-term support services are also provided to community members.

■ A sampling of Hmong and Laotian religious congregations: **Lao Buddhist Community Temple**, 2325 Hillside Rd., Riverdale (994-9270); **Columbia Drive Baptist Church**, 862 Columbia Dr., Decatur (284-2111); **Glenn Haven United Methodist Church**, 4862 Glenwood Rd., Decatur (289-3422/284-7591); **Eastside Baptist Church**, 170 Upper Riverdale Rd., Riverdale (991-2076); **First Baptist Church**, 142 College St., Jonesboro (478-6710); **First Baptist Church**, 148 Church St., Marietta (424-8326); and **Holy Cross Lutheran Church**, 377 Valley Hill Rd., SW, Riverdale (478-LAOS/478-9324).

OTHER ASSOCIATIONS PROVIDING REFUGEE SERVICES TO ASIANS

■ A sampling: **Catholic Social Services**, 680 W. Peachtree St., NW, Atlanta (881-6571); **Christian Council of Metropolitan Atlanta**, 465 Boulevard Dr., Suite 101, SE, Atlanta (622-2235); **Georgia Mutual Assistance Association Consortium, Inc.** 535 N. Central Ave., Suite 103, Hapeville (763-4241); **International Rescue Committee, Inc.**, 4303 Memorial Dr., Decatur (292-7731); **Lao Friendship Association of Georgia**, 6468 River Run Rd., Riverdale (996-5820); **Lao Refugee Committee Service of Georgia**, 852 Woods Ct. Lawrenceville (962-9984); **The Save the Children Refugee Project**, Chamblee and Clarkston (885-1578); **Vietnamese Ex-Political Prisoner Association of Georgia**, 680 W. Peachtree St., NW, Atlanta (885-7465); and **World Relief Refugee Services**, 964 N. Indian Creek Dr., Suite A-1, Clarkston (294-4352).

OTHER BUDDHIST TEMPLES & CENTERS

■ There are many other Buddhist Centers in Atlanta, although participants are not necessarily from the Asian communities. A sampling: **Atlanta Soto Zen Center**, 1404 McLendon Ave., Atlanta (659-4749) (Introductory sessions on Zen Meditation are held Sundays at 10:00am, and nonguided meditation groups are scheduled throughout the week); **Buddhist Instructional Retreat**, P.O. Box 235, Alpharetta 30239-0235 (772-9927) (24-hour Instruction by telephone); and **Losel Shedrup Ling Tibetan Buddhist Center**, 5840 Allen Ct., Atlanta (231-4128) (Meditational instruction at 7:30pm the first and third Wednesday of every month).

CHINESE CLASSES

■ **Chinese Community Center**, 5377 New Peachtree Rd., Chamblee (451-4456) offers a 10-week class for adults in Chinese language in which Mandarin and characters are taught. The center also offers classes for adults and children in Chinese cooking, dance, painting, wrestling, singing, exercise, modeling and martial arts. A weekend enrichment school for children emphasizes mathematics and Chinese language and culture.

■ **Atlanta Taiwanese Presbyterian Church**, 1039 Rays Rd., Stone Mountain (294-0498) offers Taiwanese language classes for adults and children on Sunday.

KOREAN CLASSES

■ **Korean American School in Atlanta**, 6003 Buford Hwy., Doraville (971-6856/455-3288) offers Saturday Korean language instruction for children K–high school, along with classes in history, dance, music and karate.

THAI CLASSES

■ **Wat Buddha Temple**, 3094 Rainbow Dr., Decatur (284-2416) is the location for a special children's summer program offering instruction in Thai language and culture.

SOUTHEAST ASIAN CLASSES

■ **Our Lady of Vietnam Catholic Church**, 4265 Thurman Rd., Forest Park (361-3741) offers Vietnamese language classes for children, as well as a Sunday youth activity program.

■ **Holy Cross Lutheran Church**, 377 Valley Hill Rd., SW, Riverdale (478-LAOS/478-9324) conducts some Sunday school classes in Khmer.

OTHER CLASSES

■ **Cooking**. Atlanta's most popular Asian cooking instructor is **Tan Lee Chin** (498-1163), whose private and group classes are always well-received. She also teaches Asian cooking at **Evening at Emory** (727-6000) and at **DeKalb College's Continuing Education Program** (244-5050).

■ **Martial Arts**. Numerous schools of martial arts may be found in Atlanta, each having its own philosophy and style. For example, the **Atlanta Tai Chi Association** (289-5652), which is dedicated to preserving traditional Chinese cultural activities, offers instruction in language, arts, the basic principles of modern wushu dance and gymnastics, the ancient healing arts, and Chinese philosophy. Look in the *Yellow Pages* or *Creative Loafing* for the many listings under karate and martial arts.

NEWSPAPERS, MAGAZINES, BOOKS, VIDEOS

CHINESE

■ *The Asian Post*, P.O. Box 930091, Norcross 30093 (925-4567) and *Atlanta Chinese News*, 5420 New Peachtree Rd., Chamblee (455-0880) are both Chinese language weekly newspapers. Available at Chinese restaurants, groceries and retail establishments. Free.

■ *World Journal and Chinese Daily News*, 5389 New Peachtree Rd., Chamblee (451-4509/451-4628) is a Chinese language daily newspaper. Available at Chinatown Square and some Chinese groceries and restaurants. Cost is 50¢/issue.

■ *Chinese Business Guide and Directory Southeast USA* is a bilingual directory listing Chinese associations, professionals, business establishments, and restaurants in Alabama, Florida, Georgia, Kentucky, Mississippi, North Carolina, South Carolina and Tennessee. Available at Chinese bookstores. Free.

■ **World Journal Bookstore,** Chinatown Square, 5389 New Peachtree Rd., Chamblee (451-4509/451-4628) is well-stocked with Chinese language books, magazines and newspapers.

■ **Linking Book and Video,** Northwoods Shopping Center, 5095-D Buford Hwy., Doraville (936-0829) carries a large inventory of Chinese language reading material, music and rental videos.

■ Video stores are springing up all over Atlanta, stocking a large selection of Chinese movies. A sampling: **Comedy Plus Video,** Chinatown Square, 5389-D New Peachtree Rd., Chamblee (458-3874); and **Video Central Production,** 5345-I Jimmy Carter Blvd., Norcross (263-8388). Also, quite a few of the Chinese-owned markets listed below sell Chinese language reading material, audio cassettes, CDs and rental videos.

KOREAN

■ Almost all of the local Korean newspapers are written primarily in Korean, yet the advertisements may be helpful to anyone interested in locating Korean establishments. A sampling: *The Chosun Ilbo*, 3329 Cains Hill Pl., Atlanta (233-2044); *The Korean Journal – Atlanta Edition*, 5455 Buford Hwy., #207-A, Atlanta (451-6946); *The Korean Southeast News*, 5269 Buford Hwy., Suite 17, Doraville (454-9655); and *The Korea Times Weekly*, 3163 Shallowford Rd., Chamblee (458-5060). These newspapers are available at Korean groceries and retail establishments.

■ *The Korean Business Directory* (458-5060) is a bilingual business directory listing Korean associations, religious institutions, professionals, retail establishments and restaurants in the southeast USA. Published by the Korea Times. Free.

■ **KORYO Books & Gifts**, 5181 Buford Hwy., Doraville (457-6737) stocks a large selection of Korean reading material, small gifts and religious items.

■ **New York Koryo Bookstore**, 5268 Buford Hwy., Atlanta (455-3222) has a very large selection of books, newspapers, magazines, music and religious gift items, including a special children's book section.

■ Video stores are opening up all over Atlanta, stocking a large selection of Korean movies. A sampling: **Han Guk Video/Korean Video**, 5302 Buford Hwy., Doraville (451-7832); **Korean Video & Photo**, 5732 Buford Hwy., Doraville (455-0777); and **Video Central Production**, 5345-I Jimmy Carter Blvd., Norcross (263-8388). Also, almost all of the Korean-owned markets listed below have Korean reading material, audio cassettes and rental videos.

THAI

■ Most of the groceries owned by Southeast Asian proprietors stock a variety of Thai newspapers, magazines, books, audio cassettes, CDs and/or rental videos. A sampling: **Asian Convenience Store**, 5957 Ash St., Forest Park (366-3297); **Norcross Oriental Market**, 6065 S. Norcross-Tucker Rd., Norcross (496-1656); **Oriental Food Mart** at 5091 Buford Hwy. (Northwoods Shopping Center Annex), Doraville (457-5666); **Riverdale Oriental Market**, 6465-7 Hwy. 85, Riverdale (997-3186); and **Southeastern Oriental Market**, 3275 Chamblee-Dunwoody Rd., Chamblee (451-5962).

VIETNAMESE/SOUTHEAST ASIAN

■ **Le Phan Bookstore and Video**, 4763 Buford Hwy., Chamblee (986-8886) sells Vietnamese books, magazines and rental videos.

■ **My Dung Bookstore**, 5095-H Buford Hwy. (Northwoods Shopping Center), Doraville (936-9183) stocks a selection of Vietnamese books, magazines, audio cassettes, rental videos and small gifts.

■ Southeast Asian groceries carry reading material, audio cassettes, CDs and

rental videos. A sampling: **Khanh Tam's Oriental Market**, 4051-B Buford Hwy., Atlanta (728-0393); and **Southeastern Oriental Market**, 3275 Chamblee-Dunwoody Rd., Chamblee (451-5962).

FILIPINO

■ *An Adventure in Philippine Cooking in Georgia* is an excellent cookbook compiled by the Filipino community, which is available for purchase at the Filipino-American Association of Greater Atlanta's booth at local festivals. Cost is $5.00.

OTHER

■ **The Dependable Bookman**, Mr. Woody Bates, 4010 Beechwood Dr., NW, Atlanta (237-0529) sells out-of-print and hard-to-find books about Asian history, culture, art, religion and philosophy. The mail-order business has over 7,000 books in inventory and will conduct special interest searches. Call for a catalogue.

---

sbopping centers, import stores, botels

SHOPPING CENTERS

■ **Chinatown Square** (New Peachtree Rd. between Chamblee-Tucker and Chamblee-Dunwoody Rds., Chamblee) features Chinese and Asian business establishments, retail stores, two restaurants and a terrific Asian food court. A sampling of establishments includes: **Dinho Market**, a large supermarket featuring foods from all over Asia, as well as fresh meats, seafood, kitchen wares, herbal medicines and more; **Summit National Bank**, providing banking services for the Asian, Hispanic and international community; **World Journal Book Store**, selling a large selection of Chinese language reading material; **Comedy Plus Video Store**, stocking Chinese language videos; **Elegance Fashion and Alteration**, selling all kinds of women's clothing; **Phoenix International**, stocking quality import games, gifts and household fashions; **Y.T. Herb Store**, a ginseng and herb store; **Wong's Bakery**, a Vietnamese bakery specializing in French and Asian pastries; **Oriental Pearl**, serving authentic Hong-Kong style cuisine and one of the best dim sums in town; and **Sichuan Restaurant**, traditionally decorated and specializing in highly seasoned Szechuan cuisine.
■ **Chamblee-Dunwoody Road Shopping Center** (between New Peachtree Rd. and Buford Hwy., Chamblee) includes **Southeastern Oriental Market**, a full-

sized Southeast Asian grocery store also housing a bakery and snack-bar; **Tung Dynasty Trading Co.**, trading in high quality oriental arts, antiques, furniture and decorative accessories; **Erawan,** a Thai-owned store selling a selection of inexpensive gifts, toys, appliances and household goods from Taiwan, Hong Kong and Thailand; and **Honto's**, one of Atlanta's favorite Hong Kong-style Chinese restaurants.

■ **Northwoods Shopping Center** (Buford Hwy. at the intersection of Shallowford Rd./1/2 mile inside I-285, Doraville) features several Asian owned business establishments, including: **Linking Book Video**, stocking a large selection of Chinese reading material and rental videos; **My Dung Bookstore**, carrying a selection of Vietnamese books, music and videos; **Hung-Ren Ginseng and Herb Store**, selling traditional herbal medicines, and cosmetics; **Oriental Food Mart**, stocking a selection of foods from all over Southeast Asia; and **Bien Thuy Vietnamese Restaurant**, considered by most to be the best Vietnamese restaurant in Atlanta.

■ **Pinetree Plaza** (Buford Hwy. just north of Northwoods Shopping Center, Doraville) has a variety of Asian business and restaurant establishments, such as: **Yeh Lai Hsiang Chinese Restaurant**, a Korean-influenced Chinese restaurant specializing in friendly and helpful service; **Kang Suh**, a highly-praised Korean restaurant; **Go Hyang Jip**, another Korean restaurant specializing in "grill your own" meals; and **Koto**, a newly opened Japanese restaurant and sushi bar in the former location of Gojinka.

■ **Cheshire Bridge Road** (between Piedmont and Lenox Rds., Atlanta) has a variety of ethnic markets, bakeries and restaurants, including: **Hoa Binh,** a Vietnamese/Chinese grocery store specializing in barbecued meats and fresh noodles; **Tien Tien**, a small, informal storefront selling inexpensive Hong Kong-style fare, as well as a large selection of barbecued and roasted meats; **Hot Pepper Thai Cuisine**, serving excellent Thai cuisine and specializing in spicy dishes; **Hong Kong Harbour**, serving delicious authentic Hong Kong-style cuisine and dim sum daily; and **Bamboo Luau**, also specializing in Hong Kong-style cuisine and serving dim sum daily.

■ **Koreatown Plaza** (Buford Hwy. across from Pinetree Plaza, Doraville) is a Korean-owned mall housing retail stores, offices and restaurants such as: **Nadry Gifts and Health Food**, carrying cosmetics, herbs, chinaware, dolls and other small gifts; **Korean Video**, renting a large selection of Korean language videos; **Lotte Fashion**, displaying high-style Korean women's fashions; **Rice Cake Bakery**, selling Korean rice cakes and other baked items; and **Yen Jing Chinese Restaurant**, a highly praised Korean-influenced restaurant serving authentic Chinese fare.

■ **Asian Square** (Buford Hwy. across from Pinetree Plaza, Doraville) is presently under construction and when completed, the large mall will probably have a mix of about 50 Chinese, Taiwanese, Korean and Southeast Asian businesses, professional offices, retail establishments and at least six restaurants. The mall also plans to house 99 Ranch Market, a large Asian grocery store (part of the Tawa chain) and, perhaps, an Asian Activity Center. Completion is expected in 1993. Call 458-8899 for information.

CLOTHING, CUSTOM-MADE FASHIONS & ALTERATIONS

■ A sampling: **J & A Alterations**, 1845 Cobb Pkwy., Marietta (952-3572) (men's and women's clothing); **Mikado of Hong Kong**, 1 Galleria Pkwy. (Galleria Shopping Mall), Atlanta (980-1430) (shirts and suits for men); **Hong Kong Tailors**, 5378 Buford Hwy., Doraville (458-8682) (clothing for men and women); and **Saigon Tailors**, 5085 Buford Hwy. (Northwoods Shopping Center), Doraville (451-4280) (all kinds of custom clothing).

■ **Elegance Fashion and Alteration**, 5389 New Peachtree Rd., Chamblee (986-0818) (high-style fashions for men and women); and **Lotte Fashion**, 5302 Buford Hwy. (Koreatown Plaza), Doraville (451-5568) (high-style women's fashions).

GIFTS & HOUSEHOLD ITEMS

■ **Agnes Market**, 5210 Buford Hwy., Doraville (457-7911) carries a large selection of cosmetics, jewelry, small gift items, appliances, household goods, audio cassettes, CDs and rental videos from Korea and Japan.

■ **Asian Foods, Etc.**, 1375 Prince Ave., Athens (706/543-8624) has a few imported gifts from the Philippines, such as handbags, knives and chess sets.

■ **Erawan Gift Store**, 3283 Chamblee-Dunwoody Rd., Chamblee (455-1638) sells Buddha images, handicrafts, decorative items, appliances, toys, music tapes and other small gifts from Thailand, Taiwan and Hong Kong.

■ **Global Furniture Import**, 3114 Oakcliff Industrial St., Doraville (458-2296) sells Korean lacquered furniture, decorative home accessories, gifts, cosmetics and electronic equipment to wholesalers and the general public.

■ **Import 'N' Place**, 3750 Venture Ave. (Outlet Mall), Duluth (476-0787); 2841 Greenbriar Pkwy. (Greenbriar Mall), Atlanta (349-8947); and 750 George Busbee Pkwy. (Outlet Mall), Kennesaw (421-8252) carries imported accessories, such as jewelry, handbags, sunglasses, belts, and T-shirts from Hong Kong, Thailand, Taiwan, China and the Philippines.

■ **Kam Fai's Orientique**, 351 Peachtree Hills Ave., Suite 501B, Atlanta (262-

1875) trades in antiques, porcelains, furniture, accessories, screens and other decorative arts.

■ **Mandarin Shop**, 110 E. Andrews Dr., Atlanta (233-0361) carries high quality Chinese and Oriental gifts, including jade figurines, ginger jars, jewelry and home accessories.

■ **Manos Boutique**, 1 Galleria Pkwy., Atlanta (612-9300), in Galleria Mall, carries Indonesian batik T-shirts, bags and other accessories during the spring and summer.

■ **Nadry Gifts and Health Food**, 5302 Buford Hwy., Doraville (458-5540), in Koreatown Plaza, sells cosmetics, herbs, health food, chinaware, dolls and more small gift items.

■ **Oriental Art**, 5173 Roswell Rd., N.E., Atlanta (255-2680) showcases high quality import items from Japan, China, Korea and other Far Eastern countries, such as furniture, screens, paintings, vases, home accessories and decorative garden lanterns.

■ **Oriental Depot**, 11235 Alpharetta Hwy., Roswell (664-5474) stocks ginger jars, furniture cabinets, home accessories, flowers and other gift items from mainland China.

■ **Oriental Imports**, 6624 N.E. Expressway, Suite 15, Norcross (263-9008) has a large selection of Oriental furniture, porcelains, gifts and home accessories from all over Asia.

■ **Oriental Trading Co.**, 1351 Northside Dr., NW, Atlanta (351-7873) sells porcelains, paintings, screens, jewelry boxes and other gift items from China, Japan, Taiwan, Hong Kong and other Asian countries.

■ **The Orient Express**, 2880 Holcomb Bridge Rd., Alpharetta (642-7364) carries high quality gifts from Japan, China, Thailand, Indonesia and other Asian countries.

■ **Phoenix International**, 5389-0 New Peachtree Rd., Chamblee (998-1156), in Chinatown Square, sells quality Asian imports, such as art, small gift items, mah jong sets, household accessories and jewelry.

■ **Tung Dynasty Trading Company**, 3279 Chamblee-Dunwoody Rd., Chamblee (455-8637) trades in high-quality oriental arts, antiques, furniture and decorative accessories, including porcelain vases, embroidered pillows and cloisonne jewelry.

GINSENG, HERBS & COSMETICS

■ **Koryo Herbs**, 5185 Buford Hwy. (Pinetree Plaza), Doraville (451-2999); **Hung-Ren Ginseng & Herbs**, 5095-C Buford Hwy. (Northwoods Shopping Center), Doraville (452-8289); **Kim's Oriental Herbs and Acupuncture**, 5312

Buford Hwy., #20, Doraville (455-6511); **H.S. Chinese Ginseng & Herbs**, 5280 Buford Hwy. (West Pinetree Plaza), Doraville (452-7207); **Oriental Herbs & Ginseng**, 3420 E. Ponce de Leon Ave., Scottdale (299-6508); **Y.T. Herb**, 5389 New Peachtree Rd. (Chinatown Square), Chamblee (458-8898); **Nadry Gifts & Health Food**, 5302 Buford Hwy. (Koreatown Plaza), Doraville (458-5540); and many of the larger Asian groceries carry ginseng, herbs and cosmetics..

GROCERIES, MARKETS, BAKERIES

BAKERIES

■ **Pastry Chef Bakery & Cafe**, 5975 Roswell Rd., Atlanta (843-3075). A selection of Chinese baked goods, including pork buns, sweet rolls, onion rolls and beef curry dumplings, may be purchased at this bakery, which also sells American-style baked goods.

■ **P. N. Rice Cake House**, 5273-B Buford Hwy., Doraville (451-3327). This small store in Pinetree Plaza sells kim chee and spicy Korean pickles of all kinds (really — you have got to try them), rice cakes and a small selection of Korean sweets.

■ **Wong's Bakery & Cafe**, 5389 New Peachtree Rd., Chamblee (451-4608). The Chinatown Square bakery specializes in French pastries, Asian buns and pastries, and American-style baked goods. There is a small seating area.

■ **Zion Rice Cake Bakery**, 5302 Buford Hwy., Doraville (936-0969) (458-4117). The storefront in Koreatown Plaza sells rice cakes and a few other sweets.

GROCERIES

■ **Agnes Market**, 5210 Buford Hwy., Doraville (457-7911). The large Asian grocery stocks a full selection of fish, meat and poultry, fresh produce, frozen foods, kim chee and other pickles, and a wide-range of food products from Japan and Korea. There is also a large selection of cosmetics, household goods, small gifts, audio tapes, CDs and rental videos.

■ **Asian Convenience Store**, 5957 Ash St., Forest Park (366-3297). The Thai grocery store carries a selection of groceries from Southeast Asia and rental videos from Thailand.

■ **Asian Foods, Etc.**, 1375 Prince Ave., Athens (706/543-8624). The market sells spices, groceries and small gift items from the Philippines.

■ **Atlanta Municipal Market/Sweet Auburn Curb Market**, 209 Edgewood Ave., Atlanta (659-1665). The newly renovated market sells massive quantities of meat, fruit, vegetables, cheese and grocery items. Increasingly, the stalls and snack bar area are becoming more international in tone as Asian-Americans and African-Americans operate businesses side-by-side, resulting in an unusual mix of Asian and Southern cuisines.

- **Atlanta Oriental Store**, 3118 Oakcliff Industrial St., Doraville (458-2296). The Korean wholesale food store is open to the public and sells every kind of Korean food product imaginable, as well as kitchen and dinnerware. There is also a fresh fish market, kim chee and other pickled vegetables, fresh produce and a selection of Japanese, Chinese and Southeast Asian food products.
- **Dah-Tung Trading Co.**, 659 Ethel St., NW, Atlanta (873-2066). The large wholesale Chinese grocery will also sell to the public, but some products must be bought in bulk.
- **Dinho Market of Atlanta**, 5381 New Peachtree Rd., Chamblee (454-8888). The Chinese supermarket, in Chinatown Square, is a full-size supermarket stocking fresh meats, fruits, vegetables and seafood (including eight varieties of squid alone), as well as frozen goods and groceries from all over Asia. You may also find a selection of household goods, kitchenware and a well-stocked counter with herbs and cosmetics.
- **Dong Bang Oriental Grocery and Gifts**, 380 White Ave., Marietta (424-7115). The large Korean grocery store carries groceries from all over Asia, as well as small gifts, audio cassettes, newspapers and rental videos.
- **First Asia**, 5596 Old Dixie Rd., Forest Park (361-7202). The Thai-owned grocery store has a selection of Korean, Japanese, Chinese and Southeast Asian groceries.
- **First Oriental Market**, 2774 E. Ponce de Leon Ave., Decatur (377-6950). The grocery store is well-stocked with food products from all over Asia and specializes in fresh barbecued pork, duck and other meat delicacies.
- **Happy Oriental Food Market**, 5477 Riverdale Rd., College Park (994-9461). The market sells Thai, Southeast Asian and Chinese food products.
- **Happy Super Market**, 3420-C E. Ponce de Leon Ave., Scottdale (377-9988). The Chinese grocery store is packed with all kinds of food products, as well as some fresh produce and household items.
- **Harry's Farmers Markets**, 1180 Upper Hembree Rd., Roswell (664-6300) and 2025 Satellite Point, Duluth (416-6900). Harry's stocks fresh produce, meats, cheeses, spices, coffees, dried fruits, nuts, groceries and baked goods from around the world, including a selection of Asian specialties. Take-out sushi, egg rolls, wontons and dumplings are a real treat.
- **Hoa Binh Market**, 2216 Cheshire Bridge Rd., Atlanta (636-7165). The Chinese and Vietnamese market is packed with groceries, fresh produce,

seafood and meats. Next door is a small restaurant selling freshly barbecued pork, duck and other meat delicacies, as well as home-made noodles.

■ **International Farmers Market**, 5193 Peachtree Industrial Blvd., Chamblee (455-1777). The newly-opened 90,000-square-foot facility is filled with produce, meats, fish, cheeses, coffees, spices and baked goods, with a heavy emphasis on international food products. The Asian dried goods section is perhaps the most interesting of all of Atlanta's farmers markets.

■ **Khanh Tam's Oriental Market**, 4051-B Buford Hwy., Atlanta (728-0393). The large Vietnamese grocery has a comprehensive selection of food items from Vietnam, including frozen foods and fresh produce. The store also stocks household goods, shoes, audio tapes and rental videos.

■ **Kim Sun Market**, 5038 Buford Hwy., Chamblee (457-2492). The large grocery store sells food products from Thailand, Cambodia, Vietnam, Laos and China, including fresh produce, canned goods, meat, poultry and seafood.

■ **New World Trading Co.**, 3110 E. Ponce de Leon Ave., Scottdale (373-7373/373-4989). The Korean grocery store sells groceries, fresh meat, seafood, kim chee and other Korean specialties.

■ **Norcross Oriental Market**, 6065 S. Norcross-Tucker Rd., Norcross (496-1656). The grocery store carries a large selection of Thai and Southeast Asian groceries, as well as small gift items.

■ **Oriental Farmers Food Market**, 5345-C Jimmy Carter Blvd., Norcross (368-8888). This 35,000-square-foot supermarket sells food products from all over Asia, and meats, poultry, seafood, frozen foods and fresh produce are plentiful. Two aisles of the market are stocked with a variety of cooking utensils, dishes and other household goods.

■ **Oriental Food Mart**, 5091-F Buford Hwy., Doraville (457-5666). The small grocery store in Northwoods Shopping Center Annex has a varied selection of groceries from all over Southeast Asia.

■ **P. N. Rice Cake House**, 5273-B Buford Hwy., Doraville (451-3327). The small store sells kim chee and other spicy pickled vegetables, a variety of rice cakes, rice and a few other Korean sweets.

■ **Rainbow Oriental Trade**, 962 Roswell St., Marietta (422-0086). The small Korean grocery store carries Asian food products, reading material, audio tapes, CDs and rental videos.

■ **Riverdale Oriental Market**, 6465-7 Hwy. 85, Riverdale (997-3186). The Thai grocery store sells groceries, fresh produce, small gifts, reading material, music and rental videos.

■ **Sambok Oriental Foods**, 2469 Lawrenceville Hwy., Decatur (320-6719). The large Korean grocery store carries a good supply of Korean food products, fresh produce, kim chee, reading material, music and rental videos.

■ **Shop & Go**, 2595 Lawrenceville Hwy., Decatur (938-3754). The Korean grocery store is jam-packed with unusual Korean and Japanese food products, including homemade kim chee, tofu and a large selection of household goods, rental videos and reading material.

■ **Southeastern Oriental Market**, 3275 Chamblee-Dunwoody Rd., Chamblee (451-5962). The large Asian grocery store is packed with Thai food products, as well as groceries from Cambodia, Vietnam, Laos and China. The market has its own bakery and cafeteria area, along with an extensive selection of rental videos from all over Southeast Asia.

■ **United Foods**, 765-B Clay St., Marietta (426-0155). The wholesaler allows the public to shop, but be prepared to buy some products in bulk.

■ **Windmill Shop**, White Horse Square, Helen (706/878-3444). The Helen retail store occasionally offers Indonesian spices for sale.

■ **Yong Woung Asian Market**, 2530 Chapman Springs Rd., College Park (761-6336). The grocery store offers groceries and rental videos from Southeast Asia.

■ **Your DeKalb Farmers Market**, 3000 E. Ponce de Leon Ave., Decatur (377-6400). The international farmers market considers itself a "World Mart," and rightfully so. It offers an enormous diversity of international groceries, spices, produce, cheese, meats, coffees, delicatessen items and baked goods, including an incredible variety of Asian fresh produce and dried goods.

RESTAURANTS

CHINESE RESTAURANTS

There are over 400 Chinese restaurants in the metro-Atlanta area — here is but a sampling. But first, some definitions:

Cantonese or *Hong Kong-style cuisine is from the Southeast region of China, and because the Cantonese were the first to establish restaurants outside the country, this style of cooking has become the most familiar to Americans. Specialties are, in reality, a combination of many styles, with an emphasis on stir-fried dishes and subtle flavors. Roast meats, poultry, lobster, fried fish, bird's nest soup and shark fin soup are some of the more familiar dishes originating from this region.*

Hunan cooking is from the Central region of China and Hunan specialties are hot, spicy and richly seasoned — and sometimes sweet and sour.

Peking or *Shantung cuisine is from the Northeast region of China and is the oldest and highest level of Chinese culinary art. Dishes are light, elegant, mildly seasoned rather than rich; and specialties are liberally spiced with garlic, scallions, leeks and chives. Peking Duck, soft-fried foods, spring rolls, delicious roasts and noodles are some of the more familiar dishes originating from this region.* **Mandarin***-style cuisine relates to the Peking-Shantung school of cooking, but in America, Mandarin-style actually encompasses a number of different schools of cooking.*

Szechuan *or* **Chung King** *cuisine comes from the hot climate of Western China and dishes are highly spiced, peppery, somewhat oily and richly flavored.*

(A) Designates a reputation for authentic Chinese fare.
(♦) Designates the restaurant serves dim sum (traditional Chinese breakfast).

■ *(A♦)* **Bamboo Luau's Chinatown**, 2269 Cheshire Bridge Rd. (Lenox Rd.), Atlanta (636-9131). Authentic Cantonese cuisine makes this restaurant quite popular with the Asian community. Be sure to try some "off-menu" specialties, such as house noodle soup and seafood combination in a nest. Dim sum is served Daily. Open: Lunch and Dinner: Daily.

■ **China Cafe**, 1497 Mt. Zion Rd. (across from Southlake Mall), Morrow (968-1100). This popular southside restaurant prides itself on its mango chicken and flaming steak, as well as its friendly and accommodating staff. Open: Lunch and Dinner: Daily.

■ **The China Doll**, 1230 Powers Ferry Rd. (near Delk Rd.), Marietta (955-6544). The modernistic, Mandarin-style restaurant claims to have the "best Singapore noodles in town," and apparently Cobb County customers agree. Open: Lunch: Mon.–Fri.; Dinner: Daily.

■ **China Moon**, 3527 Northside Pkwy. (W. Paces Ferry Rd.), Atlanta (237-8889). This restaurant is considered one of Atlanta's most expensive Chinese restaurants, but critics agree that the Cantonese and Szechuan specialties are superb. Open: Lunch: Sun.–Fri.; Dinner: Daily.

■ **China Royal**, 4415 Roswell Rd. (Wieuca Rd.), Atlanta (256-4119). Frank Ma's restaurant is a long-standing favorite among the northwest Atlanta crowd, who praise the consistently well-prepared Mandarin-style cuisine. Try the royal special banquet, which must be prepared in advance by the head chef. (24-hour advance notice for groups of eight or more). Open: Lunch: Mon.–Fri.; Dinner: Daily.

■ *(A)* **Chinatown Square Food Court**, 5389 New Peachtree Rd. (between Chamblee-Tucker and Chamblee-Dunwoody Rds.), Chamblee. The informal food court area has booths covering the five different regions of China and Vietnam. Spicy noodle dishes, barbecued meats, vegetarian entrees, spring rolls, soups and almost every other kind of authentic fare imaginable may be sampled. Open: Lunch and Dinner: Daily.

■ **Chopstix**, 4279 Roswell Rd. (Chastain Square Shopping Center), Atlanta (255-4868). Recently renovated and expanded, the stylish Hong Kong cafe consistently wins awards for "Best Chinese Cuisine in Elegant Surroundings." Try one of the superb daily specials. Open: Lunch: Mon.–Fri.; Dinner: Daily.

■ **East Ocean**, 6319 Jimmy Carter Blvd. (Buford Hwy.), Norcross (446-1588). This large Mandarin-style restaurant specializes in seafood dishes and has quickly made a name for itself among the Gwinnett County crowd. Open: Lunch and Dinner: Daily.

■ **Empress of China II**, 1255 Johnson Ferry Rd. (next to Merchant's Walk), Marietta (977-9798); **Empress of China III**, 4251 New Peachtree Rd. (south of I-285), Chamblee (451-1216); and **Empress of China V**, 4750 Roswell Rd. (Alabama Rd.), Roswell (992-1105). The extensive menus at these restaurants include a selection of Mandarin, Szechuan and Hunan specialties, such as Phoenix and Dragon and Sesame Beef. Open: Lunch: Sun.–Fri.; Dinner: Daily.

■ **Far East Cafe**, 2770 Lenox Rd. (High Plantation Mall between Buford Hwy. and Lenox Square), Atlanta (233-8989). The ultra-modern restaurant has quickly found a following among the Buckhead crowd, who enjoy such Hong Kong-style specialties as Kung Pao Calamari and Coral Shrimp. Open: Lunch and Dinner: Daily.

■ **Feng Nian**, 5000 Memorial Dr. (Rockbridge Rd.), Stone Mountain (296-8386). The beautifully decorated restaurant, complete with an Asian garden, waterfall and giant fish tank, serves well-prepared Mandarin and Szechuan-style food. Open: Lunch and Dinner: Daily.

■ *(A♦)* **First China Restaurant**, 5295 Buford Hwy. (south of I-285 and north of Pinetree Plaza), Doraville (457-6788). Authentic Cantonese-style fare and moderate prices have made this restaurant a favorite among the Asian community. Specialties include Bird's Nest with Chicken and a seafood war bar. Dim sum is served daily. Open: Lunch and Dinner: Daily.

■ **Golden Buddha**, 1905 Clairmont Rd. (south of N. Druid Hills Rd.), Atlanta (633-5252); **Golden Buddha II**, 3095 Hwy. 20 (Buford Mall), Buford (945-1224); **Golden Buddha III**, 2055 C Beaver Ruin Rd. (Indian Trail Rd.), Norcross (448-3377); and **Golden Buddha IV**, 3200-4 Buford Hwy. (Duluth Plaza), Duluth (497-1954). The consistent quality of the original Golden Buddha has made the restaurant a long-standing favorite, especially among the Emory University crowd. The restaurants' Mandarin-style cuisine includes some Szechuan and Hunan specialties. (A hint: At the original

Golden Buddha, try asking for some "off-menu" Korean specialties.) Open: Lunch and Dinner: Daily.

■ **Grand China Restaurant**, 2975 Peachtree Rd. (south of Pharr Rd.), Atlanta (231-8690). The Buckhead restaurant has a loyal following of customers who, for many years, have enjoyed well-prepared food and attentive service. Try your pick of any of the 200-plus entrees listed on the menu, including Mandarin, Hunan and Szechuan specialties. Open: Lunch and Dinner: Daily.

■ **The Great Wall**, 240 CNN Center (Marietta St.), Atlanta (522-8213); 3000 A-2 Windy Hill Rd. (across from the Hyatt Regency near Powers Ferry Rd.), Marietta (953-6392); and 6616 Tara Blvd. (a few blocks south of Exit 77 off of I-75), Jonesboro (961-6608). The original Great Wall is a long-standing favorite of the downtown and tourist crowd. Specials include Great Wall Prawns, Moo Shu Pork, Mongolian Beef and Peking Duck (order 12 hours in advance). The CNN location is open: Lunch and Dinner: Daily. The other locations are open: Lunch: Mon.–Fri.; Dinner: Daily.

■ **Happy Family**, 94 N. Cobb Pkwy. (north of the Big Chicken), Marietta (422-8886). Consistently well-prepared Mandarin-style cuisine has given this restaurant a loyal following among the Marietta crowd. Open: Lunch and Dinner: Daily.

■ *(A)* **Ho Ho Chinese Restaurant**, 3683 Clairmont Rd. (Buford Hwy.), Chamblee (451-7240). Ho Ho offers the most authentic fare of Atlanta's Chinese restaurants. The casual atmosphere and inexpensive prices make this restaurant a must among the brave at heart. Request items from the Chinese menu, so you may enjoy the black bean dishes, oyster pancakes, pickled pig's snout and other unusual specialties. Open: Lunch: Mon.–Fri.; Dinner: Daily.

■ **Hong Kong Cafe**, 870 Peachtree St. (inside the Howard Johnson Hotel), Atlanta (892-5231). A mixture of Cantonese, Hunan and Szechuan specialties are enjoyed by the midtown crowd. Open: Lunch: Sun.–Fri.; Dinner: Daily.

■ **Hong Kong Delight**, 5920 Roswell Rd. (Parkside Shopping Center), Atlanta (255-3388). One of Atlanta's newer Chinese restaurants has already become a big hit in Sandy Springs. Try the Chinese donuts stuffed with shrimp, stuffed chicken or one of the many other Hong Kong-style dishes. Open: Lunch: Mon.–Fri.; Dinner: Daily.

■ *(A♦)* **Hong Kong Harbour**, 2184 Cheshire Bridge Rd. (1/2 mile south of Lindbergh Rd.), Atlanta (325-7630). Authentic Hong Kong-style cuisine has made this restaurant a favorite among the Asian community. Specialties include fresh seafood dishes, black bean entrees and Chinese hot-pots and congees. The service is excellent and the staff is accommodating to young children and large groups. Dim sum is served daily. (Weekend dim sums are quite popular, so come early.) Open: Lunch and Dinner: Daily.

■ *(A♦)* **Honto**, 3295 Chamblee-Dunwoody Rd. (Buford Hwy.), Chamblee (458-8088). Restaurant critics and Chinese food lovers consistently give this restaurant top reviews. Request the Chinese menu or ask the waiters for suggestions, so you may try some of the more authentic dishes. Mussels with Black Bean Sauce, and Salt and Pepper Squid are highly recommended. Groups, meetings and parties are welcome. Dim sum is served weekends. Open: Lunch and Dinner: Daily.

■ **House of Chan**, 2469 Cobb Pkwy. (across from Loehmann's Plaza), Smyrna (955-9444). The Hong Kong-style restaurant has been called "Atlanta's suburban hide-away" and has received rave reviews from food critics for its nouvelle cuisine combining Cantonese, Mandarin and Szechuan cooking styles. Open: Lunch: Mon.–Fri.; Dinner: Daily.

■ **House of Peking**, 5382 Buford Hwy. (1/4 mile inside I-285), Doraville (458-0671). The restaurant is billed as the "only Mongolian barbecue restaurant in Atlanta." There is a luncheon buffet, an all-you-can-eat Mongolian barbecue for dinner and a regular dinner menu. Open: Lunch and Dinner: Mon.–Sat.

■ **Hsu's Gourmet Chinese Restaurant**, 192 Peachtree Center Ave. (International Blvd.), Atlanta (659-2788). The upscale and romantic restaurant serves Hong Kong-style cuisine, earning this restaurant excellent ratings by food critics. Favorites include Peking Duck and the Flamingo Nest with Phoenix and Dragon. Open: Lunch: Mon.–Sat.; Dinner: Daily.

■ **Hunan Palace**, 618 Ponce de Leon Ave. (across from the old Sears building), Atlanta (872-2918). Hunan Palace is the last of the Asian restaurants remaining in the Great Mall of China, perhaps because it continues to offer well-prepared Mandarin, Szechuan and Hunan cuisine in an elegant atmosphere. Catering and banquet facilities are available. Open: Lunch and Dinner: Daily.

■ **Hwang's Dynasty Restaurant**, 5554 Chamblee-Dunwoody Rd. (Dunwoody Hall Shopping Center near Mount Vernon Rd.), Dunwoody (395-7676). The neighborhood restaurant serves Mandarin, Szechuan and Hunan cuisine. Sunday luncheon buffet. Open: Lunch: Mon.–Fri.; Dinner: Mon.–Sat.

■ **Little Szechuan**, 5091-C Buford Hwy. (Northwoods Plaza), Doraville (451-0192), Critics rave about the dishes prepared at this newly opened restaurant specializing in highly spiced Szechuan cuisine. Try the home style tofu or stir fried Szechuan string beans. Open: Lunch and Dinner: Daily.

■ **L'Oriental**, 111 Perimeter Center West (Marque of Atlanta Hotel & Suites), Atlanta (392-1008). This upscale hotel restaurant's menu features a variety of

Mandarin and Cantonese dishes. Peking Duck and Veal with Sa Cha Sauce are among the specialties. Open: Lunch and Dinner: Daily.

■ **Lucky China**, 11680 Alpharetta Hwy. (across from N. Fulton Hospital), Alpharetta (740-1818). This Mandarin-style restaurant prepares gourmet specials every night, including some Szechuan entrees. Casual and formal dining rooms are available. Open: Lunch and Dinner: Daily.

■ **Mah Jong**, 2140 Peachtree Rd. (Brookwood Square), Atlanta (352-8339). The upscale Hong Kong-style restaurant remains a favorite among the Buckhead set. Specialties include Bird's Nest Prawns and a stuffed lettuce appetizer. Open: Lunch: Mon.–Fri.; Dinner: Daily.

■ **Mandarin House Chinese Restaurant**, 6263 Roswell Rd. (Johnson Ferry Rd.), Atlanta (255-5707). Mandarin and Szechuan entrees, such as Three Delicacies, Tin Sin Beef and Princess Prawn, continue to be enjoyed at this Sandy Springs restaurant. Open: Lunch: Sun.–Fri.; Dinner: Daily.

■ *(A♦)* **Oriental Pearl**, 5399 New Peachtree Rd. (Chinatown Square), Chamblee (986-9866). The large, mirrored dining room is often filled to capacity with a mainly Asian crowd. Excellent Cantonese-style cuisine is served, including Shark Fin Soup and other seafood specialties. Dim sum is served daily. (Weekend dim sum crowds are impressive, so come early.) Open: Lunch and Dinner: Daily.

■ **The Orient at Vinings**, 4199 Paces Ferry Rd. (near Vinings Square), Atlanta (438-8866). This contemporary restaurant serves "New Cantonese" cuisine and Szechuan specialties, such as Rainbow Shrimp, Night Clams, Szechuan Cuttlefish and Fire Cracker Pork. Special Sunday brunch. Open: Lunch: Mon.–Fri.; Dinner: Mon.–Sat.

■ **The Peking Restaurant**, 3375 Buford Hwy. (Northeast Plaza), Atlanta (634-2373). One of Atlanta's first Mandarin-style Chinese restaurants continues to serve well-prepared Chinese cuisine. Open: Lunch: Mon.–Fri.; Dinner: Daily.

■ *(A)* **Pung-Mie**, 5145 Buford Hwy. (between Pinetree Plaza and Northwoods Shopping Center), Doraville (455-0435). Restaurant reviewers rave about this Korean-influenced Chinese restaurant. Chinese dumplings, meatballs and unusual seafood fare, including jellyfish and sea cucumber entrees, come highly recommended. The staff is accommodating to families with small children. Open: Lunch and Dinner: Daily.

■ **Pyng Ho Chinese Restaurant**, 1357 Clairmont Rd. (north of N. Decatur Rd.), Decatur (634-4477). The neighborhood restaurant serves Mandarin-style cuisine and has a special Preferred Chinese Menu, listing some of their more authentic dishes. Special Sunday buffet. Open: Lunch: Sun.–Fri.; Dinner: Daily.

■ **Sam's Gourmet Chinese Seafood**, 4959 Roswell Rd. (Belle Isle St.), Atlanta (252-5880). This Cantonese-style restaurant has been praised for its exquisite seafood entrees. Critics recommend Whole Lobster in Cream Sauce and Soup of Duck with Mustard Greens. Open: Lunch and Dinner: Daily.

■ **Seafood China**, 3039 Buford Hwy. (Corporate Square), Atlanta (321-6066). The Hong Kong-style restaurant serves Americanized entrees as well as a few authentic specialties, such as Seafood Hot Pot and Buddha's Delight. Open: Lunch: Mon.–Fri.; Dinner: Daily.

■ **Shangri-La**, 1309 Powers Ferry Rd. (Powers Ferry Plaza/inside I-285), Marietta (952-5335). Mandarin-style cuisine is enjoyed at this restaurant. Ask for some "off menu" items, so you may sample some of the more authentic entrees. Open: Lunch and Dinner: Daily.

■ **Sichuan Restaurant**, 5389-A New Peachtree Rd. (Chinatown Square), Chamblee (457-6570). The second of the restaurants in Chinatown Square specializes in spicy Szechuan cooking, including specialties like Chili-flavored Chicken, Jadeite Shrimp and Chengdu Braised Sea Cucumber. Open: Lunch and Dinner: Daily.

■ **The Szechuan Gardens Chinese Restaurant**, 5458 Buford Hwy. (1/4 mile inside I-285) Doraville (455-7723). The restaurant serves Szechuan-style cuisine, as well as some Hunan, Mandarin and Cantonese dishes. Open: Lunch and Dinner: Daily.

■ **(A) Tien Tien**, 2225 Cheshire Bridge Rd. (Lenox Rd.), Atlanta (320-6829). Simple, inexpensive Cantonese and Hong Kong-style dishes are served at this informal store-front restaurant. You may also purchase fresh roasted pork, duck and other specialty meats. Open: Lunch and Dinner: Thurs.–Tues. (Closed on Wed.).

■ **Tientsin Chinese Restaurant**, 4015 Holcomb Bridge Rd. (one mile past Peachtree Industrial Blvd.), Norcross (662-8736). The neighborhood restaurant serves Mandarin, Peking and Szechuan-style cuisine. Open: Lunch: Mon.–Fri.; Dinner: Daily.

■ **Uncle Tai's Hunan Yaun**, 3500 Peachtree Rd. (Phipps Plaza), Atlanta (816-8888). This restaurant in Phipps Plaza specializes in hot and spicy Hunan specialties such as sliced lamb Hunan style and Uncle Tai's Jumbo Shrimp. This is the fourth U.S. location for the popular chain. Open: Lunch and Dinner: Daily.

■ **Ya Shu Yuen**, 5499 Chamblee-Dunwoody Rd. (Dunwoody Village/north of Mt. Vernon Rd.), Dunwoody (393-8674) and 10800 Alpharetta Hwy. (near Holcomb Bridge Rd.), Roswell (993-2007). The attractive restaurants serve Mandarin, Szechuan and Hunan cuisine, as well as Chinese-American fare. Open: Lunch: Sun.–Fri.; Dinner: Daily.

- (*A*) **Yeh Lai Hsiang Chinese Restaurant**, 5285 Buford Hwy. (Pinetree Plaza), Doraville (457-7014). The restaurant has received excellent reviews for its Mandarin-style cuisine and Korean-influenced specialties, including prawn salad and split prawns in fiery mustard sauce. The friendly atmosphere is appreciated by families with small children. Open: Lunch: Mon.–Fri.; Dinner: Daily.
- (*A*) **Yen Jing Chinese Restaurant**, 5302 Buford Hwy. (Koreatown Plaza), Doraville (454-6688). The bright restaurant in Koreatown Plaza serves excellent Chinese and Korean-influenced cuisine. Dishes blend the best of both cuisines, prices are reasonable and portions are huge. Dumplings, nida with shrimp, chef's special tofu and fried bread are some favorites. The staff is accommodating to children. Open: Lunch: Mon.–Fri.; Dinner: Daily.

KOREAN RESTAURANTS

Kim chee is not only the national dish of Korea, but is also considered a national treasure. The red-hot pickled cabbage is served with every meal in Korea, even breakfast! In Atlanta's Korean restaurants, kim chee is often served along with a combination of other pickled vegetables — daikon, cucumbers, bean sprouts — some of which are just as fiery as the kim chee.

- **Baek-Do Garden & Sushi Bar**, 5728 Buford Hwy. (Doraville Plaza), Doraville (457-8510). This large Korean restaurant features well-prepared Korean fare, barbecue and a sushi bar. Each entree is accompanied by kim chee and a selection of pickles. At night, the rear portion of the restaurant becomes a lively club featuring live entertainment and karaoke. Open: Lunch and Dinner: Daily.
- **Chofun Ok Restaurant**, 5865 Buford Hwy. (1 mile north of I-285), Doraville (452-1821). The small Korean restaurant serves traditional Korean fare, such as bulgogi (marinated rib-eye) and bee-beem-bap (shredded beef salad). Open: Lunch and Dinner: Daily.
- **Garam Korean Restaurant**, 5881 Buford Hwy. (north of I-285 at US 25), Doraville (454-9198). The award-winning restaurant serves excellent Korean and Japanese fare in elegant surroundings, along with kim chee and a variety of spicy pickles. The large sushi bar offers a full selection of sushi and sashimi. The lunch menu features Korean lacquer box specials — a wonderful treat. Open: Lunch and Dinner: Daily (The sushi bar is closed on Monday).
- **Go Hyang Jip**, 5269 Buford Hwy. (Pinetree Plaza), Doraville (458-8783). The small restaurant may be hard to find because its sign is in Korean, but be adventurous — the informal restaurant serves authentic Korean fare and spe-

cializes in "grill your own meat" at the table. Open: Lunch and Dinner: Daily.

■ **Hanil Korean & Japanese Restaurant**, 2313 Windy Hill Rd. (Cobb Pkwy.), Marietta (956-9138). Traditional Korean fare may be enjoyed along with an extensive selection of sushi and a sampling of other Japanese specialites. Open: Lunch and Dinner: Daily.

■ **Il Mee Restaurant**, 1000 N. Cobb Pkwy. (North Marietta Shopping Mall), Marietta (426-4929). Traditional Korean fare, including bulgogi (marinated rib-eye), cold spicy noodles and barbecued beef ribs, are quite popular at this restaurant. Open: Lunch and Dinner: Daily.

■ **Jang Goon Korean Restaurant**, 5119 Jimmy Carter Blvd. (Old Norcross-Tucker Rd.), Norcross (729-8396). Spicy squid dishes, bulgogi (marinated rib-eye), cold noodles, kim chee, and other authentic Korean fare may be enjoyed at this Gwinnett restaurant. Open: Lunch and Dinner: Daily (except on the second Tuesday of each month).

■ **Kang Suh**, 5181 Buford Hwy. (Pinetree Plaza), Doraville (451-8989). This restaurant has been voted most authentic Korean restaurant year after year by Atlanta's food critics, who praise the restaurant's inexpensive "gourmet" Korean fare. Feast on bulgogi (marinated rib-eye), barbecued ribs or one of the cold noodle dishes. Open: Lunch and Dinner: Daily.

■ **Lai Lai** (Asia Beef House), 2390 Chamblee-Tucker Rd. (Buford Hwy.), Chamblee (458-1940). Authentic Korean fare and Chinese favorites may be enjoyed at this unusually attractive restaurant specializing in hibachi ("grill your own") cooking at the table. Open: Lunch and Dinner: Tues.–Sun.

■ **Mirror of Korea**, 1047 Ponce de Leon Ave. (Plaza Drugs/Highland Ave.), Atlanta (874-6243). The beautifully decorated restaurant is one of Atlanta's first Korean restaurants, and customers continue to enjoy the consistently well-prepared Korean entrees, as well as the sushi bar. Open: Lunch and Dinner: Tues.–Sun.

■ **Secret Garden**, 5877 Memorial Dr. (Hairston Memorial Shopping Center), Stone Mountain (296-1699). The neighborhood restaurant serves both Korean and Mandarin cuisine. In addition to the regular menu, a dinner buffet is featured daily. Open: Dinner: Daily.

■ **Shi Gol House**, 570 Cobb Pkwy. (South Marietta Square Pkwy.), Marietta (425-1462). This restaurant serves a selection of authentic Korean and Japanese entrees. Open: Lunch and Dinner: Daily.

THAI RESTAURANTS

■ **Bangkok Thai Restaurant**, 1492 Piedmont Rd. (Ansley Square), Atlanta (874-2514). Bangkok is one of Atlanta's first Thai restaurants, and it still remains popular due to its consistently well-prepared and inexpensive traditional Thai cuisine. The curries come highly recommended. Open: Lunch: Mon.–Fri.; Dinner: Daily.

■ **Hot Pepper Thai Cuisine**, 2257 Lenox Rd. (Cheshire Bridge Rd.), Atlanta (320-1532). Recently opened to excellent reviews, this restaurant has a large selection of well-prepared spicy Thai entrees, such as Hot Peppers Mixed Seafood, Spicy Basil Leaves with Tofu and Spicy Duck Curry. Service is excellent. Open: Lunch and Dinner: Tues.–Sun.

■ **Hunan Gourmet**, 6070 Sandy Springs Cir. (Centre Court Shopping Center/Roswell Rd.), Atlanta (303-8888). Besides serving Hunan-style cuisine, this restaurant also features a whole menu of Thai entrees. Open: Lunch: Mon.–Sat.; Dinner: Daily.

■ **Jonathan Lee's Thai and Chinese Restaurant**, 1799 Briarcliff Rd. (Sage Hill Shopping Center), Atlanta (897-1700). The attractively decorated dining room serves both Chinese-American cuisine and Thai specialties, including Pud Thai (Thai noodles), Siamese Chicken and Crispy Squid. Open: Lunch: Mon.–Fri.; Dinner: Daily.

■ **King and I**, 1510 Piedmont Rd. (Ansley Square), Atlanta (892-7743) and 4058 Peachtree Rd. (Windsor Station), Atlanta (262-7985). The attractive decor and authentic dishes have earned this restaurant a popular following in Atlanta. Favorites are Yum Yai (spicy Thai salad) and Pad-se-ew Noodles (wide noodles with broccoli). Open: Lunch: Mon.–Fri.; Dinner: Daily.

■ **Palace Thai Cuisine**, 6034 S. Norcross-Tucker Rd. (south of Jimmy Carter Blvd.), Norcross (242-4015). The restaurant has quickly earned a reputation as a must for Thai food lovers. Critics recommend Nam Sod (minced pork with chili and spices) and any of the red or green curries. Open: Lunch: Mon.–Sat.; Dinner: Daily.

■ **Phuket Thai Restaurant**, 2839 Buford Hwy. (south of N. Druid Hills Rd.), Atlanta (325-4199). The upscale decor, friendly service and excellent Thai food have made this restaurant one of the more popular Thai restaurants in Atlanta. Try the Phuket Yum (spicy salad with shrimp, scallops and squid), Tom Ka (spicy chicken coconut soup) or Tom Yum Koon (shrimp and lemon grass soup). Open: Lunch: Mon.–Fri.; Dinner: Daily.

■ **Queen of Thailand**, 3330 Buford Hwy. (north of N. Druid Hills Rd.), Atlanta (982-9321). The pleasant and informal restaurant serves authentic Thai food, including Tom Ka (chicken coconut soup) and Mixed Seafood in Clay Pot. Open: Lunch: Mon.–Sat.; Dinner: Daily.

■ **Rama & Sato**, 605 Indian Trail-Lilburn Rd. (US 29), Lilburn (381-1615). Traditional Thai food, such as Pud Thai (Thai noodles) and Basil Chicken, are served at this small, friendly Thai restaurant. Open: Lunch: Tues.–Fri.; Dinner: Tues.–Sun.

- **Royal Thai Cuisine**, 6365-A Spalding Dr. (Spalding Centre), Norcross (449-7796). The small restaurant, in the former location of Chiang-Mai, already has a loyal following. Try the Fried Catfish Filet, Tom Yun Koon (shrimp and lemon grass soup) or any of the innovative curries. The staff is very friendly. Open: Lunch: Mon.–Fri.; Dinner: Daily.

- **Sukhothai Thai Restaurant**, 1995 Windy Hill Rd., Suite 14 (1/2 mile from Cobb Pkwy.), Smyrna (434-9276). Restaurant critics praise this restaurant's decor and the excellence of its cooking. Raining Shrimp, Tom Yum Kum (shrimp and lemon grass soup) and mixed Seafood Grill are some of the specialties. Ask for the special vegetarian menu. Open: Lunch and Dinner: Mon.–Sat.

- **Surin of Thailand**, 810 N. Highland Ave. (Greenwood St.), Atlanta (892-7789). The elegantly decorated restaurant is jam-packed on weekends with customers enjoying the well-prepared food in this Virginia-Highlands restaurant. Open: Lunch and Dinner: Daily.

- **Tamarind Thai Cuisine**, 3195 Roswell Rd. (between Piedmont and Peachtree Rds.), Atlanta (816-2288). This beautifully decorated restaurant serves well-prepared, expensively priced Thai cuisine. Open: Lunch and Dinner: Daily.

- **Taste of Thai Restaurant**, 5775 Jimmy Carter Blvd. (Brook Hollow Village), Norcross (662-8575). This restaurant has received excellent reviews for its inexpensive and authentic Thai dishes, including Crispy Catfish Salad and the many curry variations. Open: Lunch and Dinner: Tues.–Sun.

- **Thailand Cafe Restaurant and Lounge**, 2820 Chamblee-Tucker Rd. (I-85/west of the overpass), Atlanta (455-7370). Excellent Thai cuisine, house specialties, such as Lamb Satay (skewered meat with peanut sauce) and fried catfish, and friendly service have earned this restaurant a loyal following. This attractively decorated restaurant also features a lounge and dance floor. Open: Lunch and Dinner: Mon.–Sat.

- **Thai Gourmet**, 369 Sandy Springs Cir. (Roswell Rd.), Sandy Springs (847-9497). Classical Thai cooking is served at this restaurant specializing in fresh seafood dishes, such as Ship Wrecked and Garlic and Pepper Shrimp. Open: Lunch: Mon.–Fri.; Dinner: Daily.

- **Thai House**, 1227 Alpharetta St. (Kings Creek Shopping Center), Roswell (587-2588). The casual and friendly atmosphere of this Thai/Chinese restaurant makes it a favorite among families with small children. Chicken Curry and Larb (spicy minced beef) are two of the specialties. Open: Lunch: Sun.–Fri.; Dinner: Daily.

- **Thai Restaurant of Norcross**, 6065 Norcross-Tucker Rd. (south of Jimmy Carter Blvd.), Norcross (662-8575). The restaurant has remained very popular through the years with customers who enjoy the attractively decorated restaurant and tasty Thai dishes. Specialties include spicy hot whole fish entrees and Yum Yai (spicy Thai salad with shrimp, chicken and egg). Open: Lunch and Dinner: Daily.
- **Thai-Siam Restaurant**, 6435 Roswell Rd. (1/2 mile north of Johnson Ferry Rd.), Atlanta (250-1343). Food critics have greeted this new Thai restaurant with high praise for the authentically prepared and tasty cuisine. Open: Lunch and Dinner: Mon.-Sat.
- **Zab-E-Lee**, 4835 Old National Hwy. (just north of I-85/285), College Park (768-2705). This Thai restaurant on the southside of Atlanta consistently receives rave reviews for its extensive and inexpensive Thai entrees, as well as its many specialty soups and curries. There are a few Chinese dishes on the menu. Open: Lunch and Dinner: Daily.

VIETNAMESE RESTAURANTS

- **Bien Thuy**, 5095-E Buford Hwy. (Northwoods Shopping Center), Doraville (454-9046). The traditional cuisine is considered "among the best" by numerous reviewers and by the Vietnamese community. Try the Goi Cuon (shrimp and pork summer rolls), Com Tom Bi (rice with pork) or Bun Thit Nuong (grilled pork, cold noodles and salad). Open: Lunch and Dinner: Daily.
- **Ca-Dao Vietnamese Restaurant**, 4763 Buford Hwy. (across from the IRS Center), Chamblee (986-9542). The small and informal Vietnamese cafe is frequented primarily by members of the Vietnamese community who enjoy soups and other traditional Vietnamese fare. Open: Lunch and Dinner: Daily.
- **Cha-Gio**, 966 Peachtree St. (10th St.), Atlanta (885-9387). One of the first Vietnamese restaurants in Atlanta continues to serve popular Vietnamese-American fare, including spring rolls, noodle entrees and a variety of stir-fried dishes. Open: Lunch and Dinner: Daily.
- **Pho Cafe Hoai Viet Restaurant**, 5280 Buford Hwy. (Pinetree Plaza next to Koreatown Plaza), Doraville (986-8638). The informal restaurant is frequented primarily by Vietnamese customers, who enjoy the authentic Vietnamese cuisine. Open: Breakfast, Lunch and Dinner: Daily.
- **Saigon Restaurant**, 4051-A Buford Highway (Clairmont Rd. across from Outlet Square), Atlanta (634-2419). This restaurant has received excellent reviews for its inexpensive and authentic Vietnamese fare served in a casual and friendly atmosphere. Try Goi Cuon (shrimp and pork summer rolls),

the "do-it-yourself" spring rolls, cafe sua da (iced coffee) and more. Open: Lunch and Dinner: Daily.

■ **Song Huong**, 4795 Buford Hwy. (across from the IRS Center), Chamblee (451-2944). Excellent Vietnamese food at inexpensive prices make this restaurant a good bet for those who want to try authentic Vietnamese food in a friendly atmosphere. A few Chinese dishes are also on the menu. Live music is performed on weekends. Open: Lunch and Dinner: Daily.

■ **Thanh Vi Vietnamese Restaurant**, 5385 New Peachtree Rd. (Chinatown Square), Chamblee (451-1139). The booth in the Chinatown Square food court serves authentic Vietnamese dishes, as well as more familiar Vietnamese-American fare, such as spring rolls and barbecued beef. Open: Lunch and Dinner: Daily (open at 10:00am).

■ **Thien Thanh Vietnamese Restaurant**, 4300 Buford Hwy. (north of Dresden Dr.), Atlanta (315-9923). The small, informal restaurant serves authentic Vietnamese fare, specializing in curries and spicy dishes. Open: Lunch and Dinner: Daily.

■ **Vietnamese Cuisine**, 3375 Buford Hwy. (Northeast Plaza Shopping Center), Atlanta (321-1840). Although some restaurant reviewers claim this restaurant is the most expensive of Atlanta's Vietnamese restaurants, all agree that the dishes are quite good. Specialties include Saigon Shrimp and Bo Five Mon, a special dish that can feed four. Open: Lunch and Dinner: Daily. (Open for late night dancing on weekends.)

MALAYSIAN RESTAURANTS

■ **Tea Rose Garden**, 3280 Cobb Pkwy. (adjacent to Kroger Shopping Center/Vinings), Atlanta (953-9922). Along with its usual menu featuring a blend of Cantonese, Mandarin and Szechuan-style cuisines, this unusual restaurant serves a full menu of Malaysian specialties on Saturday and Sunday, including a variety of Malaysian curries and noodle dishes. Open: Lunch and Dinner: Daily.

BURMESE RESTAURANTS

■ **Mandalay**, 5945 Jimmy Carter Blvd. (N. Norcross-Tucker Rd.), Norcross (368-8368). Atlanta's only Burmese restaurant serves authentic and delectable Burmese fare combining the cooking styles of Thailand, Malaysia, India and China. The attractive menu features pictures of most of the entrees and includes a large number of Cantonese-style specialties for the less adventurous. For a rare treat, try one of the Burmese salads. Open: Lunch and Dinner: Mon.-Sat.

INDONESIAN RESTAURANTS

■ **Maison Gourmet**, 2581 Piedmont Rd. (Lindbergh Plaza), Atlanta (231-8552). Although the restaurant serves French and Continental-style cuisine, occasionally it presents a unique *rijst-tafel* (rice table), a feast of Dutch and Indonesian specialties requiring days of preparation. In the past, the *rijst-tafel* was offered on the last Sunday of each month. Call to find out if it will be offered this year.

FUSION CUISINE

■ **Azalea**, 3167 Peachtree Rd. (Grandview Ave.), Atlanta (237-9939). The Buckhead restaurant consistently receives rave reviews for its exceptional style of "fusion" cuisine (a blend of Asian, Italian and regional American styles). Restaurant reviewers choose the Szechuan Chicken with Lo Mein, Thai-chicken Pizza and Catfish with Black Bean Sauce. Open: Dinner: Daily.

■ **Nickiemoto's**, 247 Buckhead Ave. (Bolling Way), Atlanta (842-0334). This restaurant is praised for its creative "East meets West" cuisine, as prepared by a French chef. Specialties, such as Sizzling Catfish and Seven-spice Fried Oysters blend French, Japanese and Asian cooking styles. There is a large sushi bar. Open: Dinner: Daily.

■ Many restaurants, such as **Marra's Seafood Grill**, 1782 Cheshire Bridge Rd. (Piedmont Rd.), Atlanta (874-7347), and **Mambo**, 1402 N. Highland Ave. (University Dr.), Atlanta (876-2626), have begun adding quite a few "fusion" entrees to their menus — Marra's featuring Pacific-Rim cuisine, and Mambo's featuring Chino-Latino cuisine. Other restaurants are joining the craze. Keep your eye on this new trend in dining.

> ### ENTERTAINMENT:
> ### THEATRE, DANCE, MUSIC, CLUBS,
> ### FILMS, T.V. & RADIO, SPORTS

DANCE & MUSIC — LOCAL

■ **Atlanta Zheng (Zither) Concert** (262-7136). Joanne Loh's Zheng Concert is billed as the "one and only Zheng performance in the U.S.A." The performers, who are from China, Hong Kong, Malaysia, Singapore and Taiwan, play the Guzheng, a classical Chinese string instrument, while dressed in Chinese costumes representing different dynasties. This concert offers Atlantans a unique opportunity to enjoy Chinese culture and music. Joanne Loh also offers classes in classical zheng for children and adults.

■ Chinese dance troupes performing classical and traditional dances, such as the ribbon, fan, hat and scarf, may be enjoyed at the Chinese Community Center's New Year's Celebration, Georgia Tech's International Festival, Kingfest International, Underground's Festival of Cultures, the Festival of Trees and many other Atlanta events. Some of the groups to look out for are **Hwee-Eng Lee & Chinese Dancers** (423-1486), **Lisa Chyn Dance Ensemble** (971-5286) and **Atlanta Chinese Dance Company** (423-1486). (These groups will be glad to perform for church groups, schools and private functions.)

■ The newly formed **Atlanta Korean Children's Choir** (671-8885) has appeared at the Atlanta Historical Society and at various churches throughout Atlanta. The **Korean Dance Troupe** (451-0364) may also be enjoyed at Atlanta-area festivals.

■ The **Thai Association of Georgia Dancers** (493-1175) performs traditional dances at various international festivals and community events.

■ The **Filipino-American Dance Group** (396-1828) and the **Filipino-American Choral Group** (925-2824) perform at international events throughout Atlanta.

■ Look for the **White Water Birds** (286-9218), a Hmong dance troupe, at international festivals in Atlanta, including Underground Atlanta's annual Festival of Cultures.

■ Emory University and other area colleges often sponsor special events featuring Asian countries, such as the 1992 celebration of **The International Year of Tibet**, a global effort to save Tibet and the Tibetan people, one of history's most exotic and ancient cultures. As part of the celebration, **Emory University** hosted a week-long celebration of Tibet, which included performances of sacred music, chanting and dance; and **Georgia State Student Center** was the location for a lecture on medicine Buddha techniques. Art galleries, Image Film & Video Center, CNN Center and many other clubs and organizations also participated in this most unusual global event.

DANCE & MUSIC — INTERNATIONAL

■ World-class performers occasionally appear in Atlanta, such as the **Shanghai Acrobats & Dance Company**, which appeared at Georgia Tech; the **Bao Dao Acrobats of the Republic of China,** whose unique performance at Agnes Scott College combined acrobatics, magic and dance; and the **Festival of Indonesia: Music & Dance of the Sumatra**, a touring ensemble of 300 performing artists from eleven different Indonesian ethnic groups, who came to Atlanta and performed dance, ancient martial arts, and music from their native country. Also, the Organization of Chinese Americans sponsored **The Georgia Chinese-American Festival** at Agnes Scott College, which featured **Yin Cheng-Zong**, China's foremost pianist, and other top classical musicians from China.

FILMS

- Emory University's **Asia-Pacific Film Series** (727-6562) features films from Japan, Papau New Guinea, Indonesia, Korea, China and Hong Kong, with English subtitles. The extremely successful **Hong Kong Excitement Film Festival** is screened at the High Museum (892-HIGH) and every Friday and Saturday at midnight and Sunday afternoon at Cinevision, 3300 NE Expressway Park, Building 2, Atlanta.

CLUBS

- Chinese, Korean and Vietnamese night clubs may be found throughout Atlanta. Most feature karaoke (sing-along) entertainment. A sampling: **Gaya Restaurant**, 5805 Buford Hwy., Doraville (458-3824); Nan's Restaurant & Lounge, 3070 Presidential Pkwy., Atlanta (458-4767); **Sam Oul Lim**, 3695 Longview Dr., Chamblee (455-1819); **Shilla**, 3701 Presidential Pkwy., Atlanta (458-0843); and **Yuki Hana Oyster Cafe**, 3567 Chamblee-Dunwoody Rd., Chamblee (455-1163).
- **The Buford Korea Night Club**, 6200 Buford Hwy., Norcross (417-1490) is the first night club catering just to the Korean community. It features VIP lounges with leather couches, six bartenders and live entertainment by Korean performers.
- Many of the **Korean** and **Vietnamese** restaurants have live entertainment, karaoke and dancing on weekends.

fEsTIVALS & spEcIAL EVENTS

JANUARY/FEBRUARY

- **Chinese New Year**, Chinese Community Center, Chamblee (451-4456). Chinese food booths, traditional dances, martial art demonstrations, folk songs and children's activities highlight the lunar New Year celebration at the Chinese Community Center. The Atlanta Taiwanese Association and other smaller groups also host their own New Year celebrations.
- The **Korean, Vietnamese** and other **Southeast Asian** communities celebrate the lunar New Year with special parties, feasts, music and dance at various locations in Atlanta. Look for flyers at Asian groceries and restaurants announcing these events.

APRIL

■ **Thai New Year Celebration** (493-1175/717-7909, ext. 1992). The Thai New Year is celebrated with religious services at the Wat Buddha Temple, followed by a large dinner celebration and dance.

MAY

■ **Asian/Pacific American Heritage Banquet**. A/PAC's annual banquet is held during Asian/Pacific – American Heritage Month. The various Asian associations join together for an evening celebrating the music, dance and culture of the member associations.

JUNE

■ **Independence Day Celebration**, Filipino-American Association of Greater Atlanta (478-2057). The public is welcome to attend the annual celebration of Philippine Independence and enjoy traditional food, folk dancing and special family activities.

SEPTEMBER

■ **Mid-Autumn Festival – Harvest Festival**. Most of the Asian communities celebrate the harvest and new moon on the 15th day of the eighth month of the Chinese calendar. For example, the Vietnamese community calls their celebration **Tet Trung Thu**, and festivities include a special children's festival, where parents give their young children candle-lit lanterns, sweet bean cakes and lots of other special treats.

■ **Wok-A-Thon**, Hotel Nikko, Atlanta (365-8100). The American Institute of Wine and Food presents "Wok-A-Thon," a benefit featuring food prepared by the best Asian chefs of Atlanta. Approximately twenty different Asian restaurants participate.

NOVEMBER

■ **Buddha Celebration**, Chinese Community Center, Chamblee (451-4456). The Buddhist Bodhi Charity Foundation sponsors a cultural festival and religious ceremony celebrating Buddha. The celebration usually features Chinese art demonstrations, a bazaar and samplings of food from different Asian restaurants.

DECEMBER

■ Almost all of the Asian community associations have special holiday get-togethers during the month of December. For example: **The Thai**

Association of Georgia (493-1175/717-7909, ext. 1992) sponsors a formal holiday dinner party; and the **Filipino-American Association of Greater Atlanta** (478-2057) sponsors a formal New Year's Eve Ball.

CHINA

■ **Atlanta Taiwanese Chamber of Commerce**, 2865 Old Hapeville Rd., Suite 31, Atlanta 30354 (762-5812); **Taiwanese Coordination Council for North American Affairs**, 1349 W. Peachtree St., NE, Suite 1290, Atlanta 30309 (872-0123); and **Taiwanese Information and Communication Division – Coordination Council for North American Affairs**, 233 Peachtree St., NE, Suite 201, Atlanta 30303 (522-0481).

■ Check the *Chinese Business Guide and Directory Southeast USA* for listings of Chinese-American professional, business and trade associations.

KOREA

■ **Consulate General of the Republic of Korea**, 229 Peachtree St., Suite 500, NE, Atlanta 30303 (522-1611); and **Korean Chamber of Commerce**, 5312 Buford Hwy., Suite B-2, Doraville 30340 (454-7668).

■ Check the *Korean Business Directory* for listings of Korean-American professional, business and trade associations.

PHILIPPINES

■ **Honorary Consulate of the Philippines**, 950 East Paces Ferry Rd., NE, Suite 2980, Atlanta 30326 (233-9916).

THAILAND

■ **Honorary Consulate General of Thailand**, 3333 Cumberland Cir., Suite 400, Atlanta 30339 (988-3304); and **Thai Trade Center**, 245 Peachtree Center Ave., Suite 2104, NE, Atlanta 30303 (659-0178).

Japanese girls demonstrate the art of origami.

The Japanese
Community

HISTORY & NEIGHBORHOODS

Approximately 4,000 Japanese-Americans are estimated to reside in the Atlanta area. Many native-born Japanese-Americans have assimilated into the mainstream population and maintain few ties with other Japanese-Americans. Yet other Japanese-Americans belong to social clubs and associations which provide a means for them to continue to identify with their Japanese heritage and identity.

Most of the Japanese in our city, however, are not citizens, but are temporary residents here for business purposes. Since the 1980s, when Georgia actively began courting Japanese investment in the state, over 315 Japanese companies have located in the metro-Atlanta area, bringing with them approximately 8,000-10,000 Japanese executives, professionals, and business people as temporary residents of Atlanta. Because of the short-term nature of their residence in Atlanta, the expatriate population is not particularly cohesive, although Japanese families are offered numerous opportunities to interact with one another and learn more about Atlanta through the efforts of the Japan-American Society of Georgia. Also, with the opening of the Japanese elementary school, Seigakuin Atlanta International School (SAINTS), it is expected that Japanese families will have additional opportunities to socialize with one another.

The majority of Japanese expatriate families reside in the northside of Atlanta, with heavy populations in Marietta, Norcross, Dunwoody, Smyrna, Roswell, Lilburn and Sandy Springs. Large communities may also be found in Peachtree City and other southside neighborhoods. As Japanese investment in the U.S. continues to expand, so will the temporary Japanese community in Atlanta. For those Atlantans who may doubt that Atlanta has truly become an international city, try out the Westin Peachtree Hotel's breakfast menu, which offers a Japanese breakfast of rice, pickled plums, seafood and tea!

HISTORICAL SITES & MUSEUMS

■ **Atlanta Botanical Garden**, 1345 Piedmont Rd. (Piedmont Park at The Prado), Atlanta (876-5858). The garden has re-created a small, but charming, Japanese garden with a variety of bamboo plants and a bamboo fence. Additionally, the garden hosts bonsai shows and offers a variety of classes, including those organized by the Garden Center of Greater Atlanta in *Ikebana* (Japanese flower arranging). Call for a schedule of upcoming programs and events. Hours: Tues.–Sat. 9:00am–6:00pm; Sun. 12noon–6:00pm. (Extended hours during summer months.) Admission fee.

■ **Atlanta Museum**, 537 Peachtree St., NE, Atlanta (872-8233). The Atlanta Museum's eclectic collection includes quite a few pieces of Japanese porcelain and artifacts. World War II history buffs can also see a genuine Japanese Zero airplane in the rear of the museum. Hours: Mon.–Fri. 10:00am–5:00pm and by appointment only for groups on the weekend. Admission fee.

■ **Carter Presidential Center**, One Copenhill Ave., NE, Atlanta (331-3942). To the rear of the Carter Center lies a lovely landscaped Japanese garden with a view overlooking downtown Atlanta. Hours: Mon.–Sat. 9:00am–4:45pm; Sun. 12noon–4:45pm. Admission fee.

■ **High Museum of Art**, Robert Woodruff Arts Center, 1280 Peachtree St., NE, Atlanta (892-HIGH). The High Museum has a permanent collection entitled, "Japanese Porcelain: The Jacobs Collection," which includes over 80 pieces of 17th, 18th and 19th century Japanese porcelain. Special exhibits of work by Japanese artists may also be displayed from time to time, such as 1992's exhibit of sculpture by Mineko Grimmer. Hours: Tues., Wed., Thurs. and Sat. 10:00am–5:00pm; Fri. 10:00am–9:00pm; and Sun. 12noon–5:00pm. Admission fee.

GALLERIES

■ **The Asia Center** (876-7260). The exclusive gallery has a permanent exhibit of museum-quality artwork from Japan and China, including *netsuke* (miniature carvings), screens and scrolls. By appointment only.

■ **Japan Arts, Inc.**, 57 Basewood Cir., NE, Atlanta (393-1955). The private gallery deals in contemporary oriental art, primarily exhibiting work by Japanese artists. By appointment only.

■ Other Atlanta area galleries often house exhibits addressing aspects of Japanese culture, history and arts. A sampling: "Tsuzure-Ori" textile exhibit, which premiered at the **Atlanta International Museum of Art & Design**, Marquis Two — Garden Level, 285 Peachtree Center Ave., Atlanta (688-2467) in cooperation with the Japan-America Society of Atlanta, featuring temple hangings, priest robes, wood screens and other exquisite textile works; a show at the **BurnNoff Gallery**, 1529 Piedmont Ave., Clear Creek Center, Atlanta (875-3475) entitled "Kabuki Theater Remembered," exhibiting London's Haruyo Japanese classic figurines from Kabuki plays; and "Ichiboku Totemic Series," at **Artspace**, 50 Hurt Plaza, Suite 150, Atlanta (577-1988) displaying sculptures inspired by ancient Heian period Japanese Buddhist scriptures.

■ During **JapanFest,** held every two or three years and coordinated by the Consulate General of Japan, Emory University's Schatten Gallery, Oglethorpe University's Art Gallery and The Hotel Nikko are the locations for special exhibits of Japanese content.

COMMUNITY, RELIGIOUS & CULTURAL ASSOCIATIONS

CULTURAL ASSOCIATIONS

■ **Consulate General of Japan**, 100 Colony Square, Suite 2000, Atlanta (892-2700). Along with providing consular services to Japanese citizens and Americans, the Consulate General's Information Center provides a variety of information about Japan in the form of pamphlets, videos and exhibitions. The consul also can arrange speakers for business, cultural and academic programs; has within the consulate a library with books, photography, films and videos about cultural and social aspects of Japan; and offers a "school caravan" program for elementary, middle and high schools. Additionally, the consulate, in cooperation with local organizations and universities, organizes various social and cultural events, including concerts, cultural demonstrations and film festivals. A quarterly publication, *SIMPLY JAPAN*, provides news and announcements about the Japanese community and upcoming events.

■ **Japan-America Society of Georgia**, 225 Peachtree St., NE, Suite 710, Atlanta (524-7399). The society promotes cultural interaction between Japanese and American people by introducing Japanese culture, business, political and economic customs to Georgians, and vice versa. Activities are scheduled which bring Atlantans and Japanese expatriates together, such as Southern cooking classes, lectures on Atlanta history, and English and Japanese language classes. The society also sponsors quite a few cultural events each year, such as Japanese film festivals, music, dance and theatrical performances, social gatherings and special speaker luncheons. The **Tomodachi (Friendship) Club of Georgia**, a social organization of Japanese and American women interested in forming cross-cultural friendships, is also sponsored by the society.

■ **Japanese Women's Garden Club Hanamizuki** (961-5466). Members of this social club are Japanese women married to American and Japanese business-men who are living in Atlanta on a temporary basis. The club helps newly arrived Japanese women adjust to living in Atlanta and participates in the Festival of Trees.

■ **Japanese/American Association**, (706/227-3449 or 449-7245). This social society is open to individuals of Japanese heritage (Nisai) and Japanese-American couples. Regular meetings are held throughout Atlanta at mem-bers' homes and usually include a speaker on a cultural or social topic of interest to the members. A few special events are held during the year, including a family picnic and a Christmas party. The association may, in the next few years, merge with a newly forming local chapter of the **Japanese American Citizens League**.

■ *Hihongo o Hanasookai* (**Let's Speak Japanese Club**) (526-5313). The social club offers members an opportunity to practice speaking Japanese and to forge relationships with other Japanese-speaking people. Meetings are held monthly, and membership is open to Japanese-speaking Americans, native Japanese just learning English and students of both cultures.

■ Contact either the Japanese Consulate General (892-2700) or the Japan-America Society (524-7399) for current telephone numbers and addresses of other area social clubs such as **GO Clubs** and **Garden Associations**.

RELIGIOUS GROUPS

■ Japanese Congregations. A sampling: **Atlanta Independent Christian Church**, North Avenue Presbyterian Church, 607 Peachtree St., NE, Atlanta (987-0951) (Sunday services at 2:00pm in Japanese); **First Baptist Church of Norcross**, 706 N. Peachtree St., Norcross (448-2716) (Sunday services in Japanese at 11:00am); and **Westminster Japanese Church** (Presbyterian Church of America), 11450 Bowen Rd., Roswell (594-1382) (Sunday services in Japanese at 11:30am).

■ **Tenrikyo Hon-Ai, Atlanta Fellowship**, 332 Breezy Dr., Marietta (429-9288). The religion is based on divine revelation to Miki Nakayama in 1838. Morning and evening services are held daily in Japanese.

SCHOOLS—CHILDREN

■ **Seigakuin Atlanta International School (SAINTS)**, 3007 Hermance Dr., Atlanta (231-9699), located on the western edge of the Oglethorpe University campus, is a Japanese elementary school presently offering a program for children K–6th grades. The school follows a Japanese school year (April–March), and the curriculum follows that of Japanese schools, allowing children to move with their families to and from Atlanta without disrupting their schooling. All classes are taught in Japanese — English is studied as a foreign language.

■ **Georgia Nihongo Gakko – Saturday Schools** (923-9692/941-0533) have over 900 Japanese students, K–9th grade, studying Japanese language and culture on Saturday at Meadowcreek High School, 1300 Red Plum Rd., Norcross; or, Lindley Middle School, Pebble Brook Cir., Mableton. Japanese and English language classes are also offered for adults.

LANGUAGE SCHOOLS — ADULTS

■ Many programs in the Atlanta area provide Japanese language instruction for adults, the more popular being those classes offered by the **Japan-America Society of Georgia**, 225 Peachtree St., N.E., Suite 710, Atlanta (524-7399) (beginning-level Japanese classes on weekday afternoons); and the **Japanese Learning Center**, 165 6th St., N.E., Atlanta (876-1550) (evening classes at all levels, including a special introductory course on business Japanese).

■ **Kennesaw State College's Continuing Education Department** (423-6400) and **Oglethorpe University's Continuing Education Department** (364-8383) often offer evening Japanese language classes.

■ You may also contact the following companies that provide translation and related services: **Access Japan**, 3060 N. Pharr Ct., NW, #503, Atlanta (365-0321); **Japan-America Institute**, 6267 Oakwood Cir., NW, Norcross (448-5755); and **Japan Services, Inc.**, 57 Basewood Cir, N.E., Atlanta (393-1955).

COOKING CLASSES

■ Japanese cooking classes are sometimes offered by Chief Chef Kojo Omori of **Benihana Restaurant** (244-5050). Call for information about this year's schedule.

■ **Tan Lee Chin** (498-1163) and a few other instructors occasionally offer

Japanese cooking classes at **Evening at Emory** (727-6000) and **DeKalb College's Continuing Education Program** (244-5050).

CULTURAL ARTS

■ **The Japan-America Society of Georgia** (524-7399) and **Consulate General of Japan** (892-2700) can provide you with the names and telephone numbers of members of the Japanese community who offer classes in calligraphy, koto playing, embroidery and other cultural arts.

FLOWER ARRANGEMENT & IKEBANA

■ **Atlanta Botanical Garden** (876-5858) often offers classes in both classical and modern flower-arranging. Contact the **Japan-America Society of Georgia** (524-7399) for the names and telephone numbers of other individuals who offer classes in flower arranging.

JAPANESE KOI

■ **Atlanta Koi Club** (631-0155/939-1549) promotes, maintains, breeds and exhibits exotic Japanese koi (carp). Through regular meetings, the club provides a forum for information exchange about koi and related topics.

KYUDO (JAPANESE ARCHERY)

■ Atlanta is the only U.S. city where the public has access to learning Kyudo, a school of Japanese martial arts. Classes are offered at **Evening at Emory** (727-6000), **Georgia State Continuing Education** (651-3456) and **The Asia Center** (876-7260).

MARTIAL ARTS

■ Different schools of martial arts may be found in Atlanta, each having its own philosophy and style. Look in the *Yellow Pages* or *Creative Loafing* for listings of schools which offer karate and martial arts classes.

NEWSPAPERS, MAGAZINES, BOOKS, VIDEOS

PUBLICATIONS

■ *Yomiuri Shimbun*, the largest newspaper in Japan; *Asahi Shimbun*, the second largest newspaper; and *Nihon Keizai Shimbun*, a Japanese business publication, are all available at Japanese bookstores and groceries in Atlanta. *Yomiuri Shimbun* will even deliver the newspaper to your home. Call JETRO (681-0600) for more information.

■ Cobb International Center, Cobb Chamber of Commerce, Marietta (980-2000). The center's main goal is to serve the international business community in Cobb County. The center has published a brochure, *Family Orientation Guide,* which provides international newcomers with helpful information about living in Cobb County. A special edition exists for Japanese families listing resources of interest to the Japanese community in Cobb County. Free.

■ *SIMPLY JAPAN*, a quarterly newsletter published by the Consulate General of Japan (892-2700), contains news and announcements about the Japanese community, a calendar of upcoming events, and articles focusing on life in Japan. Free.

■ *GEORGIA Magazine's* "The Japanese Language Visitors and Business Guide to Georgia" (270-2854) is a comprehensive guide to Georgia containing advertisements and listings by Japanese restaurants, clubs, retail establishments and businesses. Although primarily written in Japanese, the guide may be useful in locating Japanese establishments in Georgia. Available at Japanese restaurants, grocery stores and retail establishments. Free.

■ *Mangajin*, P.O. Box 10443, Atlanta 30319, is an attractive magazine geared to those people interested in the Japanese language. The monthly publication, written in both English and Japanese, includes cartoons, stories, informative articles, tests and even information about Japanese language computer programs. Available by subscription at a cost of $30.00/year.

■ *The Southern Journal* (713/591-7877) is a Japanese community newspaper serving the southeast. Although the monthly newspaper is primarily written in Japanese, it is still helpful in locating Japanese restaurants and retail establishments. Available at Japanese restaurants, grocery stores and retail establishments. Free.

■ *Yellow Pages Japan in USA* (213/680-9101) is an up-to-date comprehensive guide, written in both Japanese and English, providing the telephone numbers and addresses of Japanese businesses, schools, markets, restaurants and professional services in the U.S. The section on Georgia is excellent. Available at Iwase Books and Nippan Daido grocery store for $23.50.

BOOKS & VIDEOS

■ The **Consulate General of Japan**, 100 Colony Square, Suite 2000, Atlanta (892-2700) has recently opened a Japanese Information Center in its offices, which in addition to providing a variety of information about Japan, houses a library of books, photography, films and videos about cultural and social aspects of Japan.

■ **The Dependable Bookman**, Mr. Woody Bates, 4010 Beechwood Dr., NW, Atlanta (237-0529) sells out-of-print and hard-to-find books about Asian history, culture, art, religion and philosophy, as well as books by and about Lafcadio Hearn, an American author who lived in Japan. The mail-order business has over 7,000 books in inventory and will conduct special interest searches. Call for a catalogue.

■ **Iwase Books**, 3400 Wooddale Dr. (Near Lenox Shopping Center), Atlanta (814-0462) is a modern Japanese book store featuring an extensive selection of Japanese newspapers, magazines, books, maps, posters, stationery, CDs, audio cassettes and rental videos.

■ **Nippan Daido U.S.A.**, 2390 Chamblee-Tucker Rd., Chamblee (455-3846), a Japanese grocery store, is jam-packed with a large selection of Japanese language newspapers, magazines, books, music and rental videos.

■ **Oxford Book Store**, 2345 Peachtree Rd., NE, Atlanta (364-2700) and 360 Pharr Rd., NE, Atlanta (262-3333); and **Borders Book Shop**, 3655 Roswell Rd., NE, Atlanta (237-0707) carry *The Japan Times — Weekly International Edition* and *The Asian World Street Journal.*

■ **Rainbow Video**, 6255 Peachtree Industrial Blvd., Doraville (454-7556) stocks thousands of rental videos, including a selection of Japanese television programs.

■ **Video Central Production**, 5345-I Jimmy Carter Blvd., Norcross (263-8388) has a selection of Japanese language rental videos.

shopping centers,
import stores, hotels

HOTELS

■ **Hotel Nikko Atlanta**, 3300 Peachtree Rd., NE, Atlanta (365-8100). Dispersed throughout the opulent Hotel Nikko (at the intersection of Peachtree and Piedmont Roads) is a collection of 125 pieces of Japanese art spanning three and one-half centuries. The lobby of the hotel overlooks a stunning Japanese water garden which may be the setting for afternoon tea or an elegant evening piano bar. Not surprisingly, many of the Asian associations hold their special events at the hotel. Hotel Nikko also houses Kamagowa, one of Atlanta's most praised Japanese restaurants; and Cassis, a

French-style restaurant. A small gift shop carries a selection of Japanese import items.

BONSAI

■ **Atlanta Bonsai Society** (434-9955). Members of the society meet monthly for meetings, lectures and demonstrations on bonsai. The society also sponsors a semi-annual Bonsai Show at the Atlanta Botanical Garden.

■ **Bonsai of Georgia**, 4096 Clairmont Rd., Chamblee (451-5356). The retail nursery sells bonsai trees, teaches classes and sponsors the annual Southeastern Bonsai Conference, which features a retail area selling bonsai plants, plant materials, tools, books, stands and accessories. Exhibits, lectures and demonstrations by experts from around the country are also offered at the conference.

■ **Monastery of the Holy Spirit**, Hwy. 212, Conyers (483-8705). The monks at this serene and beautiful monastery have, over the last two decades, mastered the art of bonsai and have a full greenhouse of bonsai plants for sale to the public.

■ Other retail nurseries have selections of bonsai trees for sale. A sampling: **Bonsai by the Potted Forest**, 805 Dickens Rd., Lilburn (564-0292); and **Bonsai Trees**, 352 South Atlanta St., Roswell (992-5356).

CHILDREN'S GIFTS

■ **Sanrio Surprises**, 4800 Briarcliff Rd. (Northlake Mall), Atlanta (939-7283); and **G. Whiskers**, 4400 Ashford-Dunwoody Rd. (Perimeter Mall), Atlanta (394-9293) are both colorful stores filled with Hello Kitty memorabilia and lots of very clever gift items for children by Sanrio of Japan. Local toy stores such as **The Toy Store**, 1544 Piedmont Rd. (Ansley Mall), Atlanta (875-1137) and 8560 Holcomb Bridge Rd. (Rivermont Square), Roswell (998-3094) also carry a full line of Sanrio gift items.

CUSTOM SCREENS,
JAPANESE CRAFTSMANSHIP & LANDSCAPING

■ **Shoji Custom Screens** (288-8125). Gene Riggins creates custom "rice-paper" screens for homes and restaurants and is a general contractor for Japanese-style construction.

■ **Sahara Japanese Architectural Woodworks**, 1716 Defoor Pl., NW, Atlanta (355-1976). The nationally known general contractor of Japanese-style restaurants, homes and rooms creates shoji screens, lamps, lanterns, garden bridges and pagodas. Many of Atlanta's Japanese restaurants have been designed by the firm.

FUTONS

■ Quite a few Atlanta area stores sell custom-made futons and frames. A sampling: **Dream Maker Futons**, 1144 Euclid Ave., Atlanta (523-1098); **Far East Futon Company**, 1451 Piedmont Ave., NE, Atlanta (874-0903); and **The Home Store**, 1154 Euclid Ave., Atlanta (586-9647).

GIFTS

■ **Akatory, U.S.A.**, 1893 Piedmont Rd., NE, Atlanta (876-3833). The large showroom displays an extensive selection of exquisite tableware from Japan, such as rice bowls, tea sets, saki sets, noodle bowls, dishes, vases and hibachi grills.

■ **Kutani Art U.S.A.**, 55 E. Andrews Dr., Atlanta (816-9606). The boutique specializes in a brightly colored pottery created for hundreds and hundreds of years in a small town near the Sea of Japan.

■ **Paces Paper, Inc. by Jackie**, 271 E. Paces Fery Rd., Atlanta (231-1111). The store sells Japanese hand-made paper and rice napkins.

HARDWARE/UTENSILS

■ **Highland Hardware**, 1034 N. Highland Ave., N.E., Atlanta (872-4466). The hardware store carries a selection of Japanese woodworking tools.

KAMADO (BARBECUE/SMOKERS)

■ **Pachinko House — Big Green Egg**, 3410 Clairmont Rd., Atlanta (321-4658). The unusual specialty store sells *kamado* (Japanese Barbecue/Smokers) and repairs *pachinko* (Japanese pinball) machines.

KIMONO DESIGNERS

■ **Tokyo Alterations & Gift Shop**, 4058 Peachtree Rd., NE, Atlanta (237-7063). The small store creates custom kimonos and alters men's and women's clothing. Often the store sells a selection of Japanese jewelry and small gift items.

■ Contact the **Japan-America Society of Georgia** (524-7399) for the names and telephone numbers of additional kimono designers.

BAKERIES

- **Joli-Kobe**, 5600 Roswell Rd., (Prado Shopping Center), Atlanta (843-3257). The highly praised Japanese/French bakery sells a selection of breads, croissants, tarts and gourmet pastries, blending Japanese and French cuisine-styles. A small luncheon area serves a light lunch fare of salads, meats and sandwiches.

GROCERIES

- **Kimlon Oriental Grocery & Gift**, 380 White Ave. (120 Loop), Marietta (424-7115). The Japanese grocery store stocks a full range of Japanese food products, including fresh produce, pickles, sauces, noodles, rice and a few small gifts.
- **Nippan Daido U.S.A.**, 2390 Chamblee-Tucker Rd. (Buford Hwy.), Chamblee (455-3846). The Japanese grocery store is jam-packed with a varied selection of Japanese foods, including fresh produce, frozen fish, pickled vegetables, snacks, sweets, kitchenware, household goods, gifts, newspapers, magazines, books, music and rental videos.
- The larger farmers markets and many of the Korean grocery stores carry a large selection of Japanese grocery products. A sampling: **Agnes Market**, 5210 Buford Hwy., Doraville (457-7911); **International Farmer's Market**, 5193 Peachtree Industrial Blvd., Chamblee (455-1777); and **Shop & Go**, 2595 Lawrenceville Hwy., Decatur (938-3754). Or stop by **Harry's Farmers Market**, 1180 Upper Hembree Rd., Roswell (664-6300) and 2025 Satellite Point, Duluth (416-6900) for a variety of fresh take-out sushi.

RESTAURANTS

*Hibachi-style or **teppanyaki-style** cooking refers to a combination of grilled vegetables, meat, chicken and seafood prepared at your table by a specially trained (and usually entertaining) chef.*

- **Arai Japanese**, 2055 Beaver Ruin Rd. (Indian Village Shopping Center), Norcross (246-0577). Traditional Japanese foods such as sushi, sashimi, tempura, noodles and teriyaki may be enjoyed at this authentic Gwinnett County restaurant. Open: Lunch and Dinner: Mon.-Sat.

■ **August Moon**, 5715 Buford Hwy. (1/4 mile outside I-285), Doraville (455-3464). The busy restaurant serves high-quality and unusual sushi (i.e. sea snails), as well as traditionally prepared entrees. Open: Lunch: Mon.–Fri.; Dinner: Mon.–Sat.

■ **Benihana**, 2143 Peachtree Rd. (Peachtree Park Dr.), Atlanta (355-8565) and 299 Peachtree St. (Peachtree Center — Cain Tower), Atlanta (522-9627). The national chain specializes in hibachi-style cooking at both locations. A well-stocked sushi bar is offered at the Peachtree Center restaurant. Open: Lunch: Mon.–Fri.; Dinner: Daily.

■ **Fujita Japanese Restaurant**, 5495 Jimmy Carter Blvd. (Oakbrook Shopping Center/1/2 mile east of I-85), Norcross (441-3663). Sushi, sashimi, udon and sesame chicken are house specialties at this charming restaurant. Open: Lunch and Dinner: Mon.–Sat.

■ **The Ginza Japanese Steak House**, 620 Crosstown Rd. (Kroger Shopping Center), Peachtree City (631-0005). Hibachi-style dining may be enjoyed at this southside Japanese restaurant. Open: Lunch: Mon.–Sat.; Dinner: Daily.

■ **Hama**, 2390 Chamblee-Tucker Rd. (Buford Hwy.), Chamblee (451-9883). This lovely restaurant is a favorite among the Japanese community. Try the attractive sushi bar, one of the traditionally prepared *nabemono* dishes (hot pot filled with vegetables and meat), delicious miso soup or one of the lacquer box specials for a sampling of different Japanese foods. Open: Lunch and Dinner: Tues.–Sun.

■ **Hashiguchi**, 3000 Windy Hill Rd. (Powers Ferry Rd.), Marietta (955-2337). A huge sushi bar makes this restaurant a must for sushi and sashimi connoisseurs. Traditional dining may also be enjoyed. Open: Lunch: Mon.–Fri.; Dinner: Daily.

■ **Ichiban Seafood & Steak House**, 151 Ellis St. (Courtland St.), Atlanta (659-7607). The hibachi-style Japanese restaurant offers selections of New York strip steak, filet mignon, shrimp, scallops, lobster and chicken. Open: Dinner: Daily.

■ **Kamogawa**, Hotel Nikko Atlanta, 3300 Peachtree Rd. (Piedmont Rd.), Atlanta (841-0314). Hotel Nikko's restaurant, built by temple craftsmen from Kyoto, is considered by some critics to be the most elegant in Atlanta. Both traditional and westernized Japanese dinners are served. The restaurant also offers Kaiseki, a 12–15 course dinner starting at $50.00/person. Special Sunday brunch. Open: Lunch and Dinner: Daily.

■ **Kamon**, 6050 Peachtree Pkwy. (Peachtree Corners), Norcross (449-0033). The restaurant prides itself on the extremely large sushi bar and traditional Japanese specialties, such as tempura, teriyaki, udon and sukiyaki. An all-you-can-eat buffet is offered every evening. Open: Lunch: Mon.–Fri.; Dinner: Mon.–Sat.

■ **Kobe Steak House**, 5600 Roswell Rd. (The Prado), Atlanta (256-0810). Hibachi-style Japanese meals are served at this exquisitely decorated Japanese restaurant. Open: Dinner: Daily.

■ **Koto**, 5269-3 Buford Hwy. (1/2 mile inside I-285), Doraville (451-1129). The new restaurant in Gojinka's former location at Pinetree Shopping Center serves traditional Japanese cuisine, as well as a large selection of sushi. Open: Dinner: Daily.

■ **Masa Japanese Restaurant and Sushi Bar**, 5920 Roswell Rd. (Parkside Shopping Center), Atlanta (256-0777). A well-stocked sushi bar and traditional Japanese cuisine are featured at this ultra-modern and friendly Sandy Springs restaurant. Open: Lunch: Mon.–Fri.; Dinner: Daily.

■ **Miki Japanese Restaurant**, 3330 Piedmont Rd. (across from Tower Place), Atlanta (261-6454). This beautiful restaurant, designed by Atlanta's Sahara Japanese Architectural Woodworks, features sushi, *nabemono dinners* (hot pot filled with vegetables and meat) and a *kushiyaki bar* (meat, chicken and seafood grilled by the chef to specification). Open: Lunch: Tues.–Fri.; Dinner: Tues.–Sun.

■ **Minato**, 2697 Spring Rd. (Cobb Pkwy.), Smyrna (432-6012). The relatively new restaurant serves a large selection of sushi and well-prepared traditional dishes, such as tempura, udon noodles, sukiyaki and teriyaki. Open: Lunch: Mon.–Fri.; Dinner: Daily.

■ **Misono Japanese Seafood Steakhouse**, 2500 Old Alabama Rd. (Holcomb Bridge Rd.), Roswell (993-3056). Hibachi-style dining and sushi may be enjoyed at this Japanese restaurant, formerly of the Tokyo Japanese Seafood Steakhouse chain. Open: Dinner: Daily.

■ **Mt. Fuji**, 180 Cobb Pkwy. (Marietta Trade Center), Marietta (428-0955). The restaurant serves meat, chicken, shrimp and vegetables prepared hibachi-style. Open: Dinner: Daily.

■ **Nakato**, 1776 Cheshire Bridge Rd. (Piedmont Rd.), Atlanta (873-6582). This Japanese restaurant continues to be a favorite among the tourist crowd who enjoy hibachi-style dining, the large sushi bar or traditional cuisine served in a private dining room.   The restaurant's new, attractive location overlooks a traditional Japanese garden setting. Open: Dinner: Daily.

■ **Nickiemoto's**, 247 Buckhead Ave. (Bolling Ave.), Atlanta (842-0334). Trendy sushi, tempura, teriyaki, hibachi steaks and other "East meets West" cuisine make this restaurant a popular dining spot among the Buckhead crowd. Critics rave about the Sizzling Catfish. Courtyard dining is available. Open: Dinner: Daily.

■ **Restaurant Suntory Atlanta**, 3847 Roswell Rd. (north of Piedmont Ave.),

Atlanta (261-3737). Traditional Japanese cuisine, hibachi-style dining and a large variety of sushi are served in dining rooms overlooking a traditional Japanese water garden, complete with a koi pond and waterfall. Open: Lunch: Mon.–Fri.; Dinner: Daily.

■ **Rising Star**, 1447 Peachtree St. (Pershing Point), Atlanta (875-8355). The California-style sushi bar and grill features innovative sushi combinations, soba, udon, calamari tempura and Pacific salmon. Open: Lunch: Mon.–Fri.; Dinner: Mon. –Sat.

■ **Ru Sans**, 1529 Piedmont Ave. (Monroe Dr.), Atlanta (875-7042). Traditional Japanese fare such as ramen, soba, udon, tempura and wafu-pizza offered at this restaurant operated by the very friendly former owner of Plums on Peachtree. Open: Lunch and Dinner: Daily.

■ **Sakana-ya**, 6241-A Peachtree Industrial Blvd. (Friday's Plaza at I-285), Doraville (458-0558). Atlanta's favorite Japanese restaurant, Gojinka, has reopened with a new name in a new location. You can chose between sitting at the *robata bar* (serving grilled meats and vegetables), at the sushi bar or in the large dining room which offers a full menu of traditional Japanese foods. Open: Lunch and Dinner: Wed.–Mon. (closed on Tuesday).

■ **Sakura Japanese Restaurant & Sushi Bar**, 4800 Lower Roswell Rd. (Johnson Ferry Rd.), Marietta (565-6369). This restaurant has a well-stocked sushi bar and serves a full selection of traditional Japanese fare. Open: Lunch: Tues.–Sat.; Dinner: Sun.–Sat.

■ **Satsuki Japanese Restaurant**, 3043 Buford Hwy. (north of N. Druid Hills Rd.), Atlanta (325-5285). Sushi and traditional Japanese meals are served in an authentic Japanese setting. Open: Dinner: Daily.

■ **Shiki**, 1492 Pleasant Hill Rd. (Club Dr.), Duluth (279-0097). The attractive, luxurious restaurant features hibachi-style dining, a sushi bar and a menu featuring traditional Japanese fare. Critics recommend the Sashimi Platter, Gyoza Dumplings and Grilled Salted Squid. Open: Lunch: Mon.–Fri.; Dinner: Mon.–Sat.

■ **Sushi-Huku**, 6300 Powers Ferry Rd. (Powers Ferry Plaza), Atlanta (956-9559). Japanese families enjoying a selection of sushi and traditionally cooked meals of udon, soba, teriyaki, tempura and sukiyaki may frequently be found at this small restaurant. Open: Dinner: Tues.–Sun.

■ **Teriyaki House**, 585 Franklin Rd. (Exit #112–South Loop), Marietta (499-8144). Traditional Japanese cuisine may be enjoyed, including tempura, udon, yakatori and teriyaki. The sushi bar opens at 5:00pm. Open: Lunch and Dinner: Mon.–Sat.

■ **Tokyo Japanese Seafood Steakhouse**, 1210 Rockbridge Rd. (Jimmy Carter

Blvd.), Norcross (381-6620); 3920 Canton Rd.(1/2 mile north of Chastain Rd./The Canton Promenade), Woodstock (928-9376); 1995 Windy Hill Rd. (1 mile west of Cobb Pkwy.), Marietta (438-1908); and 3230 Ga. 5 (south of I-20), Douglasville (489-1285). Hibachi-style dining and sushi may be enjoyed at these Japanese restaurants. Norcross and Marietta locations open: Lunch: Mon.–Fri.; Dinner: Daily. Woodstock and Douglasville locations open: Dinner: Daily.

■ **Toyo Ta Ya Japanese Buffet House**, 5082 Buford Hwy. (Shallowford Rd.), Doraville (986-0828). All-you-can-eat buffets feature sushi, noodle dishes, seafood, terriyaki and more. Open: Lunch and Dinner: Daily

■ **Tsukushi**, 2421 Cobb Pkwy. (Cumberland Square), Atlanta (955-2985). The small restaurant has been praised for its sushi, traditional grill menu and formal Kaiseki dinners (with advanced notice). Open: Lunch: Tues.–Sat.; Dinner: Tues.–Sun.

■ **Umezono**, 2086-B Cobb Pkwy. (Windy Hill Rd.), Smyrna (933-8808). The restaurant offers sushi, tempura, udon noodle soups and other traditional specialties, all at inexpensive prices. Open: Lunch and Dinner: Daily.

■ **Westin Peachtree Plaza Hotel**, The Café Restaurant, 210 Peachtree Rd. (International Blvd.), Atlanta (659-1400). The Café Restaurant serves an unusual treat — a traditional Japanese breakfast, complete with rice, pickled plums, seafood and green tea. Open: Breakfast: Daily (6:00am– 11:30am).

■ **Yakitori Den-Chan**, 3099 Peachtree Rd. (E. Paces Ferry Rd./Buckhead), Atlanta ((842-0270). Those who are wary of sushi bars may wish to try a *yakatori* bar featuring your choice of grilled skewered beef, chicken, seafood, tofu, and vegetables. Atlanta's food critics rave about these Japanese "kabobs." Open: Dinner: Tues.–Sun.

■ **Yokohama Japanese Restaurant**, 6280 Roswell Rd. (north of Johnson Ferry Rd.), Sandy Springs (255-4227). The restaurant features a sushi bar and traditional dishes, such as tempura, sukiyaki, teriyaki, noodles and sashimi. Kaiseki dinners (multi-course feasts) are available with advance notice. Open: Lunch: Tues.–Fri.; Dinner: Tues.–Sun.

KOREAN RESTAURANTS

■ Quite a few of Atlanta's Korean restaurants have attractive sushi bars stocking a complete selection of sushi and sashimi. A sampling: **Baek-Do Garden**, 5728 Buford Hwy. (Doraville Plaza), Doraville (457-8510); **Garam Korean Restaurant**, 5881 Buford Hwy. (north of I-285 at US 25), Doraville (454-9198); and **Mirror of Korea**, 1047 Ponce de Leon Ave. (Plaza Drugs/Highland Ave.), Atlanta (874-6243).

FAST FOOD

■ **Sumo**, 1170 Collier Rd. (Howell Mill Rd.), Atlanta (351-3999). Seven different styles of Japanese food are available for pick-up and delivery in limited areas. Open: Lunch: Mon.–Fri.; Dinner: Daily.

> ### ENTERTAINMENT:
> ### THEATRE, DANCE, MUSIC, CLUBS,
> ### FILMS, T.V. & RADIO, SPORTS

THEATRE, DANCE, MUSIC & FILMS

■ The Japan-America Society and the Consulate General of Japan sponsor a **Japanese Film Festival** (727-6562) and special cultural events at Emory University. For example, Emory recently hosted "Celebration of Japanese and American Music," a series of two concerts featuring Japanese and American conductors, pianists and composers. The concerts were accompanied by a master class on conducting by renowned Japanese conductor, **Nachiro Totsuka**.

■ Japanese performers may be enjoyed at other locations in Atlanta. A sampling: Seigakuin Atlanta International School where the **Ondekoza Japanese Drummers** have performed; 14th Street Playhouse where **UNO Man and Company**, a contemporary dance group from Japan was featured; Hotel Nikko which was the location for the performance of *Noh*, a traditional Japanese drama; and The Atlanta Dogwood Festival which featured **Issou Group**, a contemporary jazz ensemble and **Hyotoko Odori**, a seven-member theatrical troupe from Japan.

■ **Anime-x!!!** (364-9773) is Atlanta's Japanese animation fan organization. Call the 24-hour hotline for news and information about Japanese animation screenings in Atlanta.

T.V. & RADIO

■ **WPBA–TV Channel 30** broadcasts "Today's Japan," an English language Tokyo news program every weekday evening from 11:30pm–12midnight.

■ **WVEU–TV Channel 69** airs "Supertime," a Japanese language Tokyo news program every weekday morning from 7:00am–7:30am; and "600 Station," a Japanese language Tokyo news program daily from 7:30am–8:00am.

■ There are quite a few Japanese Cable Companies in Atlanta that either produce news programs or arrange for the production of Japanese films in Atlanta. Those interested should contact **Japan Cable Vision** (892-8244) or **Japan Channel, Inc.** (446-3111).

CLUBS & KARAOKE (SING-ALONG) BARS

■ **Hanamizuki,** 6265 Peachtree Industrial Blvd., Doraville (986-0444); and **Japanese Cafe Kojimachi**, 1475 Terrell Mill Rd., Marietta (850-1832) are Japanese karaoke bars that are open every evening.

■ **Japanese Conference Center Cotton House**, 3400 Wooddale Dr. (Near Lenox Shopping Center), Atlanta (841-0586) is an exclusive and expensive lounge containing VIP rooms, a conference area and a karaoke bar. Open Monday-Saturday evenings.

■ **Yaki Hana Oyster Cafe**, 3657 Chamblee-Dunwoody Rd. (Peachtree Industrial Blvd.), Chamblee (455-1163) is a karaoke bar serving Chinese and Korean snacks. Open every evening.

festivals & special events

MARCH

■ **Japan-America Society of Georgia Annual Dinner**, Hotel Nikko, Atlanta (524-7399). The society honors one outstanding member of the Japanese community and one outstanding American with the Mike Mansfield Award for their contributions toward better understanding between the cultures.

■ **Conyers Cherry Blossom Festival**, Conyers (922-1000). Japanese culture is featured at this annual festival celebrating the explosion of the pink blossoms of the Yoshino cherry tree. Events have included the Ondekoza Taiko drummers, Japanese tea ceremonies, martial arts seminars, exhibits of arts and crafts, and traditional food.

■ **Macon Cherry Blossom Festival**, Macon (912/751-7429). Japan and one or two other countries are featured during Macon's annual celebration of the blooming of over 130,000 pink and white Yoshino cherry trees. The city-wide festival features over 150 performers and demonstrators, as well as an international food fair. Yoshino cherry trees may be purchased at Central City Park in Macon throughout the festival.

SEPTEMBER

■ **Wok-A-Thon**, Hotel Nikko, Atlanta (365-8100). The American Institute of Wine and Food presents "Wok-A-Thon," a benefit featuring food prepared by the best Asian chefs of Atlanta. Approximately twenty different restaurants particiate, including many Japanese establishments.

OTHER

■ **JapanFest**, Atlanta (892-2700). Every few years, the Consulate General of Japan sponsors JapanFest, a month-long series of concerts, exhibits, films, and demonstrations celebrating the culture of Japan. Tea ceremonies, cooking demonstrations, doll shows, traditional dance and music, martial art demonstrations and storytelling are some of the featured events.

RESOURCES

■ **Consulate General of Japan**, 100 Colony Square, Suite 2000, Atlanta 30361 (892-2700); **Georgia-Nihonjin-Shokokai (Japanese Chamber of Commerce)**, 1230 Peachtree St., Suite 2440, Atlanta 30309 (876-7926); and **Japan External Trade Organization (JETRO)**, 245 Peachtree Center Ave., Suite 2102, Atlanta, Georgia 30303 (681-0600).

Practice session of one of the nine teams of the Atlanta Cricket Association.

The British Commonwealth Communities of Canada, Australia & New Zealand

HISTORY & NEIGHBORHOODS

The **Canadian** community in Atlanta is mainly a corporate community, which is not surprising since three-quarters of Canada's trade is with the U.S., and the largest single component of U.S. trade is with Canada. It is expected that Canada–U.S. trade will increase even more under the new Free Trade Agreement and create greater opportunities for Canadians to visit or temporarily reside in Atlanta. Not only does our country share a common history with its North American neighbor, but our cultures are so similar that many Canadian celebrities — artists, authors, performers, movie stars and sports figures — are often as familiar to us as our own. Atlanta-area galleries frequently exhibit works by Canadian artists; Canadian sports figures can be viewed on ESPN or even on regular network television; and Canadian entertainers, especially rock stars, may be enjoyed almost every week of the year at some location in Atlanta. We share so much in common with our neighbor to the north that differences are hardly noticed in social situations. Eh?

When thinking of **Australia** and **New Zealand**, most Atlantans probably think of the Melbourne Cup (horse racing), the Australian Open (tennis), cricket (Melbourne has a 100,000-capacity stadium), kangaroos, koalas, the Great Barrier Reef, a land of exotic beauty, aboriginal culture, and the outback. While this is certainly all a part of Australia and New Zealand, the countries have also made a cultural impact on Americans with, for example, films by Peter Weir, the actor Paul Hogan of *Crocodile Dundee* fame, and the versatile actors Judy Davis and Mel Gibson. The Australian community in Atlanta is quite small, but it has strong corporate ties, since Australian business people were wooed to Atlanta during the late 1970s and early 1980s when the economy of Atlanta was booming. As with most transplanted people, the new immigrants experienced some culture shock, so the Australian Women's Association was formed in 1991 to provide support and friendship for women from "down under."

ATTRACTIONS

■ **Zoo Atlanta**, 800 Cherokee Ave., SE, Atlanta (624-5678). In the spring of 1992, the zoo featured koalas (an aborigine term meaning "no drink") on loan from the San Diego Zoo. Plans are underway to develop a permanent habitat at Zoo Atlanta for some of these marsupials from Eastern Australia's eucalyptus forests. The number of koalas living in the wild is dwindling, and Zoo Atlanta could become part of a world-wide breeding and conservation effort.

COMMUNITY, RELIGIOUS & CULTURAL ASSOCIATIONS

CANADIAN

■ **Canadian-American Society of the Southeastern United States** (221-0617). The society primarily serves as a Chamber of Commerce for Canada, promoting business opportunities between the Southeastern States and Canada. Approximately 300 members participate in the society's monthly programs which feature guest speakers involved in trade and business. The society also sponsors social events, such as golf outings, formal dinner parties, picnics and holiday celebrations. The quarterly newsletter, *Can-Am News,* is an excellent source of information about Canadian community events.

■ **Canadian Consulate General**, One CNN Center, Suite 400, South Tower, Atlanta 30303 (577-6810). The consulate primarily functions as an official Canadian governmental office for the Southeast region of the United States, but it often cosponsors business, cultural and social events in Atlanta.

■ **Canadian Women's Club** (662-0668). The Canadian Women's Club is a social and charitable organization which hosts monthly get-togethers, special social events, and participates in Atlanta-area charitable events such as the annual Festival of Trees.

■ **Quebec Government Office**, 245 Peachtree Center Ave., NE, Marquis Tower One, Suite 1650, Atlanta 30303 (880-0250). The office's primary function is the promotion of business between the Southeast region of the United States and the province of Quebec. The office is also a good starting point for finding out information (other than tourist) about Quebec. The office occasionally hosts social and cultural activities in Atlanta pertaining to Quebec and cosponsors a French-Canadian film festival at Emory University with the Alliance Française.

AUSTRALIAN

■ **Australian Women's Association** (457-8734). Australian natives and nationals will find support and friendship in this group that meets on the 26th day of each month. (The British founded Australia on January 26, 1788.) The women celebrate Australia Day, the Melbourne Cup, and ANZAC Day (American-New Zealand Army Corps), and engage in charitable activities, such as the Festival of Trees and distributing Tucker Boxes (similar to CARE packages) to needy families. So far, the association has located about 50 Australian-born women now living in Atlanta and encourages other Australian women to get in touch with the group.

BRITISH COMMONWEALTH

■ **Daughters of the British Empire** (482-7252). The social and philanthropic society is open to female citizens of the British Commonwealth (including Canada, Australia and New Zealand), as well as their proven ancestors. Chapters of the club meet monthly and engage in fund-raising activities to support homes for the elderly in the U.S.

schools, classes, language

■ **Quebec Government Office** (880-0250). The office facilitates a summer exchange program for American university-level French teachers offering them an opportunity to study French in Quebec. The office will also assist French teachers in the Southeast (at all academic levels) in procuring books, brochures, videos and field-trip information about Quebec for educational purposes (not tourist information).

■ **International Education Forum**, 540 Cornwallis Way, Fayetteville (461-4599 or 800/346-1816). Approved by the Council on Standards of Educational

Travel, this forum arranges high school foreign exchange student programs. Among other activities, American students may attend school-year programs of varying lengths in Australia.

NEWSPAPERS, MAGAZINES, BOOKS, VIDEOS

CANADA

■ **The Canadian-American Society of the Southeastern United States** (221-0617) publishes *Can-Am News*, a quarterly newsletter with information about the Canadian-American business community, upcoming social events, and announcements of interest to the Canadian community.

■ **Oxford Book Store**, 2345 Peachtree Rd., NE, Atlanta (364-2700) and 360 Pharr Rd., NE, Atlanta (262-3333); and **Borders Book Shop**, 3655 Roswell Rd., NE, Atlanta (237-0707) often carry the Saturday edition of the *Toronto Star*.

AUSTRALIA & NEW ZEALAND

■ **Oxford Book Store**, 2345 Peachtree Rd., NE, Atlanta (364-2700) and 360 Pharr Rd., NE, Atlanta (262-3333) carries *The Weekend Australian, The Sydney Morning Herald* and *The New Zealand Herald* newspapers. **Borders Book Shop**, 3655 Roswell Rd., NE, Atlanta (237-0707) carries *The Weekend Australian* and *The Sydney Morning Herald*. **BookStar**, 4101 Upper Roswell Rd. Marietta (578-4455) stocks Australian fashion magazines.

SHOPPING CENTERS, IMPORT STORES, HOTELS

■ **Shepard's of Australia**, 3393 Peachtree Rd. (Lenox Square), Atlanta (239-9330). The store features colorful, exquisitely designed Australian women's clothing. Equally impressive is the fact that the store's owner won a top award in Australia for her exporting business.

GROCERIES, MARKETS, BAKERIES

There are no groceries, markets or bakeries in Atlanta that specialize in food products indigenous to Australia, New Zealand or Canada. However, occasionally one may find crackers imported from New Zealand, chocolate covered macadamia nuts imported from Australia, and other items in Atlanta delicatessens and farmers markets. Canadian bottled water has also recently emerged in Atlanta groceries, and the flavored drinks are competing well with bottled waters from European countries.

RESTAURANTS

No authentic Australian, New Zealand, or Canadian restaurants are located in Atlanta. **Outback Steakhouse** 2700 Delk Rd. (Powers Ferry Rd.), Marietta (850-9182); 4800 Lawrenceville Hwy. (Hwy. 29/Indian Trail Rd.), Lithonia (381-7744); and 2145 LaVista Rd. (Toco Hills/N. Druid Hills Rd.) (636-5110), an Australian-themed chain restaurant, has proven to be quite popular, serving steak, chops, chicken, seafood, "Aussie chips" and "walkabout soup." Several more Outback restaurants are planned for the metro Atlanta area. Open: Dinner: Daily.

ENTERTAINMENT: THEATRE, DANCE, MUSIC, CLUBS, FILMS, T.V. & RADIO, SPORTS

THEATRE, DANCE & MUSIC

■ Canadian performing artists frequently visit Atlanta, such as the **National Arts Centre Orchestra,** which recently performed at Symphony Hall as part of the Great Performers Series; **Dynamo Theatre**, which performed at the Arts Festival of Atlanta; **Sheelagh Keeley**, who performed in Nexus Contemporary Art Center's Fall Solo Series; and **Canada's Royal Winnipeg Ballet,** which performed at the Fox Theatre in 1991 and 1992 as part of the Coca-Cola International Series. Also, don't miss the award-winning **Cirque du Soleil**, Montreal's internationally acclaimed theatrical circus without animals, featuring a 90-member troupe of tumblers, contortionists, clowns, acrobats, and musicians, in a series of dramatic scenes set to an original rock-jazz score. The circus often sets up its colorful, climate-controlled tent in midtown Atlanta and hopes to make Atlanta a regular stop on its annual tour. **The Royal New Zealand Ballet** is scheduled to perform at the Fox Theatre in 1993.

- **Kele's Pacific Paradise** (469-6292) performs authentic songs and dances from several Pacific islands, including New Zealand.

FILMS

- **French-Canadian Films** sponsored by the Quebec Government Office, the Alliance Française and other French-speaking communities are frequently screened at Emory University and other locations in Atlanta as part of the Francophone Film Series.

SPORTS

- Atlantan's have become quite familiar with the outstanding **Toronto Blue Jays,** who clinched the baseball World Series Championship in 1992 by defeating our terrific Braves. Another Canadian baseball team, the Montreal Expo's, sometimes play at Atlanta Fulton County Stadium. For the last few years, enterprising Canadian football fans have arranged to have live satellite feed of **Canadian Football League** games at local sports bars, including the broadcasting of the **Grey Cup Game**, the Canadian Football League's championship competition. Contact the Canadian-American Society for information about locations for this year's broadcasts.
- **Atlanta Cricket Club** (971-6097/381-0727/447-9248). Cricket is a very popular sport in Australia, and natives are welcome to join the Atlanta Cricket Club, whose members include British expatriates, Indians, Pakistanis, South Africans and West Indians. The club began in 1989 and has already grown from just two teams to nine. Games are held every Sunday, May–October, at four fields in metro-Atlanta.

FESTIVALS & SPECIAL EVENTS

JANUARY

- **Maple Leaf Ball**, Canadian-American Society (221-0617). The society sponsors an annual "black-tie" dinner dance for the Canadian community and its friends, celebrating understanding, good will, and business relationships between Canada and the Southeast.
- **Australia Day**, Australian Women's Association (457-8734). January 26th is Australia Day, and this association welcomes members of the Australian community to get in touch with the organization so Australians may celebrate the holiday together.

JULY

- **Canada Day** (221-0617). The Canadian-American Society arranges for an "Old South" picnic as part of the Canadian Independence Day celebration. Festivities include dining on barbecue and other southern foods, sports events and lots of patriotic fun.

OCTOBER

- **Canadian Consul General's Annual Reception at the Official Residence** (221-0617). The consul general hosts an annual reception for members of the Canadian community and the Canadian-American Society.

RESOURCES

CANADIAN

- **Canadian Consulate General**, One CNN Center, Suite 400, South Tower, Atlanta 30303 (577-6810) and **Government of Ontario Ministry of Industry, Trade & Technology**, SE Regional Office, 1100 Circle 75 Pkwy., Suite 620, Atlanta 30339 (956-1981).

AUSTRALIAN

- **Australian-American Chamber of Commerce**, Peachtree Place Tower, 999 Peachtree St., Suite 1400, Atlanta 30303 (870-6234).

Mario Peralta performs at Atlanta's Hispanic festival.

hispanic
communities

HISTORY & NEIGHBORHOODS

The Spanish *entrada* (invasion) was the first European exploration of the southeastern United States, with the first settlement being established in St. Augustine, Florida. The *conquistador* Hernando De Soto, who made his way into Georgia in 1540, was probably the first European in the state. He came through Georgia on his way from Florida to the Misissippi River with his army, priests, servants and Indian slaves. Although he did not find the gold he sought, missing Dahlonega by just a few miles, the actions of De Soto's men (and Europeans before and after) had a devastating effect on the Native Americans by bringing hitherto unknown diseases to the continent. King Philip II of Spain claimed all of what is now the southeastern portion of the U. S. for Spain. Then the French settlers arrived in 1564, but King Philip sent in Pedro Menendez de Aviles in 1565, who successfully drove them out. For almost two hundred years, Spain was dominant; but in 1732, King George II of England granted a charter for Georgia to become a colony, and that effectively ended all Spanish claims.

To mark the 450th anniversary of De Soto's invasion of Georgia, former governor Joe Frank Harris created The De Soto Trail Commission to identify the route of De Soto's expedition across the state by establishing appropriate commemorative markers for easy identification by motorists. This trail, beginning in Augusta and going through Milledgeville, Macon, Americus, Albany and Thomasville, is now complete and connected to the trail in Florida. In the works is a bill calling for a nationally designated De Soto Trail.

In our time, a large and proud Hispanic population has made significant contributions to Atlanta. ("Hispanic" is a term that commonly refers to people from 22 Spanish-speaking countries, including Spain.) Members of the

Hispanic community have attained positions of respect and power, not only within their own community, but in the larger Atlanta community. Two stand-outs are Robert Goizueta, a native of Cuba, who is CEO and Chair of the Board of Coca-Cola Company; and Alfredo Duarte, a native of Cuba, who is an international media analyst at the Carter Center and commentator on North and South American television. Thousands of women and men have developed successful small businesses that enrich the larger Atlanta community. Atlanta Mayor Maynard Jackson recently designated May 18 as Hispanic-American Day, to honor, respect and bolster the image of Hispanics in Atlanta.

The Hispanic population in the five county Atlanta metro area has nearly tripled since 1980 and continues to grow. U.S. Census data indicates there are over 58,000 members of the community, though many sources suggest the population is traditionally undercounted and estimate the population to be anywhere from 90,000 to 150,000. The largest groups are Mexican (about 43,000), Cuban (about 18,000), Colombian (about 16,000) and Puerto Rican (about 8,500).

Families of Hispanic heritage are dispersed throughout Atlanta, although DeKalb County has about 34 percent of the residents and the largest numbers of any county in Georgia (about 15,700). The highest concentrations of Hispanics are in census tracts in South Atlanta near the federal penitentiary, DeKalb Peachtree Airport (Chamblee), and Lindbergh Plaza, but these neighborhoods represent only a small fraction of all Hispanic residents in the metro area.

MUSEUMS & GALLERIES

■ **Center for Puppetry Arts Museum**, 1404 Spring St., Atlanta (874-0398). This museum features one of the largest exhibits of puppets in North America and includes pre-Colombian clay puppets and puppets from South America. Hours: Mon.–Sat. 9:00am–4:00pm, and evenings on performance nights. Admission fee.

■ **Centro Cultural de Mexico**, 3220 Peachtree Rd., NE, Atlanta (264-1240). The art gallery is run by the Friends of Mexico with the support of the Mexican Consulate and features exhibits, as well as conferences and symposia, relating to the history and culture of Mexico. Hours: Mon.–Fri. 10:00am–6:00pm. Free.

■ **Consulate of Mexico**, One CNN Center, 410 South Tower, Atlanta (688-3258). The waiting room at the consulate displays works by Mexican artists. Hours: Mon.–Fri. 9:00am–4:00pm. Free.

■ **High Museum of Art**, Robert Woodruff Arts Center, 1280 Peachtree St., NE, Atlanta (892-HIGH). Spanish paintings are part of the museum's permanent European collection and some are usually on exhibit. Hours: Tues., Wed., Thurs. and Sat. 10:00am–5:00pm; Fri., 10:00am–9:00pm; and Sun. 12noon–5:00pm. Admission fee.

■ **Michael C. Carlos Museum** (formerly Emory University Museum of Art and Archaeology), Main Quadrangle, 571 Kilgo Cir., Decatur (727-7522). The permanent collection includes pre-Colombian Indian artifacts from North and South America. Hours: Tues.–Sat. 10:00am–4:30pm; Sun. 12noon–5:00pm. Free, but a donation of $3.00 is suggested.

■ **Folk Art Imports Gallery**, 25 Bennett St., A-1, Atlanta (352-2656). The gallery has a wonderful selection of international art, with a heavy concentration of South American arts and crafts. Included are folk and tribal arts, textiles, beadwork, pottery, baskets, masks and jewelry. Hours: Sun., Thurs. and Fri. 12 noon–5:00pm; Mon., Tues., Wed. and Sat. 11:00am–5:00pm.

■ Keep an eye on other Bennett Street galleries. Recently, **Novus Gallery** (355-4074) was host to six Argentine artists sponsored by the Argentine Consulate of Atlanta; **TULA Foundation Gallery** (351-3551) showcased works by nine Venezuelan painters; and **New Visions Gallery** (874-3881) held an exhibition, "Latin American Women: Beyond Labels," that received rave reviews for talented, burgeoning Atlanta artists.

■ Other museums & galleries: **Atlanta International Museum of Art**, Marquis Two Tower, 289 Peachtree Center Ave., Atlanta (688-2467) frequently showcases Hispanic art as diverse as "Guatemala: Artistic Traditions and Spanish Influences" and "Woodcarvers of Oaxaca"; **Emory Framing & Gallery**, 2126 N. Decatur Rd., Atlanta (634-6568) featured "Mexico, or there abouts," which included photos, prints and sculpture; **Nexus Gallery**, Nexus Contemporary Arts Center, 535 Means St., NW, Atlanta (688-1970) is committed to exhibiting high-quality contemporary art from diverse cultures, and, to this end, featured a retrospective of works by Luis Camnitzer, a Uruguayan conceptual artist, and an exhibit of contemporary Mexican photography; **High Museum at Georgia-Pacific Center**, 133 Peachtree St., NW, Atlanta (577-6940), a frequent host of works by international artists, exhibited paintings by Jorge Tacla, held a Latin Christmas celebration and screened a film on Chilean folk artists; and **Urban Nirvana Gallery & Gardens**, 15 Waddell St., NE, Atlanta (688-3329) celebrated the Mexican festival of Our Lady De Guadalupe.

BOLIVIAN COMMUNITY

■ **Asociación Boliviana de Atlanta** (373-2985/923-0709). This group was formed in November of 1991 as a social and cultural organization.

BRAZILIAN COMMUNITY

■ **La Sociedad Brasileña-Americana (Brazilian-American Society of Atlanta)** (351-6791). The society was formed in the fall of 1990 to provide people with information about Brazil and to promote the culture of Brazil though the sponsorship of various cultural events, such as the Brazilian carnival held in February, the "Festa do Sabado de Alleluia," June's "Festa Junina," and dances with Brazilian music. The society also provides business consulting and publishes a monthly newsletter. There are approximately 500 Brazilian families in metropolitan Atlanta with many residing in Sandy Springs and East Cobb.

CUBAN COMMUNITY

■ **Club Cubano de Atlanta (Cuban Club)**, 5797 New Peachtree Rd., Doraville (451-3477). This social and cultural club was founded over ten years ago to promote Hispanic literature in its monthly meetings. Members plan social and cultural activities throughout the year, provide a cafeteria and restaurant to members in the building on Friday, Saturday and Sunday, and publish a monthly bulletin. The club welcomes other Hispanics and currently has members who are natives of Argentina, Puerto Rico, and Colombia.

ECUADORIAN COMMUNITY

■ **Asociación Ecuadoriana de Georgia (Ecuadorian Association of Georgia)** (498-5482). People of Ecuadorian heritage socialize through this association and participate in educational and cultural activities, including celebrating Ecuador's Independence Day each August.

MEXICAN COMMUNITY

■ **Amigos de México (Friends of Mexico)** (688-3278). Initiated by the Consulate of Mexico in Atlanta the group solicited interest in and money for the Mexican Cultural Center in Atlanta and continues to support Mexican culture through social events and the arts. The organization is made up of both natives and others who are interested in Mexico.

■ **Centro Cultural de Mexico**, 3220 Peachtree Rd., NE, Atlanta (264-1240). The center is supported by the Friends of Mexico and the Mexican Consulate and features conferences and symposia relating to the history and culture of Mexico, hosts celebrations, such as el Día de los Muertos, and houses an art gallery.

■ **La Asociación de la Comunidad Mexicana (ACM)** (264-1240). The association hosts special celebrations and has an education committee that provides adult education courses, student scholarships and student cultural exchange programs. The group celebrates Independence Day in a big way, with a float in the downtown Atlanta parade which includes mariachis, la Reina de las Fiestas Patrias Mexicanas, folk dancers, and children wearing traditional dress. The organization also celebrates el Día de los Muertos.

PANAMANIAN COMMUNITY

■ **La Sociedad Panameña de Atlanta, Georgia, Inc. (Panamanian Society)** (284-3434). The society hosts a Panamanian Independence Day Celebration and Scholarship Drive in November to provide scholarships for high school seniors who are Panamanian natives or of Panamanian descent.

PERUVIAN COMMUNITY

■ **Cambio 90** (292-1903). This is a Peruvian organization dedicated to aiding Peru.

■ **Honorable Society of the Friends of Perú**, (727-6562). The non-profit group sponsors the Peruvian-American Institute at Emory University and seeks to improve international cooperation between the U.S. and Peru.

■ **La Unión Peruano-Americana de Atlanta (Peruvian Association of Atlanta)** (986-0058). Monthly luncheons are held the first Sunday of each month after Spanish Mass at Christ the King Cathedral, 2699 Peachtree Rd., Atlanta at 2:30pm. The group also celebrates Peruvian holidays and supports relief efforts for Peru.

PUERTO RICAN COMMUNITY

■ **Asociación Puertorriqueño de Atlanta (Atlanta Puerto Rican Association)** (436-5750). This is a social, civic and cultural organization for the approximately 8,500 Puerto Ricans living in Atlanta. Anyone interested in Puerto Rico is welcome.

■ **Puertorriqueños Americanos en Georgia, Inc. (Puerto Rican Americans)**

(394-5025). Among its activities, the association supports social services organizations and sponsors dances.

URUGUAYAN COMMUNITY

■ **El Club Social Deportivo Uruguayo Charrúa** (454-6264). Named after an indigenous tribe in Uruguay, the new social club expects to create a Uruguayan *fútbol* team and open a restaurant that will serve typical Uruguayan and other Latin American food.

LATIN-WIDE ASSOCIATIONS

■ **Casa Cultural Iberoamericana** (351-1034/237-7899). Spanish language classes are offered by this group, which also promotes the arts of Latin America and Spain.

■ **Círculo de Arte Latinoamericano (Latin American Art Circle)** (892-3600, ext. 321). The Art Circle is part of the Twentieth Century Art Society of the High Museum of Art and sponsors various artists and events at the museum, such as the Latin American Film Festival held in November.

■ **El Círculo Hispanoamericano de Atlanta (Hispanic-American Circle of Atlanta)** (438-7575). The social and cultural club celebrated its 50th anniversary in 1991! It was founded to promote and promulgate the Spanish language by providing a forum for Spanish-speaking people from Latin American countries to come together and study the language and enjoy social and cultural activities. Members wish to improve communication and understanding between American and Hispanic cultures in Atlanta. Currently about 300 families, many bicultural, are members. The club hosts two theatrical and dance works each year, in addition to smaller events, such as fashion shows.

■ **Georgia Partners of the Americas** (525-1168). This organization hosts hundreds of events throughout the year which bring people of South and North America together. A recent event was "Festa De São Joao," a Brazilian thanksgiving of harvest commemorating St. John.

■ **Image** (266-1956). The Greater Atlanta Chapter of Image seeks to support the civil rights of Hispanics and improve educational and employment opportunities. Image hosts the Metro Atlanta Hispanic Image Debutante Ball in October.

■ **Juventud Católica Hispana de Atlanta** (888-7839/498-7811) This Catholic youth group raises money for its missionary work in Mexico through various activities, such as theatrical performances.

■ **League of United Latin American Citizens (LULAC)** (928-3331/289-0948).

208

The organization provides scholarships to Hispanic college students and lobbies on issues affecting Hispanics, such as education, housing and women's issues. Meetings are held monthly on the third Thursday.

RELIGIOUS ORGANIZATIONS

Catholic Churches have traditionally been a focal point for the Hispanic community — a place for social, cultural and religious group meetings, and the location for many celebrations and festivals. In Atlanta there are 20 Hispanic Churches and over 30 English-speaking churches which have masses in Spanish. Of course Hispanics in Atlanta are represented in various Protestant denominations, especially Baptist, Mormon and Jehovahs Witness. A comprehensive listing of these churches may be found in the *Mundo Hispánico Directory* and *Páginas Amarillas Hispanas*. There are also about 100 Sephardic Jews from Spain who attend the Or VeShalom Synagogue, speak Ladino and maintain the culture of their origin. Listed here is a random sampling of religious institutions in various locales:

■ **Centro Católico Chamblee**, 5726-C New Peachtree Rd., Chamblee (454-8437); **Christ the King**, 2699 Peachtree Rd., NE, Atlanta (233-2145); **Immaculate Heart of Mary**, 2855 Briarcliff Rd., NE, Atlanta (636-1418); **Briarlake Congregación Hispana Bautista**, 3715 LaVista Rd., Decatur (634-2460); **Iglesia Bautista Hispana Americana**, 4109 Burns Rd., Lilburn, (381-8032); **Primera Congregación Hispana Bautista de College Park**, 1773 Hawthorne Ave., College Park (231-0254); **Corpus Christi Church**, 600 Mountain View Dr., Stone Mountain (469-0395); and **Holy Family Church**, 3401 Lower Roswell Rd., SE, Marietta (971-6580).

schools, classes, language

SCHOOLS

■ **DeKalb Center for Community Television** (378-6294). The center offers seminars in editing, directing and documentaries. Students may produce a program in Spanish or English on a wide range of subjects, such as community services, filming a theatrical performance, or creating a production for non-Hispanic audiences informing them about Hispanic culture.

■ **Hooper Alexander Elementary School**, 3414 Memorial Dr., Decatur (289-1933). Hooper is the location of the DeKalb County Public School System Spanish Language Magnet Program.

LANGUAGE CLASSES

■ **Artplay, Inc.**, 595 Piedmont Ave., NE, Atlanta (607-9660). Artplay offers an after-school Spanish language program for children ages 5 and older. It cosponsors a children's summer camp program at the International School for children ages 4 and older.

■ **Casa Cultural Iberoamericana** (237-7899). Call for information on private tutoring in Spanish.

■ **Latin American Association (Asociación Latinoamericana)**. Lindbergh Plaza: 2581 Piedmont Rd., Suite C1145, Atlanta (526-4603) and Gwinnett Service Center: 318 W. Pike St., Suite 410, Lawrenceville (339-4335). The association offers language classes in both Spanish and English.

■ Atlanta area colleges and universities offer daytime and evening courses in Spanish and Portuguese. A sampling: **Georgia State University, North Metro Center** (651-3456) occasionally offers classes for children in the Spanish language. For information on courses specially designed in English for Spanish-speaking business people, call 651-3650. They also have a study abroad program through the International Intercultural Studies Program (651-2450). Also, **DeKalb College** (551-3064), **Evening At Emory** (727-6000); and **Kennesaw State College** (423-6765) may offer evening Spanish and Portuguese classes to the general public..

■ Many **churches** that serve the Hispanic community offer free courses in English language.

SPANISH CONVERSATION GROUPS

■ **Freight Room Restaurant**, 301 East Howard Ave., Decatur (681-3560). On Monday at 6:30pm native speakers and students at all levels meet in a relaxed atmosphere and converse in Spanish.

■ **Tapatío Restaurant**, 1091 Euclid Ave., Little 5 Points, Atlanta (221-0265). Folks gather to practice Spanish every Friday at 6:30 pm.

OTHER CLASSES

■ **Capoeira Lessons**, Arts Exchange, 750 Kalb Ave., Atlanta (365-0675). Classes in this unique Brazilian art form are offered weekly.

■ **Mexican Folkloric Classes**, St. Lucas Episcopal Church, 435 Peachtree St., NE, Atlanta (248-0540). Saturday classes for children are led by Rolando Camacho, the choreographer of the Mexican Folkloric Ballet of Atlanta.

NEWSPAPERS

■ *El Nuevo Día*, 3754 Buford Hwy., Suite A-4, Atlanta (320-7766). Published biweekly in Atlanta, the newspaper is "Georgia's Bilingual Hispanic Newspaper," reporting on issues affecting the broad-based Hispanic community and devoting a couple of pages to local news. Free. Subscription rate is $25/yr.

■ *Mundo Hispánico*, P.O. Box 13808, Atlanta 30324-08008 (881-0441). The bilingual newspaper of the Hispanic Community in Atlanta presents local news, news in brief from various Latin American countries, and a calendar of events. It is published the first and fifteenth of each month and may be found at some libraries, Latin grocery stores, restaurants and bookstores. Free. Subscription rate is $30/yr.

■ *Los Primos*, 3949 Doral Circle, Doraville (455-1381/457-7210). *Los Primos* is a weekly newspaper written in Spanish that publishes news and information of interest to the Mexican community in Atlanta. There is a column for children which communicates the customs of Mexico and enriches children's understanding and appreciation of the Spanish language, spoken by about 400 million people. Articles on the history of the indigenous culture of Mexico appear, such as a recent one on the pyramids. Other topics have been Mexican current events, sports, films, immigration, and recent social and cultural events in Atlanta. Available at some Latin grocery stores. Free.

■ *Iberoamerica En Primera Plana*, 3808 Centennial Trail, Atlanta (448-9103). The Spanish language newsletter is a source of Latin American current events for residents of Atlanta and is available at some Latin grocery stores. Free.

■ *El Deportivo*. The Spanish language newspaper reports on league sports, especially fútbol's La Liga Latinoamericana de Fútbol and soccer's Suramérica team.

■ Spanish language newspapers from various Latin American countries are sold at many grocery stores, such as **Las Américas** and **Los Latinos**. **Oxford Book Store**, 360 Pharr Rd., Atlanta (262-3333) and 2345 Peachtree Rd., Atlanta (364-2700) usually carries *Cuba Internacional, Lo Mejor, Proceso, El Pais, El Cambio, Tiempo, Cuba Update* and the literary *Review: Latin American Literature and Arts*. **Borders Book Shop**, 3655 Roswell Rd., NE, Atlanta (237-0707) frequently carries a newspaper from Spain. Call ahead to find out if the paper you are interested in is available.

■ **Atlanta-Fulton Public Library**, 1 Margaret Mitchell Square, Atlanta (730-4636). The library maintains over 2,600 books by Spanish authors, as well as works translated into Spanish on a wide range of subjects.

■ **Cuban Club of Atlanta**, 5797 New Peachtree Rd., Doraville (381-6057). The club maintains over 600 books for adults and children, including books on Cuban history and geography, Spanish language books and Spanish classics for club members.

■ *Directorio Hispano De Atlanta (Hispanic Directory of Atlanta)*, published annually by Mundo Hispánico, Inc. (881-0441). The directory provides information on Hispanic businesses, social service agencies, social, cultural and civic organizations, churches and more. Free.

■ **Library of the Mexican Consulate in Atlanta**, 1 CNN Center, 410 South Tower (688-3258). The library carries over 2,500 books in Spanish on a wide range of subjects, including economics and literature, and Mexican newspapers and magazines.

■ *Páginas Amarillas Hispanas (Hispanic Yellow Pages)*, published annually by Casablana Publishing, Inc. (413-1431). The directory is a compilation of information about Atlanta's Hispanic organizations, facts about Latin countries, and listings of commercial services. Free.

■ Some bookstores in Atlanta carry a few novels or children's books in Spanish, such as: **Oxford Book Store**, 360 Pharr Rd., Atlanta (262-3333) and 2345 Peachtree Rd., Atlanta (364-2700); **Borders Book Shop**, 3655 Roswell Rd., NE, Atlanta (237-0707); **BookStar**, 4101 Roswell Rd., NE, Marietta (578-4455); and **Children's Book & Gift Market**, 375 Pharr Rd., NE, Atlanta (261-3442). The titles they carry seem to be continually growing in number.

VIDEOS

■ Videos can be rented at numerous locations throughout Atlanta. The following is but a sample of what is available: **All Star Video — La Casa de la Música Latina**, 1871 Cobb Pkwy., SE, Marietta (951-1002); 2581 Piedmont Rd., (Sidney Marcus Blvd.), Atlanta (231-5884); 5265 Jimmy Carter Blvd. (Cedar Village), Norcross (447-4037); and 5000 Buford Hwy. (Flea Market), Chamblee (455-1580); **Atlanta-Fulton Public Library**, 1 Margaret Mitchell Square, Atlanta (730-4636) (maintains about 150 videos in Spanish); **3 V Video Movie Rental**, 2049 Sylvan Rd., SW, Atlanta (753-6677); and **Música Latina y Videos**, 5280-F Buford Hwy. (Pinetree West Shopping Center), Chamblee (455-1580).

■ Many grocery stores have a selection of videos and cassettes, such as: **Diaz**

Market, 368 5th Street, NE, Atlanta (872-0846/875-6568); **El Norteñita**, 5522 New Peachtree Rd., Suite D-1, Chamblee (451-6971); **El Rinconcito**, 2845 Buford Hwy., Atlanta (636-8714); **El Tío**, 6065 S. Norcross-Tucker Rd. (near Jimmy Carter Blvd.), Norcross (939-7474); and **Los Latinos**, 438 N. Indian Creek, Clarkston (297-7753).

sbopping centers, import stores, botels

- **Cotton Salsa**, 4400 Ashford-Dunwoody Rd. (Perimeter Mall), Atlanta; Upper Alabama St., Underground Atlanta (659-4133); 3393 Peachtree Rd. (Lenox Square), Atlanta (816-3019); and 1000 Cumberland Mall, Atlanta (438-0694). The shop carries brightly colored handwoven textiles from Guatemala and Peru.
- **Dolci's Shoes**, 1420 Cumberland Pkwy., NW, Atlanta (435-8658); 3393 Peachtree Rd. (Lenox Square), Atlanta (264-1497); 2100 Pleasant Hill Rd. (Gwinnett Place Mall), Duluth (476-7371); 4800 Briarcliff Rd. (Northlake Mall), Atlanta (491-6849); 4400 Ashford-Dunwoody Rd. (Perimeter Mall), Atlanta (395-0665); 1000 Southlake Mall (Southlake Mall), Morrow (968-4160); Shannon Mall, 1000 Shannon Southpark, Union City (969-1465); and 400 Earnest Barrett Pkwy. (Town Center Mall), Kennesaw (429-9117). The stores carry shoes imported from Brazil.
- **Folk Art Imports Gallery**, 25 Bennett St., A-1, Atlanta (352-2656). This gallery has a wonderful selection of international art with a heavy concentration of South American work. Included are folk and tribal arts, textiles, pottery, baskets, masks and jewelry.
- **Continental Shopper**, One CNN Center, Suite 232, Atlanta (522-6201) This creative gift shop carries some items from Latin America, such as jewelry, textiles, pottery and other arts and crafts. Two additional locations are being considered.
- **El Norteño**, Buford Highway Flea Market, 5000 Buford Hwy., Chamblee (455-8794). Cassettes, magazines, Mexican crafts, clothing, and Mexican gifts are sold here. Open Friday-Sunday.
- **Manos Boutique**, 1 Galleria Pkwy. (Galleria Mall), Atlanta (612-9300). The store specializes in handmade sweaters from South America.
- **Medwin Aquatics**, 1701 Penny Lane, Lawrenceville (962-1733). Owner Stuart Medwin is a breeder of discus, a beautiful fish about the size of a pancake that originates in the Amazon River. Its life span can reach 15-20 years

and it is considered suitable for a home or office aquarium.

■ **Sassafras**, 2841 Greenbriar Pkwy. (Greenbriar Mall), Atlanta (346-3444). The store carries Latin women's apparel, as well as Eastern and Asian clothing.

■ **Tijuana Flea Market**, 6616 New Peachtree Rd., Doraville (454-7725/936-0447). Mexican clothing, magazines, cassettes and more are for sale every Saturday and Sunday.

■ **World Winds**, 3393 Peachtree Rd. (Lenox Square), Atlanta and 4400 Ashford-Dunwoody Rd. (Perimeter Mall), Atlanta (671-9646). Special kiosks at both shopping malls carry colorful items made in Central America, such as bracelets, T-shirts, shirts, sweaters and purses.

GROCERIES, MARKETS, BAKERIES

■ Many grocery stores and supermarkets in Atlanta carry Goya and Iberia products, fresh refrigerated tortillas, and packaged Mexican food. **Kroger's** and **Cub Foods** are among the larger chain operations carrying brands such as El Paso, Ortega, La Casa Fiesta, San Marcos, Jarritos, Conchita and La Costeña. **Harry's Farmers Market**, 1180 Upper Hembree Rd., Alpharetta (664-6300) and 2025 Satellite Blvd., Duluth (416-6900); **Your DeKalb Farmers Market**, 3000 E. Ponce de Leon, Decatur (377-6400); and **International Farmers Market**, 5193 Peachtree Industrial Blvd., Chamblee (455-1777) carry, in addition to fresh tortillas and packaged goods, fresh cheeses, chili peppers, herbs, fruits and vegetables native to Latin American countries. For a more diverse selection of products, you may visit the markets and bakeries listed below.

GROCERIES & MARKETS

■ **Bolero Mart**, 5674 Roswell Rd., Atlanta (843-1884). A large selection of fresh and packaged Mexican food is sold here, including fresh tortillas, jalapeños and mole.

■ **Brazil Tropical**, 4374 S. Atlanta Rd. (Exit #11 off I-285), Smyrna (319-0909). As the name implies and the green flag out front emphasizes, this store specializes in Brazilian and other South American foods. Staples such as coconut milk, palm oil, cashew apple juice and canned goods are on the shelves, as well as chocolates and tropical juices. Magazines and South American T-shirts can be purchased.

■ **Brito Produce Co.**, State Farmers Market (I-75/Exit #78), Forest Park, Building 23, Booths 5 & 6. A Hispanic farmer sells a variety of produce, including tomatillos and other products from Mexico and Latin America.

■ **Díaz Market**, 368 5th St., NE, Atlanta (872-0846). This store carries Cuban, Jamaican, Puerto Rican, Mexican, Central and South American food products, including fresh flour tortillas, cheeses, chorizos and tamales, but no produce. Also available are magazines, Spanish newspapers, videos in Spanish and Mexican cassettes.

■ **El Primo**, 1651 Smyrna-Roswell Rd., Smyrna (434-3653) and 6045 Norcross-Tucker Rd., Norcross (939-8247). This supermarket carries numerous Mexican, Salvadoran and other Latin foods, including fresh tortillas, peppers, canned and packaged products. On the weekends, it sells fajitas, patas, lengua, menudo, barbeque and more. Spanish language cassettes and Mexican magazines are also available.

■ **El Rinconcito**, 2845 Buford Hwy. (south of N. Druid Hills Rd.), Atlanta (636-8714). For more than a decade, this grocery has offered a variety of products from Latin America and the Caribbean, including Cuban coffee, chorizo, plantains, yucca root and Mexican soft drinks. Spanish language magazines, books, *Iberoamerica En Primera Plana*, *Páginas Amarillas Hispanas*, greeting cards, tapes and CDs are also available. A recent addition is a small snack-bar inside the grocery which serves authentic Puerto Rican food.

■ **El Tío**, 6065 S. Norcross-Tucker Rd. (near Jimmy Carter Blvd.), Norcross (939-7474). This supermarket and taquería carries many Mexican, El Salvadoran and other Latin products, including beer and wine, tamales, barbeque, tacos, menudo, sandwiches and more. Magazines and cassettes are sold, and patrons may play billiards.

■ **Fiesta**, 2581 Piedmont Rd. (Sidney Marcus Blvd.), Atlanta (233-8795). The store carries fresh dairy products, fresh tortillas, corn husks, spices, salsa and other canned and packaged products from Latin countries. *Mundo Hispánico* and *Los Primos* are available here. A good, cheap deli has been added.

■ **Jalisco Supermarket**, 2077 Beaver Ruin Rd., Norcross (449-7467). Jalisco stocks Colombian, Mexican, Puerto Rican and other Latin American food products, as well as cassettes and piñatas.

■ **La Bodeguita Grocery**, 3669 Clairmont Rd. (Dresden Dr.), Chamblee (451-4758). This grocery has bijo spices, banana leaves, yuca, fresh tortillas, fresh cheeses, masa, corn husks, frozen foods and Cuban deli sandwiches. Some kitchen accessories are for sale, including molcajetes.

■ **La Canasta**, 215 Copeland Rd., Atlanta (250-1522). Mexican and other Latin American products, fresh vegetables and groceries are sold at this Sandy Springs market. Spanish language videos and cassettes are also available.

■ **La Norteñita**, 5522 New Peachtree Rd., Suite D-1, Chamblee (458-8733).

Seven days a week, the store carries fresh tortillas and a complete line of Mexican food products, along with cassettes, sweets, piñatas, magazines, sarapes and more.

■ **LaPerla**, 1853 Cobb Pkwy. (Cobb International Plaza), Marietta (980-1144). The Hispanic grocery offers tortillas, bread, chorizo y huevos, magazines, newspapers and more.

■ **Los Angeles Mexican Food Market**, 4805 Old National Hwy., College Park (768-8486). The market specializes in Mexican and Latin food products, as well as cassettes and video in Spanish, piñatas and more.

■ **Los Latinos**, 438 N. Indian Creek (Campus Plaza Shopping Center), Clarkston (297-7753). Food products from Mexico, Latin America and the Caribbean, as well as newspapers, magazines, cassettes and videos are sold here.

■ **Los Primos Food Market**, 3287 Chamblee-Dunwoody Rd., Chamblee (457-7210/936-9781) and 4230 Hwy. 29, NW, Lilburn (564-0881). The market carries Mexican and Latin food products, as well as magazines, cassettes, meat, Mexican socas and tortillas, and will ship products all over the world! Social services such as amnesty and immigration advice, notary publics, passport information and legal assistance are also offered.

■ **Olé Mexican Foods**, 5565 New Peachtree Rd., Chamblee (458-5614). The market sells a variety of Mexican products, including fresh tortillas.

■ **Ojat Mart**, 5436 Riverdale Rd. (Windjammer Center), College Park (994-9388). A wide range of Hispanic food products are stocked in this market.

■ **Puritan Food Store**, 568 Boulevard, SE, Atlanta (622-2187). Enjoy fresh Cuban sandwiches, tortas, tamales and a variety of Latin products at this grocery.

■ **Tienda Las Américas**, 3652 Shallowford Rd., Doraville (458-7962). The store carries fresh dairy products, fresh tortillas, corn husks, lots of spices, fresh cilantro and peppers, salsa and other canned and packaged products from the Caribbean, Mexico, Peru, Argentina, Colombia and Uruguay. Mexican newspapers, magazines and Spanish language cassettes are also sold. The store provides telephone service to every part of the world and will exchange money from Caribbean and Latin American countries.

■ **Tony's Farmers Market**, 2335 Cheshire Bridge Rd. (Cheshire Square Shopping Center/LaVista Rd.), Atlanta (315-6656). Owned by Tony Fundora, a native of Cuba and owner of Avanti's Pesci Vino restaurant, the 7500 sq. ft. farmers market specializes in Hispanic and Cuban food, including fresh meat, seafood and produce. A deli featuring Latin and Cuban food has opened, and an in-house bakery and espresso bar are in the planning stages.

BAKERIES

■ **Don Chuy**, 5726-A New Peachtree Rd., Doraville (936-0102). Bakery items, candy and Mexican sweet bread are available.

■ **Frutii Valle, Inc.**, 2859 Buford Hwy. (south of N. Druid Hills Rd.), Atlanta (248-1958). Opened in November of 1991, this South American bakery specializes in a wide range of Colombian bread, pastries, and tropical juices and offers daily specialties, such as sancocho, lengua, frijoles and more.

■ **La Fiesta Panadería**, 6034 Norcross-Tucker Rd., Norcross (449-7917). The bakery sells empanadas, pan de dulce, roscos, panes and coffee for the early morning riser.

■ **Las Américas Bakery**, 3671 Clairmont Rd., Chamblee (457-2172). Sweet breads and other sugary treats are available.

■ **Panadería México**, 3691 B Chamblee-Dunwoody Rd., Chamblee (457-3138). Mexican and French bread, bakery items, tortas and tamales are offered, along with other Latin food products, cassettes and novels.

BUTCHERS

■ **Carnicería "El Mexicano,"** 5050 Jimmy Carter Blvd. (Carter-Rockbridge Plaza), Norcross (448-0735). This meat market carries all kinds of Latin-cut fresh meat products, as well as other Latin groceries.

■ **Carnicera Hispanica Quality Meats**, 2714 Shallowford Rd., Chamblee (936-9132). Latin-cut fresh meat products are sold.

RESTAURANTS

BRAZILIAN & PERUVIAN

■ **Las Chalupas**, 440 N. Indian Creek Dr. (Campus Plaza Shopping Center), Clarkston (292-5484). This unique restaurant offers Peruvian and Brazilian food on Saturday and Mexican food the rest of the week. Open: Lunch and Dinner: Mon.–Sat.

COLOMBIAN

■ **La Esmeralda**, 4022 Buford Hwy. (north of Clairmont Rd.), Atlanta (636-0886). Patrons enjoy authentic Colombian and Mexican meals, including empanadas, chorizo, sodas and Clausens Colombian beer, while watching Spanish television programs. Dance to Colombian discotheque on Friday and Saturday nights for an entrance fee of $6.00. Open: Lunch and Dinner: Tues.–Sun.

■ **Mia's Village Cafe**, 1931 Peachtree Rd. (Brookwood Village Shopping Center across from Piedmont Hospital), Atlanta (350-9760). The restaurant, known for its pollo asado, recently won the U.S. Chef's Open at Underground Atlanta in the continental cuisine category. The owners are from Colombia. Open: Lunch and Dinner: Daily.

CUBAN

■ **The Black Bean Cafe**, 366 Fifth St. (Durant St.), Atlanta (876-2326). Cuban and Spanish food is served in a bustling cafe setting. Open: Lunch: Tues.–Thurs.; Dinner: Tues.–Sun.

■ **Café Montserrat**, 515 N. McDonough St. (on the Square in Decatur), Decatur (373-2922). The new restaurant serves southern European cuisine and features Maria's Cuban Corner, serving ropa vieja and black bean soup. Open: Lunch: Mon.–Fri.; Dinner: Mon.–Sat.

■ **Coco Loco**, 2625 Piedmont Rd., Suite G-40 (Sidney Marcus Blvd./Buckhead Crossing Mall), Atlanta (364-0212); 6301 Roswell Rd. (Sandy Springs Plaza), Atlanta (255-5434); and 303 Peachtree Center Ave., One Peachtree Center Food Court, (Peachtree St.), Atlanta (653-0070). The Cuban and Caribbean restaurant is recommended by *Knife and Fork* and the *Atlanta Journal/Constitution* for excellent food, especially Cuban sandwiches, paella and tasty black bean soup, served in a tastefully decorated restaurant with art by co-owner Anna Guzman and background Latin music. The menu is extensive and diverse, with tropical beverages, California and Latin wines, and beers from Mexico, the Virgin Islands, Europe, Asia, and Jamaica. Lunch specials weekdays. Food court open: Lunch: Mon.–Sat. Restaurants open: Lunch and Dinner: Daily. (The Peachtree Center location serves Latin fast food for lunch weekdays.)

■ **Díaz Cuban Café**, 368 5th St. (Peachtree St.), Atlanta (872-0846). The small cafe is part of Díaz Market and serves Cuban sandwiches and entrees with daily specials. As of this writing, patrons wishing alcoholic beverages must bring their own. Open: Lunch and Dinner: Daily.

■ **El Buckhead Station Restaurant-Bar**, 309 Pharr Rd. (Bolling Way), Atlanta (841-6446). The Cuban restaurant and sports bar offers an all-you-can-eat lunch buffet. Open: Lunch and Dinner: Daily.

■ **Havana Sandwich Shop**, 2905 Buford Hwy. (south of N. Druid Hills Rd.), Atlanta (636-4094). Get quick service in this no-frills restaurant known for its delicious Cuban sandwiches and fresh Cuban bread ready for take-out. Open: Lunch and Dinner: Daily.

■ **Mambo**, 1402-B N. Highland Ave. (University Dr.), Atlanta (876-2626). Mambo's authentic Cuban cuisine consistently receives high praises from critics, especially *Atlanta Magazine*, which considers it the "Best Cuban Restaurant." Mambo uses only extra virgin olive oil and canola oil. Special Sunday Brunch. Open: Dinner: Daily.

■ **The Spanish Café**, 4847 Peachtree Rd. (across from Oglethorpe University), Chamblee (452-8544). Among other foods, this restaurant offers Cuban platters and sandwiches. Open: Lunch: Mon.–Fri.; Dinner: Daily.

■ Note: **Kool Korner Grocery**, 349 14th St. (Peachtree St.), Atlanta (892-4424). The popular store reputedly has the "Best Cuban Sandwich" in town (*Atlanta Magazine*), and the owner says they are especially good on Saturday, when he has time to put more "art" into the preparation. Take-out only. Open: Lunch and Dinner: Mon.–Sat.

DOMINICAN

■ **Caramba Café**, 1409-D N. Highland Ave. (University Dr.), Atlanta (874-1343). An exciting, recent addition to the regular Mexican menu is home-made Dominican food served on Sunday from 5:00pm–10:00pm. Open: Lunch: Mon.–Fri.; Dinner: Sat.–Sun.

LATIN AMERICAN

■ **Cafe Provincial**, 931 Monroe Dr. (8th St./Midtown Promenade — Lower Level), Atlanta (872-9896). This inexpensive and casual restaurant offers an Ecuadorian and Mediterranean menu, including yuca bread and ceviche. Special Sunday brunch. Open: Lunch and Dinner: Wed.–Mon.

■ **La Fonda Latina**, 1150B Euclid Ave. (Little Five Points), Atlanta (577-8317). Owned by Clay Harper and Mike Nelson, who also own the close-by Fellini's, this indoor restaurant with enclosed patio offers the "Best Paella" (*Atlanta Magazine*), a Latin sandwich, quesadillas and salads. The background music is salsa and the prices are very reasonable. Open: Lunch and Dinner: Tues.–Sun.

■ **Papá Tino's**, 3115 Buford Hwy. (north of N. Druid Hills Rd.), Atlanta (321-6668). This popular Latin club offers a varied Latin American dinner menu. Open: Dinner: Wed.–Sat.

MEXICAN

Mexican restaurants are popping-up all over Atlanta as the Hispanic population grows and the numbers of non-Hispanic, Mexican food lovers grow, too! There are upwards of 200 Mexican restaurants in greater metropolitan

Atlanta – too many for us to list here. So below are some of the well-known ones and others that are lesser known gems. Don't forget, of course, that Mexican fast food (like that found at **El Taco**, **Taco Bell** and **Taco Mac**) is a good alternative to the usual fast food chains Americans frequent. To sample some of the higher-quality cuisines of Mexico (Mexican cuisine is as varied as its geographical regions), venture to a restaurant listed below:

■ **Azteca Grill**, 1140 Morrow Industrial Blvd. (Market Place), Morrow (968-0907). Gourmet regional Mexican food is offered, including posole (pork stew), pollo loco, and many varieties of salsas. The green chili soup consistently receives top ratings, and chocolate chimichangas are among the most popular desserts. Open: Lunch and Dinner: Daily.

■ **Billar Restaurante El Mexicanito**, 5805 Buford Hwy. (Doraville Plaza), Doraville (452-7364) and 1885 Cobb Pkwy. (Cobb Pkwy. Plaza), Marietta (612-1946). This restaurant invites the entire family to enjoy authentic Mexican food, including pollo rostisado, all kinds of mariscos (seafood), tortas, chiles rellenos and pollo a la Veracruzana. Open: Lunch and Dinner: Mon.–Sat.

■ **Blue Coyote**, 980 Piedmont Ave. (10th St.), Atlanta (872-4061). This unusual restaurant offers interesting vegetarian selections, along with typical Mexican fare of tacos, burritos and more. Open: Lunch and Dinner: Daily.

■ **Cafeteria Y Taquería las Américas**, 3652-E Shallowford Rd. (west of Buford Hwy. in Roland Shopping Center), Doraville (454-8557). Authentic Mexican food is prepared by Mexican chefs. All brands of Mexican beer and genuine Mexican sodas are sold. Open: Lunch and Dinner: Daily.

■ **Camino Real Mexican Restaurant**, 1825 Rockbridge Rd. (US 78/Stone Mountain Festival Shopping Center), Stone Mountain (413-1664). Standard Mexican food is offered with daily specials. Lunch and Dinner: Daily.

■ **Caramba Café**, 1409-D N. Highland Ave. (University Dr.), Atlanta (874-1343). This cafe is popular with the trendy set and offers standard Mexican food and specials. An exciting recent addition to the menu is homemade Dominican food, served on Sunday from 5:00pm–10:00pm. Open: Lunch: Mon.–Fri.; Dinner: Sat.–Sun.

■ **The Chile Tree**, 469 N. Highland Ave. (south of Ponce de Leon Ave. one block south of Carter Library), Atlanta (688-0836). Yucatan and southern Mexican cuisine is served, which includes meals in banana leaves, pumpkin seed sauces and mole. Open: Lunch: Tues.–Fri.; Dimmer: Tues.–Sun.

■ **Cinco de Mayo**, 1622 Woodcliff Dr., Suite H (between Briarcliff and N. Druid Hills Rds.), Atlanta (320-0256) and 5100 Buford Hwy. (Flea Market), Chamblee. Tortas, enchiladas, nachos, tropical juices and more may be enjoyed with live mariachi entertainment on Wednesday through Friday nights at the Woodcliff location. Open: Lunch and Dinner: Mon.–Sat.

- **Dos Copas**, 2880 Holcomb Bridge Rd. (Nesbitt Ferry Rd.), Atlanta (640-8733). Traditional Mexican cuisines may be eaten with Mexican beers or California wines in a casual atmosphere. Lunch specials are offered weekdays. Open: Lunch and Dinner: Mon.–Sat.
- **Dos Guitarras Mexican Restaurant**, 4403 Cowan Rd. (Lawrenceville Hwy./Hugh Howell Rd.), Tucker (934-0110). Eat traditional Mexican food in pleasant surroundings. Open: Lunch: Mon.–Fri.; Dinner: Mon.–Sat.
- **El Azteca**, eleven locations throughout metropolitan Atlanta. Traditional Mexican food with specialties of fajitas, menudo, lengua and carnes asadas can be enjoyed at this popular chain. Open: Lunch and Dinner: Daily.
- **El Charro**, three locations around Atlanta: 2581 Piedmont Rd. (Sidney Marcus Blvd.), Atlanta (264-0613); 5000 Buford Hwy. (Shallowford Rd.), Chamblee (457-9039); and 5265 Jimmy Carter Blvd. (by All-Star Video), Norcross (448-4588). Specialties include chorizos, tamales, tolimenses, mole sauce and Colombian dishes. Open: Lunch and Dinner: Daily.
- **El Chico Mexican Restaurants**, 5150 Memorial Dr. (Race Rd., outside I-285), Atlanta (296-0882). Fresh, authentic Mexican food is served. Open: Lunch and Dinner: Daily.
- **El Eradero**, 2479 Cobb Pkwy. (near K-Mart), Kennesaw (423-1213). If you are out and about in northern Atlanta, give this Mexican restaurant a try. Open: Lunch: Mon.–Sat.; Dinner: Daily.
- **El Jalapeño**, 1399 Bankhead Hwy. (Gordon Rd.), Mableton (739-5553). Specialties include menudos, carne asada, camarones, carnitas de puerco, fajitas and ensaladas de frutas. Mexican fútbol is on TV via satellite. Open: Lunch: Mon.–Sat.; Dinner: Daily.
- **El México**, 408 Atlanta St. (Roswell Mill), Roswell (594-8674). Recommended by many critics, the restaurant serves standard Mexican dishes, including fajitas, in an artsy part of Old Roswell. Open: Lunch and Dinner: Daily. (Opens at 1:00pm on Sunday.)
- **El Mexicano Restaurant**, 1341 Moreland Ave. (near Kroger's), Atlanta (622-3501). Authentic Mexican food, such as moles, caldos and mariscos, is served with sangría and Mexican beer. The Olivares Trio plays Latin music on Sunday evenings. Open: Lunch and Dinner: Daily.
- **El Nopal**, 2500 Godby Rd. (Old National Hwy.), College Park (768-9765). This popular restaurant serves authentic, homemade Mexican food. Open: Buffet Lunch: Mon.–Fri.; Dinner: Daily.
- **El Portón**, 10675 Alpharetta Hwy. (Holcomb Bridge Rd.), Roswell (552-7571). Watch Mexican fútbol on TV via satellite while you partake of authen-

tic Mexican food. Open: Lunch and Dinner: Daily.

- **El Potro Mexican Restaurant**, 3396 Buford Hwy. (Briarwood Rd.), Atlanta (321-9860). Eat authentic Mexican food in a personable environment. Open: Lunch and Dinner: Daily.
- **El Sol Mexican Restaurant**, 4343 Dunwoody Park (Dunwoody Plaza), Dunwoody (671-1499). Eat authentic Mexican food in comfortable surroundings. Open: Lunch: Mon.–Fri.; Dinner: Mon.– Sat.
- **El Taco Veloz**, 5084 Buford Hwy. (Clairmont Ave.), Doraville (936-9094) and 5670 Roswell Rd. (1 block inside I-285), Sandy Springs (252-5100). The taqueria serves burritos, top rated chiles rellenos and tacos, carne asada and more. Take-out is emphasized here and drive-through windows are available. Open: Lunch and Dinner: Daily.
- **Frijoleros**, 1031 Peachtree St. (between 10th & 11th Sts.), Atlanta (892-TACO). Dine indoors or outside while enjoying burritos, chalupas, quesadillas or black beans in a funky environment. Open: Lunch and Dinner: Daily.
- **The Green Jalapeño Mexican Restaurant**, 5984 Memorial Dr. (Stonewood Village Shopping Center), Stone Mountain (501-0030). Mexican cuisine with Nicaraguan appetizers is offered, and Sunday features a dinner buffet where patrons assemble chicken fajitas, tacos, burritos and more. Open: Lunch: Mon.–Sat.; Dinner: Daily.
- **Jalisco Mexican Restaurant**, 2337 Peachtree Rd. (Peachtree Battle Shopping Center), Atlanta (233-9244). Jalisco is known for its quick service, prices and good Mexican food. The combination chalupa, beef enchilada, and beef burrito is popular at lunch, as is the burro supremo with chicken. Open: Lunch and Dinner: Mon.–Sat.
- **La Bamba Restaurante Mexicano**, 1139 W. Peachtree St. (13th St.), Atlanta (892-8888). Famous for its fresh fruit Margaritas and authentic fresh ingredients, the restaurant features "Old Mexico" decor and an outdoor patio. Open: Lunch and Dinner: Daily.
- **La Cazuela** has four locations around Atlanta: 4606 Jimmy Carter Blvd. (Rockbridge Rd.), Norcross (493-8341); 900 Indian Trail Rd. (Dickens Rd./Indian Trail Square), Lilburn (923-3937); 3100 Hwy. 78 (Killian Hill Rd.), Snellville (979-3317); and 3585 Peachtree Industrial Blvd. (Pleasant Hill Rd.), Duluth (497-1730). La Cazuela offers alambres, tortas de mole, churros, natural fruit drinks from Mexico, and features live entertainment Wednesday–Sunday. Open: Lunch and Dinner: Daily.
- **La Fuente**, 265 Peachtree Center Ave. (Atlanta Marriott Marquis Hotel), Atlanta (586-6028). Entree salads are offered along with a special chicken breast with cinnamon salsa, cheese, avocado and plantains. Lunch specials are

offered daily. Reservations recommended. Open: Lunch and Dinner: Daily.

■ **La Quebrada Restaurant**, 1355 Clairmont Rd. (N. Decatur Rd.), Decatur (636-4749) and 2580 Shallowford Rd. (I-85), Atlanta (982-0631). Standard Mexican dishes and daily specials are served with an emphasis on margaritas. Open: Lunch and Dinner: Daily.

■ **Las Banderas Mexican Restaurant**, 123 E. Court Square (E. Ponce de Leon Ave.), Decatur (377-6549). This Mexican food is popular with the local lunch crowd. Open: Lunch and Dinner: Daily.

■ **Las Colinas**, 6120 Covington Hwy. (Panola Rd.), Lithonia (987-3891) and 6470 Spalding Dr. (Peachtree Corners), Norcross (662-5027). Enjoy live entertainment Wednesday–Saturday with your Mexican meal. Open: Lunch and Dinner: Daily.

■ **Las Margaritas**, 1842 Cheshire Bridge Rd. (LaVista Rd.), Atlanta (873-4464). Authentic Mexican cuisine is served indoors or on a patio. Open: Lunch and Dinner: Mon.–Fri.

■ **Los Arcos**, 1171 Hairston Rd. (Redan Rd.), Stone Mountain (292-0752). The Olivares Trio plays Latin music on Saturday evenings while patrons choose from a menu listing mesquite grilled shrimp, chicken and steak, as well as 24 combination dishes. Open: Lunch and Dinner: Daily.

■ **Los Toribio Mexican Restaurant No. 4**, 2262 E. Main St. (Hwy. 78), Snellville (985-1664). Diners may choose from a variety of traditional Mexican foods, including daily specials. Open: Lunch and Dinner: Daily.

■ **Los Toros**, 1455 Pleasant Hill Rd. (Club Dr./Pleasant Hill Point Shopping Center), Lawrenceville (923-7016). Sports fans will be glad to know this restaurant features fútbol broadcast directly from Mexico via satellite. Open: Lunch and Dinner: Daily.

■ **Mazatlán Mexican Restaurant**, 4058 Peachtree Rd. (across from Brookhaven MARTA Station), Atlanta (261-7955). Authentic Mexican food is served in this new, bright restaurant. Open: Lunch: Mon.–Fri.; Dinner: Mon.–Sat.

■ **Mexico City Gourmet**, 2134 N. Decatur Rd. (Clairmont Rd.), Decatur (634-1128) and 5500 Chamblee-Dunwoody Rd. (Mt. Vernon Rd.), Dunwoody (396-1111). Critically-acclaimed gourmet Mexican food is offered, including seafood specialties, a chicken quesadilla, vegetable quesadilla and lunch specials. Open: Lunch and Dinner: Mon.–Sat.

■ **Monterrey Restaurante Mexicano**, 5406 Buford Hwy. (inside I-285), Doraville (458-1179); 3865 LaVista Rd. (Montreal Rd.), Tucker (493-3565); and 2540 Atlanta Rd. (Pat Mell Hill), Smyrna (432-1815). Standard Mexican food and lunch specials are served in a spacious room. Mexican beers are offered. Open: Lunch and Dinner: Daily.

- **Nuevo Laredo Cantina**, 1495 Chattahoochee Ave. (Marietta Blvd. & Boot Hill), Atlanta (352-9009). Colorful decor is accented with photographs of Mexico taken by the owner of the cantina. Traditional tacos, burritos and specials are offered. Open: Lunch: Mon.–Fri.; Dinner: Daily.
- **Papá Tino's Mexican Bar & Grill**, 3115 Buford Hwy. (N. Druid Hills Rd.), Atlanta (321-6668) and 309 Pharr Rd. (Peachtree Rd.), Atlanta (841-6446). Eat such Mexican specialties as cabrito (goat), chorizo, camarones (shrimp), pollo, fajitas or pescado. Listen to records spun by a D.J. at the Buford Highway location. Open: Lunch and Dinner: Tues.–Sun.
- **Santa Fe Mexican Grille**, 8560 Holcomb Bridge Rd. (Rivermont Shopping Center), Alpharetta (594-8831). The specialty is grilled Mexican chicken (pollo al carbón). Open: Lunch and Dinner: Mon.–Sat.
- **Tapatío Restaurante Mexicano**, 1091 Euclid Ave. (Little Five Points), Atlanta (688-8903). Chimichangas, shrimp fajitas, vegetarian selections, flans, fried ice cream and more may be enjoyed indoors or on an outdoor patio. Open: Lunch: Mon.–Sat.; Dinner: Daily.
- **Taxco Restaurante Mexicano**, 4500 Roswell Rd. (2 miles south of I-285), Atlanta (255-9933) and 2916 N. Druid Hills Rd. (LaVista Rd. across from Toco Hills Shopping Center), Atlanta. Authentic Mexican cuisine, an extensive menu, generous portions and reasonable prices make this a local favorite. Eat in or take-out. The Toco Hills location has a drive-through window. Open: Lunch: Mon.–Sat.; Dinner: Daily.
- **Tortillas**, 774 Ponce de Leon Ave. (east of Peachtree St.), Atlanta (892-3493). The restaurant is known for its popular "San Francisco-style" burritos, quesadillas, soft tacos and vegetarian dishes with natural ingredients. Open: Lunch and Dinner: Daily.
- **Tres Amigos Mexican Gourmet**, 1205 Johnson Ferry Rd. (Woodlawn Shopping Center), Marietta (977-7096). Enjoy Mexican gourmet food, a bar and live entertainment, which is booked on a regular basis. Free delivery. Open: Lunch: Tues.–Fri.; Dinner: Tues.–Sun.

PUERTO RICAN

- **El Rinconcito**, 2845 Buford Hwy. (south of N. Druid Hills Rd.), Atlanta (636-8714). Located inside the grocery of the same name, this small snack bar features authentic Puerto Rican food including, *pan de puerco*, empanadas and other food cooked with traditional herbs and spices. *Mabí*, a popular Puerto Rican beverage, is also available. Open: Mon.–Sat. 11:00am–6:00pm.

Among the more popular Tex-Mex restaurants are:

■ **Cactus Cafe**, 6375 Spalding Dr. (Holcomb Bridge Rd.), Norcross (441-2233). Very popular with the locals, who consider the food to be top-rate. Open: Lunch and Dinner: Mon.–Sat.

■ **Cha Cha Charley's**, 3093 Peachtree Rd. (Sardis Way), Atlanta (841-9257). This is a well-known Buckhead Tex-Mex restaurant. Open: Lunch and Dinner: Daily.

■ **La Paz Restaurant & Catering**, 6410 Roswell Rd. (outside I-285), Atlanta (256-3555). Tex-Mex and California lite cuisine is served in a two-story Old West ambiance. Open: Lunch and Dinner: Daily.

■ **Rio Bravo Cantina** has seven locations throughout Atlanta. Popular dishes include mesquite grilled meat, chicken fajitas, chili con queso and fresh tortillas served in a pleasant, cantina environment. Special family Sunday brunch. Open: Lunch and Dinner: Daily.

■ **Sundown Café**, 2165 Cheshire Bridge Rd. (LaVista Rd.), Atlanta (321-1118). Opening to rave reviews in January of 1992 and by August earning the accolade "Best Southwestern Cuisine" from *Atlanta Magazine*, the cafe has established a reputation for creative, spicy entrees, including carnitas, trout sundown, pollo loco and Aneheim shrimp. The desserts are also top-rate. Open: Dinner: Mon.–Sat.

■ **Tortilla Flats**, Kenny's Alley, Underground Atlanta, Atlanta (522-0844) and Perimeter Mall, 4400 Ashford-Dunwoody Rd., Atlanta (913-9414). Voted "Best Mexican Restaurant" in the Best of Atlanta contest, Tortilla Flats offers the usual Tex-Mex bar and grill menu. Open: Lunch and Dinner: Daily.

■ **U.S. Bar Y Grill**, 2002 Howell Mill Rd. (Collier Rd.), Atlanta (352-0033); 6660 Roswell Rd. (outside I-285), Sandy Springs (255-7770); and, 4058 Peachtree Rd. (Dresden Dr.), Atlanta (814-0070). Eat mesquite roasted cabrito (goat), chicken, seafood, and quail, among other grilled foods, in this popular restaurant and cantina. Listen to live mariachi bands on weekends. Open: Lunch: Mon.–Sat.; Dinner: Daily.

SPANISH

■ **The Black Bean Café**, 366 5th St. (Durant St.), Atlanta (876-2326). Authentic Spanish and Cuban food is offered in this small, popular restaurant. Open: Breakfast and Lunch: Tues.–Thurs.; Dinner: Tues.–Sun.

■ **Café Montserrat**, 515 N. McDonough St. (on the Square in Decatur), Decatur (373-2922). The highly-praised restaurant serves southern European and Cuban cuisine, with house specialties including tapas, boliche, ropa vieja, seafood and paella. Open: Lunch: Mon.–Fri.; Dinner: Mon.–Sat.

■ **Don Juan's Restaurant**, 1927 Piedmont Circle (I-85/Piedmont Rd.), Atlanta (874-4285). This is an authentic Castillian restaurant, serving paella, zarzuela, mariscos, tapas and more. Listen to Spanish guitar Wednesday–Saturday evenings. Reservations are required for dinner. It is an Atlanta tradition to celebrate La Fiesta del Rey Juan Carlos here, as the owners are natives of Spain. Open: Lunch: Mon.–Fri.; Dinner: Mon.–Sat.

■ **The Spanish Café**, 4847 Peachtree Rd. (across from Oglethorpe University), Chamblee (452-8544). Enjoy paella, fresh sangria, tapas and other specialties served in a cozy atmosphere with Spanish decor. Spanish and Cuban take-out food is available. Open: Lunch: Mon.–Fri.; Dinner: Mon.–Sat.

■ Note: **La Fonda Latina** (see above) serves a very highly regarded paella with large portions at a reasonable price. Other restaurants which offer one or more Spanish dishes are **Coco Loco** and **Mambo**, also mentioned above.

ENTERTAINMENT: THEATRE, DANCE, MUSIC, CLUBS, FILMS, T.V. & RADIO, SPORTS

MUSIC & DANCE — LOCAL PERFORMERS

■ **Atlanta Virtuosi** (938-8611). This versatile chamber music group, under the direction of its founder Juan Ramírez, a native of Mexico, plays music from the Eurocentric tradition and from the Spanish and Latin traditions. Sometimes performing all-Spanish programs, the group has featured Pepe Romero and Alfonso Moreno. Mr. Ramírez has recently expanded his musical vision to include a Hispanic Festival of Music and the Arts, concerts for Hispanic children, and to forming his own publishing company.

■ **Mexican Folkloric Ballet of Atlanta** (320-1129). This burgeoning ballet company has performed at the Emory International Festival held in April, Kingfest Internationale held in May and other local festivals.

■ **Orquesta Lyrica**. Atlanta's premier Latin salsa orchestra was founded in 1988 by Enrique Mercado and Hassan Ortiz, the director and a percussionist, respectively. In addition to salsa, the group performs merengues, cumbias and jazz. (The history of salsa can be traced from Africa, through the Caribbean to the United States, with influences from African-American jazz.) The orchestra plays at events all year long, such as the Latin Jazz Connection at Piedmont Park in August, the Arts Festival of Atlanta in September at Piedmont Park, and is available for special occasions.

■ Local folkloric groups perform dances and music in native costumes at festivals in Atlanta and some perform thoughout the state of Georgia. For information on local groups, contact the appropriate community association. Since new groups are forming in Atlanta every year, here is but a sampling: **Ballet Folklórico Infantil Latinoamericano, Ballet Folklórico Latinoamericano; Colombian Folkloric Group, Grupo Folklórico de Colombia, Ecuadorian Folkloric Dancers, El Grupo Infantil de Baile de Colombia** (a recently formed ballet group that presents traditional children's ballets)**, El grupo Folklórico de la República Dominicana, Folkloric Music from Peru, Peruvian Folkloric Group, Grupo Artistico Venezuela, Grupo Folklórico Peruano,** and **Grupo Folklórico de Panama**.

■ Numerous local bands are available to play at restaurants, banquets and ballrooms, and some are booked through entertainment agencies. A sampling: **Los Amigos Mexican Band, La Nueva Armonia, Marimbas Chiapas, Jose Castillo Mariachi, Santa Cecilia, Taboga, Caribbean Kermit & Marisol, Tropical Hi, Grupo Sabor, Jorge Alvarez y sus Amigos, El Destino, El Kinder, Stephanie Pettis & Rio,** and **Los Olivares Trio**.

MUSIC & DANCE – INTERNATIONAL PERFORMERS

■ Latin American performance groups are featured at the City of Atlanta's **Festival of Cultures — Latin American & Caribbean Festival** in Underground Atlanta in July and **Montreux Atlanta International Music Festival** in August; at the **Festival of Ethnic Dance** at Soapstone Center for the Arts in September; at **Arts Festival of Atlanta** in September; and the **Atlanta Symphony Orchestra** has featured Hispanic composers, such as Puerto Rican composer Roberto Sierra.

■ International performers are also booked year-round through **Georgia Partners of the Americas** (525-1168).

CLUBS & RESTAURANTS

■ **Arthur Murray Dance Studios**, 2468 Windy Hill Rd., Marietta (951-8811). Monthly Latin dances are held, and the sponsors hope eventually to offer dancing three nights per week.

■ **Chicago's International Cabaret**, 900 Circle 75 Cobb Pkwy., Atlanta (980-6300). The upscale restaurant and nightclub features contemporary American music weekdays and Latin music on the weekends, with such popular bands as Taboga and Orquestra Lyrica.

■ **Club Diaz**, 795 Powder Springs Rd., Marietta (427-9719). On Friday, Saturday and Sunday nights, dance to Mexican music, such as música norteña and rancheras. Local bands, such as Tabago, Montecarlo, Forastero and

Centella, alternate playing. (The club is also open Tuesday–Thursday.)

■ **El Azteca Night Club**, 63 Cobb Pkwy., Marietta (419-1787/458-9721). Friday, Saturday and Sunday evenings feature dances with a variety of live music.

■ **El Paraiso**, 3011 Buford Hwy. (N. Druid Hills Rd.), Atlanta (458-9721/936-0447). Tuesday–Sunday, the ballroom features Mexican bands, leg and dance contests, and eventually hopes to present Latin music, blues, jazz and reggae bands. The manager is a native of the Dominican Republic.

■ **Frederick's**, 8 Decatur St. (one block from Underground Atlanta), Atlanta (659-3403). The new club offers Latin music on records and mambo and cha-cha lessons on Wednesday and Friday evenings.

■ **International Ballroom**, 6616 New Peachtree Rd. (Buford Hwy.), Doraville (936-0447/454-7725). Dances with live Latin music (ranchera, tropical, chicana) and rock and country are held on Friday, Saturday and Sunday evenings from 9:00pm–3:00am. Professional boxing matches, wrestling and theatre may be held in the newly renovated space, which has a capacity of 2,500 guests. Check the calendar in *Mundo Hispánico* for dates, times and admission charge.

■ **Jubilations**, 2255 Delk Rd. (Holiday Inn Northwest), Marietta (425-6207). The discoteque for young people features merengue, cumbia and salsa on Friday and Saturday nights.

■ **La Cumbre**, 5800 Buford Hwy., Doraville (458-5949). The Mexican restaurant plays records of cumbia, salsa and merengue for your dancing pleasure on Friday and Saturday nights from 10:30pm–4:00am.

■ **La Esmeralda Restaurant**, 4022 Buford Hwy., Atlanta (636-0886). On Friday and Saturday evenings, patrons may dance to tropical music at this Colombian discotheque and restaurant.

■ **Mustache Mike's Food & Spirits**, 5303 Buford Hwy., Doraville (458-7496). Entertainmant is offered Friday, Saturday and Sunday.

■ **Nite Lite**, 1260 Custer Ave., Atlanta (622-0620). Mexican music is performed by live bands Wednesday through Sunday at this Grant Park area club.

■ **Palacio Tropical**, 2847 Buford Hwy., Atlanta (325-4647). Located next to El Rinconcito grocery strore, this new nightclub spins merengue, salsa, cumbia and tropical records for listening and dancing pleasure on Friday and Saturday nights.

■ **Papá Tino's Latin Club**, 3115 Buford Hwy., Atlanta (321-6668). On Friday and Saturday nights, patrons may dance to records playing cumbia, merengue and salsa. Wednesday and Sunday evenings offer a variety of live music, and Thursday features *peñas musicales* (a Puerto Rican style derived from African and Spanish traditions, in which the audience is encouraged to perform and to sing along), led by guitarist-singer Ramón Carbajal, a native of Uruguay.

■ **Sanctuary**, 128 East Andrews Dr., Atlanta (262-1377). Formerly Sounds of Buckhead, Sanctuary features Wednesday and Thursday evenings of Latin music and dancing with free cha-cha and mambo lessons.

■ **Tropicalia**, 1837 Corporate Blvd. (near Buford Hwy.), Atlanta (634-3199). Dances with recorded Latin music, including cumbia, merengue and salsa, are held on Wednesday–Sunday. Dance contests are on Sunday.

■ **Vela Place**, 245 Flat Shoals Dr., Atlanta (622-3501/681-0830). The new cantina offers live music and other activities such as billiards.

THEATRE

■ **Grupo Artístico Latino de Atlanta (GALA)** (874-9920). GALA is a volunteer theatre group under the proud direction of Visi Noya for over 23 years, that presents plays around Atlanta. A recent play, *Zaragueta*, sponsored by the Cuban Club of Atlanta and Círculo Hispanoamericano, was performed at the Cuban Club.

■ **Variety Playhouse**, 1099 Euclid Ave., Atlanta (524-7354). The Playhouse has year-round ethnically diverse programming. Recently, El Vez, the Mexican Elvis Presley, performed to an enthusiastic audience.

FILMS

■ **Atlanta Third World Film Festival**, City of Atlanta Bureau of Cultural Affairs (653-7146). The film festival screens some Latin American films (in Spanish with English subtitles) in October. There is no admission charge.

■ **Emory University**. Emory Center for International Studies (727-6562) sponsors a **Latin American Film Series** offering a diverse range of films: some by Latin American artists (some in Spanish language, others in English language), and some on a theme related to Latin America by non-Latin filmmakers. Call to receive their newsletter. An **Argentine Film Festival**, sponsored by the Latin American and Caribbean Studies Program and the Consulate General of Argentina, was held in December.

■ **Georgia State University** (688-3258). Teodoro Maus, the Mexican Consul in Atlanta who is also a filmmaker, organized **A History of Mexican Film** at Georgia State that included lectures and Mexican films. Call for information on future possibilities.

■ **High Museum of Art**, Robert Woodruff Arts Center, 1280 Peachtree St., NE, Atlanta (892-HIGH). The Latin American Art Circle sponsors a **Latin American Film Festival** that is screened at the museum in October. Films are shown in Spanish or Portuguese, with English subtitles.

■ Some places to watch for Spanish-language films with English subtitles: **Garden Hills Cinema**, 2835 Peachtree Rd., NE, Atlanta (266-2202); **The Plaza Theatre**, 1040 Ponce de Leon Ave. (Little Five Points), Atlanta (873-1939); **The Screening Room**, 2581 Piedmont Rd. (Lindbergh Plaza), Atlanta (231-1924); and the **Metropolitan Film Society**, Cinevision Screening Room, 3300 NE Expressway, Bldg. 2, Atlanta (729-8487).

TV & RADIO

■ **Univision**, a Spanish cable TV channel for metropolitan Atlanta (932-0084). This complete network has movies, sports, children's programming, noticias, deportes, novelas, comedias and specials, English classes, and music and dance programs.

■ **WAGA-TV Channel 5** (875-5551). A Spanish program is broadcast Saturday morning 11:00am–11:30am and rebroadcast Sunday morning by WPBA-TV Channel 30 from 8:30am–9:00am. This locally produced program features a diverse array of topics from local to international, including news, cultural programs, artistic performances and special interest topics. On Sunday at 11:30am, viewers may watch an informative program on Latin Atlanta.

■ **WXIA-TV Channel 11** (892-1611). The station offers a Sunday morning Spanish program.

■ **DeKalb Cable GCTV Channel 12** (most of DeKalb County) and **Channel 23** (North DeKalb). Programs in Spanish for children are shown on Friday at 5:30pm and Saturday at 10:00am. For current course offerings, call 378-6294.

■ **WAOS-AM (1600)** (944-6684). La Favorita Spanish language radio station began broadcasting in 1988 and is on the air from 6:00am-5:30pm. This station reaches listeners in Cobb, Clayton, Douglas, Fulton, Paulding, Fayette and part of DeKalb counties. **WXEM-AM (1460)** is a second La Favorita station that reaches the rest of DeKalb County, as well as Gwinnett, Hall, Barrow, Forsyth and Jackson counties.

■ **WAZX-AM (1400)** (458-4300). Radio Éxitos began broadcasting in the spring of 1991 under the direction of Javier Macias, a native of Mexico, whose family also owns Tijuana Flea Market, Taqueria México, El Azteca Ballroom and the chain of El Azteca Mexican Restaurants. This station offers a wide variety of Latin music, with an emphasis on Mexican music, information, entertainment and call-in programs. The station is broadcast 24 hours every day. Residents of north metropolitan Atlanta can receive this station.

■ **WGUN-AM (1010)** (373-2521/659-5567). *La Voz de la Esperanza* is a program hosted by Alberto Rodriguez at 10:30am on Sunday.

■ **WVEU-FM (69)**, (325-6929). Each Saturday, listeners may tune in to *Así es la Vida*, a half-hour program on life styles, politics and art.

SPORTS

■ **Soccer.** Latin American Soccer League (**La Liga Latinoamericana de Fútbol**) (885-1386) organizes games held at local parks; and **International Soccer League (Liga Internacional de Fútbol)** (923-6864) offers an academy for children ages 8–12.

■ **Basketball.** Latin Basketball League (**La Liga Latina de Basketbol**) (531-0290) organizes several teams, including two in metropolitan Atlanta and others in Gainsville.

■ **Mexican Fútbol.** See fútbol on TV via satellite at the following restaurants: **El Buckhead Station Restaurant-Bar**, 309 Pharr Rd. (Bolling Way), Atlanta (841-6446); **El Jalapeño**, 1399 Bankhead Hwy. (Gordon Rd.), Mableton (739-5553); **El Portón**, 10675 Alpharetta Hwy. (Holcomb Bridge Rd.), Roswell (552-7571); and **Los Toros**, 1455 Pleasant Hill Rd. (Club Dr./Pleasant Hill Point Shopping Center), Lawrenceville (923-7016).

■ **Boxing and Wrestling.** Watch live matches at **International Ballroom**, 6616 New Peachtree Rd. (Buford Hwy.), Doraville (936-0447/454-7725).

festivals & special events

FEBRUARY — MARCH

■ **Brazilian Carnival** (351-6791). Hosted by the Brazilian-American Society, this carnival features dancing and food.

■ **Hispanic Music and Arts Festival** (938-8611). The Atlanta Virtuosi Foundation sponsors this event which features a variety of Hispanic music (including tangos, waltzes, polkas, and popular songs) played by the renowned Atlanta Virtuosi, under the direction of Juan Ramirez, a native of Mexico.

■ **Mariachi Festival of Atlanta** (688-0851). Sponsored by the Mexican Consulate of Atlanta, this festival features the music of local mariachi bands.

APRIL

■ **Festival of Nations** (320-6111). Hispanic students attending schools in Atlanta participate, representing their native countries. The festival includes music, native costumes and food.

MAY

- **Cinco de Mayo**. Mexican Independence Day is celebrated in many locales throughout the city, especially in private homes and restaurants. One special annual event is a gala fundraiser for the Atlanta Virtuosi, featuring an authentic Mexican dinner and mariachi entertainment. Call 938-8611 for information on this special fundraiser.
- **Hispanic American Day**. Designated by Atlanta Mayor Maynard Jackson to be May 18th of each year.
- **Latin American Association** (231-0940). The association holds an annual banquet for the elderly in May, which includes dancing and entertainment.

JUNE

- **Metropolitan Atlanta Chapter of Image** (659-8220). Image, an organization that supports the civil rights of Hispanics, holds an annual awards ceremony.

JULY

- **Colombian Independence Day**, Atlanta (624-4211). A day-long celebration features a dinner-dance, entertainment, cultural exhibits at various galleries, a memorial mass and an address by the Colombian General Consul.
- **Festa Junina** (351-6791). The Brazilian-American Society commemorates St. John's Day with traditional Brazilian dishes, games, and dancing to samba, lambada, forro and frevo music.
- **Independencia del Perú** (986-0058/729-8743). Purchase tickets to the festivities, which include evening dancing at several locations throughout Atlanta. Sponsored by the Peruvian Association of Atlanta.
- **Panamanian Friendship Reunion** (215-2689/297-1983). The annual dinner-dance and picnic is sponsored by the Panamanian Society.

AUGUST

- **Argentine Festival** (659-1293). The bilingual festival has included Andean music, regional stories by Normando Ismay, slides, artworks and a bandoneon performance by Daniel Dias.
- **Ecuadorian Independence Day Celebration** (962-5945/456-9572). A picnic, games and piñatas for children are part of the day's celebration sponsored by the Ecuadorian Association of Georgia.
- **Montreux Atlanta International Music Festival**, Atlanta (653-7127). The City of Atlanta Bureau of Cultural Affairs sponsors a day of free outdoor concerts with performances by noted local and international Latin musicians.

SEPTEMBER

■ September is a month dotted with **Independence Day Festivities** — most Central American countries (Costa Rica, El Salvador, Guatemala, Honduras and Nicaragua) and the South American countries (Brazil, Chile and Mexico) celebrate national holidays this month. Contact the various country-specific community associations for the location and exact dates of this year's festivities. And throughout Atlanta, **Hispanic Heritage Month** (September 15–October 15) celebrations include art exhibitions, dances, concerts, fundraisers, and an annual reception sponsored by the Atlanta Hispanic Chamber of Commerce (992-0134).

■ **Latin American Association** (231-0940). The association hosts an annual race this month as one of its fund-raising activities.

OCTOBER

■ October is the culmination of **Hispanic Heritage Month** celebrations (September 15–October 15), and each year more organizations are participating in established festivities and others are creating new events. Check out *Mundo Hispánico* this month for an expanded calendar of events around Atlanta.

■ **Hispanic Festival**, Immaculate Heart of Mary Catholic Church, Atlanta (888-7839). Held in October, this festival celebrates the cultures of Central and South America and Spain, with Latin and Spanish foods, salsa music, and arts and crafts. Previous festivals have boasted an attendance of over 8,000 visitors.

■ **"Latin Fever"** (231-0940). The Latin American Association hosts the October dinner-dance fundraiser "Latin Fever" to raise money for the association, whose primary goal is to help Spanish newcomers successfully adjust to living in Atlanta.

■ **Metro Atlanta Hispanic Image Debutant Ball**, Hellenic Community Center, Atlanta (924-3440/266-1956). Miss Hispanic Debutante is crowned at this dance sponsored by the Greater Atlanta chapter of Image.

NOVEMBER

■ **Benefit Dinner-Dance** (231-0940). The annual benefit was begun in 1987 to benefit needy Hispanic families and is sponsored by the Atlanta Chamber of Commerce, Catholic Social Services, Image, the Latin American Association, LULAC and Mundo Hispánico and has featured the local band Taboga.

■ **Círculo Hispanoamericano** (461-1002) Círculo holds an annual folklore and costume party. Folkloric groups representing many countries perform.

■ **Panamanian Independence Day Celebration**, Panamanian Society (981-3148/762-5655). Celebrations are held in several locations in Atlanta, including a large celebration at Chicago's International Cabaret (980-6300) with a live Latin band.

DECEMBER

■ Numerous religious celebrations specific to December are held at Hispanic churches throughout Atlanta, such as Virgin of Guadalupe celebrations and traditional Latin American Christmas novena.

OTHER

■ **Special Events**, such as national holidays, are celebrated by the various Latin American associations, churches, clubs and restaurants in Atlanta — and more are being celebrated each year as the Hispanic population in Atlanta grows and the community becomes more organized. Fundraisers, special cultural awareness activities and award banquets are also multiplying. An excellent source for current festivals and special events in the Hispanic community is the calendar of events in each issue of *Mundo Hispánico*.

■ Throughout the year, many events of interest to the Hispanic community are sponsored by Emory University. The events are as diverse as plays in Spanish (*Bajarse al moro* by Alonso de Santos), music (Brazilian guitarist Carlos Barbosa-Lima and Atlanta Virtuosi's four concert series of Hispanic music), artwork (*Ecos del Espíritu*, paintings, drawings, sculpture and more, by seven contemporary Hispanic artists at the Atlanta College of Art), and conferences (*Sumos un Pueblo*). It is difficult to obtain information on a regular basis as many groups and artists are scheduled at the last minute, so the best way to get current information is on posters and flyers around the university. Also, call the Emory Center for International Studies (727-6562) to receive their newsletter which lists events that have been booked well in advance.

RESOURCES

SOCIAL SERVICE AGENCIES:

There are a number of aid associations that assist Latin American people, such as Atlanta Committee on Latin America, Atlanta Medical Aid to Central America, Clergy & Laity Concerned and Solidaridad. Others are:

■ **Agencia Latina Americana**, 1777 Northeast Expressway, Suite 235, Atlanta 30329 (636-9496). The agency provides services for immigrants, such as legal referrals, translation referrals, school registration, auto registration and medical and dental services.

- **Latin American Association (Asociación Latinoamericana)**, Lindbergh Plaza: 2581 Piedmont Rd., Suite C1145, Atlanta 30324 (231-0940) and Gwinnett Service Center: 318 W. Pike St., Suite 410, Lawrenceville 30245 (339-4335). This human service agency advocates for Hispanic people, and promotes cooperation among various Hispanic cultural groups and service organizations, to enhance the understanding of Hispanic heritage, and to facilitate the participation of Spanish-speaking people in the general Atlanta community. Translation services, classes in the English language, immigration assistance, services to the elderly, and help with other social services in the areas of health, education, employment and living are provided.

- **Catholic Social Services (Servicios Sociales Católicos)**, 680 W. Peachtree St., NW, Atlanta 30308 (888-7841) and 2601 Ward St., Smyrna 30080 (432-6880). The services offered include help with employment, citizenship exam preparation, immigration assistance, profesional translators and interpreters, and English language classes.

- **Centro El Buen Samaritano (Good Samaritan Center)**, 429 Peachtree St., NE, Atlanta 30308 (885-1386). The center provides interpreters, immigration services, job orientation, banking assistance and more. There is a social hall which Hispanic organizations may use for meetings and celebrations. The center sponsors the Latin American Soccer League.

- **Georgia Hispanic Alliance** (624-1819/872-0460). This is a political action group whose mission is to improve the image of Hispanics in the eyes of state officials and the business community in general, as well as to share and spread the richness of their cultural heritage.

- **Our Lady of the Americas Catholic Mission**, a Roman Catholic Outreach Center in Doraville, assists native Mexicans with friendship, a place to stay, and provides a sense of belonging. Weekly meeting discussions cover a range of social topics and include Bible study, singing and music.

CONSULATES, CHAMBERS OF COMMERCE & TRADE ORGANIZATIONS:

- **Atlanta Hispanic Chamber of Commerce**, 555 Pharr Rd., NE, Suite 225, Atlanta 30305 (264-0879); **Honorary Consulate of Argentina**, 229 Peachtree St., NE, Atlanta 30303 (880-0805); **Southeastern U.S. Argentine Center**, (880-0805); **Consul of Bolivia**, 2385 Drew Valley Rd., P.O. Box 18925, Atlanta 30326 (320-9312); **Honorary Consulate of Chile**, 1050 Crown Pointe Pkwy., Suite 310, Atlanta 30338 (671-8500).

- **Consulate General of Colombia**, 3379 Peachtree Rd., Suite 220, Atlanta 30326 (327-1045); **Honorary Consulate of Costa Rica**, 315 W. Ponce de Leon, Suite 455, Decatur 30030 (370-0555); **Honorary Consulate of Ecuador**, 1650 Birmingham Rd., Alpharetta, 30201 (751-3933); **Honorary Consulate of El Salvador**, P.O. Box 9795, Atlanta 30319 (252-8425); **Honorary Consulate of Guatemala**, 4772 E. Conway Dr., NW, Atlanta 30327 (255-7019); **Honorary Consulate of the Republic of Honduras**, 3091 Chaparral Pl., Lithonia 30038 (482-4769); **Industrial Development Group — Honduras**, 1000 Abernathy Rd., Northpark Town Center, Bldg. 400, Suite 1245, Atlanta 30328 (668-2266).
- **Consulate of Mexico**, One CNN Center, 410 South Tower, Atlanta 30303 (688-3258); **Trade Commission of Mexico**, 229 Peachtree St., NE, Suite 917, Atlanta 30303 (522-5373); **Consulate General of Panamá**, 260 Peachtree St., NW, Suite 1760, Atlanta 30303 (525-2772); **Society of the Friends of Peru**, P.O. Box 831231, Stone Mountain 30083 (299-8234); **Puerto Rican Consulate**, 315 W. Ponce de Leon, Suite 455, Decatur 30030 (370-0555); and **Economic Development Administration — Puerto Rico**, 2635 Century Pkwy., Suite 780, Atlanta 30345 (321-5284).

Preschoolers at play at the Atlanta Jewish Community Center.

Jewish
Atlanta

HISTORY & NEIGHBORHOODS

James Oglethorpe founded the colony of Georgia as a haven for those suffering religious persecution — a vision that included permitting Jews to settle in Georgia. The earliest Jewish settlers in the South were Sephardic Jews escaping the Spanish inquisition. These settlers reached Savannah in the early 1700s, and rumor has it that Philip Minis, born in Savannah in 1734, can claim title to being the first Jewish Georgian and the first male Caucasian of record "conceived and born" in Georgia. By the 1800s, more and more Jewish immigrants arrived from Germany and surrounding areas, followed by waves of refugees from Central and Eastern Europe, all fleeing religious persecution.

Atlanta's Jewish community is believed to have begun around 1846, making the community almost 150 years old. Steady growth of the community continued until the 1970s, when the migration of Northerners to the Sunbelt began in earnest. From that period on, the Jewish population grew in leaps and bounds, and by 1990, estimates indicated that the community was over 67,000 strong. As more Jews settled in Atlanta, the community built houses of worship where Jewish heritage and religious traditions could be preserved and taught to their children, and established social agencies to care for the elderly, infirm and others in need. This history of providing services for those in need has led to the community's active participation in "Operation Exodus," the worldwide effort to resettle Jewish refugees leaving Russia and Iran. Assisted by Jewish community volunteers, over 1,500 Russian and Iranian émigrés have already arrived in Atlanta to begin new lives. The Jewish community hopes and expects this new wave of immigration will bring even greater cultural diversity to Atlanta's Jewish community. If you are interested in participating in this monumental effort, please contact the Atlanta Jewish Federation to find out what role you can play.

Jewish synagogues, business establishments and delicatessens are conveniently spread throughout the Atlanta area. Because a large number of Orthodox Jews live in the Emory University/LaVista Road neighborhoods, where they may be within walking distance to Beth Jacob Orthodox Synagogue, not surprisingly, there is a diverse selection of kosher butchers, bakeries and delicatessens in this area. If you drive through these neighborhoods in the autumn during the Jewish holiday Sukkos, you can see the many homemade *sukkahs* (small sheds covered with leaves and decorated with grapes and other fruits of the harvest), where families and friends gather for special holiday meals celebrating the fall harvest.

HISTORICAL SITES & MUSEUMS

■ **Museum of the Jimmy Carter Library**, One Copenhill Ave., Atlanta (331-3942). A museum exhibit highlights the Camp David Peace Talks and offers an overview of the politics of the Middle East. Hours: Mon.–Sat. 9:00am–4:45pm; Sun. 12noon–4:45pm. Admission fee.

■ **Atlanta History Center,** 3101 Andrews Dr., NW, Atlanta (814-4000). The Atlanta History Museum, scheduled to open in October 1993, will feature an exhibit entitled "Creating Community: The Jews of Atlanta, 1845–Present," which will be on display from September 1993–September 1994. The exhibition will provide a comprehensive view of Jewish life in Atlanta, touching upon Jewish accomplishments in Atlanta, the place of the community in Atlanta society, and how the Jewish community has worked with the general community to be a part of the city and its future. Admission fee.

■ **Jewish Heritage Center,** The Atlanta Jewish Federation, 1753 Peachtree St., NE, Atlanta (873-1661). The federation has assembled large-scale public exhibitions of Jewish content and is in the process of creating a Jewish Community Archives. Long-term plans are in the works to expand the facility into a free-standing center of Jewish history and culture. After leaving the Atlanta History Museum in 1994, the exhibit, "Creating Community: The Jews of Atlanta, 1845–Present," will become the foundation for the permanent exhibit of the center.

GALLERIES

■ **Zaban Park Branch of The Jewish Community Center**, 5342 Tilly Mill Rd., Dunwoody (396-3250). This branch of the AJCC houses an art gallery displaying exhibits of Jewish content. For example, "Heritage & Mission: Jewish Vienna" and "Contemporary Collection of Moscow and Latvia Avant Garde

Paintings" were featured in the past year. The Zaban Branch also exhibits works of art by Israeli and local Jewish artists.

■ **Zachor Holocaust Center**, Jewish Community Center – Lower Level, 1745 Peachtree St., NE, Atlanta (873-1661). The Holocaust Center houses a permanent exhibit of Holocaust history, photography and survivor's memorabilia. Since the center is staffed by volunteers, we suggest you call ahead to make sure it is open. Free.

■ Other Atlanta area galleries occasionally have exhibits of Jewish content or display art by local Jewish artists, Russian émigrés and world-renowned Israeli artists. For example: **Emory University's Schatten Gallery**, Woodruff Library, 540 Ashby Cir., Atlanta (727-6868/727-6861); **BurnNoff Gallery**, 1529 Piedmont Ave. (Clear Creek Center), Atlanta (875-3475); **The Atelier**, 857 Collier Rd., Atlanta (355-6710); and **Arts Connection at Oxford Book Store**, 360 Pharr Rd., Atlanta (262-3333), all had such exhibits in past years.

COMMUNITY, RELIGIOUS & CULTURAL ASSOCIATIONS

■ **The Atlanta Jewish Federation**, 1753 Peachtree Rd., NE, Atlanta (873-1661). The federation is the central coordinating, planning, fundraising and community action organization for Atlanta's Jewish community. Below is a listing of some of the community centers and organizations it supports.

COMMUNITY CENTERS

■ **Atlanta Jewish Community Center**. The AJCC sponsors social, recreational, cultural and educational programs for the community, including classes, lectures, films and programs about Judaism and Israel. A wealth of concerts, plays, book fairs, festivals, classes and special events are offered throughout the year, targeted to children, teens, singles, adults and seniors. Call one of the centers below for up-to-date information or try the hotline at 421-8353, ext. 7039.

—**Midtown Branch**: 1745 Peachtree St., NE, Atlanta (875-7881). Permanent facilities include an indoor pool, gymnasiums, an exercise room, racquetball courts, tennis courts, athletic fields, an auditorium, meeting rooms, lounges, health clubs and fitness centers, a game room, a daycare center, and playground. The Peachtree Senior Adult Program is a comprehensive program for adults 60 and older, offering meals, exercise classes, lectures, volunteer work, day trips and other social activities. "Midtown Experience in the Arts," a camp program for older children, is offered during the summer.

—**Zaban Branch**: 5342 Tilly Mill Rd., Dunwoody (396-3250). Permanent facilities include two outdoor pools and pool club, children's pool, gymnasium, racquetball courts, nursery school, kindergarten, playground, summer day camps for children of all ages, an athletic field, meeting rooms, tennis courts, lounges, game room and youth lounge, jogging trails, fitness center, adult daycare, and weekend respite care for developmentally disabled children and youths.

—**Shirley Blumenthal Park/Max L. Kuniansky Family Building Branch**: 2509 Post Oak Tritt Rd., NE, Marietta (971-8901). Permanent facilities include a junior Olympic pool and pool club, a children's pool, a bathhouse, a preschool and daycare program, a mother's-morning-out program, meeting rooms, playing fields, park land and lake. There is also a summer day camp program for preschool children.

SENIOR ADULTS

■ **Club 50** (875-7881). Couples and singles 50 years of age and older may participate in year-round social, educational and cultural programming at the AJCC Zaban branch.

■ **Institute for Adult Enrichment** (875-7881). The AJCC's daytime continuing education series is held four times a year, with each series lasting four to eight weeks. These programs often include overnight excursions.

■ **Peachtree Senior Adult Program** (875-7881). Designed for the independent elderly 60 years of age and over, the comprehensive program at the AJCC's midtown branch offers social, cultural and recreational activities. A nutritious kosher lunch is provided to participants.

SINGLES

■ **Atlanta Jewish Community Center** (875-7881). The AJCC provides special programming services and social opportunities for singles 21 years and older, including ski trips, weekend retreats, volleyball tournaments, movies, ethnic dining excursions and other such group activities. Educational and Judaic cultural programs are also scheduled.

■ **Jewish Association of Single Services (JASS)** (908-3395). JASS offers a 24-hour recorded message about the latest singles events in the city.

■ **Atlanta Hillel**, Emory University, Drawer "A," Atlanta 30322 (727-6490). Atlanta Hillel serves the Jewish religious, cultural, educational and social needs of students and members of the university communities at Emory, Oglethorpe, Georgia State and Georgia Tech.

■ **Atlanta Jewish Community Center** (875-7881). The AJCC provides various athletic, social and educational activities year-round for those under 21 years of age and operates AJECOMCE summer day camp at the Zaban Branch, Midtown Experience in the Arts summer camp at the midtown branch, and Camp Barney Medintz overnight camp in Cleveland, Georgia.

■ **B'nai B'rith Youth Organization**, 5342 Tilly Mill Rd., NE, Dunwoody (396-9321). BBYO serves 8th–12th grade students by offering athletic, social, cultural and community programs.

■ **Young Judaea/Hashachar** (800/733-0637). Young Judaea is a non-political organization whose purpose is the development of Jewish identity in young people through club meetings, regional conventions, camps and Israeli programs. Clubs for 4th–12th graders meet at the Zaban Branch of the AJCC, Congregation Beth Shalom, Congregation Or VeShalom, The Hebrew Academy and locations in Marietta.

OTHER PROGRAMS

■ **The Israel Program Center** (875-7881). The center promotes awareness, knowledge and information on all aspects of Israel. Activities include Israeli folk dancing, an Israeli Memorial Day Celebration, a Yom Hatzmaut Celebration and exchange programs in Israel. The center also acts as a resource center for organizations, synagogues and Jewish schools, lending free of charge videos, movies, music and educational material in both English and Hebrew.

■ **Young Leadership Council**, 1753 Peachtree Rd., NE, Atlanta (873-1661). The YLC's aim is to develop a strong community commitment among Atlanta Jews 25–40 years of age and involve the community in educational programs, leadership development and outreach programs.

■ **Soviet Acculturation Services** (875-7881). The AJCC offers many services to recent Soviet émigrés to help them adapt to their new Jewish and American cultures while still respecting their self identity. Programs include special holiday celebrations, tax preparation workshops, family classes and a monthly Russian/English language newsletter.

■ **ORTHODOX & CHASSIDIC** (Strictly following the Torah's written and oral laws): **Anshe S'Fard** (Orthodox & Chassidic), 1324 N. Highland Ave., NE, Atlanta (874-4513); **Beth Jacob**, 1855 LaVista Rd., NE, Atlanta (633-0551); **Beth Tefillah**, 5065 High Point Rd., Atlanta (843-2464); **The Chabad Shul of Cobb County**, 2905 Post Oak Tritt Rd., NE, Marietta (565-4412); **Ner Hamizrach** (Orthodox Sephardic), 1858 LaVista Rd., NE, Atlanta (636-2473); and **Yeshiva High School**, 3130 Raymond Dr., Atlanta (451-5299).

■ **CONSERVATIVE & TRADITIONAL** (Blending traditional interpretation of the Torah with modern life): **Ahavath Achim**, 600 Peachtree Battle Ave., NW, Atlanta (355-5222); **Beth Shalom**, 5303 Winters Chapel Rd., Atlanta (399-5300); **B'nai Torah**, 700 Mt. Vernon Hwy., Atlanta (257-0537); **Congregation Etz Chaim**, 1190 Indian Hills Pkwy., Marietta (973-0137); **Or VeShalom** (Sephardic), 1681 N. Druid Hills Rd., NE, Atlanta (633-1737); **Shearith Israel**, 1180 University Dr., NE, Atlanta (873-1743); and **United Jewish Congregation of Rockdale-Newton**, Oxford College Chapel, Oxford (706/786-7011).

■ **REFORM & PROGRESSIVE** (Interpreting the Torah in a liberal and contemporary fashion): **B'nai Israel**, P.O. Box 383, Riverdale 30274 (471-3586); **Chavurat Ruach Ha'Emet** (662-4147); **Reform Jewish Students Committee**, Emory University, Drawer "A," Atlanta 30322 (727-6496); **Temple Beth David**, 1885 McGee Rd., Snellville (978-3916); **Temple Beth Tikvah**, 9955 Coleman Rd., Roswell (642-0434); **Temple Emanu-El**, 1580 Spalding Dr., Dunwoody (395-1340); **Temple Kehillat Chaim**, 10200 Woodstock Rd., Roswell (641-8630); **Temple Kol Emeth**, 1415 Old Canton Rd., Marietta (973-3533); **Temple Sinai**, 5645 Dupree Dr., NW, Atlanta (252-3073); **The Temple**, 1589 Peachtree Rd., NE, Atlanta (873-1731); and **Bet Haverim** (Reconstructionist Serving the Gay and Lesbian Communities), Friend's Meeting House, 701 W. Howard Ave., Decatur (642-3467).

■ **NON-DENOMINATIONAL**: **Atlanta Hillel**, Emory University, Drawer "A," Atlanta 30322 (727-6490); **Jewish Educational Alliance of Emory University**, Box 21369, Emory University, Atlanta 30322 (636-3362); **Jewish Home**, 3150 Howell Mill Rd., NW, Atlanta (351-8410); and **Atlanta Jewish Community Chaplaincy** (Pastoral Care for the Unaffiliated), 1605 Peachtree St., NE, Atlanta (873-2277).

DAYCARE & PRESCHOOL PROGRAMS

■ **Jewish Community Center** offers a half-day preschool program at the Zaban Branch in Dunwoody (396-3250) and the Shirley Blumenthal Park in Marietta (971-8901). Daycare programs (Keshet Day Care) are offered at all three branches.

■ **The Epstein School**, Solomon Schecter School of Atlanta, 600 Peachtree Battle Ave., NW, Atlanta (351-7754) offers a preschool program for children ages 2–4 years.

■ Certain of the **synagogues** offer daycare, preschool or Mother's-Morning-Out programs.

ELEMENTARY SCHOOLS

■ **Jewish Community Center** offers a half-day kindergarten program at the Zaban Branch of the AJCC in Dunwoody (396-3250) and the Shirley Blumenthal Park in Marietta (971-8901).

■ **The Davis Academy**, 460 Abernathy Rd., Atlanta (303-0347) is a reform Jewish day school presently offering a program for children K–2nd grade. The School plans to add an additional grade each year.

■ **The Epstein School**, Solomon Schecter School of Atlanta, 335 Colewood Way, NW, Atlanta (843-0111) offers a program for preschool children through 8th grade.

■ **Greenfield Hebrew Academy**, 5200 Northland Dr., NE, Atlanta (843-9900) offers a program for preschool children and an elementary school program for K–8th grade.

■ **Torah Day School**, 1901 Montreal Rd., Tucker (723-9559) offers classes for children in K–8th grade.

HIGH SCHOOL

■ **Yeshiva High School**, 3130 Raymond Dr., Atlanta (451-5299) is Atlanta's only fully-accredited Jewish high school for children 7th–12th grade.

RELIGIOUS & HEBREW SCHOOLS

■ **Individual congregations** and **Atlanta Hillel** at Emory University sponsor afternoon and/or Sunday religious instruction.

■ **Atlanta Scholars Kollel** [800/44-HEBRE(W)], in conjunction with the National Jewish Outreach Program in New York City, offers Hebrew reading courses and sponsors adult education discussion groups at various times and locations in Atlanta. Call for dates and registration information.

■ The **AJCC** offers an extensive selection of classes, workshops, sports programs, exercise classes and field trips for children, teens, adults, seniors and singles. Also call to find out about the active Yiddish Club.

■ A large number of acculturation classes are provided to recent **Soviet émigrés** by the AJCC, including tax preparation workshops, family classes and language classes.

■ **Emory University** (727-2697) has a Near Eastern and Judaic Languages and Literature Department. A wide range of collegiate classes in Arabic, Hebrew and Judaic language and literature are offered.

NEWSPAPERS, BOOKS, MAGAZINES, VIDEOS

■ *The Atlanta Jewish Times* (352-2400) features articles about local, national and international events of interest to the Jewish community, together with calendars listing community events and religious services. Available at bookstores and Jewish establishments throughout the city. Cost is 75¢/issue. Subscription rate is $29/year.

■ *Centerline* (875-7881), the AJCC's monthly newsletter, provides a calendar of AJCC events, including classes, workshops, festivals, religious services and special events. Free.

■ *The Jewish Georgian* (237-7400) is a bimonthly newspaper featuring news about members of the local Jewish community, a community calendar, schedules of religious services, listings of delicatessens and restaurants, and advertisements by Jewish retail establishments. Available at bookstores and Jewish establishments throughout the city. Free.

■ *Jewish Civic Press* (231-2194) is a monthly newspaper featuring articles and editorials about local, national and international events of interest to the Jewish community. Available by subscription only, for a cost of $10.00/year.

■ Some of the Jewish delicatessens carry Hebrew and Yiddish newspapers. Try **Arthur's Kosher Meats and Deli,** 120 Copeland Rd. (Roswell Rd.), Atlanta (252-4396) and 2166 Briarcliff Rd. (LaVista Rd.), Atlanta (634-6881); or

Quality Kosher Meats and Delicatessen, 2161 Briarcliff Rd. (LaVista Rd.), Atlanta (636-1114).

■ **Chosen Treasures Judaica Gallery**, 5920 Roswell Rd. (Parkside Shopping Center), Atlanta (843-1933) sells religious books, children's books, children's educational material, music and video tapes.

■ **Judaica Corner**, 2183 Briarcliff Rd., Atlanta (636-2473) is packed with Hebrew and English language religious books, children's books, children's educational material and music.

■ **The Israel Program Center** (875-7881) will lend, free of charge, videos, movies, music and educational material about Israel, in both English and Hebrew.

■ Most **synagogues** have Judaica libraries and gift shops selling a selection of Jewish books and religious items.

SHOPPING CENTERS, IMPORT STORES, HOTELS

■ **Chosen Treasures Judaica Gallery**, 5920 Roswell Rd. (Parkside Shopping Center), Sandy Springs (843-1933) carries Judaica giftware, including menorahs, mezzuzot, dreidels, seder plates, original art work, toys, linens and more.

■ **Judaica Corner**, 2183 Briarcliff Rd., NE, Atlanta (636-2473) has religious articles and gifts for all occasions packed into the small store, including jewelry, books, original art, music, games, toys and linen.

■ Most **synagogues** have Judaica gift shops selling a selection of Jewish books and religious items.

GROCERIES, MARKETS, BAKERIES

(K) Designates that food served in the establishment is Kosher
(Under Strict Rabbinical Supervision).

BUTCHERS

■ *(K)* **Arthur's Kosher Meats and Deli,** 120 Copeland Rd., Atlanta (252-4396) and 2166 Briarcliff Rd., N.E., Atlanta (634-6881). A full-selection of kosher meats, prepared meats, smoked fish and other delicatessen products are sold at this Jewish grocery.

■ *(K)* **Quality Kosher Meats and Delicatessen**, 2161 Briarcliff Rd., Atlanta (636-1114). The Jewish grocery sells a full-selection of kosher meats, prepared meats, smoked fish and other delicatessen products.

BAKERIES

■ *(K)* **Bernie the Baker** (formerly Siskinds), 3015 N. Druid Hills Rd. (Toco Hills Shopping Center), Atlanta (633-1986). The bakery sells a large selection of cakes, cookies, pastries, breads and challahs.

■ **Goldberg and Son Bakery & Delicatessen**, 4383 Roswell Rd., Atlanta (256-3751). The long-standing Atlanta favorite sells fresh bagels and baked goods, in addition to their delicatessen specials.

■ **Masada Bakery**, 1660 NE Expressway Access Rd. (between N. Druid Hills Rd. and Clairmont Rd. exits), Atlanta (320-0452). The wholesale bakery will sell cakes, cookies, pastries, breads and challahs to the general public.

■ **Palace Bakery,** 2869 N. Druid Hills Rd. (Toco Hills Shopping Center), Atlanta (315-9016). New York-style cakes, pies, cookies, pastries, breads, bagels and challahs are sold at the popular bakery adjacent to the Bagel Palace.

■ **The Royal Bagel**, 1544 Piedmont Ave., Atlanta (876-3512). Fresh-baked bagels (rumored to be the best in town), baked goods, and some deli items are available at the recently expanded bakery located in Ansley Mall. A small seating area is available.

SPECIALTIES

■ *(K)* **Bijan**, 5920 Roswell Rd. (Parkside Shopping Center), Atlanta (843-3000). Bijan offers kosher catering at its large banquet hall or for take-out. Home-cooked kugels, roast briskets, chopped liver, stuffed cabbage, roast chicken, and barley and mushroom soup are among the specialties. (Call well ahead for orders during the Jewish holidays.) On Tuesday and Wednesday, Bijan sometimes presents kosher buffet dinners for the public, featuring Persian, Italian or other specialty foods.

DELICATESSENS & RESTAURANTS

■ *(K)* **Arthur's Kosher Meats and Deli,** 120 Copeland Rd. (Roswell Rd.), Atlanta (252-4396) and 2166 Briarcliff Rd. (LaVista Rd.), Atlanta (634-6881). Kosher meats, groceries, delicatessen items and hot meals may be purchased at this deli. There is a small seating area. Open: Lunch and Dinner: Mon.–Fri.; Brunch: Sun. (until 2:00pm).

■ **Bagel Gourmet**, 2492 Mt. Vernon Road (Mt. Vernon Center), Dunwoody (396-6465). New York-style bagels, breads, sandwiches, soups, deli items and baked goods are sold at this delicatessen in the northern suburbs. Open: Breakfast, Lunch and Dinner: Daily.

- **Bagelicious**, 1255 Johnson Ferry Rd. (Market Plaza), Marietta (509-9505); 2500 Old Alabama Rd. (Village Terrace), Roswell (998-3401); and 3722 Roswell Rd. (Powers Ferry Square), Atlanta (816-0550). This delicatessen chain sells bagels, breads, salads, cold cuts, appetizers, deli items, soups and hot meals. Open: Breakfast, Lunch and Dinner: Mon.–Sat.; Brunch: Sun. (Each restaurant has slightly different hours.)

- **Bagel Palace & Deli**, 2869 N. Druid Hills Rd. (Toco Hills Shopping Center), Atlanta (315-9016). This large, popular, and recently expanded delicatessen offers bagels, baked goods, deli items and hot meals. Specialties include a large selection of smoked fish platters. Adjacent to Palace Bakery. Open: Breakfast, Lunch and Dinner: Mon.–Sat.; Brunch: Sun. (until 4:00pm).

- **Baines Deli**, 4400 Ashford-Dunwoody Rd. (Perimeter Mall), Atlanta (395-1910). The Jewish-style deli in the food court of Perimeter Mall Shopping Center offers a selection of New York-style deli sandwiches. Open: Lunch & Dinner: Daily.

- **Boychiks' Deli**, 4520A Chamblee-Dunwoody Rd. (Georgetown Shopping Center), Dunwoody (452-0516). Dunwoody's favorite deli serves bagels, baked goods, soups, sandwiches, deli items and well-prepared Jewish-style hot meals. Open: Breakfast, Lunch and Dinner: Daily.

- **(K) Cafe Brussels**, 5975 Roswell Rd. (Hammond Springs Shopping Center), Atlanta (256-0100). The European cafe, owned by a Belgian family, features freshly-baked kosher food, Belgian waffles, pastries, crépes, soups, salads and imported coffees. Live classical and jazz music may be enjoyed on the patio. Open: Lunch: Sun.–Fri.; Dinner: Sat.–Mon. (Closes late Friday afternoon before sundown for the Sabbath and reopens after sundown on Saturday.)

- **(K) Elyseé Buckhead**, 519 E. Paces Ferry Rd. (Piedmont Rd.), Atlanta (266-8998). This elegant restaurant is Atlanta's first establishment featuring kosher continental cuisine with a French accent. Catering is also available. Open: Dinner: Sat.–Thurs. (closed on Friday nights.)

- **Emah's**, 5920 Roswell Rd. (Parkside Shopping Center–Lower Level), Atlanta (255-2686). The Israeli-owned restaurant has received praises for its authentic Israeli, Jewish, Middle Eastern and Moroccan specialties, such as couscous, shish kabob, goulash, hummus and felafel. Menu changes daily. Open: Lunch and Dinner: Daily.

- **Fox's Stage Door Deli and Saloon**, 654 Peachtree St. (next to the Fox Theatre), Atlanta (881-0223). New York-style deli is offered, including excellent cheesecakes and desserts. Piano entertainment may be enjoyed before and after Fox Theatre performances. Catering is also available for parties up to 50 in a private loft area. Open: Lunch and Dinner: Daily. (Late hours after Fox Theatre performances.)

■ **Goldberg and Son Bakery & Delicatessen**, 4383 Roswell Rd. (Roswell Wieuca Shopping Center), Atlanta (256-3751). Bagels, baked goods and deli items are served at this Jewish bakery and deli. Try the Poor Boy sandwich — it can't be beat. There is a small sit-down eating area. The deli has recently opened a small concession stand at the Georgia Dome. Open: Breakfast and Lunch: Daily.

■ **The Legal Bagel**, 55 Park Pl. (First Union Bank Building), Atlanta (522-2245). The downtown sandwich shop features bagels and New York-style deli sandwiches. Open: Breakfast and Lunch: Mon.–Fri.

■ **Mabel's Table**, 2071 N. Druid Hills Rd. (just west of I-85 exit/Buford Hwy.), Atlanta (315-6231). This innovative restaurant combines Jewish delicatessen favorites with Cajun specialties. The New York-style deli sandwiches are excellent, as is the friendly service. Open: Lunch and Dinner: Mon.–Sat. (Plans include adding a special Sunday brunch and Sunday dinner.)

■ **The New Bagel Eatory**, 6333 Roswell Rd. (Marshall's Shopping Center), Atlanta (256-4411). The restaurant sells bagels, a full-line of bakery products, delicatessen items and hot meals. Open: Breakfast, Lunch and Dinner: Mon.–Sat.; Brunch: Sun. (until 6:00pm).

■ *(K)* **Quality Kosher Meats and Delicatessen**, 2161 Briarcliff Rd. (LaVista Rd.), Atlanta (636-1114). The delicatessen sells kosher meat, groceries and deli items and has a large eating area offering kosher deli sandwiches and hot meals. Open: Breakfast and Lunch: Mon.–Fri.; Brunch: Sun. (until 3:00pm).

■ **Snack 'N' Shop**, 3515 Northside Pkwy. (W. Paces Ferry Rd.), Atlanta (261-4737). This northwest Atlanta favorite sells bagels, bakery items, delicatessen sandwiches, smoked fish, soups and kosher-style hot meals. Open: Breakfast and Lunch: Mon.–Fri.; Brunch: Sat.–Sun. (until 6:00pm).

■ **Sonny's Deli**, 6623 Roswell Rd. (Abernathy Square), Atlanta (303-0030). The old-fashioned Jewish delicatessen serves a full-range of kosher-style hot and cold entrees, along with Middle Eastern specialties, such as felafel, hummous, tahina and babaghanoush. Open: Breakfast, Lunch and Dinner: Daily (until 8:00pm).

■ **Stage Restaurant Deli**, 3850 Roswell Rd. (1/4 mile north of Piedmont Rd.), Atlanta (233-3354). The original sandwich shrine in New York City has recently opened in Atlanta serving New York-style delicatessen with menu items named after local Atlanta celebrities. Also try the soups, salads and hot meals. Plans are underway for a second downtown location. Open: Breakfast: Sat.–Sun.; Lunch and Dinner: Daily.

■ **Timberlake Sandwich Shop**, 60 Luckie St. (Peachtree and Broad Building),

Atlanta (525-5265). The New York-style restaurant serves a selection of deli sandwiches to the business crowd. Open: Breakfast and Lunch: Mon.-Fri.

■ *(K)* **Wall Street Pizza**, 2470 Briarcliff Rd. (Loehmann's Plaza/N. Druid Hills Rd.), Atlanta (633-2111). All the food served at this restaurant — pizza, Middle Eastern specialties and more — is kosher. Open: Lunch: Sun.–Fri.; Dinner: Sat.–Mon. (Closes late Friday afternoon before sundown for the Sabbath and reopens after sundown on Saturday.)

ENTERTAINMENT: THEATRE, DANCE, MUSIC, CLUBS, FILMS, T.V. & RADIO, SPORTS

JEWISH SINGLES ACTIVITIES

■ *The Atlanta Jewish Times* features a special column spotlighting Atlanta's singles' events, including activities sponsored by the AJCC, advertisements by private single dating services, and announcements about social events sponsored by local entrepreneurs who organize parties for Jewish singles. A special classified ads section called "People Connector – Voice Connector," allows a single to record a personal message to enhance his or her print advertisement.

■ **JASS LINE** (908-3395) is a free single events hotline sponsored by the AJCC.

THEATRE, DANCE & MUSIC

■ **The Israeli Folkdance Club** (499-1181), in conjunction with the Israel Program Center, holds free dance workshops at the AJCC/Peachtree throughout the year. Other folk dance groups meet at the AJCC/Zaban Branch, AJCC/Cobb Branch, some of the synagogues and Atlanta Hillel at Emory University. You may also contact the club for information about special workshops by visiting Israeli choreographers, which are scheduled throughout the year. Look for announcements in the AJCC newsletter and *The Atlanta Jewish Times.*

■ **Shirim Chorale** (875-7881), the southeast's only Jewish chorale group, performs at the AJCC singing a variety of Jewish music in Yiddish, Hebrew and English.

■ Plans are underway to put together a **Russian Émigré Orchestra** and bring premier Russian performers to Atlanta.

■ The AJCC and The AJF sponsor year-round films, concerts, theatrical performances and special events. For example: **AJCC's Café Dizengoff** features an evening of Israeli songs and music; and the **Israeli Independence Day** celebration in April usually features a concert by world renowned Israeli performers.

Look for announcements in the AJCC newsletter and synagogue newsletters.

■ Jewish and Israeli performers may also be enjoyed at other locations in the city. For example, in recent years: **Itzhak Perlman** and **Israel Sholom Pops Orchestra with Theodore Bikel** performed at the Fox Theatre as part of the Coca-Cola International Series; **Habibi**, the Israeli pop recording group, performed at a local synagogue; and **The Klezmer Conservatory Band** performed an eclectic selection of Yiddish vocal and instrumental pieces at the Hyatt Regency Ravinia. (Klezmer music is sometimes humorously referred to as the "Blues of the Jews" because it began in the ghettos of Eastern Europe during the Middle Ages when bands of itinerant Jewish musicians went from town to town playing for Jewish festivals and special events.)

FILMS

■ **Jewish Film Festival,** Robert Woodruff Arts Center, High Museum of Art, 1280 Peachtree St., Atlanta (892-HIGH) is a month-long film festival cosponsored by the Consulate General of Israel and the Israel Program Center of the AJCC. At least six current award-winning Israeli films are usually screened at the film festival.

T.V. & RADIO

■ Recently, cable television stations have been broadcasting **High Holy Day Services** (Rosh Hashanah and Yom Kippur) in the fall. Contact the Atlanta Interfaith Broadcasters, Inc. (892-0454) for this year's schedule.

festivals & special events

JANUARY

■ **Russian Cultural Arts Showcase**, AJCC, Atlanta (875-7881). This cultural arts festival spotlights the Russian émigré community and features a visual arts exhibit and an evening performance of music and dance.

PASSOVER

■ **Passover Seder**, AJCC (875-7881). The AJCC sponsors three special seders during Passover — a family seder at the Zaban Park branch; a Kid's Passover Extravaganza, also at the Zaban Park branch; and a special seder for émigré families, their sponsors and hosts at the Peachtree Road branch.

APRIL

■ **Yom Hashoa – Day of Remembrance for Victims of the Holocaust** (875-7881). The AJCC hosts a religious service at Greenwood Cemetery and a civic observance at the Georgia State Capitol Building.

■ **Homecoming**, AJCC, Atlanta (875-7881). The entire community is welcome to attend this annual event, which features rides, demonstrations, program information, singing, dancing, relay races, food and lots of fun.

JUNE

■ **Celebrate Israel**, Zaban Park Branch of the AJCC, Dunwoody (396-3250). This annual celebration of Israel features an Israeli marketplace, hands-on arts and crafts activities for children, singing, dancing, Maccabean games, ethnic food and other special children's activities.

SEPTEMBER

■ **Family Funday**, Zaban Park Branch of the AJCC, Dunwoody (396-3250). A carnival, moonwalk, pony rides, a matzah ball hunt and live entertainment highlight this children's festival at Zaban Park.

OTHER

■ The AJCC and the AJF sponsor festivals and special events throughout the year. A sampling: **Road to Israel**, offering information about study and travel programs in Israel and featuring Israeli art, books, food and performances; **The Jewish Book Festival**; and **The Jewish Artist's Festival**.

■ **Synagogues** sponsor Purim carnivals, Passover Seders, Chanukah parties and other holiday celebrations. For example, Or VeShalom's annual Chanukah festival has become quite popular through the years.

RESOURCES

CONSULATES, CHAMBERS OF COMMERCE & TRADE ORGANIZATIONS

■ **Consulate General of Israel**, 1100 Spring St., Suite 440, NW, Atlanta 30309 (875-7851); **Israel Government Tourist Office**, 1100 Spring St., NW, Atlanta 30309 (875-7851); **American-Israeli Chamber of Commerce**, 1100 Spring St., Suite 410, Atlanta 30309 (874-6970); **Development Corporation for Israel** (Israel

Bond Office), 2250 N. Druid Hills Rd., Suite 230, Atlanta 30329 (634-9500).

SOCIAL SERVICE AGENCIES

■ **JACS of Atlanta** (266-7971) provides a confidential hotline and program for Jewish alcoholics and chemically dependent persons and their significant others.

■ **Jewish Educational Loan Fund** (892-0503) provides interest-free loans to Jewish students in the southeast for post-secondary schools, colleges or universities based upon need.

■ **Jewish Family Services** (873-2277) and Cobb Branch (973-3167) provides professional casework and counseling services for families and individuals with interpersonal and socio-economic problems. Geriatric counseling is also offered. Outreach programs are available in many suburban counties.

■ **Jewish Vocational Services** (876-5872) assists adults seeking employment through the use of job-related services and offers college counseling and testing for high school students and adults. A Senior Adult Workshop assists older adults in becoming gainfully employed. Special services are offered for Jewish Russian and Iranian émigrés.

■ **Massell Dental Clinic**, 18 7th St., NE, Atlanta (881-1858) provides dental services, including prophylaxes, extractions and orthodontia. Other dental specializations are available. Fees are based on family income and size.

■ **Outreach Programs** (873-1661) provide social, educational and cultural opportunities for members of the Jewish community from Latin America, Iran and South Africa. For example, **Programma de Asistencia a Judios Latinos** (Jewish Latin Outreach Program in the U.S.) provides support services for Jewish Latins and sponsors social activities for the community such as an annual Mother's Day Picnic.

RESOURCES FOR SENIOR ADULTS

■ **Dial-A-Ride Transportation** (873-2277) provides senior adults with transportation to appointments.

■ **Housemate Match** (875-7881) attempts to match those needing living space with those who have room. One person in the match must be 60 years of age or older.

■ **William Breman Jewish Home**, 3150 Howell Mill Rd., NW, Atlanta (351-8410) is a modern 120-bed nursing facility offering comprehensive residential care for older men and women, including medical, nursing, rehabilitation, recreational, spiritual and casework support services.

■ **The Jewish Tower**, 3160 Howell Mill Rd., NW, Atlanta (351-3536) is an apartment residence for the disabled, handicapped and/or those 62 years of age or older.

■ **The Louis Kahn Group Home**, 1538 Markan Dr., NE, Atlanta (873-2112) provides residential care for senior adults who require basic support services to maintain an independent life style. Services include 24-hour facility coverage, kosher meals and social programming.

■ **Meals on Wheels** (873-2277) delivers kosher meals for the homebound.

■ **Senior Adult Workshop** (876-5872) provides older adults with opportunities for gainful employment.

■ **Weinstein Center for Adult Day Services**, Atlanta Jewish Community Center – Zaban Branch, 5300 Tilly Mill Rd., Dunwoody (458-3614) offers daycare for the elderly and weekend respite care for developmentally disabled children and youths.

RESOURCES FOR THE HOMELESS

■ **Genesis Shelter**, The Temple – Selig Building, 1589 Peachtree Rd., NE, Atlanta (351-1935) is a 10,000 square foot, year-round facility for homeless newborns and their families — the first such shelter in the country. Genesis Shelter is sponsored by 16 different churches, temples and businesses in the Atlanta area.

■ **Zaban Night Shelter**, The Temple – Selig Building, 1589 Peachtree Rd., NE, Atlanta 30367 (872-3067) houses a shelter for homeless couples, sponsored and staffed by volunteers from Atlanta's synagogues and religious institutions.

OTHER

■ **American Jewish Committee** (233-5501); **Anti-Defamation League of B'nai B'rith** (262-3470); **B'nai B'rith District Five** (662-8505); **Chabad Center-Lubavitch Central Organization** (843-2464); **Jewish National Fund** (633-1132); **National Council of Jewish Women** (262-7199); and **Women's American ORT Federation** (393-8555).

■ Contact the **Atlanta Jewish Federation** (873-1661) for current numbers of other Jewish organizations which have local chapters, such as **American Friends of Hebrew University, American Jewish Congress, American Mizrachi Women, Atlanta Zionist Federation, Brandeis University National Women's Committee, Children of Holocaust Survivors, City of Home, Eternal Light-Hemschech, Generation After, Hadassah, Jewish Marriage Encounter, Jewish War Veterans, Magen David Adom, Pioneer Women, Service Guild Inc., Women's Circle** and **Zionist Organization of America**.

Pan People Steel Band

CARIBBEAN COMMUNITIES

HISTORY

An estimated 35,000 West Indians live in metropolitan Atlanta, augmented by a daily influx of immigrants from both the Caribbean region and the northeastern U.S. The more than 23 Caribbean island countries were originally inhabited by Arawaks (thought to be the creators of Jamaican jerk spice), Caribs and other Native Indian groups, but now boast a rich and diverse ethnic history, with roots extending to Africa, the Netherlands, Spain, Britain, France, and Ireland. The Chinese, Lebanese, Syrians and East Indians have also left their historical footprints in the Caribbean, influencing, among other things, the spices used in contemporary West Indian cooking.

The culinary contributions of West Indians to Atlanta reach beyond the familiar nutmeg and cinnamon of Grenada and fiery jerk (a combination of spices) from Jamaica. The contributions include Scotch bonnet pepper, curries, Blue Mountain coffee and rum (distilled from sugar cane). There are also unique tropical fruits, such as guanabana, plantains, tamarind and ackee, and uncommon vegetables, such as callaloo, igname and chayote. In Atlanta, these food products may be purchased in several West Indian markets and farmers markets, and savored in tasty meals served in trendy, Caribbean-style restaurants with reggae music in the background.

Bob Marley . . . reggae . . . Harry Belafonte . . . calypso . . . steel bands. The islands have spawned unique and exciting music enjoyed by people all over the world. Reggae was born in Jamaica, and steel bands and calypso began in Trinidad and Tobago. Atlantans may listen or dance to reggae and other Caribbean music almost any day of the year at a few local restaurants, nightclubs, special events, and festivals.

257

■ **Atlanta Botanical Garden**, 1345 Piedmont Rd. (Piedmont Park at The Prado), Atlanta (876-5858). The Fuqua Conservatory has a plethora of tropical plants one can study and enjoy while meandering on a stone path past a waterfall in the misty, enclosed environment. Hours: Tues.–Sat. 9:00am–6:00pm; Sun. 12noon–6:00pm. (Extended hours during summer months.) Admission fee.

■ **Ancestral Arts Gallery**, 780 N. Highland Ave., NE, Atlanta (872-0792). The gallery exhibits original works by African-American, African, South American, Jamaican and Haitian artists. Art books, art objects and framing are available. Hours: Tues.–Fri. 11:00am–7:00pm; Sat. 12noon–8:00pm. Free.

■ **Hammonds House Galleries and Resource Center of African-American Art**, 503 Peeples St., SW, Atlanta (752-8215). The Hammonds House is an art gallery and cultural and resource center in historic West End, located in a mid-nineteenth century Victorian-style house. Included in its excellent permanent collection of art is a stunning survey collection of important Haitian paintings. Hours: Mon.–Fri. 10:00am–8:00pm; Sat.– Sun. 12noon–6:00pm. Free.

■ **Le Primitif Galleries**, 631 Miami Cir., Suite 25, Atlanta (240-0226). This colorful gallery specializes in Haitian art, including brilliant paintings, woodcarvings, elaborately sequined fabrics, papier mâché, and oil drum sculptures whose originality, whimsicality and appeal have been compared to Calder's sculptures. Well-known first generation Haitian artists, such as Bigaud, Cedor, Gourgue and the younger artists Dambreville, Michaud, Jacques and others, are featured. The owner travels to Haiti periodically to buy directly from the artists. Hours: Mon.–Thurs. 11:00am–5:00pm; Fri.–Sat. 11:00pm–6:00pm; and Sun. 1:00pm–6:00pm. Free.

PLACES TO KEEP AN EYE ON

■ **Afrimage Arts & Promotions**, 70 Fairlie St. (5th floor Fairlie Building), Atlanta (525-5758). Afrimage has had a Haitian art collection and other special artwork, notably the African Cameo Collection. The art may be viewed by appointment only.

■ **ArtVue**, 220 Pharr Rd., NE, Atlanta (841-9130). The gallery occasionally exhibits works by Caribbean artists and recently hosted a display of Haitian artwork. Hours: Tues.–Fri. 11:00am–6:00pm; Sat.–Sun. 1:00pm–6:00pm. ArtVue prefers customers make an appointment.

■ **Bryant Galleries**, 99 W. Paces Ferry Rd., Atlanta (841-1920). Haitian art is frequently shown along with art from many countries, including the U.S. Hours: Mon.–Sat. 10:00am–5:30pm.

■ **Heritage Galleries**, 4189-D Snapfinger Woods Dr., Atlanta (284-1353). Heritage always seems to have some pieces of Caribbean art in its collection. The gallery featured Caribbean art, cuisine and music in conjunction with the annual Peach Caribbean Carnival held the end of May. Hours: Tues.–Fri. 12noon–8:00pm; Sat. 10:00am–8:00pm; and Sun.–Mon. by appointment only.

■ **The Modern Primitive Gallery**, 1402 N. Highland Ave., Atlanta (892-0556). The gallery presents works by Haitian artists, local artists, and others working in the primitive motif. Hours: Tues.–Sun. 11:00am–9:00pm.

■ **Undersea World** — *On the Horizon*. The ambitious and fascinating aquarium project, partially funded by the city of Atlanta, is still in the design and funding stages. The vision includes "marine life habitats common to the Caribbean" in one tank area.

COMMUNITY, RELIGIOUS & CULTURAL ASSOCIATIONS

■ **Atlanta Caribbean Association** (482-6781). This organization, founded in 1984, seeks to unify West Indians, foster cultural, social and economic relationships among Atlantans of Caribbean descent, and share their culture with the larger community. Members participate in the Atlanta Peach Carnival and Black History Month, among other events. The association publishes a newsletter and a business directory, *The Caribbean Pages*. Membership is open to everyone and monthly meetings are held the first Saturday of each month at Holy Cross Episcopal Parish Hall, 5:00pm–7:00pm.

■ **Barbados American Cultural Association** (593-1832). Former residents of Barbados and other interested people are invited to attend monthly meetings at the Glen Haven United Methodist Church in Decatur. Prominent members of the community are honored, and recently the Barbados ambassador to the U.S., Sir William R. Douglas, was a guest speaker.

■ **Atlanta Jamaican Association** (593-9290). This group meets once a month at the Episcopal Church of the Holy Cross in Decatur and celebrates Jamaican Independence Day in August. Members try to get involved in community issues of importance to people of Jamaican heritage.

■ **Jamaican Cultural Society of Atlanta (JCSA)** (808-1869). The society had its inaugural meeting in March of 1991 and currently meets in libraries, with the annual general meeting held each July. Call for current location and meeting time.

■ **Haitian American Community Service Association** (289-5977). The cultural and service organization serves the Haitian community in Atlanta and hosts educational forums and holiday festivities.

■ **Trinidad & Tobago Cultural Association, Inc.** (286-1621). This is primarily a social organization for natives or descendants of Trinidad and Tabago.

RELIGIOUS INSTITUTIONS

Although there is a diverse spiritual heritage in the Caribbean, including Haitian voodoo and Jamaican Rastafarianism, most natives and descendants of islanders are of Catholic and Protestant faiths. A sampling:

■ **Episcopal Church of the Holy Cross**, 2005 South Columbia Pl., Decatur (284-1211). This multi-national parish is the gathering place for several organizations, among them the Atlanta Jamaican Association and the Atlanta Caribbean Association. Jamaican Independence Day is celebrated here in August of each year.

■ **Haile Selassie I Foundation, Order of the Nyabinghi**, 504 Holderness St., SW, Atlanta (753-9019). Gatherings and Bible study are on Sunday, and the study of Rastafari and Nyabinghi is held on Tuesday and Thursday.

■ **Haitian Churches** include: **Haitian Community Church of God**, 2832 1st Ave., SW, Atlanta (762-9144/243-6772); **Haitian Ministry Theophile Church in Christ, Inc.**, 934 Custer Ave., SE, Atlanta (624-9432/478-2623) (sermons in French and Creole); and **Haitian Seventh Day Adventist Church**, 201 Washington St., Atlanta (523-5749).

■ **Ibeji Yoruba Cultural Center**, 1058C St. Charles Ave., NE, Atlanta (888-0879/755-4257). The Orishan religion practiced at this center is of African-Caribbean origin. The group maintains the culture and traditions of the Yorubas of Nigeria through art, dance, music and celebrations.

schools, classes, language

■ **The Dunham Institute**, Community Center, 321 West Hill St., Decatur (523-4474). The program includes classes in modern, jazz, Caribbean and African dance.

■ **Jamaican Dance Theater** (243-6914). Under the direction of Paulette Cousins, the theater performs dances reflective of the African heritage in Jamaica. Classes in Caribbean dance movement and history are offered to children and adults.

NEWSPAPERS

■ **Oxford Book Store**, 360 Pharr Rd., NE, Atlanta (262-3333) carries the newspaper *Caribbean Contact*.

MAGAZINES & BOOKS

■ *Caribbean Pages*, P.O. Box 794, Redan 30074 (482-6781). This business directory identifies and promotes West Indian businesses in Atlanta and is published by the Atlanta Caribbean Association.

■ **Ancestor Records & Tapes**, 306 Auburn Ave., Atlanta (681-0166). Ancestor specializes in calypso, reggae and World Beat Music.

■ **Celebrity Records and Tapes**, 4191-D Snapfinger Woods Dr. (Chapel Hall Shopping Center), Decatur (284-6870). Owned by an Antiguan native, this store specializes in Caribbean music, such as calypso, soca, steel band, reggae, jazz and gospel.

■ **Marley's**, 515 Ponce de Leon Ave., NE, Atlanta (873-2966). Records, tapes and posters abound in this small store which is an outlet for music of the Caribbean, especially Jamaica.

■ **Tropical Breeze**, 1129 Euclid Ave., NE, Atlanta (659-0884). This music and cultural shop offers African and Caribbean music on records, cassettes and CDs, as well as musical instruments, clothing, jewelry, books and alternative African-American and African films.

■ **Africaribbean Food Store**, 6067 Buford Hwy. (1-1/2 mi. outside I-285), Doraville. The store offers items from West Africa and the West Indies, such as hot pepper spices, teas, bottled Caribbean sauces and glazes, canned products (coconut milk), as well as some everyday household items.

■ **Brotherhood West Indian American Bakery**, 476 Edgewood Ave., Atlanta (523-3516). The store specializes in food from Trinidad and offers such delights as coconut rolls, cassava pones, vegetable patties and hops bread.

■ **Caribbean-USA Food Market**, 4467 Glenwood Rd., Decatur (286-9990). The market carries Caribbean food products, including West Indian spices.

■ **Choice Bakery & Roti Shop**, 3375 Columbia Woods Dr., Decatur (286-4138). West Indian food such as roti (a bread from Trinidad) and traditional American baked goods are offered at this eclectic bakery.

■ **Diaz Market #3**, 755 Ponce De Leon Ave., NE, Atlanta (875-6568). Jamaican, Cuban, Puerto Rican, Mexican and Latin American food products may be purchased, as well as magazines, Spanish newspapers, videos in Spanish, and cassettes.

■ **Global Food Distributors**, 2995 Roosevelt Hwy., College Park (768-1927). This international grocery specializes in African and Caribbean foods and products.

■ **Helen's Tropical Exotics**, 3519 Church St., Clarkston (292-7278). Helen's produces and sells special tropical food seasonings and sauces, such as Scotch bonnet pepper sauce, jerk chicken seasoning, and tropical fruit sauces, which can be found on the shelves of Atlanta's farmers markets. The mail order department will gladly send you a free sample of seasonings and a pamphlet of recipes. Helen Willinsky has written a cookbook entitled *Jerk, Barbecue From Jamaica*, which is available at local bookstores.

■ **International Kitchens**, 4880 Lower Roswell Rd., Suite 780, Marietta (971-8912). Jamaican Blue Mountain coffee and spices, as well as marmalades, jellies and more, are imported from the Caribbean. Make up your own or have the owner assist you in creating "A Touch of Jamaica" gift basket. Coffee and food products from many other countries are also offered.

■ **Island Spice Jamaica**, Suite #11, 1640 Smyrna-Roswell Rd., Smyrna (319-0749). The owners make their own spices and sell to the general public and restaurants.

■ **J J's West Indian Mart**, 3429 Covington Dr. (Covington Plaza), Decatur (288-7865). Specializing in Jamaican groceries, the market carries jerk seasonings, spices, Scotch bonnet pepper sauce, cold ginger beer, beef patties, hard dough bread and buns, and other West Indian food. They have home-cooked, take-out food including, chicken curry, spicy meat pies, and ackee, and cod lunches served on Saturdays. Two tables are available for limited seating.

■ **J. Martinez**, 3230-A Peachtree Rd. (Buckhead), Atlanta (231-5465). West Indian specialities, including Jamaican Blue Mountain coffees, are sold here for individual purchase or corporate gift giving.

■ **Montego Jamaican and West Indian Foods**, 4763 Memorial Dr., Decatur (294-9057). A patron may purchase West Indian food products at the store, including fresh Jamaican peppers, and eat lunch or dinner in the adjoining restaurant.

- **Royal Caribbean Bakery**, 4859 Memorial Dr., Stone Mountain (299-7714). The shop sells a variety of foods including vegetable patties, oxtail, spiced buns, coco bread (used for making sandwiches) and take-out Jamaican dishes.
- **T's Tropical Market**, 2863 Buford Hwy., Atlanta (728-8882). The new market carries a variety of African, Caribbean, Hispanic and American fresh, packaged and refrigerated foods.
- **Tony's Caribbean American Store**, 3590 Covington Hwy., Decatur (296-9192). Tony's offers Jamaican jerk spice and other hot pepper spices, tropical sauces for seafood and chicken, and many other Caribbean food and personal care products.
- **Tropical Delite**, 2136 Candler Rd., Decatur (284-1878). Enjoy Jamaican pastries, fresh-baked Jamaican beef patties, and other food baked on the premises.
- **Tropical Food Mart**, 2047 Stewart Ave. (Crossroad Mall), Atlanta (761-2202). The market carries ginger beer, a unique guava-pumpkin jam, and other foods, spices, and natural ingredients from Jamaica and Trinidad, as well as West Africa.
- **Tropical Foods**, 5165 Buford Hwy. (Pinetree Plaza), Doraville (451-4355). The pleasant, spacious market carries a lot of teas and spices from West Africa (especially Nigeria) and the Caribbean, as well as canned goods, frozen fish, fresh vegetables, toiletries, candy, and beautiful fabric made in Holland.
- **West Indian American Foods**, 2575 Snapfinger Rd., Decatur (987-4015). The market offers a wide variety of West Indian food, spices and fresh peppers.
- Ingredients for cooking Caribbean-style food at home are easy to come by in Atlanta. In addition to the superb locations listed above, the following farmers markets carry fresh produce and spices indigenous to the islands: **Harry's Farmers Market**, 1180 Upper Hembree Rd, Alpharetta (664-6300) and 2025 Satellite Point, Duluth (416-6900); **International Farmers Market**, 5193 Peachtree Industrial Blvd., Chamblee (455-1777); and **Your DeKalb Farmers Market**, 3000 Ponce de Leon Ave., Decatur (377-6400). Also, don't be surprised to discover Jamaican hot pepper sauce in your local market or Caribbean spices at the health food store.

■ **Bridgetown Grill**, 1156 Euclid Ave. (Moreland Ave./Little Five Points), Atlanta (653-0110) and 689 Peachtree St. (across from the Fox Theatre), Atlanta (873-5361). Enjoy reggae background music while eating spicy Jamaican and Cuban food in this popular indoor/outdoor restaurant. House specialties are Caribbean jerk chicken, BBQ jerk pork chops, a vegetarian plate and Jamaican beer. Open: Lunch and Dinner: Daily.

■ **Caribbean Queen**, 6116-D Covington Hwy. (Panola Rd.), Lithonia (808-0393). Curried goat and chicken, seafood, oxtail, and jerk chicken are some of this restaurant's specialties. Open: Lunch and Dinner: Mon.-Sat.

■ **The Caribbean Restaurant**, 180 Auburn Ave. (Piedmont Rd.), Atlanta (658-9829). An extensive menu features curried goat, jerk chicken, sweet and sour chicken, oxtail, snapper, fried conch, shrimp, grouper and more, served with rice and two vegetables. Open: Lunch: Mon.–Fri.; Dinner: Mon.–Sat.

■ **Caribbean Sunset Restaurant and Nightclub**, 60 Upper Alabama St., (Underground Atlanta), Atlanta (659-4589). This is a Caribbean theme nightclub and restaurant serving jerk chicken, curried goat and more. Open: Lunch and Dinner: Daily.

■ **Coco Loco Cuban and Caribbean Café**, 2625 Piedmont Rd. (Buckhead Crossing Mall/Sidney Marcus Blvd.), Atlanta (261-0198) and 6301 Roswell Rd., (Sandy Springs Plaza), Atlanta (255-5434). Known for its excellent Cuban sandwiches and extensive menu, this cafe also offers jerk chicken, tropical beverages, Latin wines and beers from Mexico, the Virgin Islands, Jamaica, Asia and Europe. Open: Lunch and Dinner: Mon.–Sat. and Sun. 1:00pm–9:00pm.

■ **Eat Right West Indian-American Restaurants**, 2440-H Wesley Chapel Rd. (Wal-Mart Shopping Center), Decatur (987-2104). Owned by a native of Jamaica, this restaurant specializes in West Indian cuisine. Take-out food is available. Open: Lunch and Dinner: Mon.–Sat.

■ **Indigo Coastal Grill**, 1397 N. Highland Ave. (Lanier Ave.), Atlanta (876-0676). Seafood, spicy dishes, and their special Tia Maria flan are served in a tropical atmosphere at this consistently well-rated restaurant. Open: Dinner: Daily.

■ **J J's West Indian Mart**, 3429 Covington Dr. (Covington Plaza), Decatur (288-7865). Specializing in Jamaican groceries, the market carries jerk seasonings, spices, Scotch bonnet pepper sauce, cold ginger beer, beef patties, hard dough bread and buns, and other West Indian food. They primarily offer home-cooked, take-out food, but have two tables for limited seating. Open: Lunch and Dinner: Mon.–Sat.

- **Montego Cafe**, 4763 Memorial Dr. (Rockbridge Rd./outside I-285), Decatur (294-9057). This Jamaican restaurant (adjoining Montego Jamaican and West Indian Foods) offers curries, ginger bullah cakes, Red Stripe beer and more, with reggae music in the background. Open: Dinner: Lunch and Dinner: Daily.
- **Springy's**, 710 Peachtree St. (3rd Ave.) Atlanta (607-0021). Jamaican home-made soup, jerk chicken and pork, salads, curries, and homemade desserts are created to please the clientele. Open: Lunch and Dinner: Mon.–Sat.

> ## ENTERTAINMENT:
> ### THEATRE, DANCE, MUSIC, CLUBS, FILMS, T.V. & RADIO, SPORTS

DANCE & MUSIC

- **Jamaican Dance Theater** (243-6914). Under the direction of Paulette Cousins, a Jamaican native, this group combines African, European and regional traditions into a distinctly Caribbean art form. The costumes are colorful and the music is dynamic. Enjoy performances at various festivals around Atlanta, including the Peach Carnival and Kingfest Internationale in May. Dance classes are also available to children and adults.
- **Other Performance Groups.** There are numerous local bands that play Caribbean music, especially reggae. Two popular groups are **Tropical Steel Vibes** (758-9859), a calypso and reggae band which, under the direction of Clyde Fabien, has played all over Atlanta, including the Festival of Nations at Villa International, Emory University, the Summer Concert Series at One Atlantic Center, and Underground's Festival of Cultures. Another popular local group is **Pan People Steelband** (753-8241), under the direction of Ajamu Nyomba, whose eight members play a wide range of music from reggae and calypso to jazz and classical.

NIGHTCLUBS

- **Carey's Buckhead Longbranch,** 290 E. Paces Ferry Rd., Atlanta (239-9650). Dance to live reggae music at 9:00pm on the deck.
- **Caribana International Reggae Bar**, 2043 Cheshire Bridge Rd., Atlanta (248-9712). Enjoy reggae music every evening except Monday, beginning at 9:00pm.
- **Caribbean Sunset Restaurant and Nightclub**, 60 Upper Alabama St., Atlanta (659-4589). Head to Underground Atlanta's Kenny's Alley to enjoy a

Caribbean theme restaurant and club with live reggae, calypso and soca at 9:00pm, Wednesday–Sunday.

- **CJ's Landing**, 270 Buckhead Ave., Atlanta (237-7657). Dance to live reggae every Friday and Saturday night.
- **Club Montego**, 4763 Memorial Dr., Decatur (294-9057). The Jamaican restaurant and lounge features reggae parties every Friday and Saturday evening starting at 11:00pm.
- **The Cotton Club**, 1021 Peachtree St., NE, Atlanta (874-2523). The popular club features a variety of live music, including reggae. Tickets for shows may be purchased at Ticketmaster for "big names" (like Toots & the Maytals) or at the door. Patrons must be over age 21. Call for a very informative taped message.
- **Kafe Jamaica — Caribbean Eatery**, 1049 Juniper St., Atlanta (888-0070). The eatery occasionally books reggae and Caribbean music. Call to find out if live music has been scheduled.
- **Starlight Club**, 4467 Glenwood Rd., Decatur (286-0956). Live Caribbean music, such as reggae, soca and calypso, is played on Saturday nights.

TV & RADIO

- **WRAS-FM (88.5)**. At 10:00pm on Tuesdays, listen to reggae, soca and calypso on the "Caribbean Shakedown" program.

SPORTS

- **Atlanta Cricket Club** (971-6097/381-0727/447-9248). Atlanta's Cricket Club began in 1989 and has already grown from just two teams to nine. British expatriates, Indians, Pakistanis, South Africans and West Indians compete every Sunday, May–October, at four fields in metro-Atlanta.

FESTIVALS & SPECIAL EVENTS

FEBRUARY

- **Reggae Superfest**. The celebration is just what the name implies — a festival of exciting reggae music. Keep your eye open for the location of this year's event.

APRIL

- **Caribbean Cultural Festival**, Soapstone Center for the Arts, South DeKalb

Mall (241-2453). The spring festival features music, dance, arts, crafts and culture of the Caribbean Islands (including performances by reggae, folk and dance groups from the islands) and travel information.

MAY

■ **Atlanta Peach Carnival**, Downtown, Atlanta (433-5996/344-2567). This annual folklife festival for children and adults celebrates the rich and colorful artistic and cultural heritage of the Caribbean for three days, and is highlighted by a parade down Peachtree Street with bands of costumed dancers. Woodruff Park is transformed into a Caribbean marketplace with dance, literary, visual and performing arts, retail vendors, folklife demonstrations and food. Groups from Jamaica, the Virgin Islands, Trinidad, Tobago and other islands perform during the day and at late-night concerts. A whole afternoon is set aside for a children's carnival held at the Gilbert House. Several galleries display Caribbean art in conjunction with this festival.

■ **Kingfest Internationale**, The Martin Luther King, Jr. Center for Non-Violent Social Change, Atlanta (222-8863). Several Jamaican reggae groups, such as the Paulette Cousins Jamaican Dance Theatre and Inner Circle, often appear at this festival of international performing arts and crafts.

■ **Reggae Sunsplash**, Variety Playhouse, 1099 Euclid Ave. (Little Five Points), Atlanta (524-7354). The first annual event was held in 1991 to benefit the Community Unity Homeless Mission. Local reggae groups participate in the 7-hour event.

JULY

■ **Festival of Cultures**, Underground Atlanta, Atlanta (523-2311). This annual event features different cultural groups on the weekends throughout the month of July. One weekend features a Latin American and Caribbean Festival offering lectures, food, entertainment and a display of cultural artifacts. Tropical Steel Drums, Pirates of the Caribbean Band and other West Indian groups have played during the festival.

■ **One Love Rastafari Gathering**, Mozley Park, Atlanta (627-1732). Sponsored by One Love Commission, Inc., this annual gathering includes a live concert of reggae music. Past performers have included the national reggae superstar Sister Carol.

SOCIAL SERVICES

■ **Butler Street YMCA**, 22 Butler St., NE, Atlanta (659-8085). This is the area office of the USA/Caribbean Program Support Unit.

BUSINESS

■ **Atlanta Business League Reciprocal Jamaica Trade Mission** (584-8126).

CONSULATES

■ **Consulate of Haiti,** P.O. Box 80340, Atlanta 30366 (847-0709).

Dancers performing during Kwanzaa, a week-long African-American cultural celebration.

AFRICAN-AMERICAN & AFRICAN COMMUNITIES

Africa is a continent of diverse cultures, languages, history and natural resources, and when Africans were forceably taken (largely from West Africa) to be slaves in America, those who survived managed to preserve and bring some of their cultural heritage with them. Unfortunately, most of the African legacy was lost during the dehumanizing experience of slavery. However, after the Civil War, many former slaves moved to Atlanta, and by the turn of the century, the city had become quite an educational, economic and religious center for blacks. By the 1960s and early 1970s, blacks began the monumental task of researching and reclaiming their African heritage through reconstructing their histories and recognizing the many contributions to American life made by blacks. And yet, despite the efforts of many, much of African and African-American history is not infused into our school textbooks, so most Americans remain ignorant of African history and the significant impact this cultural legacy has had in all fields, including science, politics and government, education, entertainment, visual arts, law and medicine.

Some recent efforts underway in Atlanta to promote African and African-American culture and history include the preservation of historic sites and neighborhoods, most recently Reynoldstown, South Atlanta, and the Sweet Auburn District; the creation of cultural centers, such as House of Ujamaa, Shrine of the Black Madonna, and Africa House Learning and Resource Center; the promotion of art through the Catherine Waddell Art Gallery, Hughley Gallery, and William Tolliver's Art Gallery; the development of performing arts groups, such as Jomandi Productions, Just Us Theatre Company, Ballethnic Dance Company and Total Dance Theatre; and the celebration of culture through festivals such as the biennial National Black Arts Festival. African-Americans maintain an active, visible political presence in the city, occupying the Office of Mayor of the City of Atlanta, Chairman of the Fulton County Commission, and numerous seats on the City Council and County Commission. Justice Leah Sears-Collins of Atlanta joined the Supreme Court of the State of Georgia in 1992.

Approximately 35,000 native Africans (of which about 5,000 are Ethiopians and Eritreans and 5,000 Nigerians) reside in the city of Atlanta. Many are well-educated or are students who speak English fluently, yet cultural adjustments and daily living needs, such as housing and work, are often complicated by the lack of U.S. acceptance of African professional degrees and job experiences. Plus, the African community is not cohesive, since immigrants often do not speak the same language. Despite these drawbacks, Africans have started businesses, entered professions, continued with their educations, formed community associations, created performance groups and hosted festivals so that they may share their heritage with other Atlantans. Recently, a few hundred Somalian refugees have come to Atlanta, escaping the devastating famine in their homeland, and more may be resettled here in the near future.

"Interestingly and significantly, the overwhelming choice for the best American city for Blacks is Atlanta (59.1) percent..." according to the Annual Readers Poll conducted by *Ebony* magazine in April of 1992. Our chapter highlights, among other things, some of the institutions, community groups, restaurants, festivals and performing arts groups and venues that seek to preserve and promulgate the African heritage of Atlanta's black community. We suggest readers begin with a visit to the Sweet Auburn District.

SWEET AUBURN DISTRICT

The Sweet Auburn District is currently being redesigned (along with an adjacent section of Peachtree Street) and is expected to be completed in time for the 1996 Olympics. The renaissance of this historic entertainment, social, cultural, political and business district includes the expansion of the APEX Museum and the construction of the Auburn Avenue Research Library on African-American History and Culture, that promises to be one of the best in the nation. The National Park Service has several plans in the works: Peace Pavilion, a visitor's center and museum focused around the life of Dr. Martin Luther King, Jr.; the construction of a new, much larger sanctuary for the Ebenezer Baptist Church; and the restoration of Fire Station No. 6 built in 1894. Buildings, roads and a tourist trolley are all being planned to inspire a renewal that will result in the area once again being a center of African-American culture and inspiration — truly a "special street in a special city."

(Note: The term "Sweet Auburn" was coined by social activist John Wesley Dobbs.) Some of the highlights are:

■ **The Atlanta Preservation Center** (876-2040). The center offers walking tours of this historic street where Atlanta's black entrepreneurs created a vital community of entertainment and commercial activity. Tours are offered on Saturday at 11:00pm and Sunday at 2:00pm from April through November and begin in front of the National Park Service at 522 Auburn Ave. (No reservations are necessary for groups under 15.) The center also has a brochure and free slide presentation available for group use entitled *Stories Worth Sharing: The Heritage of Atlanta's Historic African-American Neighborhoods*, which chronicles the history and achievements of Reynoldstown, South Atlanta and Mozley Park.

■ **African-American Panoramic Experience Museum (APEX)**, Collections of Life & Heritage, Inc. (John Wesley Dobbs Building), 145 Auburn Ave., NE, Atlanta (521-APEX). A must visit for all Atlantans, the APEX, founded by Dan Moore in 1985, is a permanent collection of exhibits that depicts the historical and cultural heritage of African-Americans and recognizes their contributions and achievements in helping to build Atlanta and America. Permanent exhibits in Phase I include a re-creation of the Yates & Milton Drug Store, the Paul Jones Collection of African-American Art, a state-of-the-art trolley with a beautiful video production called "Sweet Auburn, Street of Pride," and special exhibits chronicling black achievements in history, politics and science. The APEX is raising money to expand the facility (Phase II) by 90,000-square-feet. School groups and youth organizations will find that a visit to the APEX is a great field trip! Hours: Tues.–Sat. 10:00am–5:00pm; (Wed. until 6:00pm); and Jan., Feb., June, July and Aug., Sun. 1:00pm–5:00pm. Admission fee.

■ **The Atlanta Daily World**, 145 Auburn Ave., NE, Atlanta (659-1110). The public is welcome to visit and tour the first and oldest daily newspaper in the country published by black Americans. The first weekly issue was published on August 3, 1928, and in 1932, it became the first black daily paper. Hours: Mon.–Sat. by appointment only. Free.

■ **Atlanta Life Insurance Company**, Herndon Plaza, 100 Auburn Ave., NE, Atlanta (659-2100). Atlanta Life Insurance Company, the second largest black-owned insurance company in the United States, was founded in 1905 by Alonzo Herndon, a former slave. The atrium of the modern high-rise houses a permanent exhibit on the Herndon family and the history of Atlanta Life Insurance, as well as a magnificent collection of approximately 500 pieces of African-American art. Hours: Mon.–Fri. during normal business hours. Free.

■ **Auburn Avenue Research Library on African-American Culture and History**. The library is under construction on the corner of Auburn Avenue and Courtland Street next to the APEX Museum. The non-circulating collection of books, periodicals, recordings, and other materials will be open to the public, since the collection expects to have an appeal beyond academicians. It is scheduled to open in 1993.

■ **Big Bethel A.M.E. Church**, 220 Auburn Ave., NE, Atlanta (659-0248). Originally built in the 1890s, then rebuilt in 1924 after a fire, the church was a religious center and the location of Morris Brown College classes until the college acquired its own campus at the turn of the century.

■ **Ebenezer Baptist Church**, 407 Auburn Ave., NE, Atlanta (688-7263). Visitors are welcome to walk through this famous Gothic Revival sanctuary where Dr. Martin Luther King, Jr., his father, and his grandfather preached. In 1957, the church was the location of the founding of the Southern Christian Leadership Conference (SCLC) and always a focal point for the civil rights movement. The church was the site of Dr. King's funeral and is also the site of the annual ecumenical service held during King Week. Hours: Guided tours on weekdays are offered, but please call for times. Donations welcome.

■ **Martin Luther King, Jr. Birthplace**, 501 Auburn Ave., NE, Atlanta (331-3919). The simple Victorian birth home of Martin Luther King, Jr., originally purchased by his grandfather in 1909, has recently been restored and is open to visitors. Hours: Daily 10:00am–4:30pm from June to Labor Day, and 10:00am–3:30pm Labor Day to May. Free.

■ **Martin Luther King, Jr. Center for Nonviolent Social Change**, 449 Auburn Ave., NE, Atlanta (524-1956). The King Center is the official national and international monument dedicated to the life of Martin Luther King, Jr. (1929-1968), the youngest person to receive the Nobel Peace Prize. Its goal is to preserve and advance Dr. King's mission by applying his principles of nonviolence to all areas of human activity. There is an exhibition hall displaying photographs and memorabilia of Dr. King's personal and public life, and the library and archives contain one of the world's largest collections of primary source material on the civil rights movement and Martin Luther King, Jr. In the beautiful, serene courtyard of the center lies the marble crypt of Dr. King, engraved with the heartwrenching words from his famous speech, "Free at last, free at last, thank God Almighty, I'm free at last!" The center sponsors many community services and cultural events throughout the year. Hours: Mon.–Fri. 9:30am–5:30pm; Sat.–Sun. 10:00am–5:30pm with later closing hours during summer months and peak tourist season. Free.

■ **Masonic Building**, 334 Auburn Ave., NE, Atlanta. The building houses the headquarters of the Southern Christian Leadership Conference and WERD, the first black-owned radio station in the country, which was founded in 1949 by Jesse B. Blayton.

■ **National Park Service Visitor Center**, 522 Auburn Ave., NE, Atlanta (331-3920). The center has visitor information and a bookstore carrying many books on African-American history. Hours: Daily 9:00am–5:00pm.

■ **Royal Peacock Night Club**, 186 Auburn Ave., NE, Atlanta (880-0745). Opened in 1949 by Carrie Cunningham, the club was an immediate focal point for African-American culture in Atlanta, presenting top black entertainers from all over the country, such as Nat King Cole and Cab Calloway. The club continues to provide entertainment most Friday and Saturday evenings.

■ **Southern Christian Leadership Conference Headquarters**, 334 Auburn Ave., NE, Atlanta (522-1420). The SCLC was founded by Dr. Martin Luther King, Jr. over thirty years ago, and the organization still plays an important role in the civil rights movement. Hours: Mon.–Fri. 9:00am–4:30pm. Call ahead for an appointment if you would like a guided tour. Free.

■ **Sweet Auburn Welcome Center**, 145 Auburn Ave., NE, Atlanta (521-2739). Located in the APEX Museum, the center provides information on black attractions, cultural arts, business and other black institutions, and up-to-date information on black political, social and church organizations. The center also carries all of Atlanta's black-owned publications. The center is of great interest to Atlanta residents, as well as tourists.

HISTORIC WEST END DISTRICT

■ The West End is Atlanta's oldest neighborhood, dating back to 1835. **The Atlanta Preservation Center** offers walking tours of the West End and the Wren's Nest by special request. To make arrangements, phone the center at 876-2041.

■ **Hammonds House Galleries and Resource Center of African-American Art**, 503 Peeples St., SW, Atlanta (752-8730). The Hammonds House is an art gallery and cultural and resource center in historic West End, in a mid-nineteenth century Eastlake Victorian-style house. Besides housing an excellent permanent collection of Haitian and African-American art, the center sponsors numerous educational programs, forums, lectures, workshops and traveling exhibits. It also collects and shares documentation on artworks and artists in the form of videos, films, computer data bases, slides, catalogues, periodicals, publications and books. Hours: Tue.–Fri. 10:00am–6:00pm; Sat.–Sun. 1:00pm–5:00pm; and by appointment. Free.

■ **Shrine of the Black Madonna Bookstore and Cultural Arts Center**, 946

Ralph D. Abernathy Blvd., SW, Atlanta (752-6125). The center is an important place in the West End community, hosting numerous cultural events and speakers, and housing the largest black bookstore in the southeast, as well as the Karamu Art Gallery. The center also carries African imports, handcrafted jewelry, Kwanzaa materials and art prints.

■ **The Wren's Nest**, 1050 Ralph D. Abernathy Blvd., SW, Atlanta (753-7735/753-7736). The Wren's Nest is a living tribute to Joel Chandler Harris (1848-1908), author of the Uncle Remus tales featuring Br'er Rabbit and Br'er Fox. The National Historic Landmark houses the original Harris family memorabilia, books, photographs and furnishings. For years, The Wren's Nest, located in a vital African-American community, would not admit black sightseers. That changed in 1968, when a suit was filed and won under the 1964 Civil Rights Act. A guided tour of the Nest includes a slide presentation about Mr. Harris and an explanation of how his tales were influenced by stories of African folklore told by Uncle Bob Capers and George Terrell, black slaves. Indeed, these stories originated in ancient African tribal legends. The Nest is also the location for Saturday storytelling by such talents as Akbar Imhotep and Cynthia Watts, and festivals throughout the year. Hours: Tues.–Sat. 10:00am–5:00pm; Sun. 2:00pm–5:00pm, with the last tour conducted at 4:00pm. Admission fee.

RESEARCH MATERIALS

■ **Atlanta-Fulton Public Library**, One Margaret Mitchell Square, NW, Atlanta (730-1700). The Sam Williams collection of black history is available to the public. The archivist of the collection is Herman "Skip" Mason, who is also President of the African-American Family History Association, Inc. He helped develop the special exhibit "Hidden Treasures: African-American Photographers in Atlanta, 1870-1970" at the APEX Museum in 1991. At the end of the show, many photographs, oral history tapes, and other materials depicting life in the African-American community were added to the library's collection. The library also has special events during Black History Month in February and during the National Black Arts Festival held biennially in July and August. Hours: Mon. 9:00am–6:00pm; Tues.–Thurs. 9:00am–8:00pm; Fri.–Sat. 10:00am–5:00pm; and, Sun. 2:00pm–6:00pm.

■ **Atlanta History Center Library/Archives**, 3101 Andrews Dr., NW, Atlanta (814-4040). Several important collections relating to black history are available to the public at this research library, including the Grace Towns Hamilton Papers, the A. T. Walden papers, and the Justice Charles L. Weltner Collection. The archives total more than 900 manuscript collections and one million photographs, as well as books, maps and drawings. The collections document individuals, organizations, and businesses, including subject and personality files, such as the one containing magazine and newspaper clippings on Martin Luther King, Jr. Special research materials include records from Fulton county, Georgia, and the city of Atlanta. Open: Mon.-Fri. 9:00 am-5:30 pm; Sat. 9:00 am-5:00 pm.

■ **Atlanta University Center's Robert W. Woodruff Library**, 111 James P. Brawley Dr., SW, Atlanta (522-8980). The library is a repository of research materials on African and African-American history and culture.

■ **Auburn Avenue Research Library on African-American Culture and History**, Auburn Ave., NE, Atlanta (730-1700). The library, a branch of the Atlanta-Fulton Public Library System, is under construction on the corner of Auburn Avenue and Courtland Street next to the APEX Museum. Scheduled to open in 1993, this facility will be a research center dedicated solely to African-American studies. The impressive collections of the library have been gathered from all over the nation and include private papers, rare books, an extensive photograph collection, recordings, and other sophisticated and rare research materials on both famous and ordinary black people. The branch will also have a large auditorium with a full schedule of lectures, workshops and films. There will be storytelling and other activities geared to children. The non-circulating collection will be open to the public.

■ **Martin Luther King, Jr., Center for Nonviolent Social Change**, 449 Auburn Ave., NE, Atlanta (524-1956). The King Library and Archives contains one of the largest collections of documents on the civil rights movement and Dr. King's personal papers in the world. The library is open to the public, but users should call in advance to make sure there is a staff member available for assistance.

HISTORICAL EXHIBITS

■ **Atlanta Heritage Row**, Underground Atlanta, Upper Alabama St., Atlanta (584-7879). This interactive walking tour begins with the Civil War, a bunker with sound effects included, and concludes in the present with a short film of some of Atlanta's most notable figures. In between are a timeline; informative, historical newspaper articles; and videos where you can listen to Martin Luther King, Jr.'s moving "I Have a Dream" speech, John Lewis, former leader of SNCC (Student Non-Violent Coordinating Committee) and Maynard Jackson in 1970. You may take a special guided tour emphasizing the Atlanta African-American experience. Occasionally, special events are held at the museum, such as the recent discussion by Representative John

Lewis on the civil rights movement of the 1960s. Hours: Tues.–Sat. 10:00am–7:00pm; Sun. 1:00pm–7:00pm. Admission fee.

■ **Atlanta History Center**, 3101 Andrews Dr., NW, Atlanta (814-4000). The Center, which is operated by the Atlanta Historical Society, is a complex of historic houses and museum exhibits set on 32 acres of historical gardens. Through June 23, 1993, a small room devoted to the civil rights movement is on display as part of the exhibit, "Atlanta Resurgens." The 83,000-square-foot **Atlanta History Museum** will open at the Center in October 1993 with six new exhibitions, including one of traditional celebrations in Atlanta's ethnic communities and one tracing the evolution of the city's black elite and its role in the African-American community through the story of the Herndons, Atlanta's wealthiest black family. The centerpiece of the museum will be "Metropolitan Frontiers: Atlanta 1835-2000," which will tell the city's story with artifacts, mixed media, historical environments and interactive displays. (For information on the Center's Library/Archives, see listing under **Research Materials**.) Hours: Mon.–Sat. 9:00 am–5:30 pm; Sun. 12 noon–5:00 pm. Admission fee.

■ **Cyclorama**, 800 Cherokee Ave., SE, Atlanta (624-1071/658-7625). The Atlanta Cyclorama is a unique attraction that depicts the Civil War through various media. A portion of the museum houses Civil War artifacts, photographs and a small special exhibit honoring African-Americans and other minority soldiers of the war. Hours: Daily 9:30am–4:40pm, September–May and to 5:30pm, May–September. Tours are given every half hour. Admission fee.

■ **Fernbank Science Center**, 156 Heaton Park Dr., NE, Atlanta (378-4311). The center has an annual Planetarium show called "African Skies," created by David Dundee, the chair of the Space Sciences Department at Fernbank. The program has been well researched and explores the myths of creation, legends and stars from the perspective of African culture in 18 different countries. (Africans do not connect the stars to draw a figure as Europeans do.) The traveling exhibit "Images of Africa: Artifacts from Ann Bassarat Collection: Fernbank" accompanied the show in 1991. The center intends to develop more shows that highlight African-Americans in the sciences. Showtimes: Sat.– Sun. throughout February at 1:30pm. Children under the age of five will not be admitted. Admission fee.

■ **Georgia State Capitol**, 330 Capitol Ave., SW, Atlanta (656-2393). The capitol has a sculpture on the northeast side of the building depicting black Georgians' struggle for political power. Inside is a portrait of Dr. Martin Luther King, Jr. Hours: Mon.–Fri. 8:00am–5:30pm. Tours are conducted Mon.–Fri. at 10:00pm, 11:00pm, 1:00pm and 2:00pm. Free.

■ **The Herndon Home**, 587 University Pl., NW, (near Morris Brown College), Atlanta (581-9813). The Herndon Home is a Beaux Arts Classical mansion designed by Alonzo Herndon, Atlanta's wealthiest black entrepreneur, philanthropist and founder of Atlanta Life Insurance Company, and his first wife Adrienne McNeil, a drama teacher at Atlanta University. The mansion was built by skilled black craftsmen and throughout the years has stood as a symbol of black achievement. The impressive collection of furniture, rugs, glass, silver and other decorative artwork is available for viewing. Hours: Tues.–Sat. 10:00am–4:00pm. Reservations are required for groups. Free.

■ **Oakland Cemetery**, 248 Oakland Ave., SE, Atlanta (688-2107). Established in 1850, Historic Oakland Cemetery was the only municipal burying ground in Atlanta, so nearly everyone, rich or poor, black or white, was buried here until 1884. Now listed in the National Register of Historic Places, the Victorian cemetery includes the graves of black leaders Bishop Wesley J. Gaines, founder of Morris Brown College; Carrie Steele Pitts, creator of the first black orphanage in Atlanta; and William Finch, a member of the Atlanta City Council during reconstruction. An organization (Historic Oakland Cemetery Inc.) is in the process of restoring this deteriorating cemetery, improving the headstones, and marking all unmarked graves, if possible. Hours: Daily from dawn to dusk. (The office has limited hours.) Free. A walking tour brochure is available at the cemetery office for $1.25.

■ **American Minority Military History Institute** — *On the Horizon.* A group of Atlanta veterans is raising money to establish the institute in Atlanta to honor the accomplishments of African-American men and women in the military.

GALLERIES

■ **African-American Panoramic Experience — The APEX CENTER**, Collections of Life & Heritage, Inc., 145 Auburn Ave., NE (John Wesley Dobbs Building), Atlanta (521-APEX). The APEX houses the Paul Jones Collection of African-American Art and changing exhibits. Hours: Tues.–Sat. 10:00am–5:00pm (Wed. until 6:00pm); and open Sun. 1:00pm–5:00pm in Jan., Feb., June, July and Aug. Admission fee.

■ **Afrimage Arts and Promotions**, 70 Fairlie St., NW, Atlanta (525-5758). Afrimage deals in original art and posters, and assists businesses and private collectors in selecting artworks. The building itself is "dedicated to the display of the work of prominent black artists." Viewing of special collections by appointment only.

■ **Ancestral Arts Gallery**, 780 N. Highland Ave., NE, Atlanta (872-0792). Original art works by African-American, African, South American, Jamaican and Haitian artists are for sale, as well as art books and framing.   Hours: Tues.–Fri. 11:00am–7:00pm; Sat. 12noon–8:00pm.

■ **Art Effects**, 6410 Dawson Blvd., Norcross (446-6362). This gallery has original art work, limited editions, silk screen and lithographs by African-American and other notable artists. Hours: Mon.–Sat. 10:00am–6:00pm.

■ **Artist Showcase** (349-0259). The owner has a collection of originals, silk screens, lithographs and more by contemporary African-American and other prominent artists. Call for an appointment.

■ **Artistic Expressions**, 185 Mitchell St., SW, Atlanta (681-0242). The gallery specializes in African-American paintings and sculpture, provides custom framing and sells greeting cards. Hours: Mon.–Fri. 9:30am–5:30pm; Sat. 10:00am–3:00pm.

■ **Artvue**, East Village Square, 220 Pharr Rd., Suite 106, Atlanta (841-9130). Artvue exhibits art by local black artists and hosts special exhibits of Nigerian and Haitian works. Some exhibits are ongoing. Hours: Tues.–Fri. 11:00am–6:00pm; Sat. 1:00pm–6:00pm.

■ **Atlanta City Hall**, 55 Trinity Ave., Atlanta (296-1175). The magnificent atrium showcases African-American art and features the work of Wadsworth Jarrell on permanent display. Hours: Mon.–Fri. 8:00am–5:30pm.

■ **Atlanta History Center Downtown**, 140 Peachtree St., NW (at Margaret Mitchell Square), Atlanta (814-4150). The downtown center, which is operated by the Atlanta Historical Society, has small changing exhibitions highlighting Atlanta's architecture, politics, businesses and heritage, including the history of African-Americans. Recent exhibitions included: "Lift Every Voice: Atlanta's Black Artistic Heritage" and "Our New Day Begun: Atlanta's Black Artistic Heritage," both of which were offered in conjunction with the National Black Arts Festival. Open: Mon.–Sat. 10:00 am–6:00 pm.

■ **Atlanta Life Insurance Co.**, Herndon Plaza, 100 Auburn Ave., NE, Atlanta (659-2100). The large, black-owned insurance company has approximately 500 works of art on display throughout the building. Hours: Mon.–Fri. during normal business hours.

■ **Atlanta University Center's Robert W. Woodruff Library Gallery**, 111 James P. Brawley Dr., SW, Atlanta (522-8980, ext. 209). The gallery exhibits works depicting the cultural heritage of African-Americans. Hours: Mon.–Thurs. 8:30am–12midnight; Fri. 8:30am–5:00pm; Sat. 10:00am–6:00pm; and Sun. 2:00pm–10:00pm.

■ **Black Expressions in Art**, P.O. Box 724977, Atlanta 30339-1977 (349-2432). Individual or corporate customers may purchase unframed, limited edition prints or posters. Call or write to receive a brochure.

- **Ebony**, 5616 Redan Rd., Stone Mountain (879-7285). Ethnic art and custom framing are available. Hours: Tues.–Sat. 11:00am–7:00pm.
- **For the Love of Art**, 3230 Kingsdale Dr., SW, Atlanta (691-9205). Original art by African-American artists is featured. Call for an appointment. During the National Black Arts Festival, For the Love of Art hosts a special daily exhibition at Rio Mall (North & Piedmont Avenues, Midtown).
- **Frames 'N' Fine Art**, 421 Moreland Ave. (Little 5 Points), Atlanta (581-1960). The owner is a collector of handmade African dolls and sells three lines of black dolls in her gallery, as well as figurines, ethnic cards, posters and prints. Hours: Tues.–Sat. 10:30am–6:30pm.
- **Future Image Gallery**, 1000 Shannon South Park, Union City (969-9424) and Underground Atlanta, 50 Upper Alabama St., SW, Atlanta (659-2911). Future Image specializes in prints, but carries a few wood carvings and other pieces of art from Africa. Hours: Mon.–Sat. 10:00am–9:30pm; Sun. 1:00pm–6:00pm.
- **Ghee Art Studio and Gallery**, 1868 Washington Rd., Suite F, Atlanta (577-3133). Contemporary African-American art by Samuel Ghee is featured. Hours: Mon.–Sat. 10:00am–6:00pm.
- **Heritage Prints and Framing**, 4189-D Snapfinger Woods Dr., Decatur (284-1353). Heritage offers a wide assortment of art prints and provides custom framing. Hours: Tues.–Fri. 12noon–8:00pm; Sat. 10:00am–8:00pm; and Sun.–Mon. by appointment only.
- **Hughley Gallery & Objects**, 142 Stovall St. (Reynoldstown), Atlanta (523-3201). Works by African and African-American artists are showcased. A recent exhibition featured the colorful narrative and figurative art of Atlantan Tina Dunkley. Hours: Wed.–Fri. 12noon–5:00pm; Sat. 1:00pm–5:00pm; and Sun. 3:00pm–5:00pm.
- **Karamu Art Gallery**, Shrine of the Black Madonna, 946 Ralph D. Abernathy Blvd., Atlanta (752-6125). The gallery is a showcase for top black American artists and features wood carvings and other art objects from Africa. Hours: Mon. 3:00pm–7:00pm; Tues.–Sat. 11:00am–7:00pm.
- **Modern Primitive Gallery**, 1402 N. Highland Ave., NE, Atlanta (892-0556). The folk art gallery features artists from many cultures, including African-American visionaries, and has exhibited the work of well-known artists Bessie Harvey and David Butler. Hours: Tues.–Sun. 11:00am–9:00pm.
- **Oduduwa Collections Gallery**, 2300 Peachtree Rd., Suite B107, Atlanta (352-8249). Original African art is displayed and may include sculpture, painting, batik and more. Hours: Tues.–Sun. 12noon–5:00pm.
- **The Picture Framer**, 4859 Memorial Dr., Stone Mountain (296-6828). In addition to providing custom framing, the store offers a selection of limited

edition prints, graphics and original ethnic art. Hours: Mon.–Fri. 10:00am–6:30pm; Sat. 10:00am–6:00pm.

■ **The Respress Art Gallery**, 675 W. Peachtree St., NE, Atlanta (874-5180). Respress carries prints by African-American artists and also has a gift shop. Hours: Mon.–Fri. 10:00am–5:30pm.

■ **Ultimate Impact Galleries, Inc.**, 2050 Lawrenceville Hwy. (Marketsquare Mall), Decatur (634-1471). African-American, African and Native American original art, limited editions, masks, sculptures and prints are displayed in this eclectic gallery. The owner, a degreed artist, envisions expanding her shop to provide space for children to display and discuss their artwork. Custom framing is available. Hours: Mon.–Sat. 10:00am–9:30pm; Sun. 12noon–6:00pm.

■ **Victoria's Art**, 3275-B Snapfinger Rd., Lithonia (981-2298). Art by black artists as well as framing services are available. Hours: Mon.–Fri. 10:00am–6:30pm; Sat. 10:00am–6:00pm.

■ **Catherine Waddell Art Gallery**, Trevor Arnett Building, Clark Atlanta University, 223 James P. Brawley Dr., Atlanta (651-3424). The collection of art work by African-American artists was begun in the 1940s when Atlanta University started sponsoring one of the only black arts festivals in the country. Works of art shown during these annual festivals were acquired by the university over the next three decades. The festivals ended in the 1970s, but the collection has kept growing thanks to the generosity of various donors. Featuring sculpture, paintings and graphics, it is the largest permanent collection of work by African-American artists in the nation. The gallery also houses a permanent collection of historical African art. Hours: Tues.–Fri. 11:00am–4:00pm. Group tours are available by appointment.

■ **Walker Gallery**, 200 Walker St., SW, Atlanta (521-3227). The multicultural arts center and gallery features the creative works of local artists, including performing arts, as well as exhibitions. A gift shop sells Afrocentric jewelry, clothing, greeting cards and more. Hours: Tues.–Sat. 1:00pm–6:00pm.

■ **William Tolliver's Art Gallery, Inc.**, 2300 Peachtree Rd., NW, Suite C-203, Atlanta (350-0811). Original art and prints by the noted artist William Tolliver are exhibited. Hours: Tues.–Wed. 10:00am–5:00pm; Thurs.–Fri. 12noon–8:00pm; and Sat. 11:00am–4:00pm.

■ Several galleries around Atlanta periodically exhibit works by African and African-American artists, especially during Black History Month and the biennial National Black Arts Festival. A few to keep your eye on are: **The Atlanta College of Art**, 1280 Peachtree St., NE, Atlanta (898-1157); **Avery Gallery**, 390 Roswell Rd., Marietta (427-2459); **Kennesaw State College Art Gallery**, I-

75 and Chastain Road, Lower Level of Library, Marietta (423-6343); **Michael C. Carlos Museum** (formerly Emory Museum of Art & Archaeology), Emory University, 571 S. Kilgo St., Atlanta (727-4282); **New Visions Gallery of Contemporary Art**, 999 Peachtree St. (10th Street Level of the Peachtree Place Building), Atlanta (874-3881); **Nexus Contemporary Art Center**, 535 Means St., NW, Atlanta (688-1970); and **North Arts Center Gallery**, 115 Perimeter Center Pl., Atlanta (841-9130).

MUSEUMS

■ **Center for Puppetry Arts Museum**, 1404 Spring St., Atlanta (874-0398). The Center for Puppetry Arts is a repository of puppets from around the world and, in fact, is one of the largest museums of its kind in North America. Among its impressive permanent collection are genuine African ritualistic figures. The center features special exhibits, a theatre with performances for children and adults, workshops and a gift shop. Hours: Mon.–Sat. 9:00am–4:00pm and evenings on performance nights. Admission fee.

■ **High Museum of Art**, Robert Woodruff Arts Center, 1280 Peachtree St., NE, Atlanta (892-HIGH). Permanent exhibits include Sub-Saharan African art: carved figures, ceremonial swords, jewelry, masks, musical instruments and textiles. Each year the museum will have at least one special exhibit featuring African art, such as 1991's "Yoruba: Nine Centuries of African Art & Thought," including masterpieces, music and dance from one of the world's richest and oldest cultures, which is still vital in Benin and Nigeria. Also on exhibit were works by Henry Ossawa Tanner, accompanied by lectures and performances. In 1992, "Memory and Metaphor: The Art of Romare Bearden" was on display. Hours: Tues., Wed., Thurs. and Sat. 10:00am–5:00pm; Fri. 10:00am–9:00pm; and Sun. 12noon–5:00pm. Admission fee.

OTHER

■ **Zoo Atlanta**, 800 Cherokee Ave., SE, Atlanta (624-5678). The zoo has impressive re-creations of the Serengeti Plains, Masai Mara and other African wildlife reserves, which include Kiswahili language plaques. The gift shop displays some authentic African crafts and art. Hours: Daily 10:00am–5:30pm. Admission fee.

COUNTRY-SPECIFIC COMMUNITY GROUPS

Many community associations are informal social and cultural groups with presidents rotating each year. Phone numbers are usually private homes or places of business since the participants often meet casually in each other's homes. Therefore, more country-specific community groups exist than you will find listed here. Often the best way to make a contact is through networking.

■ **Association of Sierra Leonians** (752-1712). This is an educational and social group that supports relief efforts in Sierra Leone.

■ **Eritrean Community Association** (752-1667). The social and cultural association holds fundraising parties and is primarily a group for Eritreans, but others familiar with the situation in Eritrea are welcome.

■ **Ghana Association** (880-8151). Call for information about community groups here in Atlanta.

■ **Kenyan Atlanta Community Organization**. This organization provides information on the many cultures of Kenya, Uganda and Tanzania.

■ **Organization of Nigerian Professionals, Atlanta Chapter** (478-3143). Nigerians who have a bachelor's degree or the equivalent are welcome to join this organization whose purpose is professional networking. Friends are also welcome at the bimonthly meetings.

■ **Igbo Union U.S.A.** (767-6932). Native Igbo people and their families may be members of this organization whose goal is to promote solidarity among Igbos here and in Nigeria. The group holds monthly meetings.

■ **OTU Imunne** (991-6805). The Nigerian club seeks to preserve and promote the culture of Nigeria through various events held in Atlanta. The organization hosts an Igbofest in March to celebrate Nigerian culture.

CULTURAL ASSOCIATIONS & CENTERS

■ **Africa House Learning and Resource Center**, 14 W. Peachtree Pl. (1 block south of Civic Center Train Station), Atlanta (242-2035/669-0527). Africa House is a center for educational and cultural activities, computer and information services, and houses a small gallery. Previous programs have included a Yoruba language class, a young grandmother support group, computer training classes, lectures on cancer in the African-American community and AIDS treatment developed in Africa, and literary arts programs. Call for information and to receive a brochure.

■ **The African Association of Georgia** (239-8183). Launched in the fall of 1990, the organization promotes cultural exhanges, friendship and business relationships among Africa, the Caribbean and Georgia.

■ **The Arts Exchange**, 750 Kalb St., SE, Atlanta (624-4211/624-1572). The Arts Exchange is a multicultural, multidisciplinary arts resource center located in the Grant Park neighborhood (near Zoo Atlanta). The exchange is the first Georgia recipient of the Phoebe Fund grant in honor of the cultural work produced here. The center houses artists, arts organizations, the Municipal Gallery and the Paul Robeson Theatre. It also offers a wide variety of classes for adults and children in dramatics, voice, piano, dance, visual arts, martial arts, languages and more. There is an excellent full-day Summer Arts Enrichment Program for children ages 5–15 years.

■ **Gilbert House**, 2238 Perkerson Rd., SW, Atlanta (766-9049). This community center's facility is listed on the National Register of Historic Homes and is the location for classes, workshops, exhibitions, and activities for children, adults and seniors year-round. A free children's festival is held in May.

■ **Hammonds House Galleries and Resource Center of African-American Art**, 503 Peeples St., SW, Atlanta (753-8730). The Hammonds House is an art gallery and cultural and resource center located in a mid-19th century Eastlake Victorian-style house in historic West End. Besides housing an excellent permanent collection of Haitian and African-American art, the center sponsors numerous educational programs, forums, lectures, workshops, and traveling exhibits. It also collects and shares documentation on artworks and artists in the form of videos, films, computer data bases, slides, catalogues, periodicals, publications and books.

■ **House of Ujamaa**, 3182 Glenwood Ave., Atlanta (241-0385). Opened during Black History Month in 1991 and named after the fourth principle of Kwanzaa (cooperative economics), this is DeKalb's first African-American Cultural Center. Poetry readings, art exhibits, educational seminars and other activities are hosted at Ujamaa. A gift shop sells Kwanzaa symbols and gifts, and custom designed outfits for dolls with an attached note explaining the doll's African heritage.

■ **Martin Luther King, Jr. Center for Nonviolent Social Change**, 449 Auburn Ave., NE, Atlanta (524-1956). The King Center is the official national and international monument dedicated to the life of Martin Luther King, Jr. The center sponsors numerous conferences, training programs, internships, workshops, community services and cultural events, and actively promotes nonviolent solutions to family, local governmental, national and international problems. Its library and archives contain one of the largest collections of primary source material on the civil rights movement and Martin Luther King, Jr.

■ **MECCA (Metro Ebone Civic Club Association)** (482-6647). The non-profit organization hosts an annual black arts festival and engages in various projects to serve the community.

■ **Metro Atlanta Kwanzaa Association** (688-3376). The group sponsors special events, lectures, storytelling and other programs throughout Atlanta related to the African-American celebration Kwanzaa, observed from December 26–January 1.

■ **Shrine of the Black Madonna Bookstore and Cultural Arts Center**, 946 Ralph D. Abernathy Blvd., SW, Atlanta (752-6125). The center is an important place in the West End community, hosting numerous cultural events and speakers, and housing the largest black bookstore in the southeast, as well as the Karamu Art Gallery. The center also carries African imports, handcrafted jewelry, Kwanzaa materials and art prints.

■ **Soapstone Center for the Arts**, One South DeKalb Center, Suite 21, Decatur (241-2453). This burgeoning center for folk, ethnic and fine arts has as its mission "to create and present arts and cultural programs which highlight the rich diversity of the arts found in Atlanta's international and minority communities." The center offers workshops and classes in drawing, painting, dance, acting, piano, voice and more for children and adults. There is an art gallery, and recently the center has put together a touring ensemble comprised of children ages 12–16 who perform at schools, community centers and shopping malls. It currently houses the dance companies Ballethnic, D'MaDeio, and Harry Bryce African-American Dance Theatre. The center supports community outreach programs and hosts colorful festivals.

HISTORICAL CHURCHES

■ **A.M.E. Church Headquarters**, 208 Auburn Ave., NE, Atlanta (659-2012); **Big Bethel African Methodist Episcopal Church**, 220 Auburn Ave., NE, Atlanta (659-0248); **Ebenezer Baptist Church**, 407 Auburn Ave., NE, Atlanta (688-7263); **First Congregational Church**, 105 Courtland St., NE, Atlanta (659-6255) (site of the founding of the National Medical Association); **Friendship Baptist Church**, 437 Mitchell St., SW, Atlanta (688-0206) (site of the first classes of Spelman College and Morehouse College); **Hopewell Baptist Church**, 182 Hunter St., Norcross (448-5475) (the church is over 100 years old and boasts the largest black congregation in Gwinnett County); and **Wheat Street Baptist Church**, 359 Auburn Ave., NE, Atlanta (659-6820) (built in the 1920s, when Auburn Avenue was still named Wheat Street).

MOSQUES

■ **Al-Farooq Masjid of Atlanta**, 442 14th St., NW, Atlanta (874-7521) is Atlanta's largest mosque (in membership) and is a place of worship for all Moslems and a cultural and educational center for the Islamic community in Atlanta. Friday congregational prayers are at 1:45pm. Two Islamic schools are also offered, as well as weekend Islamic classes for children and adults. **Atlanta Masjid of Al Islam**, 560 Fayetteville Rd., SE, Atlanta (378-1600) holds congregation prayer each Friday at 1:00pm, and educational meetings each Sunday at 2:00pm, and has both an elementary school and high school forming the second largest Islamic educational facility in the U.S. A sampling of other Mosques: **Community Masjid of the West End**, 1128 Oak St., SW, Atlanta (758-7016). **Masjid Al-Muminuum**, 735 Capitol Ave., Atlanta (586-9562).

OTHER RELIGIOUS GROUPS

■ A sample of other congregations that serve the African community in Atlanta: **Atlanta Kidist Mariam Orthodox Tewahido Church**, c/o Central Presbyterian Church, 201 Washington St. SW, Atlanta (659-0274), an Ethiopian Orthodox Church which holds services on Sunday mornings; **Ethiopian Christian Fellowship**, c/o The Heiskell School, 3260 Northside Dr., NW, Atlanta (551-9446), holds services for Ethiopians on Sunday mornings at 11:30am; **First Baptist Church of Atlanta**, 754 Peachtree St., NE, Atlanta (347-8203) has an Ethiopian ministry; **St. Elias Eastern Orthodox Church**, 2045 Ponce de Leon Ave., NE, Atlanta (378-8191) has an Ethiopian ministry; **International Christian Fellowship**, c/o Westhills Presbyterian Church, 1450 Ralph D. Abernathy Blvd., SW, Atlanta (945-2122) has worshippers at the Sunday 1:00pm service from many African countries, including Ghana, Liberia, Sierra Leone and Uganda, so worship traditions and songs of Africa are preserved, although sermons are in English; and **Pan African Orthodox Christian Church**, 960 Ralph D. Abernathy Blvd., Atlanta (752-9572/752-5490).

schools, classes, language

■ **The Atlanta University Center**, a consortium of six institutions, is the largest private complex of educational institutions of higher learning in the world, with a predominately black enrollment. In 1929, Atlanta University, Morehouse College (for men) and Spelman College (for women) became affiliated. Morris Brown College joined in 1932, Clark College in 1940, the

Interdenominational Theological Center joined in 1958 and Morehouse School of Medicine joined in 1983. Atlanta University Center has achieved international recognition for the quality of education it offers.

— **Clark Atlanta University**, James P. Brawley Dr. at Fair St., Atlanta (990-8000). Formerly Clark College (which conferred its first degree in 1883) and Atlanta University, these two colleges merged in 1988 to become Clark Atlanta University, which is known for its mass communications program. The brilliant sociologist Dr. W.E.B. DuBois was a professor at Atlanta University for over 30 years. Keep an eye out for performances by the Clark Atlanta University Symphony and its student Jazz Orchestra. WCLK-FM (91.9), Atlanta's premier jazz station, is broadcast from here daily, beginning at 7:00am. An African summer camp is also offered.

— **Interdenominational Theological Center**, 671 Beckwith St., SW, Atlanta (527-7700). The accredited theological center, which is a federation of several seminaries, provides graduate education with an interracial and international perspective and a focus on black Christianity.

— **Morehouse College**, 830 Westview Dr., SW, Atlanta (681-2800). Morehouse was established in Augusta, Georgia in 1867 and moved to Atlanta in 1879. This four year residential college is the only all-male, historically black college in the nation. Famous graduates include Dr. Martin Luther King, Jr., Dr. Benjamin E. Mays, Lerone Bennett, and Maynard Jackson. Keep an eye out for performances by the Jazz Club and the very highly regarded Morehouse College Glee Club.

— **Morehouse School of Medicine**, 720 Westview Dr., SW, Atlanta (752-1500). Dr. Louis Sullivan, Secretary of Health of the United States, is a former President of Morehouse School of Medicine.

— **Morris Brown College**, 643 Martin Luther King, Jr. Dr., NW, Atlanta (220-0270). This historically black liberal arts college was founded in 1881 by the African Methodist Episcopal (A.M.E.) Church and remains the only college in Georgia founded by blacks for blacks. The college's strongest programs are computer science, business, the hospitality industry, and an African studies program. It has a diverse student body boasting students from 36 states and 30 foreign countries.

— **Spelman College**, 350 Spelman Ln., SW, Atlanta (681-3643). This historically black women's liberal arts college has roots in the Atlanta Baptist Female Seminary which was established in 1881. The school began receiving significant donations from the Rockefeller family in

1884, and as a consequence, was named Spelman in 1924 after Rockefeller's mother. Dr. Johnetta B. Cole is the first black woman president of the college. Spelman has a little known, but highly regarded, "Fresh Images" chamber music series held in Sisters Chapel. Special programs are offered for children and adults, including the introduction in February, 1991 of Spelman's First Annual African-American History Camp for Children (241-5003). Scenes from the campus can be seen in NBC's "A Different World," starring Atlanta's Jasmine Guy.

■ **Emory University** has an Institute for African and African- American Studies. To find out more about the program and its activities, call 727-6847.

■ **Al-Farooq Masjid of Atlanta — Masjid Dar Un Noor School**, 442 14th St., NW, Atlanta (874-7521). The school presently offers religious instruction for adults, a children's weekend Islamic school, a full-time Islamic day school for children pre-K through 6th grade, and an early-morning school where children memorize the Koran.

■ **Atlanta Masjid of Al Islam**, 735 Fayetteville Rd., SE, Atlanta (378-4219). The mosque runs Sister Clara Mohammed Elementary School and W.D. Mohammed High School, that together form the second largest Islamic educational facility in the U.S.

■ **The Atlanta Preparatory School**, 2581 Dodson Dr., East Point (344-6221). The African-American preparatory school for pre-K through high school is designed to build the children's self-esteem and provide a rigorous, advanced curriculum in African and African-American history and culture, foreign languages, mathematics and other instructional areas.

LANGUAGE CLASSES

■ The general public may look for **Kiswahili** language lessons at: **Arts Exchange**, 750 Kalb St., SE, Atlanta (624-4211/624-1572); **Soapstone Center for the Arts**, One South DeKalb Center (South DeKalb Mall), Suite 21, Decatur (241-2453); and **Spelman College**, 350 Spelman Ln., SW, Atlanta (681-3643) which offers conversational Kiswahili. **Africa House Learning and Resource Center**, 14 W. Peachtree Pl., NW, Atlanta (242-2035) sometimes offers African language classes.

SUMMER & HISTORY CAMPS

■ **The Arts Exchange**, 750 Kalb St., SE, Atlanta (624-4211/624-1572). The Arts Exchange has an excellent full-day Summer Arts Enrichment Program for children ages 5–15 years, offering an eclectic program that includes

African, jazz and other forms of dance, drawing, painting, theatre and music.

- **Clark Atlanta University** (880-8438/880-8244/344-3190). Traditional African summer camps are offered for both children and adults during June and July. Call to pre-register.
- **Spelman College** (681-3643). Spelman offers summer programs for children and adults. The annual African-American History Camp (241-5003) during Black History Month offers more than 50 classes, including information on celebrating Kwanzaa, African arts and crafts, black filmmaking and African-American history.

NEWSPAPERS, MAGAZINES, BOOKS, VIDEOS

NEWSPAPERS

Among the newspapers that cater to black Americans and are available at many locations around Atlanta, including libraries, are:

- *The Atlanta Daily World* (659-1110). The first and oldest daily newspaper in the U.S. published by black Americans is now published every Tuesday, Thursday, Friday, and Sunday. A one-year subscription is $65.00, a single issue is $.25 in Atlanta, and $.35 outside Atlanta.
- *The Atlanta Inquirer* (523-6086). Published every Thursday, a year's subscription is $14.40.
- *Atlanta Metro/The Atlanta News Weekly* (907-8949/907-8953). The *Atlanta Metro* is published once a month at a newsstand price of $.50 per issue and a subscription price of $12.00 a year. The *Atlanta News Weekly* is published weekly at a newsstand price of $.25 per issue.
- *The Atlanta Tribune* (587-0501). The newsmagazine features articles, business news, calendars, and advertisements catering to African-American Atlanta. It is published the first of every month and is available for $1.00 at some bookstores, grocery stores and other locations.
- *The Atlanta Voice* (524-6426). This newspaper was founded in 1966 and is available in libraries or by subscription for $39.00/year.
- *Muhammad Speaks Newspaper* (659-1798). The newspaper is published once every two months at a subscription rate of $11.00. In the future, it is expected that the newspaper will be published once a month.
- *Nite Image* (284-7890). "Atlanta's first entertainment, niteclub & restaurant guide for people of color" is available at restaurants and clubs. Free.

MAGAZINES

■ *Catalyst*, 34 Peachtree St., NW, Suite 2330, Atlanta (730-5780). The literary magazine is funded by the Fulton County Arts Council and features work by black Americans. A two-year subscription is $10.00.

■ *Fast Forward, For Atlantans on the Move* (851-9402). This magazine is published six times a year at a subscription price of $9.95/year. Available in some African-American shops and libraries.

■ *SAGE*, P.O. Box 42741, Atlanta, 30311-0741. The black feminist journal publishes interviews, articles and fiction related to women of color around the world. Both male and female writers are welcome to submit their work. The journal is published twice a year, with each issue presenting a central theme. The individual subscription rate is $15.00/year.

■ African journals of politics and news may be found at various bookstores around Atlanta, such as the ones listed below and **Oxford Book Store**, 360 Pharr Rd., NE Atlanta (262-3333) which carries *The African Guardian, African Link, African News* and *Afrique Magazine*.

BOOKS

■ **African-American Book Shop**, 1392 Ralph D. Abernathy Blvd., SW, Atlanta (755-3756). The shop carries a selection of adult and children's books featuring the history, culture and experiences of black Americans.

■ **Al-Farooq Majid of Atlanta — Masjid Dar Un Noor School**, 442 14th St., NW, Atlanta (874-7521). The Islamic school houses a library and bookstore.

■ **First World Bookstore**, 677 Cascade Ave., SW, Atlanta (758-7124); 780 N. Highland Ave., NE, Atlanta (875-2651); Greenbriar Mall (346-3263); and South DeKalb Mall (243-0343); Salem Crossing, Lithonia (808-1386). The store carries African-American and African adult and children's books, cards, gifts, posters, clothing and videotapes, and has occasional book signings and discussions.

■ **Hakim's Book Store**, 842 Martin Luther King, Jr. Dr., SW, Atlanta (221-0740). Adult and children's books relating to African-American history and culture are available.

■ **Islamic Book Center Service of Al-Furqan Academy**, 5675 Jimmy Carter Blvd., NW, Norcross (840-7900). The center carries adult and children's Islamic books.

■ **Pan-Afrikan Book Store**, 1269 Glenwood Ave., SE, Atlanta (622-0483). The store carries adult and children's books that focus on African and African-American experiences.

■ **The Shrine of the Black Madonna and Cultural Arts Center**, 946 Ralph D. Abernathy Blvd., SW, Atlanta (752-6125). The cultural center houses the largest black bookstore in the southeast, featuring adult and children's books, as well as art, gifts and other items.

■ **Soul Source**, 118 James P. Brawley Dr., SW, Atlanta (577-1346). Soul Source carries adult and children's books that center on the history and culture of black Americans. Downstairs is the Soul Source Cafe which serves salads and sandwiches.

**shopping centers,
import stores, hotels**

SHOPPING CENTERS

■ **Greenbriar Mall**, 2841 Greenbriar Pkwy., SW, Atlanta (344-6611). During the National Black Arts Festival, the mall abounds with art, arts and crafts, clothing, jewelry and more. **Out of Africa** is located here and **Densua's** and **Wilbourn Exclusives** are boutiques in Rich's department store.

■ **South DeKalb Mall**, Decatur (241-2431). The mall has increasingly taken on an African-American tone, perhaps most emphasized by the presence of Soapstone Center for the Arts, which offers arts and cultural programs, an art gallery, and houses several dance companies. **JC Penney Co.** carries Afrocentric clothing for children and adults and some artwork.

IMPORT STORES

■ **African Arts and Crafts**, Atlanta Flea Market, 5360 Peachtree Industrial Blvd., Chamblee (874-9740). It's just like visiting a real shop in Nairobi (except for the prices)! The merchant sells soapstone carvings, wood carvings, utensils, baskets, khangas, kikoys, bags, robes, earrings and other import items from Kenya, Tanzania and other East African countries.

■ **African Connections**, 1107 Euclid Ave. (Little Five Points), Atlanta (589-1834). The African arts gallery and boutique features fine African carvings, baskets, batiks, jewelry and weavings, including Yoruba beadwork and Asoke sculpture and textiles.

■ **African Pride**, 78 Upper Alabama St., Underground Atlanta, Atlanta (523-6520). The store carries lots of traditional and contemporary clothing, jewelry, original paintings and more from Africa.

■ **Batik**, 1148 Euclid Ave., (Little Five Points), Atlanta (577-8317). The shop abounds in African clothing, fabric and jewelry.

■ **Boutique Africa**, 879 Ralph D. Abernathy Blvd., SW, Atlanta (752-5194). The shop sells African artifacts and clothing. Open Wednesday–Saturday.

■ **Curio Designs**, 136 Marietta St., SE, Atlanta (521-9014). The owner is a designer of international cultural fashions specializing in African motifs.

■ **Densua's African Treasures and Art Gallery**, 780 N. Highland Ave. (inside Ancestral Arts), Atlanta (622-7454) and Greenbriar Mall, 2841 Greenbriar Pkwy. (inside Rich's), Atlanta (872-0792). The store carries exotic oils and incense, African apparel for adults and children, accessories, basketry, jewelry, original African and African-American art, and African games which are works of art.

■ **Idris Gift Shop**, Brockett Point Mall, 1353 Brockett Rd., Suite B-2, Clarkston (981-2406). The shop sells originals of black art, lithographs, notecards, black figurines, and African style jewelry. Open Tuesday, Thursday and Saturday.

■ **La Jude International Import**, Buford Highway Flea Market, 5000 Buford Hwy., Atlanta (451-7015). African clothing and jewelry, and European accessories are for sale.

■ **La Mart African Imports**, 4833 Old National Hwy., College Park (763-2701). Bright African fabrics line the walls of this eclectic import shop that features clothing, West African and West Indian food products, and other specialty items.

■ **Out of Africa**, 2841 Greenbriar Pkwy. (Greenbriar Mall), Atlanta (344-7100) and a kiosk at Underground Atlanta, 50 Alabama St., SW (681-3579). The import shop carries clothing (some designed by the store's owner), kente cloth, wood and soapstone carvings, jewelry and other items.

■ **Out of the Woods**, 22-B Bennett St., Atlanta (351-0446). The gallery has some tribal arts and crafts, including handmade works from South Africa.

■ **Queen Makeda Doll Collection**, 50 Upper Alabama St. (Underground Atlanta), Atlanta (659-9922). Makeda Muhammad is a doll designer and artist who creates unique Afrocentric dolls dressed in traditional and contemporary clothing.

■ **Small Treasures**, 3684 Wittenburg Ct., Decatur (981-3555). Small Treasures has ethnic ornaments, note cards, T-shirts, bags, and specializes in dolls, including limited edition Marcella Welch Heritage Series, Nubian dancers and folk art dolls.

■ **Tijara**, 992 Ralph D. Abernathy Blvd., SW, Atlanta (753-7824). African clothes, jewelry and other items are for sale.

■ **Wilbourn Exclusives**, 2841 Greenbriar Pkwy., Greenbriar Mall (inside Rich's), (346-2628). The boutique is owned by two sisters who design contemporary, loose-fitting African-American clothing.

■ **Zita Fashions**, 228-230 Auburn Ave., NE, Atlanta (215-9912). Much of the traditional and contemporary design clothing is created by the owner. Other items include fabric, hats, bags, jewelry and more.

■ **Paschal's Motor Hotel**, 830 Martin Luther King, Jr. Dr., SW, Atlanta (577-3150). The black-owned hotel is a popular locale for meetings and banquets and has a highly-regarded jazz club, La Carousel.

GROCERIES, MARKETS, BAKERIES

■ **DeKalb Farmers Market**, 3000 E. Ponce de Leon Ave., Decatur (377-6400). Frequently available are such ingredients as fenugreek, cardamom and other spices, fresh peppers, greens, lentils, and Ethiopian, Kenyan and other coffees from Africa.

■ **Global Food Distributors**, 2995 Roosevelt Hwy., College Park (768-1927). The international grocery store specializes in African and Caribbean foods and products.

■ **La Mart African Imports**, 4833 Old National Hwy., College Park (763-2701). Bright African fabrics line the walls of this eclectic import shop that features clothing, West African and West Indian food products and more.

■ **Sevanada Natural Foods Cooperative Grocery**, 1111 Euclid Ave., NE, Atlanta (681-2831). Spices and vegetables used in African cooking, and coffees from Africa are available.

■ **Sweet Auburn Curb Market**, (formerly The Atlanta Municipal Market), 209 Edgewood Ave., NE, Atlanta (659-1655). The historic market is located near the Martin Luther King, Jr. Historic District and Grady Hospital. It is filled with vendors selling massive quantities of meat, "soul food" (greens, chitlins, okra...), fruits and vegetables, cheese and grocery items. Downstairs is a large flea market.

■ **Taj Mahal Imports**, 1594 Woodcliff Dr., NE, Atlanta (321-5940). Spices from West Africa can be found in this Indian grocery store.

■ **Caribbean Markets** carry food items from West African nations, including spices needed to create authentic African dishes. See our "Caribbean" chapter.

RESTAURANTS

AFRICAN MEALS

■ **Addis**, 453 Moreland Ave. (Euclid Ave.), Atlanta (523-4748). You may eat with your fingers in this Ethiopian restaurant, enjoying zigene, yemisir and more. On Wednesday nights, partake of the all-you-can-eat special which sometimes features chicken alecha, beef watt and lentils. Open: Lunch: Sat.–Sun.; Dinner: Daily.

■ **Afram**, 2851 Buford Hwy. (south of N. Druid Hills Rd.), Atlanta (634-6445). The Nigerian cuisine includes hearty soups, stews, unique vegetarian dishes (moi-moi) and a lunch buffet Monday–Friday. Open: Lunch and Dinner: Mon.–Sat.

■ **The African Brown Bag**, 699 Ponce de Leon (Ford Factory Square/Kroger Shopping Center), Atlanta (642-3434). The French-North African restaurant offers catering and unique meals using African spices. The menu changes daily. Open: Lunch: Sun. (1:00pm–6:00pm); Dinner: Tues.–Sat.

■ **The Nile**, 1928 Piedmont Cir. (near Piedmont and Cheshire Bridge Rds.), Atlanta (874-0454). Enjoy a cup of Ethiopian coffee and dine on spicy minchet abesh, vegetable entres such as azifa, lamb and beef dishes, and enjera (bread). Open: Lunch and Dinner: Daily.

■ **Pyramid Cafe**, Briarcliff Rd. (Clairmont Rd.), Atlanta (315-1925). The small cafe serves Ethiopian-style chicken on its lunch menu. Open: Lunch: Mon.–Sat.; Dinner: Mon.–Sat. (until 7:00pm).

■ **Rainbow African Restaurant**, 243 Ponce de Leon Ave. (Myrtle St.), Atlanta (876-3630). This small Ethiopian restaurant serves varied African food in midtown Atlanta. Open: Breakfast: Mon.–Sat.; Lunch and Dinner: Daily.

■ **The Red Rooster Restaurant**, 1395 Columbia Dr. (four lights from Glenwood in Alameda Plaza), Decatur (288-7984). The restaurant serves African food, American food and occasionally barbecue. Open: Lunch and Dinner: Daily.

BARBECUE/ SOUL FOOD

Some top rated barbecue and soul food restaurants in the city are:

■ **Aleck's Barbecue Heaven**, 783 Martin Luther King, Jr., Dr. (down from Peachtree St.), Atlanta (525-2062). Enjoy great barbecue, because this restaurant's sauce and ribs were voted the best in town by *Atlanta Magazine*! Open: Lunch and Dinner: Daily.

■ **Anderson's Old Fashion Bar-B-Q**, 65 Willis Mill Rd. (MLK, Jr. Dr.), Atlanta (696-8144). The restaurant serves traditional barbecue and soul food. Open: Lunch and Dinner: Tues.–Sat.

■ **Auburn Avenue Rib Shack**, 302 Auburn Ave. (Fort St.), Atlanta (523-8315). The famous restaurant is noted for its high quality barbecue (great ribs!) and fresh vegetables. Take-out is available. Open: Tues. 11:00am–4:00pm; Thurs.

11:00am–7:00pm; Fri. 11:00am–10:00pm; and Sat. 12noon–10:00pm.

- **The Beautiful Restaurant**, 2260 Cascade Rd. (Fontaine St.), Atlanta (752-5931) and 397 Auburn Ave. (near Peachtree St.), Atlanta (223-0080). The restaurant serves fresh vegetables and salads and has a catering service. Open: Daily, 24 hours.
- **Burton's Grill**, 1029 Edgewood Ave. (Hurt St.), Atlanta (525-3415). The small restaurant is famous and very highly rated. Many people claim it serves the best fried chicken around. Open: Breakfast, Lunch and Dinner: Mon.–Sat.
- **Josey's**, 2151 S. Hampton St. (Godby St.), College Park (766-3370). Soul food is served cafeteria-style, with the ribs and squash casserole especially well regarded. Open: Lunch and Dinner: Mon.–Sat.
- **Heath's Cascade Grocery**, 787 Cascade Ave. (Mission St.), Atlanta (755-0543). Take-out food only here, but *Atlanta Magazine* still rated it "Best Soul Food" with vegetables and desserts topping the list of yummy food. Open: Breakfast: Sat.; Lunch and Dinner: Tues.–Sat.
- **Little T's on the Park**, 21 Edgewood Ave. (1 Park Place South), Atlanta (525-6822). The quality of soul food served in this restaurant is well regarded, especially the ribs, chicken and desserts. Open: Lunch and Dinner: Mon.–Fri. (until 7:00pm).
- **Paschal's Restaurant, Hotel and Lounge**, 830 Martin Luther King, Jr., Dr. (between Ashby Ave. and Atlanta University), Atlanta (577-3150). Considered an Atlanta "landmark" because of its famous clientele through the years, this restaurant serves soul food, among other selections. Open: Breakfast, Lunch and Dinner: Daily.
- **Quinnie's BBQ Restaurant**, 2856 LaVista Rd. (LaVista Grove Shopping Center), Decatur (325-1996). Barbecue ribs and chicken, fried catfish, lots of fresh vegetables, corn bread and dessert are served cafeteria-style in this spare, friendly restaurant. Open: Lunch: Mon.–Sat.; Dinner: Mon.–Fri.
- **Soul Vegetarian**, 879-A Ralph D. Abernathy Blvd. (beside West End Mall), Atlanta (752-5194) and 652 N. Highland Ave. (Virginia-Highland), Atlanta (875-0145). Unique vegetarian dishes are cooked under the guidance of the Hebrew Israelite owners. A colorful atmosphere, with waiters dressed in African attire and a diverse clientele. Open: Lunch and Dinner: Daily.
- **Thelma's Kitchen**, 190 Luckie St. (International Blvd.), Atlanta (688-5855). The small cafeteria-style restaurant serves soul food, such as barbecue ribs, fried chicken, squash, collards and other vegetables. Open: Lunch: Mon.–Fri.

THEATRE & DANCE

■ **African Cultural Dance Company** (991-9468). A local group under the direction of Alani Ogunlade performs and teaches traditional West African Dance.

■ **Alliance Theatre**, 1280 Peachtree Rd., NW, Atlanta (898-1128/898-1132). Under the direction of Kenny Leon, the theatre has produced some outstanding performances in plays by August Wilson and recently collaborated on bold productions by South African playwright Athol Fugard.

■ **Arts Exchange**, Paul Robeson Performance Centre, 750 Kalb St., SE, Atlanta (624-4211/624-1572). Local African-American and African groups perform at the Arts Exchange on a regular basis, with special events featured during African-American History Month and the National Black Arts Festival. Throughout the year, the Exchange offers films, workshops, music, dance, theatre, sculpture and more.

■ **Ballethnic Dance Company** (933-9050/241-2453). Founded in 1990 and currently a resident of Soapstone Center for the Arts, Ballethnic is Atlanta's premier African-American ballet company and only the second African-American ballet company in the world. Created with the vision of combining the tradition of the Dance Theatre of Harlem with the free expression of Alvin Ailey American Dance Theatre, the ballet performances include and appeal to children as well as adults, especially the *Urban Nutcracker.*

■ **Barefoot Ballet**. The Atlanta dance troupe of young African-American girls performs West African dance and a combination of traditional African and contemporary dance.

■ **The Comedy Act Theatre**, 917 Peachtree St. (at 8th St.), Atlanta (875-3550). Opened in early 1990, this is where "black comedy is king." Top national and local black comedians perform Tuesday–Sunday at 8:30pm.

■ **The Dunham Institute**, Community Center, West Hill St., Decatur (523-4474). The institute's goal is to provide an exciting and culturally meaningful dance and exercise program to at-risk youths in the south Decatur community to enchance their self-esteem. The director, Carol Lloyd, has modeled her school after one founded by Katherine Dunham, an esteemed African-American dancer. The institute believes that the discipline, motivation, and focus required for dance can be applied to other areas of a person's life. The program teaches modern, jazz, Caribbean, African dance and more. Dunham Institute's **African Dance Connections** performs in the public schools and around Atlanta.

■ **Fox Theatre** (881-2000) and the **Atlanta Civic Center** (523-1879) present productions developed by African-Americans throughout the year, such as the Alvin Ailey Dance Company, under the brilliant direction of Judith Jamison.

■ **Freddie Hendrick's Youth Ensemble of Atlanta** (875-7057). Formed in September 1990 for kids ages 8–18, Mr. Hendrick's believes he has the top child actors in the city. Mr. Hendrick's has years of experience in the dramatic arts as director of the Upward Bound Drama Program at Morris Brown College and teacher at Artistic Attitudes in Decatur.

■ **Harry Bryce African-American Dance Theatre** (870-9308/241-2453). Founded in 1990 and currently in residence at Soapstone Center for the Arts, this modern dance company combines African traditions with ballet and modern dance techniques. The Dance Theatre tours schools, churches and civic organizations throughout metropolitan Atlanta.

■ **Jomandi Productions** (873-1099/876-6346). Jomandi Productions' performances combine drama, dance and music to dramatize the African-American experience. Thomas Jones, founder and director, says his productions have Atlanta's most integrated audiences because general interest in ethnic art is growing. Most performances are at the 14th Street Playhouse.

■ **Just Us Theatre Company** (753-2399). Under the direction of Atlanta playwright Pearl Cleage (who has had plays performed off-Broadway), Just Us brings Atlantans theatrical performances and musical revues which combine art, music, poetry and technology. Performances are at the Atlanta Civic Center.

■ **Ma'Dieo Afrikan Theatre Ensemble**, Ma'Dieo Dance Alliance (758-3120). West African dances with the goal of preserving the dance, culture and spirit of West Africa are presented.

■ **Neighborhood Arts Ensemble**. Keep your eye out for this African-American band which is under the direction of Joe Jennings and performs at various venues around Atlanta.

■ **Soapstone Center for the Arts**, One South DeKalb Center (South DeKalb Mall), Suite 21, Decatur (241-2453). The center houses Ballethnic, Atlanta's premier African ballet company, Ma' Dieo Afrikan Theatre Ensemble, and Harry Bryce African-American Dance Theatre, and offers workshops and classes in many visual and performance arts areas, including African dance for children and adults.

■ **Total Dance Theatre**, 168 Trinity Ave., Atlanta (525-3115). The organization has very highly regarded professional adult and youth companies and recently produced the popular show "Women Hold Up Half the Sky." To encourage budding amateur artists, the Total Dance Theatre Showcase provides a monthly forum for performers to audition at the club Reflections. Call for information.

■ **Urarda Dance Africa**, Ebster Recreation Center, 404 W. Trinity, Decatur (241-0560). The group provides a program of African dance and live drums, including community workshops in aerobics, dance, and drum for children ages five and up and adults on Saturday from 10:30am–12:30pm.

■ **Other Local African Dance Companies.** A sampling: **Afrikan Dance and Theater Productions** (752-5884) and **Adebonajo Ensemble** (758-3120) offer dance, song and percussion demonstrations, workshops, and lectures, putting African aesthetics into cultural and historical perspective.

■ **International African Dance Companies** visit Atlanta each year. For example: **Odadda**, musicians and dancers from Ghana, performed in lush costumes in conjunction with the "Gold of Africa" exhibit at Emory University; **Olatunji and His Drums of Passion**, a renowned percussion group from Nigeria, performed at Morehouse College (his alma mater); **Mahlathini and the Mahotella Queens** from South Africa performed at the Variety Playhouse; and the group **Alafia** (Yoruba for peace) performed rituals, drumming, and dance from Yoruba at the High Museum of Art.

MUSIC

■ **Black Gospel, Rhythm & Blues, African-American Blues and Jazz** can be heard all over Atlanta every day of the year and are not restricted to black performers nor black audiences, though jazz was generated from African-American culture and is sometimes referred to as American classical music. African-American blues, perhaps epitomized in the music of B.B. King, has a rich African heritage combined with slave-era work chants and spirituals. Rhythm and blues was primarily influenced by black gospel and blues, all of which were the roots of rock 'n roll. **Zydeco** is also an indigenous American musical form with roots in West Africa and the West Indies, combined with Native American Indian, Cajun and European immigrant influences. **Reggae**, a musical form indigenous to Jamaica, can be heard almost every night in Atlanta (See the "Caribbean" chapter). The quality of live musical performances in Atlanta varies widely, but top national artists come to Atlanta's annual festivals, and the city does boast outstanding local African-American and African talent in all forms of music. *Creative Loafing* has perhaps the most comprehensive listing of weekly musical performances in

Atlanta but we suggest readers peruse the *Atlanta Journal/Constitution* and get on the mailing lists of arts centers and universities to be sure not to miss special performances.

■ **Music South Corporation — African-American Philharmonic Orchestra & Chorale** (362-8467). Atlanta's first professional African-American orchestra performs works by black composers in pop, gospel, jazz and classical fields. The 60-piece orchestra and 125-voice choir performs annually during Black History Month at the Atlanta Civic Center to a full house and rave reviews. Tickets may be purchased at Ticketmaster (249-6400) or Music South Corporation (346-3417).

■ **Atlanta Super Choir** (653-7160). The choir, formed in the spring of 1991 and comprised of about 33 of the best singers from 11 of Atlanta's black churches, performs both traditional and contemporary gospel and has already made a recording of their music. They have performed around Atlanta and at the Montreux Jazz Festival in Switzerland.

■ **DeKalb Youth Pops Orchestra** (241-2453). The black youth orchestra is the only one of its kind in the southeast and is in partnership with the Soapstone Center for the Arts.

■ **Mt. Ephraim Baptist Church Mass Choir** (794-1470). The choir is one of Atlanta's most famous, recording its gospel music for over 20 years and being represented on the gospel charts of *Billboard* magazine since 1989.

■ **Colleges and Universities** have special performances open to the public throughout the year. A sampling: **Morehouse College** (681-2800) has the famous Morehouse College Glee Club; **Morris Brown College** (220-0320) has a Concert Choir; **Clark Atlanta University** (990-8000) offers public performances by the Clark Atlanta University Symphony and Jazz Orchestra; and **Spelman College** (681-3643) has "Fresh Images" chamber music group and the Spelman Jazz Ensemble.

NIGHTCLUBS

Among the places where patrons may consistently find high quality blues, jazz and zydeco are:

■ **Blind Willie's**, 828 N. Highland Ave. (Virginia-Highland), Atlanta (873-2583). Enjoy blues, jazz and zydeco music performed by national and local performers nightly from 10:00pm–2:00am.

■ **Blues Harbor**, 2293 Peachtree St., Atlanta (524-3001). Chicago-style blues, zydeco and other blues styles are featured nightly at this popular venue located one block north of Peachtree Battle Shopping Center.

■ **Club Ember**, 2942 Ember Dr., Atlanta (243-7297). Located inside the Red

Inn, Club Ember features comedy nights and music every evening, including live jazz, disco and reggae.

- **Dominique's**, 505 Peachtree St., NE, Atlanta (875-9296). Dominique's downtown is beginning to have live jazz.
- **Escape**, 1153 Roswell Rd., Marietta (422-6559). Escape is a new jazz and blues club located one block east of the Big Chicken. Open Wednesday–Saturday, the club features live entertainment some nights, and dancing to records other nights. Currently, chicken wings and deli food are offered in the evenings.
- **Frederick's**, 8 Decatur St., Atlanta (659-3403). The new night spot, with a view of Woodruff Park and the downtown skyline, is located just north of the Underground and offers dancing six nights a week along with a full dinner menu. Tuesday features reggae music; Wednesday and Friday, Latin jazz; and Sunday, gospel entertainment.
- **Just Jazz**, 2101 Bennett St., NE, Atlanta (355-5423). Located behind Mick's restaurant on Peachtree St., the club features live jazz beginning at 9:00pm.
- **Marko's Lounge**, 2997 Campbellton Rd., SW, Atlanta (344-6528). Live jazz may be heard Tuesday–Sunday from 6:00pm–4:00am.
- **Neighborhood Arts Ensemble**. Organized by Joe Jennings in 1977, the Ensemble is an 18-piece African-American band in the "Big Band" tradition.
- **Pan-Af Nite Club and Restaurant**, 4974 Buford Hwy., Atlanta (452-9886). Open daily at 5:00pm, Thursday features reggae music; Friday, disco and house mix; and Saturday, African House Jam and mix.
- **The Parrot**, 571 Peachtree St., Atlanta (873-3165). The restaurant has live jazz every night except Monday.
- **Paschal's La Carousel Lounge**, 830 Martin Luther King, Jr. Dr., S.W., Atlanta (577-3150). This restaurant and lounge is a very popular locale for musical events, including jazz, which may be heard every night except Sunday.
- **Reflections**, 2004 Campbellton Rd., SW, Atlanta (752-6233). The jazz club features live jazz, in addition to twice-a-month performances by Total Dance Theatre Company.
- **The Royal Peacock Club**, 184-186 Auburn Ave., NE, Atlanta (880-0745). Originally known as The Top Hat Lounge, through the years, the club has featured the likes of Count Basie, Louis Armstrong, Cab Calloway, Ray Charles, Aretha Franklin and Dizzy Gillepsie. Recently reopened, the Peacock occasionally presents rock 'n' roll and R & B on Friday and Saturday nights. (The walls of this historic club are painted floor to ceiling with peacocks.) Call ahead to make sure entertainment is booked.
- **Sweet Georgia Brown**, 5370 Old National Hwy., College Park (766-5800).

The new sports and dance bar and grill features live jazz and blues, as well as swing, bop and mambo.

■ Also, Atlanta has a regional jazz information organization for musicians, the **Southern Arts Federation**, 1293 Peachtree St., N.E., Atlanta (874-7244). For serious blues followers and musicians, there is the **Atlanta Blues Preservation Society** (523-2583), an organization dedicated to preserving and promoting the blues; and **Blues Ink**, P.O. Box 191566, Atlanta 31119 (458-0416), a newsletter offering free ads for blues related events and blues musicans, as well as disc reviews, articles on musicians and general comments on the Atlanta blues scene.

FILM

■ **Atlanta African Film Society** (525-1136). The society hosts films and events of importance by and about black and Third World peoples and sponsors screenings, film premieres, film festivals, lectures, workshops, picnics and other special events.

■ **Atlanta Third World Film Festival** (653-7160). The festival screens more than 40 films by African-American, Native American, Hispanic, and Asian-American artists at several locations around Atlanta.

■ **City of Atlanta**. The city operates a film center that produces shows for public access Channel 12 on which many shows of interest to Africans and African-Americans are shown.

■ **IMAGE Film/Video Center**, 75 Bennett St., Suite M-1, TULA Building, Atlanta (352-4225). The center tries to serve many audiences in Atlanta by being responsive to emerging community needs. Through its impressive and highly talented Board of Directors, the center sponsors festivals, competitions, offers seminars and workshops, and through the On-Line program, provides equipment rental and fiscal sponsorships. IMAGE hosts an annual Atlanta Film and Video Festival. A past festival winner was Spike Lee. IMAGE is involved in the National Black Arts Festival. In the summer of 1990, it hosted an evening of film/video by African-Americans working in Atlanta. Membership is available and encouraged.

■ International film festivals held periodically at **Emory University** (727-6582) and the **High Museum of Art** (892-HIGH) feature films from and about Africa.

TELEVISION

■ **Black Entertainment Television** (BET) — Cable, 1899 9th St., N.E., Washington, D.C. BET features black-oriented programming. Of note: Screen

Scene is BET's new movie and television preview show that accepts projects produced by black independent filmmakers. Also, in the fall of 1991, BET began producing a week-in-review program for distribution to African nations.

■ **Local Cable Channels** that broadcast information of interest to the African and African-American communities in Atlanta are: **Channel 3**, Clark Atlanta University informational programming; **Channel 4**, Atlanta Board of Education meetings, Atlanta Public School information and trivia contests between schools; **Channel 8**, services of predominately black churches as well as local and national interviews with community leaders; and **Channel 16**, a library channel that describes library services, presents author interviews, and broadcasts Fulton County Commission meetings.

■ **DeKalb Center for Community Television**. The center hosts a series entitled "Hothouse Flowers," which is an important venue for African-American media artists.

RADIO

Atlanta is the 12th largest radio market in the country and is ranked second (to L.A.) in the desirability of its very hot radio market by enterprising capitalists. The first African-American owned radio station, founded in 1947, was here in Atlanta (the former **WERD**), but as of this writing, there are only two local stations (WCLK-FM and WTJH-AM) owned and operated by blacks.

■ **WALR-FM (Love 104)**. Urban contemporary programming is offered.

■ **WAOK-AM (1380)**. The gospel and talk radio station features host Joe Walker week nights.

■ **WCLK-FM (91.9)**. Located on Clark Atlanta University, WCLK is owned and operated by blacks as a non-commerical public broadcasting station. It hosts jazz daily beginning at 7:00am and also offers news, talk, gospel, reggae and blues. On Friday from 9:00pm–1:00am WCLK broadcasts live jam sessions from the Penta Hotel rooftop lounge.

■ **WIGO-AM (1340)**. The programming is rhythm and blues from the 1960s to the present. Some Atlanta University Center athletic events are broadcast.

■ **WTJH-AM (1260)**. This gospel station in East Point is owned and operated by African-Americans.

■ **WVEE-FM (103.3)**. The sister station to WAOK offers contemporary urban programming and serves as a vital link in the black community with its original news and entertainment. The station features top rated Mike Roberts in the morning.

■ A sample of special African and African-American history and cultural programming on additional stations: **WABE-FM (90)** presents "Afropop

303

Worldwide," showcasing music from African nations on Saturday at 8:00pm; **WGKA-AM (1190)** presents "African Update" Sunday at 7:30am; **WGST-AM (640)**, a talk and news radio station that features "Ralph from Ben Hill" (C. Miles Smith) as a nighttime host; and **WRFG-FM (89.3)** presents Jazz Monday–Friday 10:00pm-1:30am; "Round Midnight" Saturday 11:00pm–10:00am, "The Jazz Corner" Daily 6:00am–8:30am, "Improvisations," (jazz classics) Saturday at 1:00pm, and "The Seeker," an African-American cultural program of music and information on Saturday 5:00pm–8:00pm.

SPORTS

■ **Ethiopian Soccer Federation** (981-6718).

fEStIVALS & SPECIAL EVENTS

JANUARY

■ **Martin Luther King, Jr. Week**, Martin Luther King, Jr. Center for Nonviolent Social Change, Atlanta (524-1956). A week of events at the King Center and at other Atlanta locations are dedicated to the memory of Dr. Martin Luther King, Jr. The week's events of lectures, religious services and entertainment culminate with the Saturday **Martin Luther King, Jr. National Parade** in downtown Atlanta, which is televised nationally on WTBS and has attracted upwards of half a million participants. The King Center hopes that in years to come the parade will become more international in flavor, expressing the hopes and dreams of Dr. King for world peace. Monday, the official national holiday, features the **National March of Celebration.** In 1992, Winnie Mandela (head of the Welfare Department of the African National Congress) joined Coretta Scott King to lead the Monday march down Peachtree Street to the King Center. Also on the day of the official observance is the Ecumenical Service at **Ebenezer Baptist Church**.

FEBRUARY

■ **Black History Month** features numerous month-long educational activities, T.V. specials, visual art exhibitions, films and performing arts events throughout the city, honoring African-American accomplishments. Contact the APEX Center (521-2654) for more information, look in local newspapers, or call the Atlanta-Fulton County Library System (730-1775/1778) and the

DeKalb County Library System (378-7569) for a calendar of events.

■ **African-American Philharmonic Chorale Concert**, Atlanta Civic Center (362-8467). The highly-regarded professional orchestra performs works by black composers in pop, gospel, jazz and classical fields in honor of Black History Month.

■ **Afrocentric Arts and Literature Expo** (658-6617). Exhibitors present books, educational materials and art that promote African heritage. Entertainment includes an African film festival, music, dance and a stage production.

■ **Emory NAACP Block Party** (712-2295). The Emory chapter of the NAACP hosts an annual block party which features children's activities, music, food, vendors and public information on the NAACP.

■ **Malcolm X Commemorative Banquet** (319-5337). The banquet, hosted by the Malcolm X Grassroots Movement, presents self-determination awards and features a keynote address and music.

MARCH

■ **Black Expo U.S.A.**, Georgia World Congress Center (656-7600/656-7676). The expo features two days of entertainment, workshops, lectures, artists and a job fair with over 300 corporations represented.

■ **Jazz on Tap**, Georgia State University, Atlanta (971-1109/651-2536). About 27 dance companies from around the region participate in this two day jazz and tap festival sponsored by Georgia State University.

■ **Paul Robeson Annual Tribute**, Arts Exchange, Atlanta (624-4211). Dancing, vendors, food and a video of Paul Robeson (1898–1976) are among the highlights at this annual affair.

■ **Spirit of South DeKalb** (987-3500). Speeches by community and government leaders, a fun run, children's activities, performances and other entertainment in conjunction with Soapstone Center for the Arts highlight this fundraiser for South DeKalb's children.

■ **Nigerian OTU Umunne Igbofest** (991-6805). The Nigerian organization welcomes everyone to attend this celebration of Nigeria with dancing, music, food and a fashion show.

APRIL

■ **Black Expo**, Georgia World Congress Center, Atlanta (656-7600). The annual event features booths, seminars and other events related to the economic development of the black community.

■ **Manor Fest**, A.R.T. Station Trolley Barn, Stone Mountain (469-1105). An African-American Invitational art exhibition is one of the events at this festival.

- **Morehouse College Glee Club** (681-2800). The annual spring concert is held in April.
- **Oromo Night Cultural Festival**, Emory University (981-4103). Oromos are the largest national group in Ethiopia and the Horn of Africa, and the celebration of Oromo culture at Emory features traditional dance, food and a lecture on Oromo history.
- **Sweet Auburn Fest**, Auburn Ave., Atlanta (344-2567). Street vendors, a children's carnival, roller-skating in the streets, a parade, southern food, black culture seminars, health screenings, arts and crafts, and celebrities join together on historic Auburn Avenue to listen and dance to local and national performers in an annual celebration of African-American heritage.
- **Salute to Black Cultural Arts**, Douglasville Cultural Arts Council, 8652 Campbelton St., Douglasville (949-ARTS). The council hosts an annual "Salute to Black Cultural Arts" at the Arts Center this month.

MAY

- **Atlanta Jazz Festival** (653-7160). Hosted by the Atlanta Bureau of Cultural Affairs during the last weekend of May and the first weekends of June, July and August, the series offers concerts, workshops, dance performances, gallery exhibitions and videos featuring acoustic and improvisational jazz performers. Past performers have included Branford Marsalis, Sonny Rollins, the Arthur Blythe Quartet and other prominent black artists. The outdoor concerts in Grant Park and Brown Bag Concerts in Woodruff Park are free, although midnight jam sessions and other music and dance events may have an admission fee.
- **Kingfest**, Martin Luther King, Jr. Center for Nonviolent Social Change, Auburn Ave., Atlanta (524-1956). Beginning in May, and continuing every other Saturday through mid-August, the King Center hosts numerous evening and afternoon arts and performance festivals for the public. Song, dance, poetry, storytelling, theatre, comedy, and juggling are some of the performances that can be enjoyed all summer long. There is a special International Day, Gospel Day and Kid's Day.
- **Celebrate East Point Festival**, East Point (765-1179/420-9481). Music, performing arts, a street festival in downtown East Point and children's activities highlight this annual festival first hosted in 1992.
- **Children's Festival**, Gilbert House, Atlanta (766-9049). Enjoy a family afternoon with games, a children's costume parade and more.
- **Malcolm X Commemoration**, West End Park, Atlanta (319-5337). The noon parade is followed by a rally in West End Park with speakers, refreshments and vendors.

■ **Spring Open House Festival**, The Arts Exchange, Paul Robeson Performance Center (624-1572). The free event features open studios, artist discussions, performances and vendors.

■ **Wren's Nest and West End Festival**, West End Park, Atlanta (752-8992/753-7735). During the first weekend in May, the West End puts on a two-day neighborhood festival complete with a parade, walking tour, African jewelry and art, entertainment and a children's tent. Nearby, the Wren's Nest, home of the famous children's book writer Joel Chandler Harris, has its own festival with storytelling, musical entertainment and many special children's activities.

JUNE — AUGUST

■ **Atlanta Jazz Festival** (653-7160). Hosted by the Atlanta Bureau of Cultural Affairs during the last weekend of May and the first weekends of June, July, and August, the series offers concerts, workshops, dance performances, gallery exhibitions, and film videos featuring acoustic and improvisational jazz performers. Past performers have included Branford Marsalis, Sonny Rollins, the Arthur Blythe Quartet and other prominent black musicians. The outdoor concerts in Grant Park and Brown Bag Concerts in Woodruff Park are free, although midnight jam sessions and other music and dance events may have an admission fee.

■ **Kingfest**, Martin Luther King, Jr. Center for Nonviolent Social Change, Auburn Ave., Atlanta (524-1956). Beginning in May, and continuing every other Saturday through mid-August, the King Center hosts numerous evening and afternoon arts and performance festivals for the public. Song, dance, live bands, poetry, storytelling, theatre, comedy and juggling are some of the events that may be enjoyed all summer long. There is a special International Day, Gospel Day and Kid's Day.

■ **Benson & Hedges Blues Festival**, Lakewood Amphitheatre, Atlanta (653-7160). Evening concerts at Lakewood Amphitheatre are at 8:30pm. Additional week-long events include a fish fry, free concerts at Woodruff Park, performances at venues around Atlanta, and a photo exhibit at the King Center. Past performers have included the best blues musicians in the world, such as B. B. King.

■ **Liberian Independence Day Celebration**, Atlanta (762-7691). Two days of activities feature a picnic with children's events, an evening ball and a religious service. The celebration is presented by the Liberian Community Association of Georgia.

■ **National Black Arts Festival**, Atlanta (730-7315). Held biennially in August, this arts festival, the only one of its kind, celebrates the accomplishments of African-American artists in a big and exciting way, presenting over 75 concerts, plays, films, dance performances, storytelling sessions, bookfairs, workshops and art exhibits at over 40 different locations throughout Atlanta. Greenbriar Mall (344-6611) features a juried art market with works by over 100 black artists from around the world, music, dance and a host of family activities. Don't miss the Roots and Branches Folk Festival (the festival's centerpiece), parade, outdoor arts and crafts market, food and many other family events throughout the festival. For a detailed calendar, purchase the August edition of the *Atlanta Tribune.*

■ **Soapstone Center for the Arts**, South DeKalb Mall, Atlanta (241-2453). A series of free jazz concerts are held on the first Saturday of each month throughout the summer.

SEPTEMBER

■ **Arts Festival of Atlanta**, Piedmont Park, Atlanta (885-1125). In addition to musical and theatrical performances and arts and crafts booths, this popular festival includes an African marketplace.

■ **JVC Jazz/Blues Festival**, Lakewood Amphitheatre, Atlanta (627-5200/627-9704). The concerts have, in the past, headlined some of the best musicians in the world, such as Miles Davis, Wynton Marsalis, B. B. King, Buddy Guy, The Neville Brothers, McCoy Tyner and George Benson.

■ **Montreux Atlanta International Music Festival**, Atlanta (653-7160). Listen to jazz, blues, zydeco, classical, folk, pop and opera thoughout Atlanta, including free, day-long concerts in Piedmont Park over the Labor Day Weekend.

■ **West End Festival**, Howell Park, Ralph D. Abernathy Blvd. (at Peeples St.), Atlanta (505-0075). The neighborhood has held this festival for over 16 years, and recent highlights include storytelling, music, arts and crafts, food and Atlanta Preservation Center walking tours. For advanced reservations for a tour of the West End, call 522-4346.

OCTOBER

■ **Martin Luther King, Jr. Street Festival** (522-3249). The MLK, Jr. and Ashby Street Merchants Association host a festival of food, merchandise and entertainment.

■ **MECCA (Metro Ebone Civic Club Association) Black Arts Festival**, DeKalb College South Campus, Decatur (482-6647). The arts festival is an opportunity to portray positive images of blacks through a range of artwork from reproductions to originals by black artists. Music, dance and refreshments accompany the exhibition.

■ **National Black Family Reunion Celebration** (524-6269). Black pride and achievement are celebrated through educational workshops, music, food and health screenings. Sponsored by the National Council of Negro Women.

NOVEMBER — DECEMBER

■ **Christmas Festival and Open House at the Wren's Nest**, 1050 Ralph D. Abernathy Blvd., SW, Atlanta (753-7735). The home of Joel Chandler Harris is decorated in Victorian-style and offers free storytelling, school choral groups and refreshments.

■ **Gospel Music Workshop of Atlanta** (522-6331). The annual African-American Christmas concert features singers from the Atlanta Philharmonic Chorale, Atlanta Chapter Mass Choir and the Atlanta Masonic Choir.

■ **Kwanzaa** (688-3376). The week-long African-American cultural holiday was created in 1966 by Mualana (Ron) Karenga, former leader of the US organization and currently a professor at the University of California-Riverside. Kwanzaa begins on December 26 and lasts until January 1, with each day being represented by one of seven African-centered principles (the Nguzo Saba): *Umoja*, unity; *Kujichagulia*, self-determination; *Ujima*, collective work and responsibility; *Ujamaa*, cooperative economics; *Nia*, purpose; *Kuumba*, creativity; and, *Imani*, faith. Kwanzaa celebrations are held privately at home and publicly around Atlanta, including a parade in Southwest Atlanta, theatrical performances, fashion shows, workshops, marketplaces, feasts (*Karamu*), lectures, special library events, puppet shows, storytelling and many other special programs. Keep an eye on local newspapers for a current listing of events or contact Metro Atlanta Kwanzaa Association (688-3376), The Arts Exchange (624-4211), Dunbar Neighborhood Center (688-3376), The APEX Museum (521-APEX) or the House of Ujamaa (284-4330).

■ **Mayor's Ball** (881-6171). This annual fund-raiser for the United Negro College Fund is a gala affair with ticket prices ranging from $200–$3500.

■ **The Morehouse-Spelman Christmas Concert**, International Chapel at Morehouse College (681-3643, ext. 226) and Sister's Chapel, Spelman College (223-1482). In late November and early December, this traditional performance consists of a blend of Christmas carols, choral compositions and music from the African-American tradition. Free.

■ **Santa Claus**. Atlanta's first black Santa Claus arrived in Atlanta in 1991 at South DeKalb Mall with a real beard and real bowl-full-of-jelly belly. Mall management continues to hire black Santas.

OTHER

■ Keep an eye on the **Georgia World Congress Center,** which is the locale for various seminars and exhibitions of interest to Africans and African-Americans throughout the year.

RESOURCES

AFRICAN

■ **Ethiopian Job Counseling**, Lutheran Ministries of Georgia, Immigration and Refugee Services, 756 W. Peachtree St., NW, Atlanta 30308 (875-0201); **Ethiopian Mutual Assistance Association**, Box 50361, Atlanta 30302 (525-2661), a refugee assistance organization; and **Pan African Orthodox Community Service Center**, 952 Ralph D. Abernathy Blvd., Atlanta 30310 (752-6607).

AFRICAN-AMERICAN

■ **NAACP Regional Office**, 970 Martin Luther King, Jr. Dr., Atlanta 30312 (688-8868).

■ **The Atlanta Tribune** has occasional listings of local and national professional, trade, and social organizations that include a contact person, place and date of next meeting, and a phone number for further information. A sampling: **Atlanta Association of Black Journalists; Black Atlanta Transplants; Black Newcomers Network; Black Professional Secretaries Association; Black Women on the Move; Black Women's Health Project; Black Youth on the Move; Georgia Association of Black Women Attorneys; Georgia Minority Supplier Development Council; National Association of Black Accountants; National Coalition of 100 Black Women** (two local chapters); and **National Society of Black Engineers**.

■ **"Preserving the Legacy: A Tour of African-American Historic Resources in Georgia,"** a brochure published by Georgia's Minority Historic Preservation Committee may be picked up at visitor information centers or by calling 656-2840.

■ **SuccessGuide**, a book distributed by Access Atlanta (876-0490), is a listing of information on approximately 3,900 black Atlanta professionals and entrepreneurs for the purpose of promoting networking.

■ **Who's Who Among Black Professionals & Entrepreneurs in Atlanta** includes profiles of approximately 300 Atlantans whom the author feels are positive role models for black youth. It is expected that the book will be published annually.

A young boy dances with his grandfather during the Okiciyapo Powwow in Lawrenceville.

NATIVE
AMERICANS

(Indigenous Peoples of the Southeast, Eskimos, Hawaiians)

HISTORY

Indigenous peoples have occupied what is now Georgia for thousands of years. In the earliest days, they were nomadic people, hunters living in close harmony with nature, moving as the seasons and food supplies changed. In time, as the population grew, their social organization became more complex as they settled into communities and became farmers. During this era, it is believed the large animal effigy at Rock Eagle, Georgia was built.

During the Mississippian Period (900–1500 A.D.), local Native American society reached its zenith with the construction of villages that were both well-integrated and virtually self-sufficient. Their medicine, religious practices, art work, languages (including the Cherokee syllabary) and sports gave the southeastern Native Americans the distinction of possessing the richest culture of any North American Indian group. Examples of their culture can be seen at many sites throughout Georgia, including Etowah in Cartersville, Ocmulgee near Macon, and Kolomoki near Blakely.

Then the Europeans arrived. Lead by the Spaniard Hernando De Soto in 1540 and closely followed by the English explorers and others, the Europeans brought hitherto unknown and devastating diseases to the indigenous population, enslaved some and drove others from their lands and homes. There were five tribes in the south — Cherokee, Chickasaw, Choctaw, Creek and Seminole — and they adopted many of the dominant society's social practices in an effort to accomodate and thus avoid annihilation. The Cherokees developed a constitution, elected leaders and had a supreme court; many accepted Christianity; they built schools and stores.

Yet in the early 1830s, the state of Georgia declared that Indians had no rights and could own no land. Cherokees were driven from their homes and land by gunpoint. Meanwhile, the U.S. Congress passed a bill in 1830 authorizing the forced removal of Native Americans to the other side of the Mississippi River. The chief of the Cherokees, John Ross, sued the State of Georgia in the U.S. Supreme Court and won, meaning, legally, the U.S. government had to protect the Native Americans from the Georgia soldiers. However, President Andrew Jackson ignored the ruling, cajoled 100 Cherokees (out of 17,000) to sign the Treaty of New Echota in December 1835, stating, in effect, that they agreed to their removal, and convinced Congress to accept the treaty. Chief Ross continued his legal battles, but lost for the final time in 1838. As a result, 16,000 eastern Cherokees were forced into concentration camps, where they began The Trail of Tears, a journey westward which was deadly for thousands from all five tribes, who suffered from disease, exposure, hunger and enemy natives. Those who survived the ordeal were made to live in tribal territories in Oklahoma and other southwestern states where they have managed to keep their traditions, languages and histories alive.

The Native American population in the United States has recently surged according to census data. Some people attribute part of this increase to a growing pride among Native Americans to officially acknowledge their heritage. The Georgia population in 1980 was 7,619, and by 1990 was 13,348, a 75.3% increase. The metro-Atlanta five county population in 1980 was 2,226 and by 1990 was 4,107, an 84.5% increase. The total U.S. population is just under two million.

MUSEUMS & GALLERIES

■ **DeKalb Historical Society Museum**, Old Courthouse on the Square, Decatur (373-1088). The museum has about a half-dozen artifacts, including projectile points and artifacts made from soapstone, and reproductions of about a dozen various artifacts. For the serious researcher, there are approximately 100 projectile points in the collection, but not on display. The Swanton House Guild of the DeKalb Historical Society has offered textile classes, including Navajo and Inca weaving techniques. Hours: Mon.–Fri. 9:00am–4:00pm. Free.

■ **J.C. Gazaway Indian Museum**, Lower Creighton Rd. (off Hwy. 369), Cumming (706/887-2586). This personal collection of hundreds of South American and Cherokee Indian tribe artifacts may be viewed on Saturday and Sunday from 9:00am-5:00pm. Free.

■ **Georgia State Museum of Science and Industry**, Georgia State Capitol Building, Atlanta (656-2844). A Native American heritage exhibit includes artifacts and dioramas depicting four cultural periods dating back over 2,500 years. Special exhibits and cultural events are featured during Indian Heritage week in November. Hours: Mon.–Fri. 8:00am–5:30pm. Tours are conducted Mon.–Fri. 10:00am, 11:00am, 1:00pm and 2:00pm. Free.

■ **Michael C. Carlos Museum** (formerly Emory University Museum of Art and Archaeology), Emory University, Main Quadrangle, 571 S. Kilgo Cir., Atlanta (727-4282). The permanent collection includes pre-Colombian Indian artifacts from North and South America. From November 17, 1993–February 13, 1994, the exhibit "Beauty from the Earth: Pueblo Indian Pottery from the University Museum of Archaeology and Anthropology" is scheduled. Hours: Tues.–Sat. 10:00am–4:30pm; Sun. 12noon–5:00pm. Free, but a $3.00 donation is suggested.

■ **Oglewanagi Art Gallery and American Indian Center**, 842 N. Highland Ave., Atlanta (872-4213). Located in the Virginia-Highlands area, this gallery was founded by an Echota Cherokee, Tom Perkins, who travels to various pow-wows dancing and collecting American Indian arts and crafts for the Oglewanagi Gallery. The gallery offers such native crafts as pottery, blankets, leather goods, silverwork, beadwork, jewelry, weapons, prints and more. Hours: Tues.–Fri. 4:00pm–9:00pm; Sat.–Sun. 10:30am–6:00pm.

■ **Ray's Indian Originals**, 90 Avondale Rd., P.O. Box 164, Avondale Estates 30002 (292-4999). Owned by Peggy and Ray Belcher, Ray's is both a museum and a store for high-quality Pueblo pottery, Navajo textiles, clothing, baskets, jewelry, totems, fetishes, Hopi Kachinas, artifacts, books and more. Ray's Indian Originals organizes an annual auction held in Atlanta of Native American arts and crafts which draws attendees from all over the United States. Hours: Sat. 10:00am–6:00pm; other days by appointment.

■ **Indian Museum**, Four Winds Village, Old Hwy. 441 S., Tiger (706/782-6939). Located 6 miles south of Clayton, the museum displays Native American crafts, such as beaded blouses, jackets, pottery and baskets, as well as gems, rocks, and antiques. This is also a bed and breakfast and retreat facility. Hours: Daily 10:00am–5:00pm.

■ **Indigo Moon Gallery**, 1751 Marietta Hwy., Canton (706/479-1311). Over 130 artists are represented in this gallery that specializes in American Indian and Southwestern art. Hours: Tues.–Sat. 11:00am–6:00pm.

■ **Ultimate Impact Galleries**, Marketsquare Mall, Atlanta (634-1471). A diverse array of artwork is available, including Hopi Kachina dolls and original works by Native Americans from Arizona, New Mexico, and Cherokee, South Carolina. A local Stone Mountain resident's work is also featured. Hours: Mon.–Sat. 10:00am–9:30pm; Sun. 12noon–6:00pm.

Important Native American Historical Sites are located throughout the state, but none are in metropolitan Atlanta, so to understand more about the history and heritage of the indigenous peoples of Georgia, it is necessary to embark upon an enjoyable day trip.

■ Take a tour of the **Chieftan's Trail**, which tells the story of Native Americans who lived around the southern portion of the Appalachian trail long before Europeans came to the area. This 150-mile trail became a state-designated historic trail in 1988 on the 150th anniversary of the Trail of Tears. It may be traversed in a one-day drive, but if you wish to linger and learn more about the sites, you will need to plan on one or two days for your journey. The highlights of the trail are designated by a dash.

— **Etowah Indian Mounds State Historic Site**, (Exit #124 off I-75), Cartersville (706/387-3747). Follow the brown "Etowah Mounds" signs to the **Etowah Archaeological Museum,** which houses one of the best Mississippian Indian artifact collections in the United States and serves as an introduction to the lives and culture of the Mississippian Indians who thrived in this valley from about 1000–1500 A.D. There is a film which discusses the history and culture of the Etowah people and describes the significance of some of the artifacts on display in the museum. Among the artifacts excavated from the area are items that suggest the Indians decorated themselves with paint, copper and shell jewelry, tattoos, and feathers. You will see pottery and marble statues, as well as the burial site of a priest-chief excavated from a mound. The museum provides a map for a self-guided walking tour of the earthen mounds, the ceremonial center of the town. There are several special programs offered here throughout the year, such as Indian Skills Day and Artifacts Identification Day. Hours: Tues.–Sat. 9:00am–5:00pm; Sun. 2:00pm–5:30pm. Admission fee.

— **William Weinman Mineral Museum**, (Exit #126 off I-75 at the junction of GA 411), Cartersville (706/386-0576). Native Americans used the great mineral wealth found in this part of Georgia in their ceremonies and everyday lives. The museum, the only in the Southeast devoted entirely to minerals, rocks, and fossils, showcases these gifts from the earth. Among the displays is the Paleontology Hall, which houses numerous cases of fossils and Indian artifacts unearthed nearby. The museum provides educational and research facilities and specimen identification services. Hours: Tues.–Sat. 10:00am–4:30pm; Sun. 2:00pm–4:30pm. Admission fee.

— **Chieftan's Museum**, (Riverside Parkway between U.S. 27 and GA 53 spur), Rome (706/291-9494). This 19th century plantation house, now a national historic landmark, is where Cherokee leader Major Ridge lived and worked with his family along the Oostanaula River. Members of the Ridge family were store owners, ferryboat masters and planters who owned slaves. Major Ridge, the Cherokee Ambassador to Washington, D.C., struggled with the conflict of trying to retain his heritage while simultaneously adapting to and adopting some of the white man's culture. He was assassinated by fellow Indians for signing the 1835 Treaty of New Echota which ceded Indian territory to the U.S. government. There are two galleries that display changing exhibits of artwork by Native Americans, and artifacts from an archeological dig are on the trading post site. There is also an exhibition describing Hernando De Soto's expedition through Georgia in 1540 and offering insight into the Indian culture of that time. Hours: Tues.–Fri. 11:00am–4:00pm; Sun. 2:00pm–5:00pm. Admission fee.

— **New Echota, Cherokee Capital**, (one mile east of I-75 on Hwy. 225 at Exit #131), Calhoun (706/629-8151). New Echota was designated the Cherokee capital in 1825 by the Cherokee national legislature. (The Indians were forced to leave the original Echota, near Knoxville, by encroaching white settlers.) New Echota soon became a thriving town. Laid out by Cherokee surveyors, it included a public square, government buildings, supreme courthouse, council house and National Printing Office, with homes, schools and stores surrounding the center of town. This independent Indian nation once covered much of the southeast including northern Georgia and parts of Alabama, Tennessee and North Carolina. The Supreme Court of the Cherokee nation was located here and the reconstructed courthouse may be toured. In 1821, Sequoyah developed a written syllabary (a phonetic alphabet) which was used in 1827 to write their government's constitution. In 1828, the Cherokees began publishing a bilingual newspaper, the *Cherokee Phoenix*, and eventually printed over 700,000 pages of books in Cherokee. The reconstructed print shop and a sheet of their newspaper can be seen at the Museum. In 1838–1839, the Cherokees were forceably uprooted from their homes and cruelly marched westward on the Trail of Tears. The area fell into ruin, with many buildings being burned or demolished. However, in the 1950s, reconstruction began, and in 1962 it was designated a state historic site to educate the public, serve as a legacy to Cherokee accomplishments and pay tribute to the thousands who died on the Trail of Tears. There is also a library here with information on Cherokee history and culture, a slide show and other museum exhibits. Echota is the site of Cherokee Homecoming Day in September and Cherokee Christmas. Hours: Tues.–Sat. 9:00am–5:00pm; Sun. 2:00pm–5:30pm. Admission fee.

— **Chief Vann House**, Vann House Historic Site (3 miles west of Chatsworth at the junction of GA 225 and GA 52A), Spring Place (706/695-2598). This enormous, two-story brick mansion, built in the federal style, was once the home of Chief James Vann. Though the chief apparently contributed to the education of the Cherokee leaders by employing Moravian Christian missionaries as teachers, he was not a well-loved person. Vann House Day is in July, when there are demonstrations of Native American arts and crafts, such as fingerweaving and basketweaving. During Moravian Christmas, held in December, the Vann House is decorated as it would have been in 1805, and two special evening candlelight tours are offered. Hours: Tues.–Sat. 9:00am–5:00pm; Sun. 2:00pm–5:30pm. Admission fee.

— **Fort Mountain State Park**, (located in the Chattahoochee National Forest 7 miles east of Chatsworth on GA 52), Chatsworth (706/695-2621). This is a great resting place for those traversing the Chieftan's Trail, offering camping, cottages, picnicking, hiking and swimming. There is a rock wall 855-feet long at the summit of the mountain. It is thought that this wall was a ceremonial center for natives who lived here over 1,000 years ago. Throughout the year, various programs are offered, including panning for gold, folk music and lectures. Hours: Daily 7:00am–10:00pm. Park office hours: 8:00am–5:00pm. Free.

— **Tate House Property**, (located ten miles south of Jasper on GA 53), Tate (800/342-7515). The land on which the 20th century marble house sits was once Cherokee land. The only structural remains of Cherokee life are the Old Harnago Tavern and the spring house, which was built in 1830 and is one of the oldest buildings in north Georgia. Return to Long Swamp Creek Powwow and Indian Festival are annual events. Hours: Wed.–Thurs. 1:00pm–3:00pm; Fri. 11:00am–3:00pm; Sat. 11:00am–4:00pm; and Sun. 11:00am–5:00pm. Call ahead to make sure the property has not been scheduled for a special event that is closed to the general public.

■ **Columbus Museum of Arts & Sciences**, 1251 Wynton Rd., Columbus (706/322-0400). The museum houses one of the best Indian artifact collections in the state of Georgia. Exhibits display artifacts of Indian culture in central Georgia and Alabama. The museum manages the Singer-Moye ceremonial mounds located in Stuart, Georgia. To visit these mounds, you must first call the museum to make arrangements. Columbus is the site of a huge Native American festival in October. Admission fee.

■ **Fort King George Historic Site**, Darien (912/437-4770). This area was inhabited by Native Americans for more than 10,000 years. Located on a river bluff, the museum relates their history, as well as the history of the Spaniards, English and Scots who came later. In September, "Native Americans of the Georgia Coast" is a special event during which Florida Indians set up camp. Free.

■ **Indian Springs State Park**, Butts County (706/775-7241). These mineral springs were important to the Creeks who inhabited this area. The Indian Springs Hotel across from the park (on U.S. 23) is where the Treaty of Indian Springs was signed in 1825. The treaty ceded all Creek land in the state of Georgia to the state. William McIntosh, who signed the treaty, was assassinated by his fellow tribesmen. Free.

■ **Kolomoki Mounds Historic Park**, (off U.S. 27), Blakely (912/723-5296). Kolomoki is a large, seven mound complex that served as the center of a Mississippian Indian village around 900–1500 A.D. The mounds were used for ceremonies, as dwellings for rulers and community buildings. The recently renovated museum has drawings, pottery and artifacts from one burial mound. A museum display reenacts a funeral ceremony. There is a special event in April. Hours: Tues.–Sat. 9:00am–5:00pm; Sun. 2:00pm–5:30pm. Free.

■ **Lanier Museum of Natural History**, 2601 Buford Dam Rd., Buford (706/932-4460). The museum exhibits trace the history of the people and land of northern Georgia and include hands-on activities for children. Nearby is a log cabin built by Cherokee Indians, archeological remains of former Indian inhabitants, an observation tower and a nature trail. Hours: Tues.–Fri. 12noon–5:00pm; Sat. 10:00am–5:00pm. Free.

■ **Ocmulgee National Monument and Museum**, 1207 Emery Hwy., Macon (912/752-8257). This is touted as one of the largest museums of Native American history in the United States. In the visitor's center, you may see a film "People of the Macon Plateau," dioramas, artifacts and exhibits that describe what is known about the original Mississippi Indian's culture, and the Creek Indians who succeeded them and occupied this site until their forced expulsion in the 1830s. The Mississippi Indians built enormous earthen mounds for ceremonial and burial purposes. The highest in this particular region is a ceremonial 45-foot high plateau built around 1000 A.D. There is a reconstructed ceremonial "earthlodge," nature trails on the grounds and a gift shop. Special events are scheduled for March and September. Hours: Daily 9:00am–5:00pm. Admission fee.

- **Rock Eagle Mound**, (9 mi. north on U.S. 441/129), Eatonton (706/485-2831). Located at the 4-H Center and owned by the University of Georgia, Rock Eagle is believed to have been a ceremonial center. Rock Eagle refers to a rock pile forming an effigy of a soaring bird which is 10 feet high and 102 feet long, with a wingspan of 120 feet. Free.
- **John Ross Home**, 212 Andrews Ave., Rossville. This two-story log home of Cherokee Chief John Ross was built in 1779 by his grandfather. Chief Ross fought the expulsion of the Indians from the southeast through the legal system, taking his case all the way to the U.S. Supreme Court. Free.
- **Sautee-Nacoochee Indian Mound**, (located at the junction of GA Hwys. 75 and 17, south of Helen). This is a Native American sacred burial site on the National Register of Historic Places where about 75 skeletons have been unearthed, as well as numerous Indian artifacts dating as far back as 10,000 B.C. There is a gazebo marking the place where ceremonies were conducted. The mound itself was probably built during the Woodland period (1000 B.C.–800 A.D.). Cherokees later built a village here. Today, the Bear Clan gathers here monthly to keep their traditions alive and to attempt to have the bones excavated from the mound returned by the Heye Foundation which currently possesses them. Free.
- **Track Rock Gap**, Union County (706/695-2621). See petroglyphs of circles, crosses, animals, and human footprints on this rock thought to be carved by prehistoric Indians. Free.

COMMUNITY, RELIGIOUS & CULTURAL ASSOCIATIONS

AMERICAN INDIAN

- **Oglewanagi Gallery and American Indian Center**, 842 N. Highland Ave., Atlanta (872-4213). Located in the Virginia-Highlands area, the non-profit American Indian Center has a gallery, meeting room, an American Indian reference library, and uses its proceeds to fund a mainstreaming program for American Indians in Atlanta. They have several programs, including talking circles, counseling sessions and discussion groups. In the future, the center also hopes to serve as a half-way house for those with alcohol and other substance abuse problems. The center is affiliated with the North Georgia Inter-Tribal Association, a social, support and self-help organization.

■ **Hawaiian Club** (396-7717). *Hui O Aloha,* founded about three years ago, is a social club open to Hawaiians and those interested in Hawaii. The club seeks to perpetuate Hawaiian culture through music, dances, picnics and fun. Membership is $15 and entitles you to receive their newsletter, *Ka Leo,* which occasionally contains information on the Hawaiian language (which is dying as a result of its neglect in the public school system). The club is developing a Polynesian revue composed of 28 professional dancers, singers and musicians.

schools, classes, language

■ **Camp Rock Eagle**, Rock Eagle 4-H Center, Eatonton (371-2821/457-8575). The DeKalb County 4-H summer camp for kids ages 9–12 features powwows and an educational program about Native Americans.

■ **GAIA Institute**, 5484 Trimble Rd., Atlanta (256-9002). Located off Johnson Ferry Rd. near GA 400 and I-285, the institute offers support groups, lectures, and programs in Native American traditions, including drumming. Sacred Drums of the Earth, a performance group, meets here the first Saturday of every month from 8:00pm–1:00am. A $5.00 donation is requested. Call for current information.

■ **Oglewanagi Gallery and American Indian Center**, 842 N. Highland Ave., Atlanta (872-4213). The only American Indian Center in Atlanta hosts cultural classes, bead classes, lectures on native writing and more. Call for upcoming events.

■ **Loy Johnson** (377-2799). Ms. Johnson is a teacher of Native American ritual and healing chants.

■ **Unicoi State Park**, (Two miles NE of Helen via GA 356), Helen (706/878-2201). "Earth Skills," offered in April, is a week-long, pre-registration workshop with participation in primitive skill development, such as forging, matchless fire building, leather, medicinal plants and basket weaving. There is a shorter, two-day Earth Skill workshop held in October. Call for more information and to pre-register.

AMERICAN INDIAN

■ **Atlantis Connection**, 1402 N. Highland Ave., Atlanta (881-6511). The New Age bookstore sells, among many other items, Native American jewelry, ritual items, and related books and tapes. The store expects to include Eskimo art and books on Eskimo history and culture in the near future. A Monday night lecture series has included "Native American History and Culture."

■ **Attanasio & Associated Educational Materials**, 4595 Dudley Lane, NW, Atlanta (843-2644). The company publishes bilingual textbooks and teaching materials in several languages, including Navajo.

■ **Oglewanagi Gallery and American Indian Center**, 842 N. Highland Ave., Atlanta (872-4213). A mini-library is available to the public and the store sells the *Lakota Times* newspaper.

■ **Ray's Indian Originals**, 90 Avondale Rd, P.O. Box 164, Avondale Estates 30002 (292-4999). Numerous books by and about Native American history and culture, as well as novels, are for sale or loan.

■ **The History Store**, P.O. Box 358, N. Parks St. on the Square, Dahlonega 30533 (706/864-7225). The bookstore is loaded with Native American history books for both children and adults and carries books on other subjects as well. There are Native American, geologic, mineral, and historic maps and — a rare find — a good selection of Native American music on cassettes, including flute and powwow music. The store carries many curiosity items from post cards to replicas of historic photos and documents. You may send away for a catalogue for $1.00.

■ **Indian Springs Trading Post & Museum**, Old 441 (Scenic loop at Tallulah Gorge), Tallulah Falls (706/754-6611). The Trading Post stocks books, including numerous Cherokee craft books, jewelry, pottery and sculpture.

■ *The Native American Journal*, NAJ, 190 Moonshadow Ct., Roswell 30075. A journal of Native American heritage and culture may be purchased for $2.00.

■ **Tekakwitha**, P.O. Box 338, Helen 30345 (706/878-2938). Books for children and adults, and greeting cards may be purchased at this large and diverse store.

HAWAIIAN

■ The *Maui News* and the travel magazines *Aloha* and *Hawaii* are usually available at **Oxford Book Store**, 360 Pharr Rd., NE, Atlanta (262-3333). The *Honolulu Star* is at **Oxford Book Store**, 2345 Peachtree Rd., NE, Atlanta (364-2700).

AMERICAN INDIAN

In addition to **Oglewanagi Gallery** and **Ray's Indian Originals** described above, the following shops offer Native American arts and crafts or books for sale:

■ **Atlantis Connection**, 1402 N. Highland Ave., Atlanta (881-6511). This New Age bookstore sells, among many other items, Native American jewelry, ritual items, books and tapes.

■ **Aztec Jewelers**, 2156 Henderson Mill Rd. (Briarcliff Village Shopping Center), Atlanta (934-2900). The store displays a selection of high-quality silver and turquoise jewelry including earrings, fetishes, necklaces, watch bands and belt buckles.

■ **Chestatee Crossing**, On the Square, Dahlonega (706/864-9099 or 800/326-9613). The spacious Native American arts and crafts store has mostly pottery and paintings, but also carries some jewelry, teas, books and rugs.

■ **Coyote Trading Company**, 439 Seminole Ave., Atlanta (221-1512). Fine Native American jewelry, weavings, sand paintings, pottery, fetishes, ritual items, incense burners and more may be found at this tucked-away shop in Little Five Points.

■ **Indian Springs Trading Post & Museum**, Old 441 (Scenic loop at Tallulah Gorge), Tallulah Falls (706/754-6611). The Trading Post stocks books, numerous Cherokee and other craft books, jewelry, pottery and sculpture.

■ **The Nature Company**, 3393 Peachtree Rd. (Lenox Square), Atlanta (231-9252) and 4400 Ashford-Dunwoody Rd. (Perimeter Mall), Atlanta (551-0266). The Lenox Square store carries a variety of nature items, such as rocks and minerals, as well as popular nature-related T-shirts, tapes, posters, jewelry, toys and books. A high-quality collection of Native American artifacts, turquoise, and Zuni fetishes of various sizes and prices is on display. The Nature Company has a small kiosk at Perimeter Mall which may, occasionally, carry Native American artifacts.

■ **Southwest Connection**, 22-B Bennett St., Atlanta (351-0446). The shop has a collection of art dating from pre-Colombian times to the present day. Look for Native American jewelry, cloth, clothing, handbags, pottery, textile wall hangings, prints and more.

■ **Tekakwitha**, P.O. Box 338, Helen 30345 (706/878-2938). This store, on the main street in Helen, has arts and crafts representing over 60 different Native American tribes, such as beadwork, jewelry, baskets, kachinas, moccasins, dolls and pottery, as well as craft supplies, cards, music tapes, and books for children and adults. The store also offers custom leatherwork.

■ **Tracy Southwest**, 3500 Peachtree Rd. (Phipps Plaza), Atlanta (237-5929). High quality jewelry, sculpture, rugs, paintings, posters and Christmas ornaments by Native American artists are featured in this gallery whose home base is Santa Fe, New Mexico.

■ **Veronica's Attic**, 220 Sandy Springs Cir. (Springs Landing Shopping Center), Atlanta (257-1409). This eclectic shop carries Native American jewelry.

ESKIMO

■ **The E.R. Maynard Co**, 2106 Windsor Dr., Snellville (978-0845). Mr. Maynard sells Inuit Art out of his home. Call between 10:00am–5:00pm for an appointment.

■ **Out of the Woods**, 22 Bennett St., Atlanta (351-0446). Various Eskimo and Inuit art is available, which may, from time to time, include dolls, fetishes and masks.

■ **Ray's Indian Originals**, 90 Avondale Rd., Avondale Estates (292-4999). Owned by Peggy and Ray Belcher, Ray's is both a museum and a store for high quality Native American art. Ray's occasionally has some Eskimo art. Call for information.

GROCERIES, MARKETS, BAKERIES

There are no Native American groceries, markets or bakeries in Atlanta. For information on indigenous American Indian cooking methods, ingredients, regional and tribal variations, all in historical context, take a look at a beautiful new cookbook *Spirit of the Harvest: North American Indian Cooking*, by Beverly Cox and Martin Jacobs. You will learn that the basic diet was simple, yet nuts, berries, seeds and herbs were creatively used to flavor otherwise bland venison and fish. Most of the basic ingredients needed to prepare these authentic recipes are readily available to Atlantans, and the colorful photographs and accompanying essays will undoubtedly entice you to try some.

From the earliest days, when there were more than 2,000 thriving Native American tribes, the food available to the people was as diverse as the environment. Northwest Indians got much of their food from the sea; Plains Indians relied on buffalo, bear and deer meat; Hopis farmed squash, corn, beans and more in the desert; Creeks in the southeast ate fruit, nuts, corn, sweet potatoes; Northeast Indians relied on hunting deer, moose, wolves and rabbits, ate corn, and loved the taste of maple syrup; those near the sea fished, ate seals and shellfish. We know the invading Europeans learned much about the indigenous food and agricultural methods from Native Americans.

Today, in Atlanta, a fun way to get a sense of the history of Native American cooking is to attend one of the many **festivals** held throughout the year, where the food will surely tempt your palate.

POLYNESIAN-STYLE

■ **Trader Vic's**, 225 Courtland St. (Atlanta Hilton Hotel), Atlanta (659-2000). A favorite among tourists, the restaurant serves Polynesian and Continental-style favorites accompanied by creative drinks, such as rum giggle and scorpion. Open: Dinner: Daily.

**ENTERTAINMENT:
THEATRE, DANCE, MUSIC, CLUBS,
FILMS, T.V. & RADIO, SPORTS**

AMERICAN INDIAN

■ Dancing, music, and traditional sports and games are an integral part of American Indian culture, and are proudly preserved and shared at the larger festivals and special events listed in the next section.

■ Storytelling has always been an essential way of transmitting the culture and history of Native Americans from one generation to the next. Though it is a dying art form in our age of rapid and complex mass communication systems, Atlantans such as **Lloyd Arneach**, a Cherokee, keep it alive by appearing at special storytelling events at Callanwolde Fine Arts Center, Oglewanagi Indian Center, and in the Atlanta public school system.

■ **Sacred Drums of the Earth** (256-9002). The Atlanta chapter of this New

York-based organization has presented drum concerts in the Atlanta area. The primary goal of this group is to bring together the percussion and drumming styles of the "four directions and the four races" of the world. The GAIA Institute is the local meeting site for this group. Meetings are held the first Saturday of every month (except August) from 8:00pm–1:00am. Everyone is welcome — bring drums or just come with your hands and feet.

HAWAIIAN

■ **Kele's Pacific Dancers** (589-0644). Booked through "Young Audiences of Atlanta," the dancers perform all over the city, mainly in the schools, but also at festivals and private occasions. They perform native Hawaiian, New Zealand, Tahitian and Samoan dances, including the ancient hula, poi, Samoan fire dance and modern hula.

ƒESTIVALS & SPECIAL EVENTS

JANUARY

■ **Native American Forum on Unity and Justice**, Martin Luther King, Jr. Center, 449 Auburn Ave., Atlanta (255-5727). This forum is part of the King Week festivities and includes lectures and workshops discussing multiculturalism from the Native American perspective and the impact of Native American culture on the rest of American society.

■ **Olde Storytelling Festival**, Callanwolde Fine Arts Center, Atlanta (872-5338). Look for storytellers of Native American culture.

MARCH

■ **Brown's Mount Indian Cultural Festival**, Macon (912/477-3729). Occurring at the same time as Macon's Cherry Blossom Festival, this festival features nature trails, picnicking, Native American music and dance, as well as arts and crafts.

■ **Lantern Light Tour**, Ocmulgee National Monument, Macon (912/752-8257). This one-mile moonlit guided walk goes through the woods to the ceremonial mounds and ends with a spectacular view of Macon. The tour guide describes Native American life and culture of years ago.

■ **Okefenokee Spring Fling**, Okefenokee Swamp Park, Waycross (912/283-0583). Okefenokee means "land of the trembling earth," so named because of the masses of peat and vegetation that float on the surface of the water giving the appearance of solid ground. Indigenous peoples inhabited this area as early as 20,000 B.C., and between 500 B.C. and 1000 A.D., built over 25 mound villages. Timucuan Indians lived here from 1550-1700. Seminoles later came here to escape the encroaching white settlers, but in 1838, they were forceably removed from the area by the state of Georgia. Learn about this history through exhibits, wildlife lectures, films, arts and crafts, music, food and a 20-minute guided motorboat tour. The festival is held the weekend before Easter each year.

APRIL

■ **Artifacts Identification Day**, Etowah Indian Mounds Historic Site, Cartersville (706/387-3747). Anyone may bring in an artifact and professionals will assist in dating and identification.

■ **Earth Skills**, Unicoi State Park, Helen (706/878-2201). This is a weeklong workshop in primitive leather working, creating fire by friction, forging, medicinal and edible plants, basketweaving and more. Participants are provided with an overview of what Native American society and culture were like. Pre-registration is required.

■ **Indian Heritage Day**, Stately Oaks Mansion, Jonesboro (478-6549). The recipient of the prestigious Southeastern Tourism Award, Jonesboro's spring festival features living history activities, entertainment, arrow making, face painting, blowgun demonstrations, finger weaving, a green corn ceremony and other festivities. In the evening, there is a one-hour mock council meeting conducted by Native Americans. The activities take place on the grounds of Stately Oaks at the authentic Creek Indian Village.

■ **Indian Weapon Skills Day**, Kolomoki Mounds State Park, Blakely (912/723-3398). Demonstrations include the construction and use of traditional Indian weapons.

■ **Mossy Creek Barnyard Arts & Crafts Festival**, (Exit #44 off I-75), near Perry (912/922-8265). The semi-annual festival features Native American art, and promoters contend the Indian crafts are museum quality. This event offers a wide range of American folk art and demonstrations including Indian pottery and basketry, rug hooking, music, clogging, a petting farm, mule and wagon rides, food and much more.

■ **Return to Long Swamp Creek Powwow and Indian Festival**, Tate House, Tate (south of Jasper) (800/342-7515). A three-day celebration of Native American culture and spiritual traditions includes traditional dancers, food, crafts, and athletic events featuring members of the Cherokee, Chippewa and Sioux nations.

MAY

■ **Cherokee County Indian Festival & Powwow**, Hwy. 5 (Boling Park, Exit #8 off 575) Canton (706/735-4930). The festival celebrates the culture and spiritual traditions of Native Americans with food, crafts, athletic events, a wildlife exhibit, tepee competition, and fire dancing. Cherokee, Chippewa and Sioux are represented.

■ **Indian Cookin'**, Etowah Indian Mounds Historic Site, Cartersville (706/387-3747). Learn traditional cooking techniques, herbs and recipes used by the Mississippian peoples, and sample the food at this event.

■ **Southeastern Indian Cultural Festival**, Chehaw Park, Albany (912/430-5275). Billed as the largest Native American cultural celebration in the southeast, with ten Indian nations being represented, this festival features traditional games, skills, dances, crafts and food.

JUNE

■ **Gathering of the Tribes** (429-9252). The International Earth Religion Leadership Conference hosts speakers, workshops, and an American Indian marriage ceremony to further the goal of developing harmony among all religious groups.

■ **Indian Days**, Helen (706/878-2521 or 706/878-2938). The festival features Native American dancers, exhibits, and demonstrations of crafts. Proceeds are donated to a Native American orphanage.

■ **Indian Games Festival**, Etowah Indian Mounds Historic Site, Cartersville (706/387-3747). Traditional games of southeastern Native Americans are played, such as chunkey, games of chance and Indian stick ball.

JULY

■ **Festival of Cultures — American Festival**, Underground Atlanta, Atlanta (523-2311). Music, dancing and lectures inform the audience about Native American history and culture.

■ **Vann House Days**, Vann House Historic Site, Spring Place (706/695-2598). Living history demonstrations include basketry, beadwork, carving, finger weaving, quilting and more. Tours of the Vann House and surroundings are available.

AUGUST

■ **Native American Heritage Days**, Crooked River State Park, St. Mary's (912/882-5256). This festival commemorates the Native Americans who once lived in southeast Georgia through special games, music and other activities.

■ **Nacoochee Valley Indian Cultural Festival & Powwow**, Helen (878-2938). Three days of dances, arts and crafts (25 booths), skill demonstrations and food (buffalo burgers, alligator, Indian fry bread) prepared by Native Americans from across the United States and Canada, afford visitors an insight into Indian culture.

SEPTEMBER

■ **American Indian Cultural Festival**, Oculmgee National Monument, Macon (912/752-8257). Each fall this festival features dancing, crafts and skill demonstrations.

■ **Cherokee Homecoming Day**, New Echota Historic Site, Calhoun (706/629-8151). Every year about 100 Cherokees (mainly from North Carolina, but some from as far away as Oklahoma) demonstrate dancing, music and song, blow guns, cooking, crafts and games at their former national capital. There are educational programs to show how the Cherokee lived in the 1800s which include Cherokee language demonstrations. A small admission fee includes all day participation, as well as a museum tour.

■ **Creek Homecoming**, Etowah Indian Mounds Historic Site, Cartersville (387-3747). In 1992, the Creek nation returned to the Indian mounds for the first time in nearly 300 years for a festive day of dancing, eating, games and demonstrations. (Their capitol is currently in Okmulgee, OK.) This special event may occur again in upcoming years.

■ **Indian Cooking Program**, Etowah Indian Mounds Historic Site, Cartersville (706/387-3747). Techniques of food preparation and the uses of herbs and recipes are demonstrated.

■ **Indian Days**, Indian Springs (706/775-6734). The events at this annual festival vary from year to year, but it is always a family affair with exhibits and, usually, music and dancers. Across the street is the oldest state park in Georgia, which boasts miniature golf and swimming for the kids.

■ **Native Americans of the Georgia Coast**, Fort King George Historic Site, Darien (912/437-4770). Native Americans from Florida visit Darien and set-up camp much as their forefathers did more than a century ago.

■ **Native Americans of the Southeast**, Unicoi State Park, Helen (706/878-2201). This event provides a historical overview and highlights the cultural aspects of Native American society. A variety of cultural skills are demonstrated, such as blow guns, darts, and natural dyes.

OCTOBER

■ **Artifact Identification and Weapon Demonstration Day**, Kolomoki Mounds

Historic Park, Blakely (706/723-3398). Events include a tour of the mounds, artifact identification, weapon demonstrations and flint knapping.

■ **Columbus Indian Cultural Festival**, Columbus College Campus, Columbus (706/571-4180 or 327-1566). This is a large festival with a strong educational component. There are 35 demonstrations, including blow guns, Cherokee games, beadwork, Choctaw dancers, Cherokee storytelling, flute music, Katawba pottery and basketweaving. There are booths with traditional and contemporary food. A Native American interpreter discusses the similarities and differences among Southeast and Southwest Indians. The special highlight of this festival is a stick ball game between a Cherokee and a Choctaw team. The festival takes place the second weekend in October.

■ **Earth Skills**, Unicoi State Park, Helen (706/878-2201). This is a two-day workshop in primitive leather working, creating fire without matches, forging, medicinal plants, basketweaving and more. Participants are provided with an overview of what American Indian society and culture were like.

■ **Indian Recognition Month**, Indian Springs State Park, Indian Springs (706/775-7241). Each Saturday in October, visitors will see demonstrations and hear lectures on Native American culture.

■ **Indian Skills Day**, Etowah Indian Mounds Historic Site, Cartersville (706/387-3747). Native Americans demonstrate skills used in basketry, pottery, hide tanning, flint knapping, weaponry and more.

■ **Intertribal Powwow**, Clayton State College, Morrow (961-3510). Held for the first time in 1992, the theme of the powwow, "The People of Turtle Island: A Native American Celebration," was expressed through dancing, music, storytelling and crafts. Whether or not this powwow will become an annual event is uncertain at this time.

■ **Medicine Wheel Gathering**. Native Americans from all over the country gather for a weekend of ceremonies, rituals, and over 20 workshops. In 1991, the Southeast Gathering was held at Saddle Rock Camp, Lookout Mountain, Tennessee. For information on the upcoming gathering, contact: Medicine Wheel Gatherings, P.O. Box 5719, Takoma Park, MD 20912 (301/270-6909) or GAIA Institute in Atlanta at 256-9002.

■ **Mossy Creek Barnyard Arts & Crafts Festival**, (Exit #44 off I-75), near Perry (912/922-8265). This semi-annual festival features Native American art, and promoters contend the Indian crafts are museum quality. This event offers a wide range of American folk art and demonstrations including Indian pottery and basketry, rug hooking, music, clogging, a petting farm, mule and wagon rides, food and much more.

■ **Native American Dance Festival**, Florence Marina State Park, Omaha

(912/838-4244). The festival celebrates Native American folklore, dance and regalia.

■ **Native American Days**, FDR's Little White House, Warm Springs (706/655-3511). This is a family-oriented event featuring Native American music and dancing. Currently, no arts and crafts are scheduled.

■ **Native American Heritage Appreciation Day**, Amicalola Falls State Park, Dawsonville (706/265-2885). American Indian life, along with skills, tools, and weapons, is demonstrated.

■ **Running Water Indian Festival**, Rome (706/232-1714). Food, music, arts and crafts, and lectures are featured.

NOVEMBER

■ **Artifacts Identification Day**, Etowah Indian Mounds Historic Site, Cartersville (706/387-3747). Anyone may bring in an artifact and professionals will assist in dating and identification.

■ **Harvest Festival**, Galleria Park and Gardens, Atlanta (953-3750). Music, dance, weapon demonstrations, apple pressing, a petting zoo and a re-creation of an authentic Native American village highlight this festival.

■ **Indian Heritage Week**, Georgia State Capitol, Atlanta (656-2844). In addition to the permanent collection of Native American artifacts, special exhibits are presented during this week. Bob Two Hawks, a Native American Culturalist, lectures and provides demonstrations. This is a week that school children look forward to, as Bob Two Hawks is known for his ability to relate to children and provide meaningful and interesting demonstrations, such as making a matchless fire.

DECEMBER

■ **Cherokee Christmas**, New Echota Historic Site, Calhoun (706/629-8151). Buildings are decorated in 18th century style, and traditional Cherokee foods are offered with apple cider. A special holiday edition of the Cherokee newspaper is published. No Native American tribes are represented at this event.

RESOURCES

■ **The Georgia Department of Natural Resources** (3GA-PARK) manages the State Historic Sites and Parks and publishes a special events brochure.

Mardi Gras celebration in Underground Atlanta.

CAJUN AND CREOLE COMMUNITIES

Cajuns trace their roots to a group of people who initially migrated from France to French Acadia, Canada. But when the English claimed the area in 1765 and renamed it Nova Scotia, the Acadians fled to Louisiana where there was already a considerable French population. Through decades of intermarriage with others in Louisana, including Native Americans and European immigrants, the Acadians evolved into a unique culture called "Cajun" (a shortened version of "Acadian"). Their language, Cajun French, is a unique blend of the French of their heritage and the French spoken in Louisiana. The Acadian cooking methods and ingredients adapted to and integrated the local agricultural products available in Louisiana, and the result is a delicious, if unsophisticated, cuisine. Cajuns developed a country-style of music that makes use of the traditional fiddle, guitar, triangle and diatonic accordian — exemplified in the music of the late Dewey Balfa. Cajun dance is a unique two-step, waltz, and more modern jitterbug. It is estimated that upwards of 41,000 Cajuns live in the greater metropolitan Atlanta area. *Laissez les bon temps rouller!*

There is not a clear consensus on the definition of the word Creole. Many historians consider it to be merely a matter of semantics (originating with the Spanish *criollo*). However, in modern-day usage, it describes people of a similar ethnic heritage as Cajuns, but with the addition of African and West Indian heritages. Of course, Cajuns and Creoles have intermarried through the centuries, so distinctions have become quite blurred. But Creole cuisine certainly is a unique blend of various cooking methods, herbs, spices and other ingredients from many cultures. The meals are spicier, in general, than Cajun cooking. Nevertheless, in Atlanta, Cajun and Creole are frequently used terms to describe the same foods. Creoles, who have influenced the development of jazz (jass) and other forms of music, often use many of the same musical instruments as the Cajuns, but play a different type of accordian and add a rub-board. The different Creole heritage (African, West Indian and French) has given rise, through the past 80 years or so, to a distinct form of music — zydeco, popularized by Clifton Chenier (a Grammy Award winner), and many others. Zydeco dance is faster and more complex than Cajun dance. Zydeco may be heard in venues around Atlanta almost every weekend of the year.

COMMUNITY, RELIGIOUS & CULTURAL ASSOCIATIONS

■ **Atlanta Cajun Dance Association**, 2704 Laurelwood Rd., Atlanta 30360 (451-6611). The very active group participates in and schedules Cajun language and dance classes, dances, and benefits for WRFG-FM. It also celebrates **Mardi Gras** and hosts special events on a regular basis, such as **Cajun Dance Weekend**, held during Super Bowl weekend at the end of January, which features dance music, Cajun French language lessons and catered Cajun food. The association brings top performers to Atlanta, including **Steve Riley and the Mamou Playboys**, who were recently voted the best Cajun band in Louisiana. A prominent association leader and dance teacher is a host on WRFG's Sunday morning Cajun and zydeco program. Call to receive a copy of the ACDA's informative newsletter — there is always something happening!
■ **The Louisiana Club** (962-2492). The 185-member club helps Louisiana transplants adjust to life in Atlanta and hosts an annual Mardi Gras Ball. Meetings are held at St. Patrick's Catholic Church in Norcross.

SCHOOLS, CLASSES, LANGUAGE

■ **Cajun French Language Lessons** are offered through the Atlanta Cajun Dance Association (451-6611). Cajun French was threatened with extinction not so long ago. In 1916, the state of Louisiana made English the official language of the school system, so Cajun and Creole children who persisted in speaking French were punished. It didn't take too many decades before people developed a negative image of anyone speaking French, including children. So to be economically and socially successful, it became necessary for

Cajuns and Creoles to neglect the French of their heritage and concentrate on mastering English. A world-wide Francophone effort was begun in 1955 to reinstate the French language in Louisiana, but the consequences of self-denigration were widespread and long-lasting. Putting this in perspective, one can appreciate how valuable it is that the ACDA actively perpetuates and promotes the Cajun French language.

■ **Cajun Dance Lessons** are offered through the Atlanta Cajun Dance Association (681-1236/451-6611). Lessons include the Cajun waltz, two-step, Creole, zydeco and Cajun jitterbug. (Cajun two-step is not the same as the Texas two-step.) Beginner, intermediate and advanced classes are offered.

■ **Cajun Music Lessons** are offered through the Atlanta Cajun Dance Association (451-6611). Accordian, fiddle, guitar and rhythms (triangle) may be studied.

NEWSPAPERS, MAGAZINES, BOOKS, VIDEOS

■ **Books** on Cajun cooking, music history, and music instruction are available by calling 451-5365.

SHOPPING CENTERS, SPECIALTY STORES, HOTELS

■ **Cajun Musical Instruments**, such as authentic Cajun triangles, spoons, zydeco rub-boards, and children's and adult's accordians; **Cajun Mardi Gras masks and hats**; and **earrings** are available by calling 451-5365.

GROCERIES, MARKETS, BAKERIES

■ Cajun and Creole spices, as well as pre-packaged jambalaya, sausages and gumbo soups, are available in some large supermarkets (e.g., Kroger) and almost all of Atlanta's farmers markets. (Of interest: The word gumbo is derived from the Bantu African word *ngombo*, meaning okra. Okra was first cultivated in Africa, and is, of course, the basis of gumbo soup. Gumbo is also a patois spoken by some French West Indians and some blacks and Creoles in

Louisiana.) If you are a novice in this cuisine and could benefit from background information and delicious recipes, pick-up one of the best subregional cookbooks currently available, *Chef Paul Prudhomme's Louisiana Kitchen.*

<hr>

RESTAURANTS

■ **A Taste of New Orleans**, 889 W. Peachtree St. (between 7th and 8th Sts.), Atlanta (874-5535). The Creole restaurant received good ratings by *Bon Appetit*, *Atlanta Magazine* and *The New York Times*. Try the fish moutarde, gumbo, crawfish cakes, oysters en brochette, or red beans and rice with Andouille sausage . . . and save room for dessert! Open: Lunch: Mon.–Fri.; Dinner: Mon.–Sat.

■ **Arthur's Ragin' Cajun Cafe**, 1360 Powers Ferry Rd. (Terrel Mill Rd.), Atlanta (850-8673). Authentic Cajun dishes prepared by an award-winning chef feature seafood bouchin, etouffee crawfish, shrimp and crab, red beans and smoked sausage, stuffed catfish, bread pudding with rum sauce, lunch specials, and an all-you-can-eat crawfish boil on Saturday from 2:00pm-5:30pm. Live Cajun music and dancing are featured Wednesday through Saturday evenings. Open: Lunch: Mon.–Fri.; Dinner: Tues.–Sat.

■ **Baker's Cafe**, 1134 Euclid Ave. (Little 5 Points), Atlanta (223-5039). The Little Five Points restaurant serves sandwiches and such Creole and Cajun specialties as rice and beans and blackened fish. Special Sunday brunch. Open: Lunch and Dinner: Wed.–Sat.

■ **Cafe du Monde**, Lower Alabama St., Underground Atlanta, Atlanta (681-2719). The cafe chain is based in New Orleans and specializes in beignets and cafe au lait made with chicory. Open: Lunch and Dinner: Daily.

■ **Cajun Bayou**, 6470 Spalding Dr. (Holcomb Bridge Rd.), Norcross (263-7872). The seafood restaurant features stuffed and soft-shell crab, stuffed shrimp, seafood gumbo, fresh oysters and other authentic Cajun dishes. Open: Lunch and Dinner: Daily.

■ **Cajun Bob's**, 2390 Delk Rd. (Scottish Inn/I-75), Marietta (952-3365 ext.200). A variety of po' boys served on Louisiana "Batar" french bread are the staples here. Open: Lunch: Daily.

■ **Cajun Joe's**, 6125 Covington Hwy. (Panola Shopping Center), Lithonia (808-9733). The restaurant serves a good chicken gumbo. Open: Lunch and Dinner: Daily.

■ **Fanny Moon's**, 151 Kenny's Alley, Underground Atlanta, Atlanta (521-2026).

Cajun meals, which include jambalaya, black bean soup, and gumbo, may be enjoyed while patrons listen to live New Orleans jazz, blues, and mojo music. Open: Dinner: Tues.–Sat.

■ **Fat Tuesday Express and Cajun Cafe**, Kenny's Alley, Underground Atlanta, Atlanta (523-7404). Louisiana-style soups, sandwiches, red beans and rice, and gumbo are served at this location of the chain restaurant. Open: Lunch and Dinner: Daily.

■ **French Quarter Food Shop**, 923 Peachtree St. (8th St.), Atlanta (875-2489). Deemed to serve the "Best Cajun Fare" by *Atlanta Magazine,* and popular with Louisiana transplants and the Atlanta Cajun Dance Association, the funky Cajun restaurant is known for its true Cajun chefs and varied menu, including great beignets, jambalaya, muffaletta, etouffees, gumbos and po' boys all at reasonable prices. Take-out and catering are available. Open: Lunch: Mon.–Sat.; Dinner: Tues.–Sat.

■ **Huey's**, 1816 Peachtree Rd. (Collier Rd.), Atlanta (873-2037). The restaurant considers itself a New Orleans-style restaurant serving food influenced by Cajun and Creole cooking. The beignets, offered with 45 toppings, are especially well-regarded. Open: Lunch: Daily; Dinner: Tues.–Sun.

■ **Mable's Table**, 2071 N. Druid Hills Rd. (I-85 in front of Travelodge), Atlanta (315-6231). Unique by most people's standards, Mable's restaurant and lounge features New York deli for lunch and classic Cajun cuisine for dinner. The menu includes muffaletta, jambalaya, po' boy sandwiches, crab cakes, creoles and daily chef's specials. Open: (Cajun) Dinner: Mon.–Sat.

■ **McKinnon's Louisiane Restaurant**, 3209 Maple Dr. (Peachtree Rd.), Atlanta (237-1313). High-quality, traditional Creole and Cajun cooking has earned this restaurant the honor of being the oldest eatery of its kind in Atlanta. *Atlanta Magazine* contends McKinnon's offers the "Best Gumbo" in town. Enjoy the sing-a-long piano bar. Open: Dinner: Mon.–Sat.

■ **Meno's Cajun Café**, 113 E. Church Square (Ponce de Leon Ave.), Decatur (377-4405). A popular restaurant, Meno's serves gumbo, jambalaya and caters special events. Open: Lunch: Mon.–Fri.; Dinner: Mon.–Sat. (opens at 3:00pm on Sat.).

■ **New Orleans Café**, 7887-A Roswell Rd. (The Shoppes of Morgan Falls), Atlanta (396-9665). The restaurant serves such Cajun specialites as muffaletta, shrimp remoulade, godchaux salad, etouffee and jambalaya. Open: Lunch: Mon.–Fri.; Dinner: Mon.–Sat.

■ **New Orleans Sub Shoppe**, 67 Park Place (across from Woodruff Park downtown), Atlanta (523-0454). Po' boys with sausage and jambalaya are big hits at this shop. Open: Breakfast and Lunch: Mon.–Fri.

DANCE BANDS

■ **Hair of the Dog** and **Atlanta Swamp Opera** are local Cajun bands that may be heard around Atlanta. Contact the ACDA (451-6611) to find out the location of their next appearance.

CLUBS

■ **Blind Willie's**, 828 N. Highland Ave., Atlanta (873-2583), a popular Virginia-Highland club, is a frequent venue for zydeco bands and, occasionally, Cajun music.

■ **Blues Harbor**, 2293 Peachtree Rd. (1 block north of Peachtree Battle Shopping Center), Atlanta (524-3001) is a hot spot for zydeco bands.

■ **Cotton Club**, 1021 Peachtree St., NE, Atlanta (874-2523) periodically features a zydeco band. Call to hear a recording of upcoming events.

■ **Decatur Arts Festival**, Old Courthouse, Decatur (371-8386) is held annually during Memorial Day weekend and has featured Cajun music.

■ **The Freight Room**, 301 E. Howard Ave., Decatur (378-5365), more of a coffeehouse than a club, is one of Atlanta's most frequented folk music clubs and occasionally hosts Cajun groups.

■ **Variety Playhouse**, 1099 Euclid Ave. (Little Five Points), Atlanta (524-7354) is occasionally the locale of an exciting Cajun band, and the dancing sometimes spills out into the street!

STORYTELLING

■ **Lella Maurer** is a professional storyteller who knows Cajun tales and has performed at the Southern Order of Storyteller's "Olde Christmas Storytelling Festival" held in January at Callanwolde Fine Arts Center.

T.V. & RADIO

■ **WRFG-FM (89.3)**. Every Sunday listen to zydeco and Cajun music from 10:00am–1:00pm. The station is weak, so you may need to be a little creative with your antenna to receive it. The station is non-profit, and the initials stand for "Radio Free Georgia." For requests, call 523-8989.

FEBRUARY & MARCH

■ **Mardi Gras Parade** (392-1272). An evening parade of colorful groups of walking krewes, floats and bands begins at the corner of Peachtree and Baker Streets and proceeds down Peachtree Street to Kenny's Alley at Underground Atlanta, where a boisterous party is held. Lots of people wear costumes and traditional beads, and doubloons are thrown into the crowd. Everyone is welcome to join in the revelry!

■ **Mardi Gras** celebrations are held around Atlanta at local restaurants (Fat Tuesday, Meno's Cajun Café, etc.) and hotels through the Atlanta Cajun Dance Association. The American Cancer Society also holds an annual Mystic Krewe Ball fundraiser.

■ **Cajun Mardi Gras Weekend**, Athens, Georgia (706/546-8748). Sponsored by the Athens Folk Music and Dance Society, festivities include dancing to Cajun dance bands and world famous Cajun musicians, Cajun food, and dance and cooking workshops. If you enjoy Cajun music, this is *the* event to attend. Call if you need assistance with weekend housing arrangements.

AUGUST

■ **Cajun Festival**, Atlanta (943-8971). Enjoy a full day of live Cajun music and dance, storytelling, a fair with Cajun food, clowns, face painting and other entertainment, as well as a Cajun dinner and dance in the evening.

OTHER

■ Many special events are scheduled year-round by the **Atlanta Cajun Dance Association** (451-6611). Call to be placed on their newsletter mailing list.

RESOURCES

■ **Atlanta Area Friends of Folk Music**, 29 Lester Rd., Lawrenceville 30244. Membership (925-8089); coffeehouse (892-1492); and newsletter (320-9203).

■ **Atlanta Cajun Dance Association Newsletter**, 2704 Laurelwood Rd., Atlanta 30360 (451-6611).

Russian Pentecostals prepare for a celebration.

the international
community —
an overview

Hopefully you have found just what you were looking for in the preceding chapters. But if you would like an overview of Atlanta's international and ethnic communities, then browse through this chapter to discover a special event, gift shop, film festival or, perhaps, farmers market, which appeals to you. Be adventurous — try a festival you never would have thought to try before: perhaps you will enjoy your piece of baklava at Taste of Atlanta, or marvel at the displays at the Festival of Trees depicting how the holiday season is celebrated in different countries around the world, or even find yourself participating in a Filipino bamboo dance at Emory's International Festival. We can assure you that no matter where you go, you will feel the friendliness and warmth of your fellow Atlantans.

> ### history, neighborhoods,
> ### historical sites,
> ### museums & galleries

HISTORICAL SITES & MUSEUMS

The majority of Atlanta's museums and historical sites focus on the Civil War and other aspects of local history; however, bit by bit, new attractions and museums are opening which address global themes or emphasize the cultural diversity of Atlanta's growing population.

■ **Atlanta Botanical Garden**, 1345 Piedmont Rd. (Piedmont Park at The Prado), Atlanta (876-5858). Garden exhibits include a small Japanese garden and the Fuqua Conservancy, a stunning glass-enclosed building simulating five distinct world environments and housing thousands of plants that grow in the various climates. Maps throughout the conservancy indicate which parts of the world have the various climates and which plants visitors are viewing. Classes, lectures and slide shows often feature bonsai, ikebana (Japanese flower-arranging) and European gardens and gardening. Unusual tours are sponsored by the garden, featuring visits to spectacular gardens in France, the Netherlands and other European countries. Call for an update on programs and events. Hours: Tues.–Sat. 9:00am–6:00pm; Sun. 12noon–6:00pm. (Extended hours during summer months.) Admission fee.

■ **Atlanta Museum**, 537 Peachtree St., NE, Atlanta (872-8233). The museum has a hodge-podge of collectibles from around the world, including such diverse pieces as Chinese porcelains, Ethiopian antiquities and Native American artifacts. Hours: Mon.–Fri. 10:00am–5:00pm and weekends for groups (by appointment only). Admission fee.

■ **Center for Puppetry Arts**, 1404 Spring St., Atlanta (874-0398). The center is the most comprehensive puppetry museum in the U.S., and its museum houses an extensive collection of puppets from around the world, including pre-Colombian clay puppets, ritualistic African figurines and a variety of puppets from Asia, the former Soviet Union, South America, North America and Europe. There is a special exhibit room for traveling shows and memorial exhibits along with a hands-on gallery, especially appealing to children. Hours: Mon.–Sat. 9:00am–4:00pm and evenings on performance nights. Admission fee.

■ **CNN Studio Tour**, Omni Center, 100 Techwood Ave., SW, Atlanta (827-2400). CNN has made its mark as the only global television network being broadcast in over 100 countries. During a tour of the CNN studio, you will also be informed about TBS' influence in other global events, such as the Goodwill Games. Hours: Daily 9:00am–5:30pm. Admission fee.

■ **Fernbank Museum of Natural History**, 767 Clifton Rd., NE, Atlanta (378-0127). This spectacular museum, lying amid the Fernbank Forest, offers Atlantans a showcase of planet Earth and the natural sciences. Exhibits are people-oriented and bring a new approach to learning about the natural history of our world. Hands-on exhibits, interactive displays and the most modern communications and learning techniques are scattered throughout the museum. The permanent exhibit, "Our Changing Earth," uses the State of Georgia as a springboard to understand the major developments of life on Earth. Two children's galleries teach concepts of natural history using bright, hands-on exhibits. The museum also houses an IMAX Theater (with a 3-story high screen), a Naturalist Center and a gift shop. A full schedule of classes, workshops, special events and summer camp programs are being developed. Hours: Mon.–Sat. 9:00am–6:00pm; Sun. 12noon–6:00pm. Admission fee.

■ **High Museum of Art**, Robert Woodruff Arts Center, 1280 Peachtree St., NE,

Atlanta (892-HIGH). Atlanta's premier museum of art showcases permanent and special exhibits of art, artifacts and antiquities from around the world, in a building that has won praise for its architectural design. Films, lectures and special events frequently accompany temporary exhibitions. The lower level of the museum contains a children's area with hands-on exhibits that delight adults as much as they do children. Hours: Tues., Wed., Thurs. and Sat. 10:00am–5:00pm; Fri. 10:00am–9:00pm; and, Sun. 12noon–5:00pm. Admission fee.

■ **High Museum at Georgia–Pacific Center**, 133 Peachtree St., NW, Atlanta (577-6940). The attractive extension to the High Museum is often the location of works of art, archaeological items and unusual exhibits of international content. These special exhibits are frequently accompanied by related innovative workshops, classes and performances. Hours: Mon.–Fri. 11:00am–5:00pm. Free.

■ **Michael C. Carlos Museum** (formerly Emory University Museum of Art & Archaeology), Emory University, Main Quadrangle, 571 S. Kilgo Cir., Atlanta (727-4282). The museum's permanent collection includes art and artifacts from ancient civilizations of the Near East and Mediterranean. Spectacular special collections can also be enjoyed, such as "Islamic Art and Patronage: Treasures from Kuwait," a recent exhibit of about 100 pieces of art, jewelry, books, rugs and artifacts from the 8th–18th centuries. These pieces were on exhibit in St. Petersburg during the Iraqi occupation of Kuwait and are believed to be the only pieces remaining from the National Museum of Kuwait. An impressive expansion has tripled the museum's existing space and includes a cafe and instructional space. From the spring of 1993 through August 1996, the renovated museum will house "Sacred Spaces, Famous Faces," an exhibit on the history of athletic competition and ceremonies in ancient Greece. Hours: Tues.–Sat. 10:00am–4:30pm; Sun. 12noon–5:00pm. Free, but a donation of $3.00 is suggested.

■ **Museum of the Jimmy Carter Library**, One Copenhill Ave., Atlanta (331-3942). Quite a few of the museum's exhibits deal with global issues of peace and human rights and emphasize Jimmy Carter's accomplishments in these areas during his presidency. The Carter Presidential Center, adjacent to the Jimmy Carter Library, is a foundation founded and led by Jimmy Carter dedicated to furthering world peace and human understanding. Recent programs have included initiatives to eradicate parasitic diseases in Africa and immunize children in the developing world. The center's primary focus these days is The Atlanta Project, a massive effort to focus our country's resources on the disadvantaged in Atlanta. Museum hours: Mon.–Sat.

9:00am–4:45pm; Sun. 12noon–4:45pm. Admission fee.

■ **Zoo Atlanta**, 800 Cherokee Ave., SE, Atlanta (624-5678). The zoo is undergoing a phenomenal multi-million dollar redevelopment program to exhibit animals from around the world in natural environmental habitats. Already completed are exhibits giving visitors a chance to imagine themselves on a world-wide safari of the jungles, rain forests and savannah plains of Africa and Asia. The expansion will include The Arctic Coast and Sea Lion Cove, featuring polar bears, sea lions and birds; an International Petting Farm of domestic animals from around the world; and South American Tropics, a jungle addition to the Reptile House, showcasing anteaters, tamarins, sloths and other animals from the Amazon. Hours: Daily 10:00am–5:30pm. Admission fee.

■ **Atlanta Historical Society's Museum of Atlanta History** — *On the Horizon*, 3101 Andrews Dr., NW, Atlanta (814-4000). The Museum of Atlanta History, scheduled to open in the fall of 1993, will feature exhibits providing comprehensive views of the history of various ethnic groups in Atlanta. A special exhibit, "DAYS TO REMEMBER: Atlanta's Cultural Calendars," will be on display when the museum opens and will feature photographs, costumes and celebratory objects representing many of the special events celebrated by Atlanta's diverse cultural populations. The year-long exhibit will be accompanied by special programs illustrating concurrent community holidays. (For example, a Hmong dance troupe might perform at the museum in December, which is when the community celebrates the New Year.) Atlanta's ethnic communities have eagerly participated in the exhibit, and Georgia State University's Department of Applied Research in Anthropology has painstakingly researched background material. A 1994 commemorative calendar in poster form, containing photographs from the exhibit and listing holidays celebrated by Atlanta's ethnic communities, will be available for purchase at the exhibit. Hours: Mon.–Sat. 9:00am–5:30pm; Sun. 12noon–5:30pm. Admission fee.

■ **DeKalb County's International Village** — *On the Horizon*. Fund-raising is underway in DeKalb County to create an "international village." Proposed plans have included the concept of an enclosed area within the village containing exhibits showcasing the ethnic diversity of DeKalb County. For further information contact the DeKalb Chamber of Commerce (378-8000).

GALLERIES

■ **Atlanta College of Art Gallery**, Woodruff Arts Center, 1280 Peachtree St., NE, Atlanta (898-1157). The college's gallery frequently displays exhibits of international content, such as "As Seen by Both Sides: American and

Vietnamese Artists Look at War," and another exhibit cosponsored by Amnesty International which captured the dilemma of refugees worldwide.

■ **Atlanta International Museum of Art and Design**, Marquis Two Tower – Garden Level, 285 Peachtree Center Ave., Atlanta (688-2467). The small gallery showcases dimensional art, design and craftsmanship for everyday use by the world's societies, both past and present. Recent exhibits have included collections of Japanese textiles, Mexican folk art and English silver. Hours: Tues.–Sat. 11:00am–5:00pm; Sun. 1:00pm–5:00pm. Free, but a donation is suggested.

■ **Contemporary International Museum of Art (CIMA)**, 15 Main Street, Buford (932-2666). Housed in the renovated Bona Allen Building in downtown Buford, CIMA's focus is both contemporary and international. At this point, the gallery is showcasing contemporary work by regional, national and internationally acclaimed artists and houses about 11 artists' studios. Plans for the future include expanding CIMA into a multimillion dollar museum which will house a permanent collection of work by Robert Rauschenberg, an International Communication Arts Museum, an outdoor sculpture garden and three large exhibition galleries featuring work by the international artist community. Hours: Mon.–Wed. by appointment; Thurs.–Sat. 10:00am–6:00pm. Free.

■ **Emory University's Schatten Gallery**, Woodruff Library, 540 Ashby Cir., Atlanta (727-6868/727-6861). The gallery's high-quality exhibits focus primarily on the art, history, politics, religion and culture of international communities in Atlanta and worldwide. The gallery is in the lobby of Emory's main library. Call for hours.

■ **Oglethorpe University's Art Museum — *On the Horizon.*** Oglethorpe's new art museum in the Philip Weltner Library is scheduled to be completed in 1993. Works of art from around the world will be featured, including a special collection of international jewelry, textiles, books and manuscripts. Call 261-1441 for more information.

INTERNATIONAL ASSOCIATIONS

■ **Amnesty International USA**, 740 W. Peachtree St., NW, Atlanta (876-5661). This international human rights organization works impartially for the release of prisoners of conscience (those arrested for their beliefs who have not used or advocated violence); for fair and prompt trials for all political prisoners; and for an end to torture, executions and "disappearances." The Southern Regional Office of Amnesty International in Atlanta serves volunteers in 11 southern states. People may participate by joining or forming community, campus, or high school groups or by joining one or more Amnesty letter-writing networks — The Urgent Action Network, Freedom Writers and the Government Action Network. The Southern Regional Office can provide speakers on human rights issues and offers for sale or rental all Amnesty International human rights reports and videos, some of which are available in Spanish, French and Arabic. In the past, the organization has sponsored exhibits addressing issues of human rights on an international level (the failed revolution at Tiananmen Square, the dilemma of refugees worldwide, etc.), but because of funding restrictions, new exhibits have been put on hold.

■ **Atlanta Council of International Organizations**, P.O. Box 56076, Atlanta 30343 (378-3719/427-7680). The council is a non-profit association which has as its goal the fostering of better communications among the growing number of international organizations in the Atlanta area. Members meet regularly to exchange information about international activities. The council publishes the *Atlanta Multicultural Directory*, a manual of over 225 pages of information about Atlanta's ethnic communities. Listings include Atlanta's social and cultural organizations; English for Speakers of Other Languages (ESOL) programs; international research programs in area universities; church and religious programs for internationals; refugee and international agencies; and performance groups. Cost is $12.00. The council also distributes a monthly newsletter *The Dateline.*

■ **Atlanta Sister City Committee** (894-4590). The Atlanta Sister City Committee is appointed by city officials for the purpose of recommending new sister-city relationships and supporting the on-going activities of the various existing committees. Atlanta presently has eleven sister-city relationships worldwide!

■ **Christian Council of Metropolitan Atlanta**, 465 Boulevard, SE, Suite 101, Atlanta (622-2235). The association offers a variety of services for internationals residing in Atlanta and publishes the *Directory of Refugee Services in the Metropolitan Atlanta Area*, a comprehensive directory listing resources for the refugee community. The directory includes facilities which offer English for Speakers of Other Language (ESOL) programs, public health facilities, local refugee assistance organizations, multicultural ministries, volunteer agencies and a few professional and commercial references. Cost is $7.50.

■ **Club International** (250-5201). This "social exchange" is open to people from around the world who want to share their "native culture and expand their cultural horizons." Regular monthly dinner meetings are held at different ethnic restaurants, and many other activities are scheduled throughout the month, such as Halloween parties, foreign policy discussion groups and Zen meditation gatherings. Call to be placed on the mailing list.

■ **The Friendship Force**, Suite 575, South Tower, One CNN Center, Atlanta (522-9490/222-2001). Atlanta is home to the international headquarters of The Friendship Force, an organization established by Wayne Smith and President Jimmy Carter, and recently nominated for the Nobel Peace Prize. Friendship Force is dedicated to promoting peace and goodwill by establishing friendships throughout the world. Members worldwide participate in exchanges — delegations from clubs in the U.S. travel to foreign countries, and internationals from foreign clubs travel to the U.S. — all exchanges having the purpose of learning more about the customs and culture of the host country. Thousands of Friendship Force members worldwide engage in exchanges each year. Those who are interested in learning more about this unique organization or desire an opportunity to participate in an exchange (as a host or an ambassador), should call headquarters to find out the telephone number of your local area Friendship Force Club.

■ **Georgia Council for International Activities**, 999 Peachtree St., Suite 770, Atlanta (873-6170). The council is a non-profit organization which affords internationals an in-depth exposure to life in Georgia and an opportunity to meet with their professional colleagues and focus on a broad range of subjects, such as foreign policy, the environment, American studies or the media. Atlantans who wish to serve as volunteer "hosts" to visiting internationals are encouraged to contact the organization and sign up as a volunteer. The council also offers assistance to international travelers in the city, providing a Language Bank (378-2041) and serving as a resource center for professional and emergency services. Two women's groups are also sponsored by the council — **The International Women Associates** which meets monthly to orient international newcomers to Atlanta and assist them in developing friendships in the Atlanta area; and **The International Business Women's Network** which meets monthly and provides a support group for international working women.

■ **International Club of Atlanta**, (250-1049). This newly formed social club brings together Atlantans from all different national, cultural and religious backgrounds. Numerous monthly activities are sponsored by the club, including bridge games, discussion groups and international dinners and dances featuring food and activities from all over the world. Although membership dues are pricey, most of the club's many activities are free to members.

■ **International Women's Club of Atlanta** (252-2728, ext. 6). The club's stated purpose is to promote goodwill and better understanding among women of different cultural backgrounds. To further this goal, the club supports the Atlanta International School, Ballet Rotaru and the Southern Center for International Studies.

■ **Southern Center for International Studies**, 320 W. Paces Ferry Rd., NW, Atlanta (261-5763). The non-profit educational institute is an independent center for thought and opinion on international affairs and U.S. foreign policy, with a mission to broaden the understanding of its members in foreign affairs. To this end, members are offered invitations to high caliber programs on foreign, political and economic conditions. Members also have access to the center's current events library which provides research services, executive information packages, copies of the center's publications and program tapes.

■ **University and College International Student Programs**. Atlanta area universities and colleges have international student offices which provide support to the various international organizations at the university. Membership in these organizations is usually not limited to international students, so anyone interested in learning more about a particular culture can become involved. The international offices can also provide contact persons for information about other international associations for students and study-abroad programs.

schools, classes, language

CHILDREN'S LANGUAGE SCHOOLS

■ **Atlanta International School**, 4820 Long Island Dr., Atlanta (843-3380), a private school in northwest Atlanta, offers multicultural education for Atlantans and overseas students K–12th grade. Students have an opportunity to become immersed in English and either French, Spanish or German. Students can also prepare for international baccalaureate examinations. The school's population hails from about 54 foreign countries.

■ Atlanta Area Public Schools have begun developing international study programs in their high schools. Recently, elementary schools in the City of Atlanta, Cobb County and DeKalb County have initiated language programs for younger children. For example, **DeKalb County's Hooper Alexander Elementary School Spanish Language Magnet Program**, 3414 Memorial Dr., Decatur (289-1933) is a magnet school offering elementary-age children in the county an opportunity to study the Spanish language in-depth.

ADULT FOREIGN LANGUAGE CLASSES

■ Most Atlanta colleges and universities offer noncredit courses on evenings and Saturdays, a good number of which focus on foreign languages or international politics, history and culture. A sampling: **Evening at Emory** (727-6000) has offered classes in Chinese, Japanese, German, French, ethnic cooking, foreign history, kyudo (Japanese archery), Russian politics and has even sponsored tours of Atlanta's dim sum restaurants; **Kennesaw State College** (423-6400) has offered classes in Portuguese, Japanese, Chinese, French, Spanish, Russian and Italian; **Georgia State University** (651-3456) has offered classes in French, Russian, German, Japanese and Spanish; and **Oglethorpe University** (364-8383) has offered classes in French, German, Italian, Spanish, Dutch, Arabic, Swedish, Russian and Japanese.

■ The *Yellow Pages* lists a large number of private companies in Atlanta which offer foreign language classes, such as the well-known **Berlitz Language Center** at 3400 Peachtree Rd., NE, Atlanta (261-5062), offering instruction in almost every foreign language; and **Language Services International** at 2256 Northlake Pkwy., Tucker (939-6400), also providing private instruction by native speakers in almost every foreign language.

■ *Creative Loafing* always has a few announcements about private language classes or clubs.

COLLEGE & UNIVERSITY
FOREIGN LANGUAGE PROGRAMS

■ Atlanta's colleges and universities offer many opportunities for students to immerse themselves in international affairs and foreign languages. A sampling: **Emory University** has, among others, a Department of Soviet, Post-Soviet and East European Studies, a Latin American and Caribbean Studies Program, an African-American and African Studies Program, and a Near Eastern and Judaic Languages and Literature Department; **Kennesaw State College** offers an International Affairs major; **Agnes Scott College** offers programs in Spanish, French, German, and Classical Languages and Literature; and **Clark Atlanta University** offers a French, German and Spanish language major.

STUDY-ABROAD PROGRAMS

■ Many student exchange organizations have local contacts in the Atlanta area. A sampling: **AIFS Scholarship Foundation** (292-7791) provides information about becoming a host family for a semester or school year to a teenage student from a European country; **International Educational Forum (IEF)** (996-2085 or 800/346-2826) arranges for families in Atlanta to serve as hosts for three, five or ten months for teenage students from Europe and Asia; and **International Student Exchange Programs (ASSE)** (455-7632 or 800/333-3802) provides information about serving as a host family or becoming an exchange student overseas.

■ Atlanta's universities and colleges have **International Student Program Offices** which can provide information about study-abroad programs.

■ See the *Atlanta Multicultural Directory* (378-3719) for additional listings.

ENGLISH FOR SPEAKERS OF OTHER LANGUAGES (ESOL)

■ Atlanta area school systems offer ESOL programs for adults and children, and a few even offer comprehensive refugee assistance programs. For example, the DeKalb County School System has an **International Center**, 3688 Chamblee-Dunwoody Rd., Chamblee (451-8049) where children who do not speak any English are first placed so they can participate in a comprehensive ESOL program before being mainstreamed into regular classrooms. The **DeKalb County School System** (292-7456) also has an extremely successful program which teaches English as a second language to over 7,000 adults each year.

■ Atlanta's colleges and universities offer ESOL programs during evening hours, such as **Evening at Emory** (727-6000), **Kennesaw State College** (423-6400) and **Oglethorpe University** (364-8383).

■ **City and county public libraries** have ESOL audio-visual materials available to assist in learning English and improve speaking, reading and writing skills.

■ See the *Atlanta Multicultural Directory* (378-3719) and *Directory of Refugee Services in the Metropolitan Atlanta Area* (622-2235) for additional listings.

TRANSLATION SERVICES

■ **Atlanta Association of Interpreters and Translators** (587-4884) and **Georgia Council for International Visitors' Language Bank** (873-6170) provide emergency translation services in a large number of languages. Atlanta's larger hotels are also offering translation services for internationals staying at the facilities.

■ See the *Atlanta Multicultural Directory* (378-3719) for additional listings of organizations and private companies offering translation services.

ASSISTANCE WITH THE ENGLISH LANGUAGE

■ **Mr./Ms. Grammar at Georgia State University** (651-2906) will answer any question regarding the English language, weekdays from 9:00am–7:00pm and on weekends from 9:00am–2:00pm.

INTERNATIONAL COOKING CLASSES

■ Many of Atlanta's cooking schools and kitchenware stores offer cooking classes featuring international cooking techniques and recipes. For example, **Everything Culinary**, 2140 Peachtree Rd., Atlanta (355-4306) offers demonstration classes by some of Atlanta's most famous chefs; and **Ursula's Cooking School**, 1764 Cheshire Bridge Rd., Atlanta (876-7463) offers a series of four demonstration classes featuring Ursula Knaeusel's own recipes of seasonal foods from around the world.

NEWSPAPERS, MAGAZINES, BOOKS, VIDEOS

LOCAL PUBLICATIONS

■ *Around Atlanta With Children* by Denise Black and Janet Schwartz. This indispensable book provides families with 300 pages of comprehensive information about places to go and things to do in Atlanta. *Around Atlanta With Children* gives in-depth coverage to a number of international and cultural festivals, performances and special events in the metropolitan area, and features descriptions of historical sites, museums and other places of interest to immigrants, international visitors and others wishing to delve into their own and Atlanta's rich heritage. The book may be found in area bookstores, toy stores, children's stores and gift shops. $12.95.

■ *The Atlanta Guidebook* **"The Definitive Guide To the South's Premier City"** compiled by Candace Springer and published by Longstreet Press, Inc. The pocket-size guidebook, with a handy pull-out map, provides general information about metro-Atlanta and its environs. $6.50.

■ *Atlanta Journal and Constitution's Saturday Leisure Guide (Weekend Section)* (522-4141). The *Leisure Guide* provides comprehensive calendars listing international and cultural events in the metro-Atlanta area. Informative feature articles highlight ethnic and international festivals, performance groups and restaurants. The *Weekend Section* is included in the Saturday paper. Newsstand price is 50¢/issue. Subscription rate is approximately $95.00/year for the Saturday and Sunday newspapers.

■ *Atlanta Magazine* (872-3100). The magazine's overview of the month's major events usually includes some of the international community's events. Restaurant reviews are excellent, and at least once a year the magazine has a special issue devoted to Atlanta's best ethnic dining. Published monthly. Cost is $2.50/issue. Subscription rate is $18.00/year.

- *The Atlanta Regional Music Directory* (370-1312). This guide of over 60 pages provides the names, addresses and telephone numbers of area performers, support services for musicians, music stores, concert halls, music-related businesses and special events throughout the year. The directory is published by Image Music Productions and is available at area music stores. Free.

- *Creative Loafing* (688-5623). *Creative Loafing* is the best source for announcements about Atlanta's international associations; its detailed calendars of performances, exhibits, meetings, festivals and special events cannot be beat. The newspaper always features reviews highlighting Atlanta's smaller and lesser-known ethnic restaurants. Published weekly. Available at stores, newsstands and restaurants. Free.

- **Emory Center for International Studies Newsletter**, P.O. Box 22181, Emory University, Atlanta (727-6562). A bimonthly newsletter highlights the many films, lectures, discussions, cultural events and conferences sponsored by the center. Call to be placed on the mailing list. Free.

- *The Hudspeth Report* (255-3220). "The Pulse of Atlanta" provides an overview of some of the upcoming month's entertainment, including concerts, performances, restaurants, nightspots, celebrities, special events and sports. Published monthly. Available at over 600 stores, newsstands and restaurants. Free. Subscription rate is $18.00/year.

- *Where Atlantans Dine* **1993 – 4th Edition** by Helen & John Friese. The book provides thorough reviews of over 200 Atlanta restaurants, a good number of which are ethnic restaurants. The book can be found at most book stores. $9.95.

- *Zagat's Atlanta Restaurant Survey* (212/977-6000) edited by Christianne Lauterbach and Kay Goldstein. The restaurant guide rates over 400 Atlanta restaurants based upon surveys given to 700 reviewers. Some of Atlanta's most popular ethnic restaurants are covered. The book can be found in most area bookstores and newsstands. $9.95.

- Other area periodicals, such as *Alternatives, Music Atlanta, Southern Voice* and *Trends,* occasionally highlight Atlanta's international and ethnic resources.

FOREIGN LANGUAGE MATERIAL

- The following libraries have a large selection of newspapers, periodicals, foreign language books and some foreign language rental videos from around the world: **Atlanta-Fulton Public Library**, Main Branch, 1 Margaret Mitchell Square, NW, Atlanta (730-INFO); **Emory University Library**, 540 Ashby Cir., Atlanta (727-6872); **Georgia State University Library**, 103 Decatur St., Atlanta (651-2185); and **Georgia Tech Library**, 225 North Ave., Atlanta (894-4500).

- **International Records**, 231 Peachtree St. (Peachtree Center Shopping

Mall), Atlanta (584-5490) sells jazz, pop-rock and hard-to-find classical CDs, tapes and albums from around the world.

■ **Oxford Book Store**, 2345 Peachtree Rd., NE, Atlanta (364-2700) and 360 Pharr Road, NE, Atlanta (262-3333); and **Borders Book Shop**, 3655 Roswell Rd., NE, Atlanta (237-0707) carry a large selection of foreign newspapers, including the *International Herald Tribune* and *The European*. They also stock an impressive selection of international fashion and literary magazines. Other area bookstores, such as **BookStar**, 4101 Roswell Rd., NE, Marietta (578-4455); and **Brentano's**, 4400 Ashford-Dunwoody Rd. (Perimeter Mall), Atlanta (394-6658) carry a selection of international fashion magazines.

■ *World of Reading, Ltd.* (233-4042) features French, Spanish, German, Dutch, Japanese, Russian and Hebrew language books, games, tapes and computer programs for adults and children. Some language instructional material is also available. Call for a copy.

■ **Movies Worth Seeing**, 1409 N. Highland Ave., NE, Atlanta (892-1802) carries, perhaps, one of the best selections of foreign movies with English subtitles. Or try Blockbusters, The Movie Store, Turtles or your neighborhood video store.

INTERNATIONAL SHOPPING, IMPORT STORES

■ **Buford Flea Market**, 5000 Buford Hwy., Chamblee (452-7140). The large flea market has a hodge-podge of booths selling imported items from around the world, including Chinese slippers, oriental rugs, Latino music, women's clothing from India and Mexican sombreros. The flea market is open on Friday, Saturday and Sunday.

■ **Continental Shopper**, One CNN Center, Suite 232, Atlanta (522-6201). This creative gift shop has an array of reasonably-priced import items from around the world, including clothing, jewelry, artwork and gift items. Two additional locations are being considered.

■ **Folk Art Imports Gallery**, 25 Bennett St., A-1, Atlanta (352-2656). Discover a delightful selection of folk and tribal arts and crafts, including fine art, sculpture, textiles, pottery, baskets, masks and jewelry, with a heavy concentration on South American work.

■ **High Museum of Art Gift Shop**, Robert Woodruff Arts Center, 1280 Peachtree St., NE, Atlanta (892-HIGH). The high-quality museum gift shop carries an unusual selection of expensive jewelry, art, books, toys and gifts from around the world.

■ **The Metropolitan Museum of Art**, 3393 Peachtree Rd. (Lenox Square), Atlanta (264-1424). This upscale gift shop sells reproductions and adaptations of treasures displayed in the New York Metropolitan Museum of Art. For example, you may purchase sculpture reproductions, decorative objects in silver, glass and porcelain, jewelry or textiles. Descriptive, historical texts are included with each reproduction or adaptation purchased. Calendars, appointment books, posters, stationery, children's books and other small gifts may also be purchased.

■ **Onion Dome Imports**, 2221 Peachtree Rd., NE, Atlanta (352-3881). The small store is jam-packed with low-priced import gifts from around the world, including a large selection of jewelry, clothes, handbags and accessories.

■ **Out of the Woods**, 22-B Bennett St., Atlanta (351-0446). Although the gallery specializes primarily in American folk art, it also has a small selection of tribal arts and crafts. Native-American art and handmade work from South Africa and Tibet are represented.

■ **Pier One Imports** (over 15 locations in metro-Atlanta) (Main Tel: 988-9223). The national chain carries an extensive selection of inexpensive import items from the world over. Jewelry, women's clothing, rugs and dhurries, wicker furniture, household items, kitchenware, pillows, small toys and gifts are some of the items carried.

■ **Window to the World**, Epworth Methodist Church, 1561 McLendon Ave., Atlanta (294-4643). International handicrafts from over 35 countries are sold the second Saturday of each month by a non-profit association that creates craft jobs in developing nations. Baskets, jewelry, carvings, scarfs, pottery and wall-hangings are some of the crafts featured.

■ **World Bazaar** (4 locations in metro-Atlanta) (436-3295); **Grand Harbor Imports**, 5370 Hwy. 78 (Stone Mountain Shopping Center), Stone Mountain (498-6086); and **Portside Imports**, 3930 N. Druid Hills Rd. (Shamrock Plaza), Decatur (321-5300) and 1291 Morrow Industrial Blvd. (across from Southlake Mall), Morrow (968-3171), all carry a selection of wicker furniture, baskets, brass gifts, artificial flowers and other small import items from around the world.

GROCERIES, MARKETS, BAKERIES

GROCERIES & MARKETS

■ **Happy Herman's**, 2299 Cheshire Bridge Rd., NE, Atlanta (321-3012) and 204 Johnson Ferry Rd., NW, Atlanta (256-3354). Atlanta's longest-standing gourmet grocery store stocks a large selection of international groceries, delicatessen items, wines, beers, chocolates and pastries from around the world. Both stores have small seating areas.

■ **Harry's Farmers Market**, 1180 Upper Hembree Rd., Roswell (664-6300) and 2025 Satellite Point, Duluth (416-6900). The large farmers market stocks fresh produce, meat, cheese, spices, coffees, dried fruits, nuts, groceries, packaged gourmet meals-to-go and baked goods from around the world. Take-out sushi, egg rolls, wontons and dumplings are a real treat! Rumor has it that Harry's is looking for a third location in Buckhead.

■ **International Farmers Market**, 5193 Peachtree Industrial Blvd., Chamblee (455-1777). The 90,000-square-foot facility is filled with produce, meats, tanks of fresh fish, cheeses, coffees, spices and baked goods, with a heavy emphasis on international food products. The Asian grocery section has perhaps the most unusual selection of all of Atlanta's farmers markets. The deli section is well-stocked with New York-style smoked fish, deli meats, sandwiches and salads. You can usually count on fewer crowds and better service at this market, especially on weekends.

■ **Julian's Market**, 985 Monroe Dr., Atlanta (872-1760). This new gourmet market features quality breads, pastries, chocolates, fresh-cooked pasta, imported and domestic cheese, deli items, coffees, teas, spices and many other gourmet delicacies from around the world.

■ **Sausage World & Deli**, 5353 Lawrenceville Hwy., Lilburn (925-4493). This sausage market cranks out an international array of meats, such as bangers, kielbasa, bratwurst, chorizo, andouille and a large selection of Italian sausages.

■ **Sweet Auburn Curb Market** (The Atlanta Municipal Market), 209 Edgewood Ave., Atlanta (659-1665). The newly-renovated market sells massive quantities of meat, fruit, vegetables, cheese and grocery items. Increasingly, the stalls and snack bar area are becoming more international in tone as Asian-Americans and African-Americans operate businesses side-by-side, resulting in an unusual mix of Asian and Southern cuisines.

■ **Your DeKalb Farmers Market**, 3000 E. Ponce de Leon Ave., Decatur (377-6400). The international farmer's market considers itself a "World Mart" and rightfully so. It offers an enormous diversity of international groceries, spices, produce, cheese, meats, coffees, delicatessen items and baked goods. A cafeteria-style restaurant also serves hot meals, samosas and other international snacks.

Atlanta has a wealth of high-quality restaurants specializing in both tradition-al and innovative ethnic cuisine which we describe in our various chapters. However, if you are uncomfortable ordering from an unfamiliar menu, but would like to experiment with food from different countries, you might try visiting one of the food courts found in major shopping malls and office buildings throughout the city. For example, try the food court at **Underground Atlanta**, (Old Alabama St. between Peachtree St. and Central Ave.), Atlanta (523-2311) which has a booth representing almost every kind of ethnic fast-food imaginable — New York-style deli, Japanese teriyaki, Italian pizza, Mexican favorites, Chinese specialties and a French-style cafe.

For a more upscale dining adventure, experiment at one of the more imag-inative, eclectic restaurants which serve unusual combinations of ethnic cui-sine on their menus. For example: **Mabel's Table**, 2071 N. Druid Hills Rd. (just west of I-85/Buford Hwy.) Atlanta (315-6231) pairs New York-style deli-catessen along with authentic Cajun and Creole specialties; **Rockbridge Diner**, 414 N. Hairston Rd. (Rockbridge Rd.), Stone Mountain (299-8784) has a chef from Mauritius who creates such diverse dishes as chilled mango soup, bouillabaisse and chicken quesadilla; and **Le Midi International Café**, 2770 Lenox Rd. (Plantation Heights Shopping Center), Atlanta (261-6280) serves an array of foods representing various cuisines of Europe and Asia in an elegant cafe atmosphere.

THEATRE , PUPPETRY & STORYTELLING

■ **Center for Puppetry Arts**, 1404 Spring St., Atlanta (874-0398) is the most comprehensive puppetry center in the U.S., featuring master puppeteers from all over the world. Puppetry performances at the center employ pup-petry styles, techniques and stories from various cultures in presentations for adult and children's audiences. Performances are interpreted historically and culturally, so even adults may be intrigued by a unique representation of a popular fairy tale. Beginning in the summer of 1993, the center hopes to begin hosting a four-year international puppetry festival, each segment lasting six weeks and concentrating on a different part of the world. Ticket office hours are Monday–Friday from 9:00am–5:00pm and Saturday from 9:00am–4:00pm.

- **The Southern Order of Storytellers** (633-3277) is a group of professional storytellers who perform regularly throughout Atlanta at bookstores, libraries, art centers, festivals and special events. The SOS also presents the Olde Christmas Storytelling Festival every January, the Atlanta Storytelling Festival in the spring at the Atlanta History Center, and performs weekly at The Wren's Nest. Increasingly, members of the SOS have begun specializing in multicultural and international folktales. Call the SOS Hotline to find out where you can hear **Akbar Imhotep**, **B.J. Abraham** or one of the many other superb storytellers in our city.

LOCAL MUSIC & DANCE

- **Atlanta Area Friends of Folk Music** (923-5817/892-1492) has as its goal, the preservation and promotion of American and world folk music and arts. It sponsors monthly get-togethers, publishes a monthly newsletter highlighting Atlanta-area and national folk performances and festivals, hosts occasional concerts and sponsors **Fiddler's Green Coffeehouse** held the third Saturday of every month at the Garden Hills Recreation Center (at Pinetree Dr. and Rumson Rd.), Atlanta (875-8942) featuring folk songs and music.
- Other coffeehouses that feature folk music are: **Lena's Place Coffeehouse**, Central Congregational Church, 2676 Clairmont Rd., Atlanta (936-4102) held on the second Saturday of every month; **Northwest Unitarian Congregation Coffeehouse**, 1025 Mt. Vernon Hwy., Sandy Springs (951-5500) held on the first Saturday of every month; **Pat's Place**, St. Patrick's Episcopal Church, 4755 N. Peachtree Rd. (outside I-285), Atlanta (455-6523) held on the third Friday of every month; and **Trinity Coffeehouse**, Trinity United Methodist Church, 265 Washington St. (near the State Capitol), Atlanta (659-6236) held on the fourth Saturday of every month.
- **Atlanta Folks, Inc.** (396-5033) represents about twenty local multiethnic folk dance groups from fifteen different countries. Members are available to perform at international and cultural events in the city. Atlanta Folks also sponsors the Atlanta Folks Festival held in November of every year.
- **Atlanta International Folkdancers** (378-2648) is a recreational folk dancing group which sponsors folk dance classes and activities for beginners at St. Matthew's Lutheran Church (Briarcliff and N. Druid Hills Rds.) on Thursdays (378-2648). Classes for more experienced dancers are on Mondays at Leafmore Community Club, 1373 Altamont St., Decatur (284-

0106/292-7176); and on Saturdays at Beacon Hill Dance Company's theatre, 410 W. Trinity Pl., Decatur (876-3296). Enjoy circle, line and couple dances from around the world. The International Folkdancers also sponsor an annual International Dance Workshop featuring workshops, demonstrations, international food, costumes and gifts.

■ Atlanta is fortunate to have many symphonies, bands, operas, chamber music ensembles, choral groups, ballets and dance companies whose performances encompass a wide-range of international compositions. Besides the internationally acclaimed **Atlanta Symphony Orchestra** (892-2414) and **Atlanta Ballet** (892-3303), keep your eye on the **Atlanta Chamber Players** (651-1228), **Atlanta Virtuosi** (938-8611), **International Ballet Rotaru** (365-0488), **Apollo's Musicke** (325-4735) and **The Pandean Players** (427-8196), to name just a few.

INTERNATIONAL PERFORMANCES

■ **Atlanta International Jazz Festival**, Atlanta Bureau of Cultural Affairs (653-7160). Held during the last weekend of May and the first weekends of June, July and August, the series offers concerts, workshops, dance performances, gallery exhibitions and film videos featuring local, national and international jazz artists. The outdoor concerts in Grant Park and brown bag concerts in Woodruff Park are free, although midnight jam sessions and other music and dance events may have an admission fee. Schedules are available a month in advance.

■ **Coca-Cola International Series** (881-2100) presents world-class performers from around the world. In recent seasons, the series has included the Vienna Boys Choir, Stars of the Bolshoi, Danish National Radio Symphony Orchestra and Canada's Royal Winnipeg Ballet. Performances are at the Fox Theatre.

■ **Montreux Atlanta International Music Festival**, Atlanta Bureau of Cultural Affairs (653-7160) is patterned after the famous Montreux Jazz Festival in Switzerland. Opera, classical, pop, folk, jazz, improvisation and zydeco performers from around the world participate at the annual event held in August and September.

■ **Windstorm Productions** (874-2232) presents world-renowned ethnic, folk and international music concerts at Emory University, The Variety Playhouse and other locations in Atlanta.

■ **Alliance Theatre**, 1280 Peachtree Rd., NW, Atlanta (892-2414); **14th Street Playhouse**, 173 14th Street, NE, Atlanta (266-0010); **Seven Stages Performing Arts Center**, 1105 Euclid Ave., NE, Atlanta (523-7647); and **Variety Playhouse**, 1099 Euclid Ave., NE, Atlanta (524-7354) strive to represent Atlanta's ethnic diversity by presenting a large variety of international and multicultural performances on a regular basis. Dance, music and other performing arts are represented.

FILMS

- **Emory University's International Film Festivals** (727-6562) and **Georgia State's Cinefest** (651-3565) screen an eclectic mix of foreign films on a regular basis. Call to be placed on Emory's mailing list and watch for Cinefest's schedule in area newspapers.
- **Metropolitan Film Society** (729-8487) sponsors monthly screenings of high-quality, non-mainstream films from around the world. Screenings are usually at the Cinevision Screening Room, 3300 NE Expressway Office Park, Building 2, Atlanta. Call to be placed on the mailing list.
- **High Museum**, Robert Woodruff Arts Center, 1280 Peachtree St., NE, Atlanta (892-HIGH) is the location for quite a few international film festival series throughout the year, such as The Jewish Film Festival, the Latin American Film Festival and the Hong Kong Excitement Film Festival.
- **IMAGE Film/Video Center**, 75 Bennett St., NW, Suite M-1, Atlanta (352-4225) offers year-round screenings of film and video work by local, national and international artists. Festivals, competitions, seminars and workshops are also offered. Since May of 1977, IMAGE has hosted the annual **Atlanta Film and Video Festival** which introduces audiences to the most exciting and innovative independent film and video media being created. Membership is available and encouraged.
- **Third World Film Festival**, Atlanta Bureau of Cultural Affairs (653-7160), screens more than 40 films during four weekends in October at the Atlanta-Fulton County Public Library and other venues in Atlanta. The festival features high-quality films and videos by African-American, Latino, Indian, Asian and Native American artists.
- **Worldwide Travelogs** (872-2679) presents in-depth tours of the featured countries. Films are screened throughout the year at Toco Hills Theatre (N. Druid Hills and Clairmont Rds.) and the Marietta-Cobb Civic Center (S. Marietta Pkwy. at Fairground St.). Call to be placed on the mailing list.
- And don't forget that **Garden Hills Cinema**, 2835 Peachtree Rd., NE, Atlanta (266-2202); **Screening Room**, 2581 Piedmont Rd. (Lindbergh Plaza), Atlanta (231-1924); and **Lefont Plaza Theatre**, 1049 Ponce de Leon Ave., Atlanta (873-1939), all screen foreign films on a regular basis.

T.V. & RADIO

- **WRAS-FM (88.5)** (651-2240). Georgia State University's station has, in the past, aired "Universally Speaking," a listing of campus and city events featuring broadcasts in different languages; and "Musical Shores," another program featuring international music and news. The station is unclear at this time as to whether these programs will be resumed in the near future.

FESTIVALS & SPECIAL EVENTS

JANUARY

- **Travel Fest** (633-9609). During the annual fundraiser for the Vince Dooley Easter Seal Society in Atlanta, guests receive a "passport" to travel around the world and experience international cuisine and entertainment. Silent and live auctions usually feature international vacation packages.

MARCH

- **Athens International Festival**, Athens Chamber of Commerce, Athens (706/546-1805). The Chamber of Commerce and University of Georgia sponsor four days of visual and performing arts from around the world. Included are international displays, a fashion and talent show, art lectures, garden exhibits, coffee and wine tastings, ethnic cuisine and performances of international music, dance and comedy.
- **Macon Cherry Blossom Festival**, Macon (912/751-7429). With over 160,000 Yoshino cherry trees in full bloom, Macon, the Cherry Blossom Capital of the World, celebrates spring with arts and crafts, entertainment, tours, parades, a ball and international celebrations. Japan and one or two other countries are featured each year, and festivities highlight the culture, entertainment and cuisine of the selected countries.
- **Georgia Council for International Visitors' Annual Fundraiser**, Atlanta (873-6170). The council hosts a fund-raising dinner saluting a foreign country each year, such as a recent "Salute to the Netherlands" which featured Dutch and Indonesian food, a re-creation of an authentic Dutch street and klomp (wooden-shoe) dancing.

APRIL

- **Cultural Crossroads**, Arts Clayton, Clayton County (473-0848). Arts Clayton sponsors this performance festival to feature the ethnic diversity of its community. Call for this year's calendar of performance events.

■ **Celebration of Cuisine**, Atlanta Ballet International Night, Atlanta (873-5811). This upscale benefit for the Atlanta Ballet offers guests an opportunity to partake in gourmet ethnic food with interesting dining companions.

■ **Atlanta Dogwood Festival**, Piedmont Park, Buckhead and Midtown (952-9151). The Dogwood Festival celebration features an International Village which provides a vehicle for performers and artists from many countries to present a true image of their cultural identities.

■ **International Cultural Festival**, Emory University Quadrangle, Atlanta (727-3300). Students from more than fifty countries participate in this friendly outdoor festival to share information about their homelands. Folk dancing, a fashion show, traditional food, martial arts demonstrations and displays of jewelry, crafts and travel information are all featured at this festival.

■ **Villa International Atlanta's Festival of Nations**, Emory University, Atlanta (663-6783). International Villa at Emory University presents an international food fair with information booths, crafts and displays, storytelling, face-painting, a magic show, a cake-walk, an auction and international entertainment.

■ **Georgia State University International Festival**, Georgia State Campus, Atlanta (651-2450). The four-day festival features information booths and food from the many nations represented, plus a Friday evening performance of international dance, fashion and music.

■ **A Taste of Atlanta**, CNN Center, Atlanta (248-0066). The three-day celebration of "eating" features samples from more than 50 of Atlanta's restaurants, including many of Atlanta's ethnic haunts. Jaffa Gate, U.S. Bar Y Grill, Lawrence's Cafe, Haveli, Bugatti, Nakato and Reggie's British Pub have participated in recent festivals. Live entertainment, children's activities, clowns and street entertainers make this event a favorite for hungry Atlantans.

MAY

■ **Atlanta Storytelling Festival** (814-4000) at the Atlanta History Center. Presented by the Atlanta Historical Society and the Southern Order of Storytellers. Dozens of the nation's best professional tellers of tales share authentic folktales, myths, ballads, legends and fables from around the world—along with musicians, food and fun for the whole family. Call for further information.

■ **Georgia Tech's International Festival**, Georgia Tech Campus, Atlanta (894-7475). The four-day celebration features international food, music and dance performances, films, documentaries and cultural activities sponsored by the International Student Department at the University.

- **Atlanta International School's Annual Dinner** (843-3380). The school's annual black-tie dinner spotlights a different nation each year. A recent theme was "Journey Through India," featuring Indian food, music and dancing, as well as a shopping bazaar of Indian art and artifacts.
- **DeKalb College's International Festival**, Clarkston (299-4126). The college celebrates its rich cultural diversity with lectures by international faculty members, displays from the students' native countries, colorful costumes, music, dance and food.
- **Atlanta Storytelling Festival**, Atlanta History Center, Atlanta (814-4000). Although the majority of the storytellers performing at this festival are southern performers and celebrities, recently, many of the storytellers have added multicultural and international folk tales to their repertoire, including a large number of Native American stories and myths.
- **Clarkston International Festival**, Market Street, Clarkston (297-4946). Cultural dances, karate demonstrations, international music, arts and crafts, and other activities highlight this festival celebrating the cultural diversity of the Clarkston community.

SPRING/SUMMER

- **Salute to America July 4th Parade – WSB-TV**, Downtown, Atlanta (897-7452). The largest Independence Day Parade in the U.S. features elaborate floats entered by many of Atlanta's ethnic communities. Look for the spectacular floats created by Asian/Pacific American Council of Georgia (A/PAC) and La Asociación de la Comunidad Mexicana (ACM).
- **Festival of Cultures**, Underground Atlanta, 50 Upper Alabama St., Atlanta (523-2311). Underground Atlanta celebrates a different culture (i.e. Asian, Latino, Native American, etc.) each weekend from late June through late July. Music and dance performances may be enjoyed throughout the weekend, as well as cultural exhibits, art displays and demonstrations designed to increase public awareness and appreciation of the featured culture.
- **DeKalb International Choral Festival**, DeKalb Convention and Visitor's Bureau (951-1888). More than 800 singers and musicians from around the world gather for a week-long cultural celebration of song in June at different venues throughout the county. A festival finale is usually held at Georgia's Stone Mountain Park and televised locally.
- **Kingfest Internationale**, Martin Luther King, Jr. Center for Nonviolent Social Change, Atlanta (524-1956). Kingfest Internationale, part of the summer-long Kingfest Festival, is a day-long celebration of Atlanta's ethnic culture, featuring arts and crafts, lots of food and continuous entertainment by

local and international performers. Song, dance, live bands, poetry, story-telling, theatre and comedy are some of the events that are often featured.

■ **Atlanta International Food & Wine Festival** (873-4482). The festival has recently undergone a major change in format and is now held at various locations in Buckhead. Over 500 different wines from some of the world's most famous vinters are available for sampling during "grand tastings," "premium tastings" and "full-course banquets."

FALL

■ **Arts Festival of Atlanta**, Piedmont Park, Atlanta (885-1125). Atlanta's most famous outdoor arts and crafts festival features three stages of continuous music, dance and theatrical performances by local, national and international companies. Along with artists' booths from all over the country, there is an African marketplace and numerous concession stands selling food prepared by ethnic restaurants.

■ **Festival of Nations**, Gwinnett Council for the Arts (962-6642). October is international month in Gwinnett County, and the council for the Arts usually sponsors international art exhibits throughout the county. During most years, the council hosts an international bazaar featuring the food, art and entertainment of other nations. An elegant dinner party featuring gourmet and international dining is the highlight of the event.

■ **Festival of Ethnic Dance**, Soapstone Center for the Arts, South DeKalb Center, Decatur (241-2453). The festival, usually held in the fall, has featured over ten different international dance groups from such diverse countries as Peru, Senegal, Laos, Jamaica and Greece. Future plans include expanding the festival to include arts and crafts and an even greater variety of international entertainment.

NOVEMBER

■ **The Atlanta Folks Festival**, Emory University's Glenn Methodist Church (396-5033). About fifteen multiethnic folk dance groups perform in native costume during this annual folk dance festival.

DECEMBER

■ **Festival of Trees**, World Congress Center, Atlanta (264-9348). The Festival of Trees showcases hundreds of elaborate Christmas trees, wreaths, vignettes and gingerbread houses created by Atlanta businesses and civic associations. Each year many international organizations participate by decorating a booth depicting how the December holidays are celebrated in their native countries. The international community helps provide continuous entertainment throughout the festival week.

OTHER

■ When the Atlanta Historical Society's Museum of Atlanta History opens in the fall of 1993, it will feature a year-long exhibit called, "**DAYS TO REMEMBER: Atlanta's Cultural Calendars**." This innovative exhibit will feature photographs, costumes and celebratory objects depicting the many special events of Atlanta's diverse cultural populations. The museum has put together a 1994 commemorative calendar in poster format, which will list events celebrated by Atlanta's many communities. This very special calendar should prove to be an excellent resource for those who wish to learn about the holidays and special events of Atlanta's many communities.

RESOURCES

■ **Atlanta Chamber of Commerce International Department**, 235 International Blvd., NW, Atlanta 30303 (586-8460). The chamber attempts to advance international trade and investment opportunities for Atlanta's business community. A variety of international services are available, including a newsletter containing information of interest to the business community, a book listing international resources and announcements about upcoming events.

■ **The Cobb International Center**, Cobb Chamber of Commerce, P.O. Box Cobb, Marietta 30067 (980-2000). The organization's goal is to promote Cobb County as an excellent place to locate international businesses and to serve the international business community already located in the county. One of the many services offered is the publication of the *Family Orientation Guide*, a brochure providing international newcomers with information about services available in Cobb County. The guide is available in Japanese, Spanish, French and German.

■ **Directory of Georgia's International Services**, International Business Council, Georgia State University, 1 Park Place South, Suite 1001, Atlanta, Georgia 30302-4045 (651-2950). Georgia State's Directory provides lists of Georgia's exporting and importing companies; freight agents; management consultants, lawyers, accountants and banks specializing in international affairs; translator and interpreter services; foreign consuls and trade

364

offices; and other varied services available to international businesses in Georgia. Cost is $25.00.

■ **Georgia Department of Industry, Trade and Tourism**, 285 Peachtree Center Ave., Suite 1000, Atlanta 30303 (656-3590). The state has a wealth of information about foreign trade and investment in Georgia, along with information about international businesses in Georgia. The staff is friendly and helpful to those interested in learning more about international business opportunities.

■ **Women's Chamber of Commerce of Atlanta**, 1776 Peachtree St., Suite 525, Atlanta 30309 (892-0538). The International Committee of the Women's Chamber of Commerce seeks to promote international development and cultural awareness in Atlanta by having Atlanta's business women work on projects with international organizations and their representatives in the Atlanta area. The Atlanta Dogwood Festival is one of the events sponsored by the organization.

■ **World Trade Club Atlanta**, 240 Peachtree St., NW, Suite 2200, Atlanta 30303 (525-4144). The World Trade Club is a business and social organization whose purpose is to promote the exchange of world trade. Members of the international club can dine in the main dining area featuring international menu selections, or use one of the many private meeting rooms to entertain or make contacts with the international community in Atlanta. Other membership privileges include use of "Network," a communications system offering members an opportunity to receive international trade information; access to reciprocal clubs in 57 different foreign countries; and invitations to speaker programs with international CEOs and foreign diplomats.